Faith
in the
Night Seasons

By
Chuck & Nancy Missler

Koinonia House

Faith in the Night Seasons

© Copyright 1999 by Nancy Missler

Third Printing May 21, 2001

Published by Koinonia House
PO Box D
Coeur d'Alene ID 83816-0347
ISBN 1-57821-068-2

All Scripture quotations are from the King James Version of the Holy Bible.

PRINTED IN THE UNITED STATES OF AMERICA

Dedication

This book is dedicated to our beloved son Chip for sharing 39 wonderful and precious years with us. May God hold you close until we see you again.

We love you,

Mom and Dad

A Special Thanks

> "When thou passest through the waters, I will be with
> thee; and through the rivers, they shall not overflow thee:
> when thou walkest through the fire, thou shalt not be
> burned; neither shall the flame kindle upon thee. For I
> am the Lord thy God...and I have loved thee."
> (Isaiah 43:2-4)

First of all, we want to thank our loving Father who <u>has</u> brought us
through the waters, *through* the rivers and *through* the fire so that
they didn't overflow us, and we weren't burned, just as He promised.
May this book bring glory to Him.

We would also like to thank Bill Welty for his incredible
contribution to this manuscript. To Lew Phelphs, John Loeffler, Lisa
Bright and Tracy MacDonald for their time and love and support. And
finally, to Claudia Lovejoy for her invaluable help with the early parts
of this manuscript.

Table of Contents

"Who is among you that feareth the Lord, that obeyeth the voice of His servant, that *walketh in darkness, and hath no light?*" (Isaiah 50:10)

Foreword
by William P. Welty

I think it's no coincidence that in His very first publicly recorded statement about what it means to follow Him, Jesus Christ totally and irrevocably eliminated human ability, human intelligence, human accomplishment, human beauty, human talents, human righteousness, human effort, or human will as meaningful criteria for true spirituality. The *first sentence* of His Sermon on the Mount makes this fact unmistakably clear: "How blessed are those who are destitute in spirit, for the kingdom of heaven belongs to them!" (Matthew 5:4, ISV) With respect to enumerating the characteristics of true discipleship, it would seem that the only human element that Christ truly values is spiritual bankruptcy, which for the purpose of this *Foreword* I define as that certain, mandatory, and abject condition of total poverty of spirit and soul that marks the beginning of true Christian maturity.

And I confess publicly that with regard to true Christian maturity I am a spiritual invalid. More truthfully, I am a spiritual coward. I fear real Christian maturity. I cannot keep my hand to the plow. I fear wisdom. And I fear the truly godly. If I have run and grown weary in the company of the immature, how will I fare with the truly strong?

As I write these words, I'm a member of a Laodicean church community (the southern California evangelical community) in a Laodicean church age (the last years of the twentieth century). Like the Word Faith heretics of the 90s (AD 1990s, that is), I proclaim loudly that "I am rich, I am increased with goods, and I have need of nothing." But inwardly, like my Laodicean namesakes of the 90s (AD 90s, that is), I do not realize that I am wretched and poor and miserable and blind and naked. May God have mercy on my soul, for like the prophet Isaiah, I am a man of unclean lips and I live among a people of unclean lips.

And so it came about, as God so often works things in the lives of His people, that I found myself being invited to review a pre-publication draft of Nancy Missler's work **Faith in the Night Seasons**. It would seem Chuck and Nancy Missler had been pleased with other evaluations that I had done for previous books. So Nancy sent me the draft. And coincident to that sending there began a personal tutorial of the principles set forth in **Faith in the Night Seasons**. The tutor: God Himself. And I am the reluctant, rebellious, weary, and disobedient student. The wretched, poor, miserable, blind, and naked disciple.

I was not always this wayward. I was introduced to Christ in high school through the campus ministry of Youth for Christ. I went on to college and then graduated from Trinity Evangelical Divinity School, one of the finest Christian seminaries in the world. I began working with non-profit corporations that were doing the Lord's work as a consultant for a highly respected Christian philanthropist.

And then, about eight years after leaving seminary, I began working on a telecommunications satellite project. My involvement in that project eventually turned out to become a remarkable example of how God provides for His people. In March 1996 I sold my stock in the satellite project to a major American aerospace company, turning over all of the proceeds to a charitable gifting structure. The charitable gifting structure then endowed the Learn Foundation so that it could begin translation of the *Holy Bible: International Standard Version.*

Then, just before Nancy Missler asked me to read the draft of **Faith in the Night Seasons**, all hell broke loose:

1. About the time I was selling the stock interests for which I served as trustee to that big aerospace firm, that firm used its influence to cancel my satellite company's construction contract with another vendor and assign the contract to itself. The other vendor sued my former company in binding arbitration before a Christian arbitration organization. I was called as a witness. As a result of my testimony to "the truth, the whole truth, and nothing but the truth, so help me God," the original vendor won its case. Nearly $17 million in damages was awarded against my former company. Another $35 million judgment may come about soon.

2. Not happy with the outcome of the arbitration, the big aerospace firm then decided to sue me--in my opinion they're doing this because I told the truth. I learned about their lawsuit the *very day* Nancy Missler's note arrived asking me to review the draft of **Faith in the Night Seasons**.

3. Meanwhile, the more than $70,000 per month due and payable to the charitable gifting structure which was funding the ISV translation project was diverted into a holding account and withheld from the Learn Foundation. The Learn Foundation's properties went into foreclosure. Work on the ISV ground to a halt.

4. And so as I write this Foreword, more than three years of hard work on the ISV project, along with nearly ten years of other work on the satellite project, seem poised on the edge of destruction.

And the opening quotation from Isaiah 50:10 cuts like a knife: "Who among you fears the Lord, obeys the voice of his servant, walks in darkness, and has no light?"

For those who try to love, serve, and obey God, yet walk through night seasons where there is only darkness, Nancy Missler's edifying discussion of *Faith in the Night Seasons* will be a welcome word of encouragement. Citing practical and personal experience, along with the words of many Scriptural, historical and well-known believers who have lived through the dark nights of the soul and spirit, Nancy Missler's gentle encouragements will prove to be of enormous benefit to anyone who wonders what's going on in their Christian life when troubles displace peace, and when light gives way to darkness.

Faith in the Night Seasons forcefully argues that God faithfully works to His glory and our greater good through the dark nights of the soul and spirit, teaching us to walk by faith when God seems to be the farthest from us.

I find my background in theology and Biblical languages to be inadequate for undertaking a review of *Faith in the Night Seasons*. The only reliable test of its usefulness to the growing Christian is to carry it with you through the experience of God-directed darkness itself. To those who find themselves in that trying night season, reading *Faith in the Night Seasons* is its own reward. This work is no academic treatise. It's not a theoretical handbook laid out with the precision of a systematic theology. But if you need a *guide map* rather than a theological treatise, much will be gained by reading--and re-reading--*Faith in the Night Seasons*.

William P. Welty, M.Div.
Executive Director
The Learn Foundation
Translators of the Holy Bible: International Standard Version®
Spring, 1999

Preface

By Chuck Missler

This is a book about faith--*faith in the Night seasons*. It's about having faith in God when our lives and everything around us appears to be crumbling and falling apart. How do we have faith and trust in God *then?*

God is working out His perfect will into the tapestry of each of our lives, and even though we might not fully comprehend what He is doing, we must trust His skill as the Master Craftsman. Father, indeed, knows best. The question is, do we *really* trust Him? Sometimes it seems that He finds a new way to ask us that question every day.

God's will for each of us is not only doing what He asks, but also accepting, with praise and thanksgiving, *all* that He allows. God alone holds the final piece to our puzzle, and only He knows "the end from the beginning."

> "For surely I know the plans I have for you, says the LORD, plans for your welfare and not for harm, to give you a future with hope." (Jeremiah 29:11 NRS)

This book will attempt to discern what the Scripture says is God's will. Not only His will in the "good" times, but also His will in our dark times. Understanding God's will in these night seasons will help give us the faith we need to get through them. If we understand what God is trying to accomplish in each of our lives, then it will be easier to weather the storms.

If we don't understand what God is doing, we will either fall away in the darkness and lose our faith, or we will end up frustrated and defeated as we try to battle harsh events in our own strength. As Hosea says, "The people who do not understand will fall." (4:14)

It is certainly true: a lack of understanding leads to confusion and doubt. And doubt will affect everything we think, say, and do. Let's remember, faith is not believing in spite of the evidence; faith is *obeying in spite of the consequences.*

It is our prayer that this book might help us to *see* through the darkness with sanctified eyes, to have the boldness to enter God's presence and the faith to remain there, regardless of what is going on around us.

In the following pages, we will explore (with many personal stories and much practical application) what God's will is; what true faith is;

what the night seasons are; why God allows them; what He is accomplishing through them; and finally, but most importantly, *what some of the incredible blessings are that come because of them.*

As with Nan's previous books, my editorial involvement has been minimal. This book, too, is principally the result of her diligence and one of the many fruits from the dark valley we have traversed together, with Him.

Love, joy and peace do not come from the absence of trials, but simply from the presence of Jesus.

In His Name,

Chuck Missler
Coeur d'Alene, Idaho

Prologue

"I have heard of Thee by the hearing of the ear: but now mine eye seeth Thee." (Job 42:5)

The Eagle Story

Someone once told me a story about a wounded eaglet that was rescued by a kindly farmer. He found the bird in one of his fields, and so took him home, tended to his wounds, and then placed him outside in the barnyard to recover.

Strangely enough, the young eaglet soon adapted to the habits of all the barnyard chickens. He learned to walk and cluck like them. He learned to drink from a trough and peck the dirt for food, and for many years he peacefully resigned himself to this new life on the ground.

But then one day, one of the farmer's friends spotted the eagle and asked, "Why in the world is that bird acting like a chicken?" The farmer told him what had happened, yet the man could hardly accept the situation.

"It's just not right," said the friend. "The Creator made that bird to soar in the heavens, not scavenge in the barnyard!" So he picked up the unsuspecting eagle, climbed onto a nearby fencepost, and tossed him into the air. But the confused bird just fell back to earth and scurried off in search of his feathered friends.

Undaunted, the man then grabbed the eagle and climbed to the top of the barn. As he heaved him off the roof, the bird made a few halfhearted squawks and flaps before falling into a bale of hay. After shaking his head a few times, the eagle then made himself comfortable and began mindlessly pecking at pieces of straw.

The friend went home that night so dejected he could barely sleep as he remembered the sight of those powerful talons caked with barnyard mud. He couldn't bear the thought, so the very next day, he headed back to the farm for another try. This time he carried the eagle to the top of a nearby mountain where the sky unfolded in a limitless horizon.

He looked into the eagle's eyes and cried out, "Don't you understand? You weren't made to live like a chicken! Why would you want to stay down here when you were born for the sky?" As the man held the confused bird aloft, he made sure the eagle was facing into the brilliant light of the setting sun. Then he powerfully heaved the bird into the sky, and this time the eagle opened his wings, *looked at the sun*, caught the updraft rising from the valley, and disappeared into the clouds of heaven.[1]

Do you know that we, too, were born for the sky? The Lord has called us to live in the heights, yet too many of us have huddled together in the barnyard, contentedly scurrying for the safety of our families, our finances, our careers and our comfortable crumbs of faith.

This book is dedicated to all those believers whose barnyards have been destroyed, and to the faithful ones who have walked, or are now walking, in darkness. The hour is late, beloved friends. It is not time to mourn our losses, but rather time to set our eyes upon heaven, spread our wings and *fly straight towards the Son.*

Never mind weariness, illness, lack of feeling, irritability, exhaustion, snares of the devil, jealousy and prejudice. Let us soar together, like an eagle above the clouds, *with our eyes fixed on the Son.* God uses the eagle throughout the Scriptures as a perfect example of "freedom." An eagle has a special third-eye-lens that enables him to look at and fly directly towards the sun and thus, frees him from his enemies as they try to follow.[2] And, the same thing can be true with us. As we keep our eyes focused directly on *the Son* during our "night seasons," we, too, can become free--free from our own thoughts and emotions, free from our circumstances, free from other people's responses and free from the enemy's attacks.[3]

Having *faith in the night seasons* is the only answer to possessing this overcoming victory.

Let's make our journey together.

Introduction

Walking in Darkness

There once lived a man who feared God and continually turned away from evil. God Himself said, "...there is none like him in the earth, a perfect and an upright man." (Job 1:8) He was blessed with many children and much wealth, and the favor of the Lord rested on him like a fine cloak. As he himself so beautifully describes: "...I was in the prime of my days...the friendship of God was over my tent...my steps were bathed in butter, and the rock poured out for me streams of oil!" (Job 29:4,6 NAS)

Could it be that this man, so loved and favored by God, was the same man who later cried out, "...nights of trouble are appointed me. When I lie down I say, 'When shall I arise?' But the night continues..." (Job 7:3,4 NAS)[4] How could a man so blameless and so upright ever experience such a night of darkness? Job never strayed from God in unbelief, yet God allowed this precious man to endure a season of sorrow. Why?

That is the question which saints, mystics and theologians have been asking throughout the ages. Why does God allow nights of sorrow to come to men and women of faith? It seems to contradict everything we know and believe about a loving and protecting Father.

But look further into the story of Job. He himself shines a powerful light upon this mystery when he speaks to God at the very end of his affliction, "I have heard of Thee by the hearing of the ear; but now mine eye sees Thee...." (Job 42:5 NAS)

Something incredible happened to Job during that very darkness. The word "see" is the word *ra'ah* in Hebrew, which also can mean to "experience." Ironically, it was the darkness that ultimately caused Job to spiritually "see" or experience his Creator *as he never had before.* During that long night of loss, God's faithful servant was transformed into God's intimate friend. And the Bible ends his story with these remarkable words, "...the Lord blessed the latter end [days] of Job more than his beginning." (Job 42:12 NAS)

As we consider the book on the life of Job, most of us would probably say, "That's an amazing story of redemption and resurrection, but I sure hope it never happens to me." Yet today, as I travel around the country speaking and sharing with other believers, I meet so many who are enduring a similar season of sorrow or hardship.

These are not disobedient people who have spurned the counsel of the Lord, but rather these are faithful men and women who have continually sought Him for direction, loved Him and even taught others about Him, as Job had. When God allows crushing circumstances to enter our lives, if we are not prepared and do not understand what is happening, we can often find our faith shipwrecked and our trust shattered.

"Now, I See"

How well I understand this pain, because after 35 years of walking closely with the Lord, I, too, experienced a Night season in my soul (see Chapter One) that almost devastated me. Strangely enough, this unexpected darkness did not descend upon me as punishment for sin or chastisement for disobedience. I had feared, honored and obeyed the Lord for many years, so I identified completely with the words of Isaiah 50:10: "Who is among you that *feareth the Lord*, that *obeyeth the voice of His Servant*, that *walketh in darkness, and hath no light*?" (emphasis added)

Since I had no understanding concerning this night season, I desperately sought guidance as to what was happening to me. How could I get through this dark time? How long would it last? Had others before me gone through a period like this? Was this normal for all Christians? What was God doing? What was His will in all the confusion?

While holding fast to the Book of Job and the hundreds of other Scriptures on night seasons that I had found (see Appendix), I scoured the bookshelves for virtually anything that would shine a light on my situation. Most contemporary Christian writings, however, offered little or nothing on the subject, and I began to feel that I was lost and alone.[5]

I yearned for comfort and understanding, but strangely enough, the only references to the dark night that I could find apart from the Bible were in the works of two Catholic mystics, St. John of the Cross and Jeanne Guyon. Although I'm neither a Catholic nor a mystic, I searched their books for glimmers of understanding and ultimately gained something far more important. God used these dear saints to let me know that I was not alone. No matter how much these people differed from me theologically and culturally, God used their words to let me know that many, many others before me had experienced this very same thing. Through these writings, God encouraged me to keep on trusting, keep on obeying and keep on enduring.

These precious saints had not only survived their own dark nights, but had gleaned amazing treasures from that very darkness. Rather than being destroyed by their suffering, these saints had been enriched by it, and their testimonies gave me insight and courage.

As I continued to read and seek understanding concerning this dark night, I discovered a peculiar dark thread woven into the tapestry of many Christian lives. Little by little, God began to show me a recurrent theme in the lives of Jesus, Joseph, Moses, David, Paul, Martin Luther, Oswald Chambers, John Wesley, Hudson Taylor and countless others.

They, too, had been discipled by a season of emptiness and sorrow. And for them, as well as for me, the darkest hour came just before dawn. It's true. Our weeping does last for a night, but oh what strength of faith and joy awaits us in the morning![6]

> "Thou hast turned for me my mourning into dancing: Thou hast put off my sackcloth, and girded me with gladness; to the end that my glory may sing praise to Thee, and not be silent. O Lord my God, I will give thanks unto Thee for ever." (Psalm 30:11-12)

For me, the dark night was simply the forerunner of greater Light. My night season came forth from a Creator who yearned for me to *see* Him and to experience Him as Job finally saw and experienced Him. "*I had heard of Thee by the hearing of the ear; but now mine eye sees Thee.*" It came forth from a Father who wanted me to know His presence, His friendship and His Love in a way I never had before--truly, being filled with "*the fulness of Christ*"[7] and living *the abundant Life.*[8]

The Purpose of This Book

The purpose of this book, then, is to encourage those of you going through your own night seasons and those of you yet to experience a time like this, that you not be confused, frightened or scared, but that you persevere through to the *incredible riches* God has planned for you as you begin to know Him in an even more intimate and deeper union. As He has promised, "Fear thou not; for I am with thee: be not dismayed; for I am thy God: I will strengthen thee; yea, I will help thee; yea, I will uphold thee with the right hand of My righteousness." (Isaiah 41:10)

In the end, you will see like Ezekiel did, that God has not done "without cause" all that He has done.[9] And, you will also come to understand the depth, the width and the height of God's unconditional Love for you. "...Yea, I have loved [you] with an everlasting Love: therefore with lovingkindness have I drawn [you]." (Jeremiah 31:3)

This does not mean to say that *everyone* will come to intimacy with God in the same precise way or that everyone in his or her journey will pass through a dark night, but for those of you who do, I pray this book will help to clarify exactly what God is doing and why. I pray that the words on these pages will comfort you and help you to understand what God requires of you, and, most importantly, how you can get through your night as quickly as possible.

In Chapter Two we will see that almost every major man and woman of God, especially those in the Bible, have gone through similar night seasons. Some say that these dark nights are God's way of preparing us for a special ministry.[10] I believe, it's simply God's way of teaching us naked faith so that we might enjoy intimacy with Him.

My heart's cry, then, through these pages, is to assure you that God has neither abandoned you nor slated you for destruction. Jeremiah tells us, "For I know the thoughts that I think toward you, saith the Lord, *thoughts of peace*, and not of evil, to give you an expected end." (29:11, emphasis added) God is the One who will see you through, because He is the One who promises never to leave you nor forsake you.[11]

The Lord is in the process of "conforming us all into His image." Romans 8:29 tells us that this is His basic will. Once we allow Him the freedom to implement this transformation in our lives, the result will be twofold: *abundant life* in our soul and *intimacy* with Him in our spirit-- i.e., the fulness of Christ. In order to accomplish this, however, there are two major things He must begin to do in each of our lives: *cleanse us from sin* and *purify us from our self-centered ways*. All Christians have *eternal Life*, but very few Christians experience *abundant Life* and the fulness of Christ![12] These blessings come, not through the absence of trials and tribulations, but simply with the presence of Jesus.

The process by which God brings this intimacy about is called *sanctification*. As 2 Thessalonians 2:13 says, "...God hath from the beginning chosen you to *salvation through sanctification* of the Spirit and belief of the truth...." (emphasis added). In some people, sanctification is a life long process. In others, it occurs quite rapidly. *The key is our cooperation and our willingness. If we relinquish our wills and our lives completely to God, walk in faith and by His Spirit, the sanctification process can go unhindered and there will be no need for a night season at all.*

So, this book is not written to frighten anyone, but simply to help believers understand what God's will is, how we can have an unshakeable faith so that He can implement His will in our lives, and ultimately, how we can attain an intimacy with Him that we have never before known.

As Oswald Chambers has noted, "...the darkness...comes not on account of sin, but because the Spirit of God is leading us away from walking in the light of our consciences to walking in the light of His love."[13] Until we understand that our night seasons are "Father-filtered" and come directly from the hand of God to accomplish His will in our lives, we are in danger of sliding into a bottomless pit of self-pity and confusion.

To those of you who might question whether it's even possible to walk through a night season without losing faith in God's Love, I can answer a resounding "Yes!" Although your prayers will be uttered through tears, and your praise will indeed be a sacrifice, you must choose to believe Lamentations 3:33 which declares that *God does not willingly afflict His children*, but only to accomplish His loving purposes.

Although this is a decision only you can make, I believe I can best weep with those who weep and comfort and encourage those who are hurting, by sharing the things that I suffered and the things that I have learned during my own night of sorrow and loss. As I said before, during my night season, I yearned for a Biblically-based book that would explain exactly what God was doing in my life...and why. In the coldest hours of my night, I needed to be told that a "dawn" would surely break for me. Most of all, I needed to know that what I was experiencing others had experienced before me, that I was not alone and that God would be faithful to bring me through, regardless of how I felt or what I thought.

So this book is my way of telling you that you are not alone. Others have walked where you are walking, and have lived to tell the story of God's faithfulness and Love. Remember, the same God who accompanies you through the Valley of the Shadow will one day fill your cup to overflowing. God faithfully and lovingly works through the dark nights of our soul and spirit to bring us into an intimacy with Him that is above and beyond anything we have ever imagined. As Job stated, "I had heard of Thee by the hearing of the ear, but *now mine eye sees Thee*." My prayer is that this book will help you to see and understand God's ways in your own desert time.[14]

God's way--the way that leads to life--Scripture tells us is very narrow and few will seek it. But, if you are longing, as I am, to "...know the Love of Christ which passes knowledge..." and to "be filled with all the fulness of God" (Ephesians 3:19), then it is my hope that this book will help to strengthen you on your journey. It's not meant to be an academic treatise, but simply a guide book sharing the potential joy of *experientially knowing Christ in His fulness*. Nothing in life can compare with an intimate love relationship with the Lord of the universe. Nothing can satisfy more than this kind of union. Everything else pales into insignificance compared to this. Nothing else matters! Thus, my most fervent prayer is that when you have turned the final page, you will know that God has not done *without cause* all that He has done.

I am neither a theologian, nor a scholar. I am simply a sister, a mom and a grandma in the Lord, so this book is not a book of theology. It's simply written to express one person's view as to why we have night seasons, what God's will is in the middle of them and how He wants us to respond to them. You have the same Teacher as I do. I urge you to check out everything that is written here. As Acts 17:11 states, "These were more noble than those in Thessalonica in that *they received the word with all readiness of mind, and searched the Scriptures daily,* [to see] *whether those things were so....*" (emphasis added).

I would also like to echo the words of Frances Frangipane, who noted in his book *Holiness, Truth and the Presence of God*, "I do not presume to have written this book without error. Much effort has been given to presenting the truth of Christ without flaw, but I will be deeply indebted to those saints who are kind enough to share their insights with me. The final proof that our doctrines are correct are evidenced in our lives."

And finally, throughout this book, I will constantly refer to surrendering, relinquishing and "giving things over to the Lord." In the Prayer Section in the back of the book, there is a chapter called *Prayer Journal*, with a "sub-heading" entitled *The Inner Court Ritual* (page 360-361). I believe that these steps, the actual ones that the priests of Solomon's Temple took in order to deal with their sin and be reconciled to God, are the very steps that the Lord has laid out for us in Scripture, in order to deal with our sin and our self to be reconciled to Him. Please refer to them often. Even as you are reading, if God brings something to your mind, use these steps to take care of the issue immediately.

My prayer is that the Spirit of Truth will guide every word in this book and that every one of them might be God breathed.[15] I pray also that the Holy Spirit might use this book to:

"...cast up the highway; gather out the stones; [and] lift up a standard [Jesus] for the people." (Isaiah 62:10)

"...[help] build the old waste places...raise up the foundations of many generations; and [to help repair] the breach, [and restore the] paths to dwell in." (Isaiah 58:12)[16]

Section One:
"Fully Persuaded"

"He staggered not at the promise of God through unbelief; but was strong in faith, giving glory to God; And being *fully persuaded* that, what He had promised, He was able also to perform." (Romans 4:20-21)

Chapter One
My Own Night Season

My Shattered World

It was July of 1990. We had just found out that we owed the IRS several million dollars (yes, million!); that Chuck's company was about ready to go into bankruptcy; that we were going to lose our "dream" home; that our insurance was going to be canceled; and that our cars and other valuables were going to be repossessed.

My world was about to be shattered, and there was nothing at all that I could do about it! There was nowhere to run for comfort, and no one I could turn to. Alternating between numbness and total disbelief, I kept thinking, "How could this be happening to us? Disasters like this happen to people in their 20s and 30s, not responsible adults in their 50s!"

I was so devastated by all that was occurring (especially, since these were circumstances I personally had nothing at all to do with), that I decided to run to the only Person I knew where I could find help. And that was to God Himself.

Back in those days, we lived in Big Bear Lake in the mountains of Southern California, and my favorite place to go and seek God began right across the street from our house--a trail that led to the top of the mountain. So, I put on my old hiking clothes, grabbed my Bible and began my hike.

It was one of those perfect summer days. The sky was a brilliant blue and as a warm breeze blew gently at my back, I climbed higher and higher into the familiar hills. Through the beautiful pine trees, I could see glimpses every once in a while of the shimmering lake far below.

We loved living in Big Bear. At this point, we had been there almost five years and it had been the most idyllic time we had had in our marriage. After twenty moves in thirty years, Chuck and I were more than ready to settle down. Our four very active, and now grown, children loved skiing, sailing and hiking, so they came often for weekends and holidays. We appreciated the little town of Big Bear so very much, as well as our wonderful church home and our many dear friends.

We lived in a spectacular home with a 180-degree view on the lake. What made it so special was that the house was built on huge boulders the size of small cars and some even larger. The house was literally secured into the rocks themselves. We used to kid about living "on the rock." We had bought this little piece of heaven intending to retire there.

Although Chuck was still active in business, he'd arranged his schedule so that we could be in Big Bear five days a week and then spend the other two days in our small Orange County apartment down the hill. It was the perfect answer while he was making the transition to retirement. We planned to live in that "dream home" for the rest of our lives.

The original house that we had bought five years earlier was too small for us on a permanent basis, so we had just spent two years doing extensive remodeling. We had spent hours and hours handpicking all the perfect colors for paint, carpets and wall coverings. We had only just moved back into the house a few months earlier when all the traumatic events began.

Meeting with God

As I hiked up the hill, I could see the lake glittering in the sunlight between the trees. I found a perfect knoll where I could sit, seeing for miles around me. I was just happy to be there with Jesus, away from all my problems.

As I began to pray and read the Scriptures (Genesis 12)--which talks about Abram building an altar to the Lord--the Spirit moved me to build an altar. I gathered as many stones as I could find, piling them on top of each other to a height of about three feet. I named it my Bethel.
I often wonder if that pillar is still there.

I sat back, turned my eyes towards the sky and began to think about my life. Up to this point, our lives had been very blessed, even though early on we had had a few marital and family problems. On the whole, however, we had had a wonderful life. We had been married a little over thirty years, we had four beautiful children, a beautiful home, a fantastic job and future and many, many friends. Now, so very abruptly--so very quickly--all that had changed.

We not only were experiencing the bankruptcy, the IRS mess and the loss of our home, cars and insurance, but also at this same time, many of our close friends had turned their backs on us. As soon as the local media began broadcasting news of our bankruptcy, the rumor mills began.

Although we fully expected to be given a cold shoulder by the secular world, we weren't prepared for the reaction we received from some of our dear Christian brothers and sisters, some of whom had invested in Chuck's company. These were our beloved Christian friends--ones whom we had counseled through their own marital and family difficulties. So it was such a shock that at the time we needed their support and their love the most, they would forsake us. Within a few days of the announcement on the radio and in the newspapers, our reputations were virtually ruined.

For me, the loss of my Christian brothers and sisters was the most agonizing part of the whole ordeal. When we had millions of dollars, our friends were too numerous to count. But when we owed millions and were in desperate straits, many of these "friends" quickly disappeared. If it hadn't been for the encouragement of a few faithful families and a couple of people whom we barely knew, Chuck and I would have felt completely abandoned by the Body of Christ. It was an absolutely crushing experience!

Trying to pick up the pieces of our lives was like trying to sweep up after an explosion. My own ministry had by this time dwindled down to just a few speaking engagements and the books that I had so longed to write had been shelved because of all of our own personal problems. (This was way before *The King's High Way Series*)

As I meditated on all these losses that had just occurred in my life, God directed me to 1 Peter which talks about a fiery trial of faith about ready to begin (1 Peter 1:7; 4:12) and Psalm 102:3 in which David cries, "My days are consumed like smoke and my bones are burned...." These Scriptures were <u>not</u> very encouraging, but they explained a little of what seemed to be taking place.

Even before the final crash of Chuck's company, when everyone else was saying, "Don't worry, it's going to be fine," every time I would pray, I seemed to receive Scriptures that indicated just the opposite--it wasn't going to be fine; we were going to go down in flames. So, God had already forewarned me. I just should have been better prepared for the crash.

God ministered in many ways to me on the mountaintop that day, but the most wonderful thing He did was to give me some incredible personal promises through His Word. As I listened carefully for His words of divine guidance and encouragement, I was stunned by a string of almost unbelievable promises. Through the Scriptures and His Spirit, God spoke to me of a future ministry far beyond my wildest dreams. As I marked each Scripture fast and furiously, I understood how young David must have felt when Samuel anointed him for a destiny he couldn't even imagine.

These were promises that I needed to hear at that time, in order to weather the coming storms. At first I was awed by what I read and heard God's Spirit say to my heart and mind. But over the next several weeks as I prayed and read the Word over and over again, God continued to confirm what I had heard on that mountaintop.

Trial of My Faith

Yet as I waited and watched for the fulfillment of those promises over the next few years, I began to grow impatient. After walking with the Lord for over thirty years, I knew I had to rely on His perfect timing, but I also was a twentieth-century Christian, and this was one of those times when I was desperate for quick answers. My world had shattered almost overnight, so I naturally assumed that the Lord would move just as quickly to bring all these new promises to pass.

Because of this assumption, the hardest part for me over the next seven years was that those glorious promises God had given me up there on that mountaintop never came true. As I experienced God's Word coming true in all the circumstances surrounding the demise of Chuck's company and the loss of our home, etc., the personal promises did not become reality. Not only did they not come true, my life experiences proved to be just the opposite--everything in my world crumbled and crashed. Like Job, instead of blessings, more and more trials just kept coming.

> "...when I waited for light, there came darkness."
> (Job 30:26)[17]

After the eventual loss of our home, we rented another house in Big Bear, not far from our daughter Lisa. In 1992, a year and a half after the bankruptcy, that rented house turned out to be on the epicenter of a 6.8 earthquake, during which most of our furniture and valuables were destroyed. Actually, we were the lucky ones. Houses on both sides of us twisted off their foundations by as much as ten feet, and even though our house sustained a lot of damage, it was miraculously still standing. There were, however, huge cracks in the walls and the foundation and everything in the house that could break broke.

It took Lisa and me eight hours to shovel our way from the kitchen door to the kitchen sink. We had to wade through a knee-high sea of broken china and glass, shattered appliances and unidentified pieces of the house. Most of our furniture and precious family mementos that had survived the bankruptcy were now reduced to rubble--in addition to all the goblets and china from our millionaire days. As I surveyed the buckling sidewalks and shattered windows, I couldn't even bear the thought of starting over *again*. As far as I was concerned, our life in Big Bear had finally come to an end.

After the earthquake and through a series of God-directed circumstances, we ended up moving to Northern Idaho. Although we loved the Northwest, we ultimately had to move another <u>six</u> times before we were finally able to find a permanent home. All of this moving and all of this devastation happened in less than two years, taking a tremendous toll on me in every way. Like the author of Lamentations, I felt that "...my strength and my hope is perished from the Lord." (Lamentations 3:18)

Even in our new situation in Idaho, God allowed all my hopes and dreams *in every area of my life* to be frustrated and destroyed. Every arrangement I tried to make blew up in my face. All my expectations went unmet, and my plans were continually confounded.

While clinging steadfastly to the promises that God had given me on the mountaintop, I kept expecting my situation to get better, but it only got worse. I'd somehow survived the shaking of homes, our finances and our loss of "friends," but now I began to experience devastating circumstances through much-loved family members, through respected pastors and mentors, through trusted partners and long-time confidantes as well as in my own personal struggle for ministry. I am not at liberty to relate all the specific details of my darkest hours, because it would offend these beloved people. Suffice to say, the "test of fire" that had forever changed my life on the *outside*, was now being turned up on the *inside*, causing incredible anguish and torment.

Some of the emotions that I noted in my journal during this time are descriptive of my feelings:

"God has abandoned me." "My prayers are not being heard." "I fear I have lost His Love." "Doubt and confusion are suffocating me" "I'll never be able to trust again." "I am overwhelmed with depression, discouragement and disappointment." "I feel like giving up."

Some of the other descriptive words I used in my journal were: "destroyed," "desolate," "self-centered," "self-pity," "anxiousness," "joyless," "lost," "coldness," "bitterness," "broken," "dismayed," "lifeless," "betrayed" and "forsaken."

Job 19:8-10 describes my feelings perfectly, "He hath fenced up my way that I cannot pass, and He hath set darkness in my paths. He hath stripped me of my glory...He hath destroyed me on every side, and I am gone...."

My world seemed to be crumbling on every side, and yet I still clutched at the memory of those glorious promises. I waited for the Lord's blessing, and yet that day never seemed to dawn for me. Each painful trial was followed by another trial, and as I waited...and waited...and waited for a break in the clouds, I truly began to understand the meaning of the word *weary*.

Had I Misunderstood God?

Had I somehow misunderstood God? Were those promises only meant to pertain to my spiritual life? No, the Scriptures I had received on the mountain top that day had been far too specific to be "spiritualized." Then, why the incredible delay? Why was I having to endure such a long season of sorrow and dryness? Would I ever again feel the joy of my salvation? I felt as if the words of Ezekiel pertained directly to me: "[My] bones are dried [up], and [my] hope is lost: [I am] [completely] cut off...." (Ezekiel 37:11)

Up to this point, I had never heard of the "dark night" or "night seasons" as the Bible calls them (Job 30:17), nor did I fully understand the sanctification process or what God was trying to accomplish in my life. Thus, I fought Him every step of the way which, of course, not only made matters worse but also much more painful for me. Every time something else "bad" would happen, I'd come out fighting. At times, I felt as if God had set me as His mark. And, in a way, I guess He really had. Only, it was because He loved me and wanted me to experience *real* abundant Life.

I had always loved and served God faithfully. Why would He allow all this devastation in my life? What was happening to me? I knew that I was not in rebellion against God. I had not given in to self-pity, nor was I holding onto unforgiveness, yet there was so much confusion growing inside of me. Although I had faithfully practiced confession and repentance for many years, sharp pieces of doubt were beginning to rise up from the depths of my soul. There seemed to be no explanation for what I was experiencing.

I'd made it through the bankruptcy and the earthquake, but when the heat of adversity started affecting all my intimate relationships, my ministry, my personal expectations and belief systems, I went into a tailspin. The candle of my faith was burning low, and doubt kept trying to rise up to take its place. I couldn't understand what God was doing or why. Had I done something to deserve all this and when was it all going to end?

The Need to Be Fully Persuaded

So often at the bottom of our struggles in the dark night is doubt and unbelief. It certainly was with me. We measure the validity of a promise by our own earthly standards which, of course, leave us wide open for doubt. *Doubt affects everything we think, say and do.* How can we trust and have faith in God today, if we don't think He has been faithful to His promises of yesterday? We can't! Doubt in God's faithfulness not only causes us indescribable inner torment, it also prolongs our agony.

When I am totally honest with myself and I peel away all the garbage, I realized that I had trusted God, yes, *but not to the point of abandoning all my earthly sources of comfort and security.* I had faith in God, yes, *but not to the point of setting aside all other supports and laying them at the cross.* I had relied upon God, yes, *but not to the point of accepting that fact that I didn't understand what God was doing, and trusting Him anyway.* I still had my own human expectations, my own presumptions and my own ambitions, and when these "supports" began to be taken away, I crashed. Big time!

Nothing reveals our true selves so well as the advent of hard times! In order to expose what is hidden below the surface of our pleasant religious exterior, God often must turn up the heat.

All of us want to be able to see and understand what God is doing in our lives, why He is doing it, what the outcome will be, and when exactly the end will occur! This, unfortunately, is not faith, but simply presumption on our part. Real faith is <u>not</u> seeing, <u>not</u> understanding, <u>not</u> feeling and <u>not</u> knowing. Real faith is simply trusting, no matter what we see happening, no matter what we understand to be true, and no matter what we feel like, that *God will be faithful to His Word and perform His promises to us in His timing and in His way.*

This faith is the kind that Abraham possessed, who "...staggered not at the promise of God through unbelief; but was strong in faith, giving glory to God; And being *fully persuaded that, what He had promised, He was able also to perform.*" (Romans 4:20-21 emphasis added)

Faith is allowing God to be God. Faith is allowing God to do in our lives all that He needs to do (good or bad from our point of view), in order to accomplish His perfect will. Faith is allowing God to strip, flay and crucify us, if that's what is needed to accomplish His will in us. *Faith is simply accepting God's night seasons as part of His will towards us.* Job came to know what true faith was all about when he declared, "though [You] slay me, yet will I trust [You]."

The turning point in my life came when I finally realized that *abandonment* to God's will and having *human expectations* cannot co-exist in my soul. *Abandonment to God's will is laying everything down at the foot of the cross and leaving it there, whereas, human expectation is picking it back up again and running with it.*

Knowing God's Will

God's primary goal and purpose for our lives as Christians is that Christ may be formed *in* us and lived out *through us.* "For whom He did foreknow, He also did predestinate to be *conformed into the image of His Son.*" (Romans 8:29) Once this transformation begins to occur in our lives, we not only will experience God's *abundant Life* in our soul, but we'll also enjoy *intimate fellowship* with Him in our spirit. In other words, we'll begin to "know" the fulness of Christ--experiencing Him in His totality, inside and out.

God wants us to *know* Him so intimately and so completely that we won't be moved away from Him when difficulties arise in our lives. As David declared, "I foresaw the Lord always before my face; for He is on my right hand, *that I should not be moved* [away]." (Acts 2:25)

Ignorance of God's will in our lives is the origin of much of our troubles. Thus, one of the purposes of this book is not only to help us see and understand what God's basic will is, but also to realize that everything He allows in our lives is orchestrated to accomplish that will. Therefore, if we can see all of our circumstances as being "Father-filtered," then, we can receive them as part of His plan and remain at rest in them. If, however, we don't understand what He is doing, especially in our night seasons, we'll get wiped out even before we begin.

"Night seasons" are not ordinary trials, but specific transition times where God moves us away from depending upon "self" to depending totally upon Him. They are seasons where He strengthens our faith and teaches us to walk only by His Spirit. *Faith is the only means by which He can appropriate His will in our lives.*

If we could only view, just for a moment, our spiritual lives from God's perspective, we would see that the darkness He allows is good and truly *an act of His Love.* It's the process He uses to *replace us with Himself.* He knows that this night of faith will not only produce a cleansing of our soul and spirit, but also a oneness with Him that we have never known before. If we understand what He is trying to accomplish, then the momentary confusion and darkness we might experience won't shake the certainty of our being loved and we won't crumble or lose our faith in the dark. We can agree with Luke's declaration:

> "I foresaw the Lord always before my face, for He is on my right hand, *that I should not be moved.*" (Acts 2:25)

So, don't read any further unless you are longing, as I am, to see *"the Lord always before [your] face"* because this way of faith is not easy. It will confound your logic, destroy your schedules, annihilate your religious attitudes, frustrate your patience and probably alienate some of your acquaintances. It's certainly not the kind of faith that the world teaches. It's not even the kind of faith that some churches teach. This kind of faith demands *all* from us and requires great love for God. *But, by learning to have **faith in the night seasons**, we will be headed for the summit of Life where we shall see our Beloved face to face.*

Joy in the Morning

All of God's promises in His Word are true. However, *His way of accomplishing these promises in our lives is regulated by our faith and our unconditional abandonment to His will.*

As I am learning to stay surrendered His will and allow Him to do in my life all that He needs to do in order to reproduce Himself in me, He is radically changing my life from the inside out. I am beginning to experience all the incredible blessings of His abiding presence. There's a continuous joy, peace and rest, in spite of my circumstances, that is beyond my understanding. There is an empowering of His Spirit--with new discernment and new revelation--that wasn't there before. There is an intimacy and a friendship and a closeness and a oneness with Jesus that I've never had before. I have fallen so in love with my God that I truly am beginning to see Him "always before my face."

Jesus, of course, was the *only* One who was ever able to have perfect and consistent fellowship with God. As long as we are in our human bodies, there will always be more sin and self to be dealt with. But, as we daily allow God to show us what He wants us to surrender to Him, we will be able, in an ever-increasing way, to experience His presence and His fulness.

It seems the more I learn to truly be abandoned to His will and live for the moment, the more I am witnessing God's beginning to fulfill *every one* of those magnificent promises that He gave me up on that mountaintop in Big Bear so many years ago.

Truly, I have learned that weeping does last for a "night," but oh what joy awaits us in the morning! (Psalm 30:5) As Jeremiah states, "There is hope in [the] end." (31:17)

Chapter Two
Are Night Seasons Part of God's Will?

Kingdom of God

If you have longed for greater intimacy with the Lord, and longed to see Him "always before [your] face," *the journey you must take is an inward one.* As believers, we don't have to travel far to find the kingdom of God,[18] because Luke 17:21 declares it lies "within" us.[19] This is where God now makes His dwelling.[20]

> "Whosoever shall confess that Jesus is the Son of God, God dwelleth in him, and he in God." (1 John 4:15)

Thus, in order to really experience intimacy with God and His moment-by-moment presence, we must learn to live in that inner chamber of our spirit where God now dwells. "I will put My Spirit within you, and cause you to walk in My statutes...and ye shall be My people, and I will be your God." (Ezekiel 36:27-28)[21] This is the place where *God teaches, guides and communes with us* and the place where *we worship, praise and love Him.* In other words, it's only through our <u>spirit</u> that God's presence can be known.

Now, when I say "inward journey," I do *not* mean a "self-ward" journey, or detachment and flight from the world, but rather, a process of sanctification by which we *can* meet with God in our spirit and experience His fulness. However, because this realm of the spirit operates outside of the reach of our human understanding, we cannot approach it logically or emotionally. We cannot see, hear, smell, taste or feel our way along this narrow path, thus, the journey inward can sometimes be very dark and confusing. In other words, there is no introspective technique we can use, no seminar we can attend, and no instruction manual we can study in order to reach this place of spiritual intimacy with Jesus. We must learn to walk purely by *"faith,"* <u>not</u> by our feelings, our sight or our understanding. This journey is accomplished only by learning how to totally abandon ourselves to God by faith.

Those of us who want this deeper relationship with God will find the inward journey towards intimacy much different from any other spiritual path we have ever been on. Many of us will struggle against it because we don't realize what God is doing. And, because of our ignorance, our journey inward can often turn out to be a *night of confusion and darkness.*[22] Indeed, Job describes it as "...where the light is as darkness." (10:22)

What Exactly are "Night Seasons?"

Trials and problems come to all Christians because of personal sin, the sins of others, the schemes of the devil, or the fallen state of the human race. According to the Bible, a true "night season" is none of these! A Biblical night season is a God-sent, Father-filtered period of time where He specifically strengthens our faith so that we might come to know Him in His fulness. (See James 1:2-2:26) It doesn't really matter were our trials come from, because our response should be exactly the same: repent of any known sin; love others wisely with God's Love; put on the whole armor of God; and, keep on walking by faith through the eyes of our spirit.

The thing that makes a "night season" so unique and so different from other trials is that there seems to be no disobedience or no known sin. Remember Isaiah 50:10: "Who is among you that *feareth the Lord*, that *obeyeth the voice of His servant*, that walketh in darkness, and hath no light?" (emphasis added) Notice something important here: this person not only fears the Lord, but he also obeys His voice. In other words, there is no known disobedience or sin involved, and yet, this person still walks in darkness.

The next distinctive characteristic about night seasons is that heaven "seems" silent. No matter how much we pray, seek God and read His Word, He doesn't seem to communicate with us as He once did. We don't "hear" Him, "see" Him or "feel" Him as we have in the past. In other words, a night season is a series of trials where we think that God has left us or abandoned us.

Night seasons are Father-filtered periods of time where God teaches us by *depriving us of the "natural" light we have always relied upon* (our own seeing, feeling and understanding). Even as mature Christians, most of us still walk by the "flesh"--by our own emotions and though the eyes of our own understanding. This is why so many of us don't know God intimately and why we have had such a lukewarm relationship with Him. God, on the other hand, loves us too much to allow us to remain in this dispassionate state. He knows that the only way we will ever attain immovable intimacy with Him is by learning to walk in *naked faith*--faith that is not dependent upon our sight, our feelings and our experience, but on Him alone. Thus, the classroom that He uses to each us this lesson is called "the dark night" or "night seasons."

God instructs us by "darkening" us--by withdrawing the natural light we are so used to. During this time of instruction, He leads us away from depending upon *self* and what we can see, feel and experience, to depending totally and completely upon *Him* and nothing else. This stripping away is why it's called "naked" faith.

According to the Biblical account, a night season is a time where God lovingly removes all our natural and comfortable support systems (internal and external), in order to replace them with total and unshakeable faith in Him. It's a time where He allows circumstances into our lives that darken our understanding, that negate our feelings and that put to confusion all our own plans and purposes. In just a few pages, we will recount the story of Joseph in the Old Testament as an example of this kind of perfect trust.

Listen to how Madame Guyon describes a night season in her book *Final Steps in Christian Maturity*:

"There comes a time in the believer's life when the Lord withdraws the joy. He will seemingly withdraw the graces. At the same time, the Christian may also find himself in a period of persecution--persecution, no less, than that coming from Christians in religious authority. Further, he may find much difficulty in his home or private life. He may also be experiencing great difficulties with his health. Somewhere there will be a great deal of pain or other losses too numerous to mention. The believer may also be undergoing experiences which he feels are totally unique to himself. Other Christians, in whom he has put his trust, may forsake him and mistreat him. He may feel that he has been very unjustly treated. He will feel this toward men and he will feel it toward his God, for--in the midst of all this other pain and confusion--it will seem that God, too, has left him!

"Even more believers give up the journey when the Lord seems to have forsaken them in the spirit and left their spirit dead--while the world and all else is crashing in on them, friends forsaking them, and great suffering and pain abounding everywhere in their lives. But, the true land of promise always lies beyond a vast wasteland. Promise is found only on the far side of a desert. When you can go beyond that place and not seeing your Lord, believe He is there by the eyes of faith alone; when you can walk further and further into Christ when there are no senses, no feelings, not even the slightest registration of the presence of God; when you can sit before Him when everything around you and within you seems to be either falling apart or dead; and when you can come before your Lord without question and without demand, serene in faith alone,

and there, before Him, worship Him without distraction, without
a great deal of consciousness of self and with no spiritual sense of
Him, *then will the test of commitment begin to be established.* Then
will begin the true journey of the Christian life."[23]

Trusting God in the Darkness

Since most of us are unable to learn these lessons through our reason,
our intellect or our emotions, God must teach us by darkening areas of
our soul, forcing us to rely upon our faith and the *eyes of our spirit.*

Although it's hard for us to imagine that God, *who is light* [24] could
ever dwell in and work through darkness, the Bible tells us that, at times,
He does.[25] This darkness is His "secret place." (Psalm 18:11) In 1 Kings
8:12, it says, "The Lord said that He would dwell in the thick darkness."
And in Exodus 20:21, Moses approached "the thick darkness where God
was." The Bible tells us that God not only "forms the light," but He also
"creates the darkness." (Isaiah 45:7)[26] *Darkness and light are the same
to Him.*[27]

This is simply saying that the things of God are far beyond the human
eye and the human ear. They are dark to us because they are beyond our
human understanding. Thus, if we are to continue our inward journey
towards intimacy with God and experience His fulness, we must choose
to walk purely by faith *in the darkness*, clinging to the assurance that
God has allowed whatever is happening in our life for a purpose and that
His will is being accomplished. Being able to unconditionally trust God
in the darkness is essential, because if we give in to doubting His Love
and care at this time, we can easily lose our way.

Many of us will struggle in this new realm of faith just as a swimmer
fights the powerful current that draws him into deeper water. Unless he
quiets his fears and calmly rests in the water, the swimmer will drown.
The believer, likewise, will drown in this dark time unless he learns to be
still and to quiet his soul.[28] God is simply using the darkness to
accomplish His will: to form Christ in us so that we might enjoy not only
His abundant Life, but also intimate fellowship.

Yet, many of us completely misunderstand this aspect of discipleship.
Because we cannot grasp God's mysterious ways, *we often distrust His
motives.* When God allows painful circumstances into our lives, we
hastily assume that He is punishing us or that He has forsaken us, yet
nothing could be further from the truth. He is simply attempting to free
us from our soulish limitations and lead us into the wider realm of His
Spirit.[29]

So many of us lack understanding of this spiritual discipline, that we naturally assume the darkness has come forth from the enemy, and that it is intended for our destruction. Nevertheless, Alan Redpath, the notable English writer, assures us that, "The devil has nothing to do with (these dark times). God has brought us to this experience. *He wants [simply] to replace us with Himself.*"[30]

I love that! God uses these dark times to simply "replace us with Himself." This is the whole Christian life in a nutshell! This is God's will: to empty us of ourselves so He can fill us with Himself.

Because this replacement process is so painful, however, God knows that many will walk away from Him bitter and confused. He also knows that others will reject Him for a season, and still others, forever. But, for the joy that He has set before those who are willing to go all the way with Him, God risks being misunderstood.

Personal Examples

Even though we all long to have the kind of intimacy that Jesus had with His Father, many of us have, instead, settled for a pale imitation of Christianity. We have become imprisoned by our "soulish" and emotional understanding of God. We declare that we are willing to pay the price for a deeper relationship with Him, yet we writhe in agony when God begins to re-arrange our lives. Until we are willing to let our precious alabaster boxes be completely broken and Jesus' Life formed in us, we will *never* fully experience the intimacy, the fulness and the oneness with God that He desires.

As I travel around the country speaking and sharing with other believers, I hear about so many devastating circumstances that God has allowed. I receive hundreds of letters and phone calls from Christians all over the country who are in night seasons. As these precious people attempt to sort through the wreckage of their broken dreams, hopes and plans, they feel weighted down by bitter disappointment, doubt and even a sense of abandonment. They feel much like Job when he uttered in pain and ignorance, "What have I done to Thee, O watcher of men? Why hast Thou set me as Thy target?" (7:20 NAS) "Thou hast laid me in the lowest pit, in darkness, in the deeps...." (Psalm 88:6)

The following stories are a few examples of the confusion and desperation these people are feeling. Are we somehow missing God? Are we hearing Him incorrectly? Are we jumping to conclusions, or *are the "night seasons" that God allows into our lives truly part of His will towards us*?

First, there is our own example. The circumstances that precipitated our bankruptcy, and that ultimately triggered my own night of faith, were absolutely perplexing. In 1989, Chuck was president and CEO of a small technology company that was awarded a contract to supply computers to all the school children in Russia. Many larger companies had bid for this contract, so when Chuck's company won the deal, we were convinced it was the Lord's hand. In fact, Chuck was so sure it was God's will and so excited about the opportunity, he used most of our own personal money to help finance the deal. After continual "green lights" for the next six months, all of a sudden, the whole deal suddenly and unexpectedly fell apart, leaving us completely dumbstruck and financially destroyed. Was God in this? Was this His will?

Second, there is the story of a dear friend who had fallen in love with a beautiful young woman. This man had not only prayed consistently about the relationship, but he also had searched the Scriptures and sought counsel from other believers. When he was absolutely convinced the Lord was in it, he asked the young woman to marry him. She readily accepted, but the night before the wedding, she unexpectedly walked out on him. Our friend was totally crushed. As a result, he went into a spiritual and emotional tailspin. Did this man somehow take a wrong turn, or was God's will at work in these painful circumstances?

Then there is the circumstances of our friends who'd spent their life savings to buy a restaurant. It had been their lifelong dream to own a diner, and after praying and seeking the Lord, they felt sure He was prompting them to move ahead. However, a year and a half after putting everything they owned into that restaurant to make it succeed, it went bankrupt. Was God in this situation?

Next, there is the letter I received from a gentleman who told me about the lucrative job offer he'd accepted in another state. After the Lord confirmed the move in *many* ways, he and his wife confidently sold their home and took the kids out of school. After buying a new house and even relocating their in-laws, the "job of promise" suddenly fell through and this man was unable to find work for months. Again, did this man somehow miss God's voice?

Then, there is the incident of the devout Christian parents whose teenage son, afflicted with cerebral palsy from birth, was suffering with severe pain in his back. After seeking several medical opinions and spending months in constant prayer, these parents felt God directing them towards a specific surgical procedure for their son. Instead of relieving the pain, however, this surgery only compounded the problem and even created physical complications that hadn't existed before.

Thus, the parents were left emotionally "shell-shocked" by this unexpected turn of events. Did they somehow "miss" God?

And finally, there is the woman who prayed for and wanted, more than anything else in the world, to be a mother and to have children. She loved God with all her heart, yet after the miscarriage of three babies, she was left devastated and feeling totally abandoned by Him. Listen, as she expresses her disappointment: "...when you have been a Christian for 15 years, however, where do you go? (Whom do you turn to?) Intellectually and experientially, you know that everything else is false and yet the God *you thought you knew* was not who He turned out to be... After our heartfelt pleadings were met with stony silence and a closed door, I had to face the fact that God *could*, but was *choosing not to*, act."

Why It's So Important to Know God's Will

Are we somehow missing God? Was He in all of these tragedies? Would a loving Father really allow situations so devastating? Are these events truly part of God's will towards us?

Ten years ago, I would have said, "No way!" But, as I search the Scriptures for understanding, I find passages like Job 30:26, "When I looked for [or expected] good, then evil came unto me." And, Lamentations 3 says, "He hath led me, and *brought me into darkness*, [but] not into light...He hath *broken my bones*...He hath *set me in dark places...He hath hedged me about*, that I cannot get out...*He hath enclosed my ways* with hewn stone; *He hath made my paths crooked*." (verses 2, 4, 6-7, 9) And Isaiah 59:9-10, "...*We wait for light, but behold obscurity*; for brightness, but we walk in darkness. We grope for the wall like the blind, and we grope as if we had no eyes; we stumble at noonday as in the night...." And finally, Job 19:8, "*He hath fenced up my way* that I cannot pass, and *He hath set darkness in my paths*." (emphasis added) Many more Scriptures on the dark night are listed in the back of the book (after the Prayer Section).

All of the people in the above personal examples, including Chuck and me, were absolutely convinced that God had been involved in their decisions. They had prayed the whole way and felt assured that He had given them specific direction to step out in faith. Yet in the end, many of them were left with emotional, and often financial, heartbreak and chaos.

Are you also one of these people?

I cannot answer for all the other people listed above; I can only answer for Chuck and me. But I can say for both of us, in hindsight, all the devastating things that God has allowed in our lives over the last seven years have turned out, like Job said, *to open our eyes and enable us to intimately see Him* in ways we never had before.[31]   And we also recognize, as Ezekiel did, that God has not done *without cause* all that He has done. (14:23)

God loves each of us so much that He will do whatever is necessary in each of our lives to accomplish His will--to replace us with Himself, so that we might experience both abundant Life and this kind of unshakeable intimacy.   If we understand what God is trying to accomplish in our lives and can see our circumstances as sent directly from Him in order to implement His will, then we can receive them as part of His plan, find the faith we need to get through and remain at rest in them.   However, if we don't understand God's will, especially in our night seasons, then we'll get wiped out even before we start.

Loren Sandford has just written a good book on the dark night of the soul.   In it, he declares, "Scripture shows us a repeated pattern in which man *receives a call, experiences success, is driven into exile* (dark night) and then, finally *returns to fulfill his destiny* in the Lord."[32]

A Scriptural Example: Joseph

A perfect Scriptural example of this pattern is Joseph in the Old Testament.   He received a call from God, was given special giftings (success), went through a night season of exile, and, eventually, was instilled as Prince of Egypt, his true destiny from the Lord.   Joseph is an example of one who understood God's purposes for a "dark night" and had the faith to triumph through it.

The story goes like this: God gave Joseph an incredible dream that contained some mind-boggling promises for the future, yet this dream left his brothers seething with jealousy. After throwing Joseph into a pit, they sold him to a caravan of Ishmaelites on their way to Egypt.   Joseph eventually was bought by Potiphar, a high-ranking Egyptian official, whose wife repeatedly tried to seduce the devout young Hebrew. When she finally accused the innocent Joseph of trying to molest her, Potiphar angrily threw the young man into prison, where he remained for years. When Joseph was finally released, as a result of divinely-orchestrated circumstances, he had been in bondage for a total of *thirteen years!*

Questions that naturally come to our mind are: Had God really spoken to Joseph through that dream? What about all those incredible promises?   Did God change his mind? Did He abandon Joseph during those thirteen years in prison? I don't think so. I don't believe anything that happened to Joseph during that time was a surprise to God. He knew exactly what Joseph would do and He also knew exactly what He wanted to accomplish through Joseph's life (i.e., fulfill his destiny by bringing the Israelites to Egypt). If you carefully read the Scriptures about Joseph's imprisonment, you will see that all who saw Joseph during those thirteen years recognized that "God was with him."[33] Joseph somehow understood God's will and thus, had the faith to allow God to work through him, even in his darkest night.

God not only creates the brightness of day, He also creates the darkness of night.[34] Thus, He not only is the Author of our joy and gladness, but also He's the Author of our night seasons. Too many Christians have chosen to recreate God in their own image. They logically tell themselves, "A loving father would never willingly allow his children to suffer hardship, and neither would a heavenly Father!" However, if we put God into a box built by our own human understanding, how will we ever survive the night seasons of our faith? How could Joseph have survived those thirteen years if not for his unwavering faith and belief in the goodness of God?

If we only believe in a God of easy comfort, how can our faith ever withstand the heat of harsh circumstances? Without roots that go deep into the soil, the grass will surely wither. And the same thing is true with us. If our faith is not unconditionally rooted in God's Love, then we, too, will wither and die during our dark night.

Other Scriptural Examples

As we search the Scriptures, we find that almost every great man or woman of God experienced their own night season or dark night. On the very night God made His eternal covenant with *Abraham,* the Bible tells us that a "terror and great darkness fell upon him." (Genesis 15:12 NAS) *David,* still reeling from the sound of all Jerusalem's singing his praises, had to flee to the wilderness and hide inside a cave like a common criminal.[35] Just days after his incredible victory over the prophets of Baal, *Elijah* hid under a tree and begged God to kill him.[36] After being born a prince of Egypt, God allowed *Moses* to be stripped of his home, his privileges, his wealth, his power and his pride and made him to dwell 40 years in the desert as a common shepherd.

And, even *Jesus,* with the "hosannas" still ringing in his ears, experienced an agony so intense that it caused him literally to sweat blood.[37] However, after the crucifixion, there came the incredible story of Jesus' resurrection. And at the end of Moses' long night season, God ultimately exalted him and gave him the unique privilege of seeing God "face to face."[38] When God called him from the burning bush, Moses couldn't even speak without stuttering, yet this was the man God ultimately chose to become His friend.[39] In like manner Joseph, after thirteen years of learning humility, endurance and overcoming faith, was exalted to a position of incredible authority.[40]

This seems to be God's pattern over and over again in the lives of His chosen vessels: A dark, emptying-out time and then, a full, infilling time of blessing, where they have the privilege of seeing and experiencing God as never before. Truly, God is faithful and "...according to all that He promised; there hath not failed one word of all His good promise, which He promised." (1 Kings 8:56)

Abraham, David, Elijah and Moses were the kind of men spoken about in Isaiah 50:10-11, "Who...feareth the Lord [and] obeyeth [His] voice...[but] walketh in darkness, and hath no light." Yet, because these men went on and, "...*trust[ed] in the name of the Lord, and stay[ed] upon [their] God*" in their night seasons, God was able not only to accomplish His will, but also to fill them with His fulness.

God's will for each of our lives is not only *doing* what He asks, but also *accepting with praise and thanksgiving all that He allows.*

Night Seasons of Other Prominent People

Many theologians and saints throughout history have also experienced and written about their own "night seasons." You can find this recurring theme in the biographies of Charles Spurgeon, Martin Luther, Francis Schaeffer, St. John of the Cross, Madame Guyon, Oswald Chambers, Augustine, John Wesley, Watchman Nee, Catherine Marshall, Dietrich Bonhoeffer, Brother Lawrence, Hudson Taylor, Charles Finney, George Fox, William Law, Jesse Penn Lewis, Francois Fenelon and many others.

These men and women eventually learned to *see through the darkness* with God's eyes and, as a result of their faithful endurance, they were able to boldly enter into His presence and find the peace and joy and rest they were looking for. Tozer called it "the ministry of the night" and Spurgeon "a child of light walking in darkness." Oswald Chambers even wrote a poem entitled "Dark Night of the Soul" in his book *Abandoned to God:*[41]

> "Cut it off. My heart is bleeding,
> And my spirit's wrung in pain,
> Yet I hear my Jesus pleading,
> Cut it off or all is vain.
>
> So I've stopped my ears in terror
> Lest self-pity make me quail,

Lest at last I take the error
And God's purpose thwart and fail.

I am bowed to death in sadness,
For the pain is all too great,
But the dear Lord must find pleasure
In the way He maketh straight."

Listen to how Francois Fenelon (in the 1600s) describes the dark night in his book *The Seeking Heart*:

"God will eventually test you in all areas of your life, but He will not let your trials become greater than you can bear. Let God use trials to help you grow. Do not measure your progress, your strength or what God is doing. His work is not less efficient because *what He is doing is invisible*. Much of God's work is done in secret because you would not die to yourself if He always visibly stretched out His hand to save you. *God does not transform you on a bed of light, life and grace. His transformation is done on the cross in darkness, poverty and death.*"[42]

The above believers were honest men and women like Job. They were praying servants who truly loved the Lord and had compassion for the poor. Like Job, they had a lifestyle of confession and repentance, and had faithfully reared their children in the fear of the Lord. Yet, after a long season of trials and tribulations, many of these men, like Job, would confess that they never really "knew" God intimately. Yes, they had feared, worshiped and honored Him; they had believed in His holiness, His power and His character; they had written books *about* Him; and they had even counseled others. But, at the end of their long dark night, many would admit, just like Job, "*I [had only] heard of Thee by the hearing of the ear, but now mine eye seeth [You].*" (Job 42:5 emphasis added)

God longs to replace us with Himself so that we might *intimately* know and see Him! Not just know *about Him* from sermons we hear, books we read, or songs we sing, but truly *experience a oneness with Him* that we have never known before--an intimacy that brings with it a joy and a peace that passes all understanding. As David expressed, only "...in Thy presence is fulness of joy." (Psalm 16:11)

How Much Do You Trust God?

The bottom line is: *How much do you trust God?*

We so often sing about His Love and His Mercy, but do we really believe in it and trust in it? A child trusts in the love of his mother, even though she must, at times, discipline him and take him to the doctor for shots. Real love involves trust. *When someone really loves and cares for you, you trust that they have your best interests at heart, even though you don't always understand their expression of love.* God asks us to do the same with Him. He asks us to unconditionally trust in His Love for us, no matter what we see, feel, experience or understand to be happening.

The God of the Bible is a loving and compassionate Father, who will use all the events in our lives to rid us of *sin* and *self*, so that He might replace us with Himself and, thereby, fill us with His fulness. He continually is stretching and shaping our faith so that we will be able to endure any circumstance that He allows, and so that we will be able to say with absolute conviction, "Though [You] slay me, yet will I trust [You]." (Job 13:15) *This is the kind of faith that overcomes the world and brings with it a peace that passes all understanding.*

The inward life of the spirit can only be gained by a passionate and consuming love for God. How much do you love Him--enough to surrender *everything* to Him? This is a question each of us must answer for ourselves. The walk of faith necessary for experiencing His presence and His fulness is not easy. It means not only going through the *narrow gate*, but also walking along the *hard path*. In the words of Jesus, "Straight is the gate, and narrow is the way, which leadeth unto life, and few there be that find it." (Matthew 7:14)

How about you? Do you love God enough to open that narrow gate and walk down that hard path?

Listen to a poem that St. John of the Cross wrote back in the 1600s called ***The Dark Night***:

"One dark night,
fired with love's urgent longings
-ah, the sheer grace!-
I went out unseen,
my house being now all stilled.

In darkness, and secure,
by the secret ladder, disguised.
-ah, the sheer grace!-
In darkness and concealment,
my house being now all stilled.

On that glad night
in secret, for no one saw me,
nor did I look at anything
with no other light or guide
than the One that burned in my heart.

This guided me
more surely than the light of noon
to where He was awaiting me
-Him I knew so well-
there in a place where no one appeared.

O guiding night!
O night more lovely than the dawn!
O night that has united
the Lover with His beloved,
transforming the beloved in her Lover.

Upon my flowering breast,
which I kept wholly for Him alone,
there He lay sleeping,
and I caressing Him
there in a breeze from the fanning cedars.

When the breeze blew from the turret,
as I parted His hair,
it wounded my neck
with its gentle hand,
suspending all my senses.

I abandoned and forgot myself,
laying my face on my Beloved;
all things ceased; I went out from myself,
leaving my cares
forgotten among the lilies." [43]

Key Points of This Chapter:

- God desires intimacy with us--to fellowship and commune with us.
- In order to experience this, we must go "inward" to where He dwells.
- This journey inward can be dark and sometimes confusing.
- We must learn to walk by faith and not our sight, senses or feelings.
- Every great man or woman of God has experienced *night seasons*.
- Intimacy and life in the Spirit can only be gained by a passionate love for God.

Section Two:
What is God's Will?

**"...this is the will of God, even your sanctification..."
(1 Thessalonians 4:3)**

Chapter Three
God's Will and Man's Free Choice

Four Aspects of God's Will

In order to thoroughly explore night seasons, their origin and purpose, we need to go back to the beginning. What is God's basic will for our lives and how does He achieve it? In other words, why has He called us to be Christians in the first place?

As we seek to explore God's will, it's important that we base our information only upon what the Word of God says, and not upon our own human understanding, because often they are contradictory. God's ways are not our ways. As He reminds us in Isaiah 55:8-9, "...My thoughts are not your thoughts, neither are your ways My ways, saith the Lord. For as the heavens are higher than the earth, so are My ways higher than your ways, and My thoughts than your thoughts." This is simply saying that God's ways of doing things are often completely opposite to what we would do, and thus, they can be very confusing to our own rational and logical mind.

1 Peter 4:2 tells us that we are to "live the rest of [the] time...[no longer for] the lusts of men, but to the will of God." The question is: How can we live the rest of the time to the will of God, unless we first understand just exactly what that will is?

According to the Bible, there seems to be *four* different aspects to God's Will:

1) *His Sovereign Will*--God's ultimate redemptive goals and purposes that are often hidden from mankind
2) *His Revealed Will*--God's will already disclosed through His Word, the Bible
3) *His Will For Mankind*--Salvation--union with Christ and thus, freedom from the dominion of sin
4) *His Will For Believers*--Sanctification of our soul and thus, intimacy with Him.

Let's review these four aspects of God's will in detail, because again, if we understand what His will is and what He is trying to accomplish in each of our lives, then we won't struggle so hard when our night seasons come.

God's Sovereign Will
(His ultimate redemptive goals and purposes)

Ephesians 1:9-10 says, "Having made known unto us the *mystery of His will*, according to His good pleasure which He hath purposed in Himself; That in the dispensation of the fulness of times *He might gather together in one all things in Christ, both which are in heaven, and which are on earth: even in Him.*" (emphasis added)

This Scripture tells us that God's sovereign will is not only the redemption of all things, but it's also a "mystery." In other words, mankind does not fully understand how God is guiding the universe and the human race toward His ultimate goals. Thus, much of God's sovereign will is still a mystery, hidden from us.

God's sovereign will is that the natural world be restored to its original glory and that man be redeemed for fellowship with Him, even though it is a mystery as to how it will all be implemented. The word *redeem* actually means "to release, to free, to liberate or to restore one from captivity." It carries the meaning of purchasing or buying back (out of the market, never to return) by paying a ransom. This perfectly describes God's ultimate plan for creation. The earth and everything in it was made for God and He desires to redeem (or purchase back) all things to Himself.

As a result of Adam's tragic disobedience and the resulting fall of mankind, man's sacred union and fellowship with God was broken and sin permeated the world. Yet from the Lord's perfect Love came forth *His plan of redemption.* By His "determinate counsel and foreknowledge,"[44] God chose to literally become a man and to die for the sins of mankind. That God Himself would undertake the task of personally atoning or covering for the sins of all people is astounding. Christ's death cleanses us from all sin[45] and by His onetime sacrifice, He has perfected for all time those who come to God through Him.[46]

Only through God can creation be set free from the slavery and the corruption of the fall and only through Him will mankind ever know "the glorious liberty" of being the children of God.[47]

The idea behind the word *redemption* is twofold: It refers to both *a deliverance* and to the price paid for that deliverance, *a ransom.* We are delivered from the penalty of sin and from the power of Satan and evil, by the price (or the ransom) Jesus paid on the cross for us. We are redeemed from sin to a new relationship with God and a new life of Love by our own appropriation of that atonement.

The *Open Bible* tells us that:

"The whole of the Bible, whether the Old Testament or the New Testament, looks to the mighty, redemptive atonement of Christ. His blood sacrifice is the ransom paid for our deliverance. He took our sinful nature upon Himself in order that He might satisfy the demands of the law. His sacrifice is accepted as the payment for the debt the sinner owes to God, and His death is accepted as the full payment for the individual's deliverance."[48]

Have you ever wondered why God would go to such lengths to redeem His fallen creation?

The answer can be summed up in one word: *Love.* As Song of Solomon 8:7 says, "Many waters cannot quench [God's] Love, neither can the floods drown it." Love is the only thing in the universe as strong as death (verse 6) and therefore, the cross was simply and purely an act of unconditional Love. *God's motivation always comes from Love, because He, Himself, is Love.*[49]

Love is the reason God created us in the first place and Love is the only key to our locked identity. We can never expect to "find ourselves" apart from an ever-deepening relationship with our Creator.

> *"Man is not the center. God does not exist for the sake of man. [Nor does] man exist for his own sake,"* writes C. S. Lewis. *"We were created for His pleasure. We were made not primarily that we may love God (though we were made for that too), but that God may love us."*[50] (emphasis added)

This is the very heart of God's redemption.

God's Revealed Will
(The Word of God--the Bible)

God's *Revealed Will* is His Word, the Bible. He even puts His Word *above His Name*! As Psalm 138:2 says, "...for Thou hast magnified Thy Word above all Thy Name."

The great discovery undergirding our ministry is that the 66 books we call the Bible, even though they were penned by over 40 authors over a period of several thousand years, are a carefully designed message system that provably has its origin from outside our time dimension![51] God authenticates His message by describing history in advance.

Perhaps the most dramatic example of this foretelling is the history of Israel. The nation's origin, its successes, its failures and its ultimate destiny are all laid out in detail. The Bible chronicles the disobedience of the Children of Israel and their ultimate fulfillment.

The central theme of this amazing chronicle is the declaration (and the subsequent fulfillment) of a Kinsman-Redeemer: the Coming One who would be the centroid of all history. The purpose, the tragedy, and the ultimate victory are all detailed.[52] His genealogy, His birth, His ministry, and every detail of His sacrificial death–and subsequent resurrection–were all spelled out in advance, as well as His ultimate establishment on the Throne of David on Planet Earth and the subjection of all things.

The Bible also details the destiny of the various nations. The rise of the major dominant kingdoms are all profiled in advance. Thus, the ultimate climax of human history, and the resolution of all things, are committed in a clearly specified scenario by a God who makes--and keeps--His promises!

God's revealed will for mankind is expressed in Matthew 22:37-40:

> "Thou shalt love the Lord thy God with all thy heart, and with all thy soul, and with all thy mind. This is the first and great commandment. And the second *is* like unto it, Thou shalt love thy neighbor as thyself. On these two commandments hang all the law and the prophets."

The whole of the Bible–all of God's revealed will–is summed up in learning to love Him and learning to love others. We are created for a love relationship with Him. Everything about knowing God and experiencing Him will be out of order if we don't *first* have that intimacy with Him.

God's Will for Mankind: Salvation
(Union with Christ and, thus, freedom from the dominion of sin)

God's sovereign will is the redemption of all things. God's revealed will is His Word, or the Bible. *God's will for mankind is* salvation--the eternal union of our soul with God.

> "The Lord is not slack concerning His promise...but is longsuffering toward us, not willing that any should perish, but that all should come to repentance." (2 Peter 3:9)[53]

One of the first things the Bible tells us is that human beings are by nature sinful and in need of the righteousness of God, that all mankind has sinned and fallen short of the glory of God.[54] "There is none that understandeth, there is none that seeketh after God. They are all gone out of the way...there is none that doeth good, no, not one." (Roman 3:11-12) The biblical account of man's historic fall out of a state of righteousness and holiness into a state of sin and condemnation explains the dark side of man. People lie, cheat, steal, murder and rape *because they are sinners by nature.[55]*

Sin is a power that came into the world through Adam's disobedience, and sin rules the world, enslaves and controls people.[56] Sin's effect on all mankind is *separation from God.* Therefore, in order to be reunited with God, we must be cut off from sin and set apart to righteousness.

If we are to approach God and be reconciled to Him, we must do so on God's terms--*we must have new lives in which our sins have been forgiven and obliterated.* Scripture tells us that we cannot save or redeem ourselves. Sin can only be overcome by a sacrifice.[57] Redemption and the forgiveness of sins only comes through the blood of Christ.[58]

Salvation means to be made whole again or to be delivered from sin. Salvation is free, but it's not cheap. It's a gift costing us nothing. However, it cost God *everything.* Jesus, God's Son, became a sacrifice and took sin's penalty for us. Therefore, should we choose to accept it, God's free gift to us--salvation--is the eternal union of our soul with His.

Salvation occurs when we admit that we have sinned and we ask God (Jesus Christ) to forgive us of our sins and become our personal Savior. John 3:16-17 are two of the most important and pivotal verses of the entire Bible: "For God so loved the world, that He gave His only begotten Son, that whosoever believeth in Him should not perish, but have everlasting life. For God sent not His Son into the world to condemn the world; but that the world through Him might be saved."[59]

At the very moment we accept and receive God's *free gift of Life*, the Holy Spirit comes to dwell at the core of our being,[60] we become united with Him in spirit and we receive His eternal Life.[61] *Eternal Life or life without end is simply God's supernatural Life in us--His Love, His Wisdom and His Power.*

Christ has done it all. Our sin has been paid for, the sentence of death has been eradicated and we have been given new Life. We just need to *receive* this Gift of Love.

Again, the *Open Bible* sums it up:

"It is one thing to be convinced of the need for salvation and the
new Life, but it is an entirely different thing to *acquire* the new
life. When we are "saved," we are said to be *new creatures in
Christ* (2 Corinthians 5:17); to have been born-again (John 3:3); to
have passed from death to life (John 5:24); to have been
transferred from the rule of darkness to the kingdom of God's Son
(Colossians 1:13); and to have been adopted by God (Galatians
4:5). These wonderful results of having new life in Christ are
offered freely to all who trust in Christ for salvation."[62]

[If you are not sure where you stand with God right now, and you
want to be assured that the separation between you and Him is
reconciled, then please take a moment to see the *Peace with God* prayer
in the Appendix. If you are doubtful of your relationship with Him, it
doesn't hurt to pray this prayer again and make sure of your calling. *It's
the most important decision you will ever make.*]

God's Will in the Life of a Believer: Sanctification
(Purification of the body, soul and spirit)

God's sovereign will is the redemption of all things; His revealed will
is His Word; His will for mankind is salvation and union with God; and
finally, *His will for the believer is sanctification*--the purification of our
body, soul and spirit--so that Christ can be formed in us and we can
experience intimacy with Him. This fourth aspect of God's will is the one
Christians understand the least and, thus, will comprise the focus of the
majority of this book.[63]

"And the very God of peace sanctify you wholly; and I pray
God your whole spirit and soul and body be preserved
blameless unto the coming of our Lord Jesus Christ."
(1 Thessalonians 5:23)

The purpose of *salvation* is so that we might be reconciled to God and
be delivered from sin.[64] God wants us freed from sin so that we might
fellowship and commune with Him. Incredible as it may seem, *God seeks
our fellowship and our communion. He wants to dwell among us.*[65] We
were created for that purpose. "Thou are worthy, O Lord, to receive glory
and honor and power: for Thou hast created *all* things, *and for Thy
pleasure they are and were* created." (Revelation 4:11 emphasis added)
Thus, God's whole purpose in creating mankind was for loving fellowship.

"Therefore *leaving* the [elementary] principles of the
doctrine of Christ, let us *go on* unto perfection [completion];

not laying again the foundation of repentance from dead works, and of faith toward God...." (Hebrews 6:1)

Sanctification is the process by which God brings this perfection and this completion about. Scripture tells us that when we first believe in Christ, we are sanctified "positionally." In other words, it's a fact that we are set apart and holy unto God. However, in order to experience this sanctification and all the benefits that go with it, we must allow God to conform us into His image, so that we <u>can</u> enjoy an intimate, love relationship.

The purpose of sanctification is twofold: *outwardly* to reflect Christ in all that we do (abundant Life),[66] and *inwardly* to experience His presence (the fulness of Christ).[67] I will be mentioning "abundant Life" and "the fulness of Christ" often throughout this book. Let me define what I mean. *Abundant Life* is simply experiencing God's Life, His Love, Wisdom and Power, in and through us, in place of our own.[68] *Fulness of God* is being totally filled up with Him, inside and out. As Colossians 3:11 expresses it, "Christ [has become] all and in all."

Why the Sanctification Process?

God desires a love-relationship with us. He yearns for the kind of intimacy and experiential union we might enjoy with our spouse. He not only wants us to experience His Love, Wisdom and Power flowing through us (abundant Life), He also wants us to experience the joy of His continual presence, the beauty of His holiness and the security of His Love, meaning the fulness of Christ.

The Lord desires to dwell among us and to personally communicate with us--Spirit to spirit. He desires to lead, guide and direct our footsteps. The whole purpose of the Ark of the Covenant in the Old Testament was so that *He could dwell among His people.* Matthew 12:6, however, tells us that "one greater than the temple" is now here, and He wants to fellowship with us continually in the Holy Place of our hearts-- *through our spirit.* Listen to Jesus' heart as He prays, "Father, I will that they also, whom Thou hast given Me, be with Me where I am; that they may behold My glory...." (John 17:24)

God wants us to be able to see Him and experience Him, as Job did. However, in order for this to occur, *purity and holiness must be the requirement.*[69] As Hebrews 12:14 says, "Follow peace with all men, and holiness, without which no man shall see the Lord."

Our greatest failing is not realizing who God is and what His character is like. God is *not* human. He is God, and as such there is an *infinite gap* between the highest in us and the lowest in God. The gap between us is *unbridgeable* from our side.[70] If the gap is to be bridged at all, it must be from God's side--for He is holy. To be holy means to be set apart. God is set apart from the power, the practice and the presence of sin, and is set apart to absolute righteousness and goodness. *There is no sin in God, and He can have nothing at all to do with sin* other than to judge it.

Therefore, if we are ever to approach God, *we must do it on His terms.* Somehow, we must be sanctified and made holy--just as He is holy. Any holiness that falls short of God's holiness will not be able to stand in the presence of God.

The Process of Becoming Holy

Sanctification is the procedure by which we become holy. It's the means by which we are set apart, separated and consecrated from anything that is unholy. Sanctification is the process God has designed to conform us into Christ's image, so that we *can* reflect Him in all that we do. In other words, in order to be conformed into Christ's image, we must *first* be made clean, purified (or holy) body, soul and spirit.[71]

Oswald Chambers once identified sanctification "as the very holiness of Christ."[72]

Since God is the One who made us, He alone holds the key to our true happiness. And, although this may come as a shock to many twentieth-century Christians, the Scriptural essence of sanctification is to surrender all that we are to God and allow Him to reproduce Himself in us.[73]

Our fulfillment, our meaning, our worth and our significance all rest on this transformation. Someone once said, "we have not only been chosen to prostrate ourselves and reverence God; *we have been chosen to reflect Him in everything we do.*" God wants us to live every moment of every day like an ambassador declaring His will.

Unfortunately, *sanctification does <u>not</u> happen automatically. It all depends upon our own moment-by-moment choices.* "Having, therefore, these promises, dearly beloved, let us *cleanse ourselves* from all filthiness of the flesh and spirit, perfecting holiness in the fear of God." (2 Corinthians 7:1 emphasis added) *Faith choices*--non-feeling choices where we say, "not my will, but Thine"--are the only choices that allow God's will, meaning the sanctification process, to be accomplished in our lives. (Matthew 26:39)

A Scriptural Example: Peter

The life of Peter is a perfect example of the process of *sanctification*. When Peter first encounters Jesus, he is a strong, fiery man given to passionate outbursts. Even though this fisherman starts off as little more than an arrogant blunderer, the Lord gradually transforms him into a hero of faith. Who but God could take Peter's foot out of his mouth and fill him with an inspired message of salvation? (Acts 2) Who but God could take this fearful man and transform him into a disciple of undaunted courage? (Acts 2-3)

Peter could have run away in defiance every time he was rebuked by Jesus, but he *chose* to humble himself and remain a disciple. He could have isolated himself in fear and shame after his betrayal of Jesus, yet he *chose* to realign himself with the risen Lord. When persecution ignited in Jerusalem, Peter could have once more denied his faith, yet he *chose* to stand for Christ. After Paul publicly rebuked him for being a hypocrite in Galatians 2:11-14, Peter could have turned away in bitterness, but instead he *chose* to repent.

Over and over again, we see Peter cooperating with God's process of sanctification by choosing to make *faith choices* or non-feeling choices to follow God's will. If our lives truly belong to God, we, too, must be willing to choose to lay everything, the good, the bad, and the ugly, at His feet, abandoning ourselves to His will being accomplished in our lives.

John 12:25 tells us that whosoever shall seek to save his life shall lose it, and whosoever shall lose, or surrender, his life shall preserve it.

Once we recognize that faith choices are imperative and the only way we can remain open and pliable to God's will in our lives, then the sanctification process can proceed. If, however, we make *emotional choices*, meaning sight and feeling choices to follow our <u>own</u> will and desires and not God's, then we not only shut God out of our lives, but we also thwart the sanctification process.[74]

Because this process involves a complete surrender, moment by moment, of our wills and our lives,[75] many Christians choose to disregard this aspect of God's will.[76] They think because they are "saved" that's all that's needed and, thus, they go about living their lives according to their own wills. Other Christians verbally promise God to "forsake all else and follow Him," but when He begins to take measures to implement their promise, they scream and yell and immediately retract it.

"And they come unto Thee as the People cometh, and they sit before Thee as My people, and they hear Thy words, *but*

they will not do them: for with their mouth they shew much
love, but their heart goeth after their covetousness."
(Ezekiel 33:31 emphasis added)

*Our failure to respond to God's call of sanctification, however, does not
stop His loving ways of accomplishing His will in our lives. The Lord is
relentless in His purpose of transformation because He knows it's the only
way we will ever be fulfilled in this lifetime.*

Sin and Self

God's ultimate plan is to sanctify or set His people apart from the
flesh, the world and the devil, and fashion us into *human conduits* freely
overflowing with His Love. As Christians, we must learn to escape the
prison of sin and self and enter a love union with Christ so that His Life
can flow through us to others. As 1 Timothy 1:5 asserts, "The end [goal,
purpose, mission] of the commandment is *Agape* [God's Love] out of a
pure heart...."

Sanctification is simply the process by which Christ's Love is formed
in us, and we learn to walk by the leading of the Spirit and not the flesh.

In order to accomplish this purification, however, there are two things
that God must do: 1) By His blood, He must cleanse our souls and bodies
(the flesh) of all *sinful acts*; and, 2) By His Spirit and His Word working
together, He must purify our soulish and *self-centered ways*. Sin and self
are the two things that stop God's Life from being formed in us.

Let me define these two things, because they are different and we will
be addressing them throughout this book. Sin is all of the *unrighteous
and unholy acts* that we do--sexual immorality, impure thoughts, lustful
pleasure, hostility, quarreling, jealousy, anger, envy, drunkenness, etc.[77]
Sin is anything that we do that is contrary to what the Word of God
commands. As we said before, sin is what separates us from God.
Whereas, self is all of our *self-centered ways*--our self-protective attitudes,
our self-oriented motivations, our belief systems, our habits and our own
natural strengths (our natural, human nature). Self is not necessarily
sinful, but if left alone and not crucified, it will eventually lead us back to
sin. (We will discuss *self* at greater length in Chapter Ten.)

Therefore, in the sanctification process, God wants us to surrender,
relinquish and give over to Him not only *everything* that is sin, but also
everything that originates from self. Liberation from sin is only the first
step! Self must also be highlighted, exposed and crucified. Self-
centeredness is the essence or the foundation of all sin and, thus, the
direct opposite of God's Love.

Because of Jesus' death on the cross, our sin has already been dealt with,[78] but our self-centered soulish ways are still very much present. Just because the problem of *two natures* has been answered by the cross does <u>not</u> mean the problem of *two lives*, God's supernatural Life verses our own natural self-life,[79] has! God wants us not only cleansed from "sin," *but also from "self." Part of the sanctification process is that God wants us to surrender to Him everything that is "<u>natural</u>," as well as everything that is "<u>sinful</u>."*

Now, *"positionally,"* as we said, we have already become sanctified because of what Christ has done for us on the cross and the holiness that He has already imputed and ascribed to us.[80] But, *"experientially"* this is <u>not</u> the case at all. Until we are, moment by moment, purified body, soul and spirit, we will <u>not</u> be able to enter or enjoy the presence of God.

So, the whole purpose of sanctification is not only to reflect Him in all we do, both in our souls and bodies, but also to have intimacy with Him in our spirits.

Please, bear in mind that Jesus was the only One who was able to do this perfectly. We can never become perfectly sanctified as long as we are in our human bodies. There will always be more sin and self to be dealt with. But, as we daily allow God to show us what He wants us to surrender to Him, we will be able--in an ever-increasing way--to experience His presence.

Thus, our responsibility is to offer ourselves--present our bodies as living sacrifices--so that God can show us the sin and the self still remaining in us. Although we *begin* this sanctification procedure when we first become believers, we only *finish* it when we are spiritually, mentally, emotionally and physically consecrated to God.[81]

As 2 Thessalonians 2:13 puts it, "...God hath from the beginning chosen you to *salvation through sanctification* of the Spirit and belief of the truth." (emphasis added)

We will explore the sanctification of our spirit further in Chapter Nine.

God Loves Us

The first point I want to really emphasize throughout this book is that God loves us. He loves us with an eternal and an unconditional Love.[82] He loves us so much that He died for us. *There is absolutely no greater Love than that.* God made us and He wants the very best for each of us. But, only <u>He</u> knows exactly what that "best" is and what it will take to implement that in our lives. Consequently, we need to unconditionally trust Him and know that everything He allows in our lives *comes only as a result of His Love.* In other words, all the circumstances of our life, every single event, occurs only by His loving permission.

> "When thou passest through the waters [trouble], I will be with thee; and through the rivers, they shall not overflow thee: when thou walkest through the fire, thou shalt not be burned; neither shall the flame kindle upon thee. For I am the Lord thy God...[You are] precious in My sight and ...I have loved thee." (Isaiah 43:2-4)

God's Love, however, can come in different forms. In the Old Testament, His Love is called *chesed* in the Hebrew and it means, not only God's *loving and compassionate Love,* but also His *strict and discipline Love.* Both aspects are considered His Love. Just as occasionally we need to love our children with *tough* love, God often must do the same with us. It doesn't mean that He loves us any less. *In fact, it often means He loves us more.*

Fenelon, the 16th century theologian, once stated, "The more God loves [us], the less He spares [us]!"[83]

Hebrews 12:5-8 also validates this, "My son, despise not thou the chastening of the Lord, nor faint when thou art rebuked of Him: *For whom the Lord loveth He chaseneth,* and scourgeth every son whom He receiveth. If ye endure chastening, God dealeth with you as with sons; for what son is he whom the father chasteneth not? But if ye be without chastisement, *whereof all are partakers*, then are ye bastards, and not sons."[84]

The imperfections in our lives are the reason for God's refining process. Once these impurities are gone, then God's Love can be experienced in a new and magnificent way and our joy will return. As 2 Corinthians 4:17-18 puts it, "For our light affliction, which is but for a moment, worketh for us a far more exceeding and eternal weight of glory."

Even though at first God's ways might seem harsh to our human mind, it's only because we cannot comprehend the glory that God wants to weave into our lives, once the hard shell of our soul has been shattered. Only then will we know the healing, the strengthening, the empowering, the rest, the peace and joy that comes from God's presence.

God is continually and lovingly chiseling away at the marble slab of our soul, like the old sculptor who was asked by his apprentice, "How do you carve a horse?" The old man looked at the boy matter-of-factly and answered, "That's easy. I just chip away anything that doesn't look like a horse." That pretty well describes what the Lord is doing in each of our lives--chipping away anything that doesn't look like Jesus.

"[God] does not afflict willingly nor grieve [His] children," Lamentations 3:33 tells us, but only as is needed, to accomplish His perfect will in us--our sanctification.

An Example: Mickey

Let me attempt to draw a spiritual analogy: Several months after a friend's hand was severely burned, his doctor stripped away all the scar tissue and then created a small pouch under the top layers of skin upon the man's breast. After the doctor carefully inserted the hand, he then stitched it into place and immobilized it for the next six weeks. During that time, the man's body slowly and steadily created new blood vessels, which naturally grafted the healthy skin onto the injured hand.

Although this process was very painful in the natural, I believe it somehow parallels the spiritual sanctification process that God takes each of us through. After first stripping us of our soulish ways, the Lord spiritually places us upon His breast and asks us to be still and know that He is God. We, however, cry out, "How long, O Lord? How long do I have to stay like this?" He simply answers, *"Till it is no longer you who live, but Christ who lives in you."*

Although this process seems cruel to us, our loving God is simply trying to replace us with Himself. What seems good to us may not be good in God's eyes, and what seems bad to us, may not be bad to God. He longs to hear us say, "Once I was self-centered, but now I'm God-centered. Once I trusted in my own strength, but now I trust in You. *Once I only heard about You, but now I see You."*

Many of us assume that we've already arrived at this place, yet when God begins to touch our lives in ways that we didn't expect, we suddenly comprehend the smallness of our faith. Nothing reveals our true selves like the advent of hard times. In order to reveal what is hidden below the surface of our pleasant religious exterior, God must turn up the heat. Not only is this the only process capable of refining gold, but also it's the only process capable of refining a human being.

Since, many of us do not *willingly* respond when the Holy Spirit prompts us to unconditionally surrender our lives and die to self, God takes matters into His own hands. He is the Potter and we are the clay. Therefore, He begins to push and pull and stretch and cut and shape us

back into His original design. He places us in life's oven where it's very
dark and very hot, hoping we will emerge from the fire, finally willing for
His perfect will to be done in our lives.

C. S. Lewis phrases it:

> *"While what we call 'our own life' remains agreeable, we*
> *will not surrender it to Him. What then can God do in our*
> *interests but make 'our own life' less agreeable to us?"*[85]
> ...[He] *whispers* in our pleasures; *speaks* in our conscience;
> but *shouts* in our pain."[86]

God wants us not only doing all that He asks, but also accepting, with
praise and thanksgiving, all that He allows. All that He gives, we must
receive. All that He allows, we must embrace. In other words, whatever
He permits in our lives must be exactly what we need at that moment.
Only He knows how to ultimately weave His perfect will into our lives
and how to produce the image of Christ in us.

Psalm 148:8 talks about, "a stormy wind fulfilling His Word [and His
will]."

Will We Trust God?

God finds new ways every day to ask us, *"Will you trust Me?* Will you
trust Me to do *towards you* all that I need to do, in order to accomplish
My perfect will *through you?"*

In our dark seasons of life, God doesn't ask us to understand
everything that He is doing, but simply to trust and believe in His Love
through what He is doing.

Brother Lawrence once said:

"If He is truly King, then this suffering could not come to [us]
against His will. I believe that such things come to us to make us
more completely His, and that rightly accepted and borne, they
bring great sweetness and consolation into our lives.   This
suffering is not an enemy to be fought against, but an ally in the
spiritual warfare to be gladly received and used. 'For me to live is
Christ, and to die is gain.' *Therefore, anything, life, joy, pain,*
death that brings me nearer to Him cannot be bad. If we are
accustomed to living in the presence of God and if we believe that
everything comes to us with His permission, then those two facts
will help to alleviate our suffering."[87]

Listen to that again, "*if we are accustomed to living in the presence of God and if we believe that everything comes to us, comes with His permission, then those two facts will help to alleviate our suffering.* This is another key to the Christian life.

Most of us still rate the events of our lives as either a "good" thing or a "bad" thing, but when we're finally able to merge all the event of our lives into the category of a *God thing*, then we will be where He wants us.

God wants us open and pliable to whatever He needs to do in our lives in order to accomplish His will. He wants us not only surrendering the moment to Him, but also surrendering our reactions to that moment to Him. We all need to get to the place where Job was when he said, "Though [You] slay me, yet will I trust [You]." (13:15)[88]

An Example: Diana

Whenever I think about ultimate trust in God, I immediately think of a dear friend of mine named Diana Bantlow. Diana was just two years old in the Lord when she was diagnosed with leukemia and given only six months to live. She had a beloved husband who adored her and two precious children, Hillary, three, and Stephanie, one.

Diana, moreover, had tremendous faith in God. And, she knew that because God loved her, He would not allow anything into her life that wasn't "Father-filtered" and that wouldn't eventually bring Him glory. So, throughout her ordeal, no matter what the circumstances were and no matter how much pain she was in, she continually chose to trust her God and to abandon herself to His will.

Now you know that she must have experienced things like fear, doubt and anger because she was human. But because she loved God and trusted Him unequivocally, she kept making those non-feeling choices--no matter how she felt or what she thought--to do His will.

Even though Diana had enough faith to literally "move mountains," and had been prayed for many times by the elders of her church, God in His sovereignty, chose not to heal her physically. He knew that the example of her faith and the witness of His Life through her frail condition would affect more lives than anything else. And, it's true. As I have shared Diana's story at different seminars over the last 20 or so years, many people have come up to me and told me how they had known Diana and how her life had touched them.

In particular, two nurses from California came up after one seminar and shared how they had both attended Diana in the hospital the last few weeks of her life. They told me that they both had come to know Jesus Christ as their Lord and Savior as a result of seeing *His Life* through Diana, even though she was dying.

They recounted, as they would go into her room to administer her pain medication, Diana would softly whisper, "No, thank you, my Father is taking care of me." Then she would go on and whisper, "And may He bless you abundantly in all you do today." Both these nurses shared how uncharacteristic this is of terminally ill patients. Either the patient is totally "out of it" (almost semi-conscious) and unaware of what is going on around him, or he is emotionally and mentally distraught as the reality of death approaches. They both related this was not at all the case with Diana. They saw in Diana a Love, a peace and a joy that "passed all human understanding." And they yearned to have what she had. Both eventually accepted Christ as a result of Diana's witness.

As it came closer to Christmas, Diana told everyone that God was going to allow her to go "home" for the holidays. Now she thought God meant her physical, earthly home, but on Christmas day 1974, God took His precious child "home" to the one He had prepared for her from the beginning of time. (John 14:2)

We must all get to the place where we can accept even the *bad things* (from our point of view) as being good, because they are from God.[89] As George MacDonald tells us, "I fear you will never arrive at an understanding of God so long as you cannot bring yourself to see the good that often comes as a result of pain." God has a plan for our lives and sometimes that plan includes suffering.

1 Peter 4:19 urges, "Wherefore, let them that suffer according to the will of God commit the keeping of their souls to Him in well-doing, as unto a faithful Creator."

God is the One who warms us in the sun and it is God who sends the rain. It is God who feeds us and it is He who also withholds our food. He sends the winter and He also allows the hot summer days. God, by His Love, does all of the above. "I form the light, and create darkness; I make peace, and create evil; I, the Lord, do all these things." (Isaiah 45:7)[90]

Our responsibility is simply to yield ourselves to the inner workings of God's Spirit and know that everything He does in our lives *comes from his Love*.[91] We are being asked to trust Someone who has the power to keep us from all danger, threat and violence. The question is, "Will we trust Him unconditionally to do so?"[92]

"As a shepherd seeketh out his flock in the day that he is among his sheep that are scattered; *so will I seek out My sheep, and will deliver them out of all places where they have been scattered in the cloudy and dark day.*" (Ezekiel 34:12)

We might ask ourselves the same questions that Fenelon raises, "Why am I afraid to break out of my chains? Do the things of this world mean more to me than You [God]? Am I afraid to give myself to You? What a mistake! It is not even I who would give myself to You, but *You who would give Yourself to me!*"[93]

Our Own Free Will

Having just explored the four aspects of God's will, we now want to briefly explore *man's individual will*--i.e., our free choice.

God has given man a free will, much like His own. Our free will is the most important element of our design, because within that will lies the power to choose between life and death, good and evil, faith and fear, darkness and light, God and Satan.[94] Our will is the master of all of our faculties and upon our will everything else depends. It controls our reason, our intelligence, our emotions and our abilities. Our will directs everything within us, and is the "gate" through which all things must pass.

The reason our own will is so very important to God, is that unless we choose by an act of our will to allow God to accomplish His will through us, He is unable to do so. (Of course, God can always *do as He pleases*, however, we must cooperate with Him in order for the sanctification process to proceed.) God has not set Himself up as our Divine Dictator, but rather as loving Discipler, and thus, He has given us the free choice to either deny Him or to follow Him. His perfect will is that we render back to Him that which we have so long claimed as our own--namely, our own will.[95]

Our will is important because *it's the bridge over which our faith must travel.* As we have said before, we don't necessarily have to understand all that God does in our lives, but simply have the faith and the trust to choose to obey His will. As my dear husband says, *"Faith is not believing in spite of the evidence, but obeying in spite of the consequences."*

Life is simply a series of ongoing choices. For the nonbeliever, it's a daily choice between good and evil; for the believer, it's a moment-by-moment choice of faith (to follow God's will) or emotions (to follow our own will). Choosing by faith to follow God, is placing ourselves in the hands of God and freely allowing Him to direct our paths. Choosing according to our emotions, is willfully quenching God's Spirit and shutting Him out of our lives completely.[96]

Moment-by-Moment Choices

Moment by moment, we have the awesome responsibility of either choosing to "walk after the Spirit" or choosing to "walk by the flesh."[97] We can define the "flesh" as everything that occurs naturally in our soul and body--everything that is "not of the Spirit" or that is "not of faith." God tells us in Romans 7:18 that our flesh is corrupted beyond repair.[98] His answer to this problem, was to give us His Life. Only His Life in us, can enable us to overcome the "motions of our flesh" and to please Him in all that we do.[99] Thus, until we learn to "crucify our flesh," there will be a continual war between our flesh and our spirit.[100]

> "For the flesh lusteth against the Spirit, and the Spirit against the flesh: and these are *contrary* the one to the other: so that ye cannot do the things that ye would." (Galatians 5:17)

Over and over again in Scripture, we see the wonderful and terrible consequences of man's free will (free choice) enabling us to either follow *God* or follow *self*. David tearfully humbles himself at the feet of God (Psalm 51), but Saul proudly plots to get his own way (1 Samuel 15). Joseph continually turns away from Potiphar's wife (Genesis 39:7-9), but Samson rushes into the arms of Delilah (Judges 16).

At the exact moment John the Beloved is choosing to lay his head upon Jesus' breast, Judas is choosing to betray Him (John 13:23-27). Mary of Bethany spends a year's income to anoint Jesus with costly perfume (Mark 14:3-9), yet Ananias and Sapphira lie in order to withhold a small portion of their income (Acts 5:1-11). A poor widow gives her last few coins to the Lord (Luke 21:2-4), but the rich young ruler won't let go of his great wealth (Luke 18:18-25). Partheon Magestrates travel a great distance to worship the babe in a manger (Luke 2:1-2), but the Pharisees won't walk six miles into Bethlehem to meet their Messiah!

As Christians, God has given us the freedom to either choose, moment by moment, to follow His Spirit and believe and trust in Him, or to follow the flesh and believe and trust in ourselves. He has given us the authority to choose to open ourselves up to Him and be willing to abandon ourselves to His will; or, the authority to shut ourselves off from Him and follow what we think, feel and desire.

An Example: Wendy

Here's a wonderful example that illustrates the power of our choices.

A friend of mine, named Wendy, had to travel on business from Durango, Colorado, to the next town which was at least 40 miles away. This part of Colorado is spectacularly beautiful, but quite desolate as far as cities or population. There is nothing between Durango and the next town.

Wendy had received *The Way of Agape* audio tapes a few months previously and had been periodically listening to them. She thought this long drive would be a perfect opportunity to finish the series, so she took them along with her. As she became so engrossed in what she was hearing on the tapes (all about our constant, moment-by-moment "faith" choices), that she didn't realize she was nearly out of gas and that she had just driven past the last gas station in Durango. There would not be another station for 40 miles.

Sure enough, about 15 or 20 miles outside of Durango, she ran out of gas. The car literally stopped. She pulled over to the side of the road and became totally distraught as she realized her precarious predicament. Since she was going to a business appointment, she was all dressed up (heels and all), so there was no way she could walk any distance. And even if she could have, there was no place to go for help. The few cars that <u>did</u> pass her, she said, terrified her. They were mostly men with beards and long hair, driving 4X4 trucks with shot guns racked in their rear windows. (Sounds like our cars and trucks in Idaho.)

As she sat there contemplating her situation, God impressed upon her heart what she had been listening to on those tapes--about making faith choices (non-feeling choices) to give any and all situations over to God. It became apparent to her that, even in this scary situation, she had a choice. She could either become paralyzed with fear (which she was already beginning to experience) and make *emotional choices* to follow the flesh; or, she could make *faith choices* to relinquish herself to God and trust Him to perform His perfect Will through her (just like she was hearing on the tapes).

She decided to try the latter. Without "feeling" anything, she chose by faith to give God her fear and apprehension and to trust Him to protect her and make a way for her. After her prayer, she decided to try the ignition one more time. She gently turned it on and, surprisingly, the motor sputtered and then started. She was ecstatic! She put the car into first gear and crept down the highway on the far right side. The farther she went, the more elated she became. She had made the appropriate faith choices, God had heard her prayers, and He was now performing a miracle right before her eyes.

My friend, Wendy, drove that "empty" car all the way (about 20 miles) to the next city. She told me later that when she would come to a hill, she simply made more faith choices to commit herself to God, softly stepped on the gas pedal and there always seemed to be just enough "oomph" to make it over the hill.

When she finally did arrive at the next city, she stopped at the first gas station feeling absolutely overjoyed. The gas station attendant even asked her if she was all right, because she looked so radiant. She was able to witness to him and tell him the whole story.

Wendy made it to her appointment a little late, but nevertheless, she arrived safely and learned an incredible lesson about God's faithfulness. Now, I don't recommend putting God to the test and going out of town without gas. But, to me, this is a perfect example of the importance of faith choices in our lives. We free God to perform miracles when we trust Him enough to constantly choose His way.

Another important thing to remember is that we are <u>not</u> responsible to change our negative feelings. There's no way we can do that! We're only responsible to put in charge the Person who <u>can</u> change our feelings, and that's God. And we do that by making faith choices.

The Power of Our Human Will

Can you see the incredible power of the human will? Our life is not determined by our circumstances, our church attendance, our social standing, our finances or even our belief systems; *the character of our life is simply determined by the daily choices we make.*

Sin isn't birthed in our mind or in our body; it's begun within our will! God has given us a fearful and awesome responsibility with our "free will." *Thus, acts of our free will, or our momentary choices, determines the degree of our sanctification.*

The goal of our instruction, as Matthew 22:37 tells us, is *to love God--* to choose, moment by moment, to totally give ourselves over to Him (sin and self)--so that He can then replace us with Himself. We were created, not only to *be* loved, but also *to love.* Thus, the only thing that will ever re-direct our will and lead us to the fulness of Christ is love for God. In other words, the more we fall in love with Jesus, the more we will be able to freely give Him our will. And, surrendering our will, moment by moment, is the only thing that will allow Him to complete the sanctification process in our lives.

Our supreme purpose as Christians is not only to learn to become vessels of God's Love to others, but also to return that Love to Him.

"We...do not cease to pray for you...*that ye might be filled with the knowledge of His will* in all wisdom and spiritual understanding; That ye might walk worthy of the Lord unto all pleasing, being fruitful in every good work, and increasing in the knowledge of God; Strengthened with all might, according to His glorious power, unto all patience and longsuffering with joyfulness; Giving thanks unto the Father, Which hath made us meet to be partakers of the inheritance of the saints in light: Who hath delivered us from the power of darkness, and hath translated us into the kindom of His dear Son..." (Colossians 1:9-13)

Key Points of This Chapter:

- There are four different aspects of God's will.
- Sanctification--the process of becoming holy so that we can show forth His Life and have intimacy--is God's will for the believer.
- Holiness, however, does not happen automatically. Because God loves us, He must first expose our sinful acts and our self-centered ways.
- We, then, must choose to surrender and relinquish these things.
- Our free choice determines our sanctification, our intimacy with Him and the character of our life.

Chapter Four
Knowing God's Will Personally

How Does God Let Us Know His Specific Will?

Hopefully, exploring God's *sovereign* will, His *revealed* will, His *will for all mankind* and His *will for believers* has been helpful. But, what about daily knowing God's specific, individual and personal will for our lives? "Should we take that new job offer?" "Would it be better if we move to that new city?" "Will our daughter be happier in that other school?" "Should I marry....?" "Do you want me to have that operation?" "...Take that medication?" "...Go here?" "...Do this?"

How can we know God's specific will for these kinds of things?

The first and most important ingredient in knowing God's individual will is having a love relationship with Him--loving Him with all our heart, mind and soul. Through this relationship and the intimacy it affords us, God reveals His will, His purposes and His ways. Our spiritual direction will only come from this love-relationship. Human logic and reason cannot be sources for spiritual guidance in our lives. As Christians, we cannot trust in our <u>own</u> understanding, any more than we can trust in our own righteousness. There is a much greater scheme of things that is not yet given to our human understanding, and this plan can only be revealed spiritually.

There are at least *four* different ways that we can know God's personal will.

The first and the most important way, is *through the reading of His Word*. This is the purest, the simplest and the surest way that God speaks to us. Besides the unparalleled gift of His Son, the Bible is the Lord's greatest gift to mankind, and yet few believers know the full range of its wisdom and power.

George Muller, the famous English teacher who, by faith alone, established a ministry to feed and house thousands upon thousands of orphans said, "Our *outward* man is not fit for work unless our *inward* man eats God's Word."

In addition to the written Word, God also speaks to our spirits *through times of prayer and fasting*. These are the times when we are *still* before the Lord and we can hear Him much more clearly. Often, when we are frazzled and tyrannized by the urgent, we're unable to hear the gentle sound of a breeze, and it's the same way with God's voice. We cannot hear His still, small voice when our minds are consumed with our daily responsibilities. For this reason, it's imperative to daily still and quiet our souls in order to receive His guidance.

Another way we can know God's Will is by staying cleansed and *yielded to God's Spirit.* Only through God's Spirit communicating to our spirit can we hear His voice and that He can personally lead, guide and direct our way.

And finally, we can know God's Will through the *counsel of other Christians,* and by the *confirmation of circumstances* that He allows in our lives.

Let's explore in greater detail each of these ways of personally knowing God's will.

God Speaks to Us Through His Word

The Bible tells us that God has a plan and a purpose for each of our lives and that His plan is specific and personal. Listen to Psalm 37:23: "The steps of a good man are ordered by the Lord and He delights in his way,"[101] and Psalm 32:8, "I will instruct [you] and teach [you] in the way which [you] shall go."[102]

The first place we should go, then, to get guidance from the Lord is to His Word.[103] The Bible is a personal Love-letter from God through which He teaches, exhorts, rebukes, encourages, corrects, inspires, trains and guides us.[104]

Before we even open our Bibles, it's imperative to pray, cleanse our hearts and ask God to open our spiritual understanding so that we <u>can</u> hear His voice and know His will.[105] Also, it's helpful to *memorize Scriptures*, then no matter what hardships we are in or where we are, it can bring life and guidance.[106] If we have God's Word memorized, then, we can still meditate on His Word, even when we are away from home and our Bibles.

Reading the Word of God daily is how we are going to know God's specific will for that particular day. I don't mean just opening our Bible and haphazardly reading a passage or two, but having some sort of consistent daily reading plan. There are many good books that have "suggested" reading plans. Go to a Christian bookstore and see which particular book and plan appeals to you.

When I first began a daily reading program, I started by reading three chapters a day--one in the Old Testament, one in the New Testament and one in Psalms or Proverbs. At the time, that seemed like a reasonable commitment to make. Over the years, I've gradually added more chapters to my daily reading.

I also find it extremely valuable to keep a *daily journal* (see the suggested *Prayer Journal* in the Appendix). When I am struggling to know God's specific will on some issue, I write out my questions to the Lord in my journal (making sure to ask for His guidance on only *one* question at a time). Then, I read my daily reading.[107] Sometimes His answers will come immediately. At other times, I must wait a few days or even a week, but whatever the time frame, I have learned to persevere because I know God will be faithful to reveal His specific will, in His timing and in His way. In my over forty years as a Christian, He has never failed me.

As I read my daily reading, I prayerfully *expect* God to answer me concerning my specific questions. When I find a Scripture that seems to apply to one of my issues, I write it down and put a question mark beside it. When God confirms that Scripture at least two or three more times, then I believe I have His answer and I'm also confident that He will give me the strength I need to "walk out" His Word.

The Scriptures seem to suggest to seek the Lord *three times* for His answer to a specific question.[108] If He doesn't answer by the end of the third time, He is either saying "No" or "Wait." If we don't have the liberty to wait for His specific answer, we might follow the steps outlined at the end of this chapter, "Discerning God's Will When We Have To Move Quickly."

Here are four simple suggestions for hearing God's will through His Word:

> **ERASE & PRAY** (submit our own will and pray for God to guide us).
> **READ & REMEMBER** (read God's Word and remember His principles).
> **CONSIDER & MEDITATE** (consider specific Scriptures, then write them down and meditate on them).
> **DECIDE & CHECK** (make your decision, and then check for spiritual peace).

The Lord will tell us specifically what to do and specifically what not to do. He will teach us, He will guide us, He will exhort us and He will give us the discernment we need through reading the Word.

A Personal Example

People will often ask me, "Can you really trust God's words in the Bible to direct your daily life?" Let me give you a personal example, and then you can judge for yourself.

I am usually asked to commit to a speaking engagement at least six months to a year in advance. At that time, I take that speaking request before the Lord. After praying and asking Him to show me His specific will about that upcoming engagement, I write down the Scriptures He gives me, and then let the Holy Spirit guide me in my final decision (I pray and do this three times until I'm assured it's His will).

A few years ago, while I was in prayer about a certain upcoming seminar, the Lord not only gave me many Scriptures confirming that I was to go, He also gave me several Scripture verses that left me very puzzled, one of which was Jeremiah 27:14-16,"*Hearken not unto the words of the prophet that speaks to you...for they prophesy a lie unto you. For I have not sent them, saith the Lord, yet they prophesy a lie in My Name...Hearken not to[their] words...*for they prophesy a lie unto you."

I obediently wrote down all the Scriptures He gave me in my prayer journal (as I always do). However, I put a question mark beside the Jeremiah Scripture.

Nine months later, on the very first night of that particular seminar, a man came up to me and introduced himself as a prophet. He then described a vision he'd had concerning me. Now, ordinarily, I wouldn't have paid much attention to this gentleman's dream until I checked it out with the Lord, except that this prophecy *totally contradicted* an incredible word that I had received just three months before. I was absolutely convinced that the first prophecy was of God, *because it lined up perfectly with all the Scriptures that God Himself had given me.*

What was spooky about this man's prophesy, was that he used the exact metaphors of the first prophecy, but they totally negated and contradicted it. I listened with intrigue, but was totally taken back by the discrepancy. Which prophecy should I listen to? Which one was from the Lord?

On the way back to the hotel room, I confessed my confusion to the Lord and asked for His understanding. That night I tossed and turned, but God completely woke me up in the middle of the night to remind me of the Scripture that He had given me nine months before. I had totally forgotten about it! I jumped out of bed, grabbed my journal and there on my page was Jeremiah 27:14-16,"*Hearken not unto the words of the prophet that speaks to you...for they prophesy a lie unto you. For I have* <u>*not*</u> *sent them, saith the Lord, yet they prophesy a lie in My Name...Hearken* <u>*not*</u> *to their words...for they prophesy a lie unto you.*"

Needless to say, God instantly gave me peace that this "prohet's" vision was <u>not</u> of Him.

God <u>does</u> speak very specifically through His Word...*but only if we are willing to listen!*

The Promises of God in the Bible

This experience of mine brings up a good question: *Can we take the promises of God in the Bible literally?* When we come across a promise in Scripture, can we apply that specific promise to our own lives?

Before we even consider making this application, we must first seek an accurate interpretation of that particular Scripture. In other words, we must <u>not</u> mishandle God's Word. Misinterpreting the Word of God is always dangerous--and sometimes deadly. Flipping the Bible open and randomly pointing to a passage, or taking a particular Scripture out of context, or even using a Scripture "promise box," is somewhat like consulting a spiritual Ouija board. It's a form of divination, and should not be trusted.

Once again, the safest way to know if we can apply a Scripture to our own life situation is to be involved in a daily reading plan. As I mentioned before, if we come across something in our daily reading that relates to our situation, we should write it down in our journal. If it's applicable to our situation, the Lord will confirm it at least two or three more times, again *through our daily reading*. (In other words, we don't have to jump all over God's Word in order to find compatible Scriptures, *He* will bring the appropriate ones to us!) Next, He will validate those Scriptures through our prayer time, through our submission to His Spirit, and through other counselors. Only then will we know that specific Scripture is from Him and for our particular situation.

Keep in mind that, even though God's promises are true, their fulfillment in our lives often lies beyond our understanding. God is so limitless that His eternal view of the events here on earth is vastly different from our own. Therefore, when we hear His words, we must approach them very carefully. In other words, the way God might fulfill His promises to us may totally confound our understanding, challenge our thought processes, and even disappoint our earthly hopes.

As the Lord Himself declares in Isaiah 55:9, "...As the heavens are higher than the earth, so are My ways higher than your ways..."

Sometimes God's promises cannot be understood in a "literal" sense, so we must be careful not to bind specific verses to our finite human interpretation. The scope of God's Word goes far beyond our own lives, and the Scriptures we receive might point to a fulfillment that's much wider and much broader and much grander than anything we could ever imagine. David Hazzard beautifully explains in his book *You Set My Spirit Free*:

> "For many of the people long ago, God's prophetic words did not come to pass in the way they expected. That was because, like us, they did not seek God's higher view first and interpreted what He told them from their own self-serving viewpoint--in the wrong way, that is. They also looked for absolutely literal fulfillment of God's Word, ignoring the fact that He was addressing spiritual conditions."[109]

Examples of God's Promises Fulfilled in His Way

Here are some examples:

In Genesis 15:7, God told Abraham, "I am the Lord who brought thee out of Ur of the Chaldees, to *give thee this land to inherit it.*" Abraham believed that to be God's personal promise to him, because in Genesis 15:8, he asks the Lord, "whereby shall I know that I shall inherit it?" Because Abraham was thinking with his rational mind, he naturally misinterpreted God's promise. The possession of the land would not occur in Abraham's lifetime, but some 400 years later through Abraham's offspring.

What a tragedy it would have been if Abraham had sought to immediately possess the land in his own strength! And how disillusioned his children would have been if they'd watched their father die before the promised fulfillment. But because Abraham continued to ask, seek and knock upon the door of the Lord, God revealed not only His will, but also understanding of His will.[110]

Another example of God's "perfect way" of fulfilling His promise takes place in the life of Jacob. While journeying to Egypt to reunite with his son, Joseph, God appears to Jacob and tells him, "...fear not to go down into Egypt; for I will there make of thee a great nation. I will go down with thee into Egypt; and I will also surely bring thee up again." (Genesis 46:3-4)

If you were to hear God speak those same words to you, wouldn't you naturally assume that He was going to let you return home in your lifetime? Why, then, did Jacob *die* in Egypt?[111] Because it was God's will that this prophecy be fulfilled at a later time, when Moses led Jacob's offspring out of Egypt and into the Promised Land! When Jacob lay dying, did he curse God for being unfaithful? No, he had come to *unconditionally trust in the Love of God,* so he died still believing in God's promise to him. Sure enough, years later his children brought his body back to Israel where he was buried, just as God had promised.[112]

One last example: Remember the two men on the road to Emmaus who were in such despair because Christ had just been crucified? (Luke 24:13-21) As they walked together, the risen Lord approached them. They supposed Him to be "a stranger in Jerusalem," so they shared their heartbreak. "We thought that *it was He [Jesus] who was going to redeem Israel.*" They had clung to the amazing promises of Christ, and naturally assumed that He was going to quickly overthrow the Romans and set up His kingdom in Jerusalem. But on the day of His crucifixion, their earthly hopes were shattered.

There was no way they could ever have imagined, through their logical minds, that Christ's promises were true, but pertained to His Second Coming![113]

"Lord, You Promised!"

Hebrews tells us that there are many other Old Testament men who believed God's promises, but *never* saw them fulfilled.[114] God's Word to these men did *not* turn out as they each expected, because many of them understood them in their own natural and literal way. This is exactly how I felt about the specific promises that God gave me on that mountaintop in 1990! Because He did not fulfill them according to my own understanding and my own time reference, I began to struggle with despair and defeat.

How many of you are in a similar situation?

How many of you have waited for God to fulfill specific promises concerning physical healing, spiritual revival, business deals, ministry opportunities, salvation of loved ones or personal finances and yet, never had an answer? As we wait for these promises to be fulfilled, our hearts can literally become sick and our faith can be shaken to its core.[115]

We logically dismiss our deferred hope by saying, "Well, I guess God really didn't make that promise." And before too long, we're also saying, "Maybe I've *never* heard God correctly. In fact, maybe God doesn't even care about me!" Misunderstanding gives birth to *impatience*, impatience gives birth to *disappointment*, disappointment gives birth to *doubt*, doubt gives birth to *unbelief*, and unbelief gives birth to *bitterness*. That's Satan's formula for transforming a believer into an apostate.

Although God never does anything without reason, human beings cannot always fathom His reasons. "For the Spirit is living and full of meaning, far more than literal words themselves, and it has the miraculous ability to affect lives far beyond all we can imagine or expect."[116] The Lord's Love for us is perfect and, therefore, it's critical that we trust Him to fulfill His promises in *His* way and in *His* time.[117] Let us not be dismayed or disappointed by the mysterious ways of God, for He dwells in light inaccessible...hid from our eyes and His ways are past finding out.

As Max Lucado so eloquently states, "When we can't see His hand, we should always remember to trust His heart."

There is also a wonderful quote in Jack Hayford's book *Pursuing the Will of God*, that perfectly describes the dilemma we often find ourselves in when God's promises are not fulfilled in the way we thought they would be:

"Sometimes when life throws us a curve, or maybe a whole flurry of them, we experience sentiments similar to this... *"Lord, You promised so and so, and I even heard You speaking to my heart..."* or *"I read this in the Word and You seemed to say it was something for me..."* or *"The Spirit of God prompted me with this thought, and I thought I understood this thing about my life and my future, but Lord, I don't see anything happening. It puzzles me. Did I make a mistake? Is something wrong with me?"*

Many of us would profit by going back and helping Noah build the ark for a hundred years. Noah just went about his business, hammering nails, slopping pitch, and punching that old time clock *for a century*, not seeing any evidence that what he believed would happen was taking place. *But he hung in there through those long, dry years. And the rains came, just as God had said. Boy, did they come!"*

I remember so well the testimony of a woman who had believed the Lord would save her husband after she herself accepted Christ. He finally did receive the Lord--two weeks before he died. And that was *forty years* after her conversion. She prayed for her man and trusted the Lord for his salvation for forty years! The Lord *does* get the job done...but not necessarily on our timetable."[118]

Holding on to God or His Promises?

All our confusion about hearing and believing God's promises occurs because we are relying on our <u>own</u> understanding, instead of resting on His Word. When we do so, we limit God and we hedge Him in on all sides.

God assured the prophet Habakkuk that His promises would come to pass at the appointed time (2:3), yet only He alone knows the secret of that appointed time. What makes us think we can understand His perfect plan? Our natural mind, which is so influenced by our soulish thoughts, emotions and desires, often tells us that God's promises are late. Even the psalmist cried out in despair: "Doth His promise fail for evermore?" (Psalm 77:8)

The Bible assures us, however, that *God is never late.*[119] He is the Lord, and He will always do things perfectly in His timing; thus, it's up to us to change our *wrong perceptions* about Him. (These are some of the "self-centered" ways that God is desirous of purging from our souls.) We must lay all our misconceptions at the foot of the cross. We must believe in His faithfulness and His lovingkindness. Once again, when we can't see His hand, we must trust His Heart. This is the only way to survive the "silence" of the Lord. God will never lie,[120] nor will He fail to fulfill His promise at the "appointed time."

So what is our part in this waiting process? Our part is simply to believe and trust in Him. Let us choose to be like Abraham who "did not waver in unbelief, but grew strong in faith, giving glory to God, and being *fully persuaded* that what He had promised, He was also able to perform." (Romans 4:20-21 NAS) For God will always "be mindful of His covenant." (Psalm 111:5)

The question we must always ask ourselves is: *are we holding onto God or to His Promises?*

An Scriptural Example: David

God wants us to seek Him *first* and then, the promises, the guidance and the direction will come.

There's a wonderful story in Scripture about a boy who loved God much more than he loved God's promises. David was nothing more than a shepherd, but one day while he was minding the flock, an old man appeared, told him he was going to be king of Israel, and then anointed him. (1 Samuel 16:12-13)

Can you imagine some dignitary walking into your workplace and telling you that you're going to be elected president? That's exactly what happened to David!

How would you handle a promise like that? Many of us would probably give 20 minutes notice, buy a bigger car and head straight for Washington. Yet David went right back to his sheepfold! He could have become obsessed with God's promise for his future, but instead he sang: "Thy loving-kindness is better than life." (Psalm 63:3) *It seems that David loved the Lord much more than he loved his own destiny, and this love is what made him "a man after [God's] own heart."* (1 Samuel 13:14)

So, even though the promises are from God and are true and will be fulfilled in God's timing and way, it's important that we not find revelation in them until they actually come to pass. That way, we are always seeking God first, not His promises.

Since misunderstanding and misusing God's promises happens so frequently, why then does He even bother to communicate with us? The answer is really very simple: Because He is God, because He loves us and because He wants to fellowship with us. He alone knows the future course of human history, and when He chooses to share His secrets with men, He proves Himself to be all-knowing, all-seeing, all-wise and all-loving. Scripture assures us that God's promises are true, and in the end, *everything* He has spoken will be understood.[121]

So, the first way God reveals His specific will to us is through His Word. God's Word tells us what to do and what not to do. He even exhorts us to consume (eat) His Word so that it actually can become a part of us. "Thy words were found and I ate them, and Thy words became for me a joy and the delight of my heart..."(Jeremiah 15:16 NAS)

God Speaks to Us Through Prayer and Fasting

God not only communicates His individual will to us through His Word, He also speaks to us through prayer and fasting. Sometimes we think of prayer as some mysterious spiritual regimen when, in fact, it is nothing more than simply *talking to our Creator.* Prayer is asking God what He wants us to do--what His will is--and then, listening for His answers.[122]

> "If any of you lack wisdom, let him ask of God, who giveth to all men liberally, and upbraideth not, and it shall be given him." (James 1:5)

Prayer is often linked to fasting, which is abstaining from some form of daily nourishment. When we fast, we literally "starve" our body in order to feed our spirit. Fasting is an incredible way of hearing God's voice more clearly. When our flesh is weakened, our spirit is more sensitive to the Spirit of God. Throughout the Bible, fasting was used to "heighten" or "quicken" the perception of those longing to discern God's will.

Fasting was a regular discipline for men like Daniel, who "...gave [his] attention to the Lord God to seek Him by prayer and supplications, with fasting...." (Daniel 9:3 NAS) Later in this same chapter, God's answer to Daniel comes through the angel Gabriel, who says, "O Daniel, I have now come forth to give you insight with understanding. At the beginning of your supplications the command was issued, and I have come to tell you...." (Daniel 9:22-23 NAS) Even though Daniel was an incredible man of God, *he still had to unlock the door to spiritual understanding through the discipline of prayer and fasting.*

Before I teach, I always spend one day fasting for God's specific will concerning the particular group of people I am about to address. I pray and ask Him what He wants me to know about this engagement, and how He wants me to pray for the people involved. I also ask Him for insight concerning their spiritual condition, and any specific discernment I might need. Since I have a medical reason that prohibits me from fasting for long periods of time, I make the very most out of my one-day fasts! I spend the entire time alone with the Lord, continually talking to Him, loving Him and listening to Him. My times of prayer and fasting have become a delight, simply because I love to be in His presence and to commune with Him.

Some examples in Scripture of those who fasted are *Jesus* (Matthew 4:2), *Moses* (Deuteronomy 9:9, 18, 25-29), *Elijah* (1 Kings 19:8), *Daniel* (Daniel 10:3), *Ezra* (Ezra 10:6), *Nehemiah* (Nehemiah 1:4-11) and *Paul* (2 Corinthians 6:5; 11:27).

God Speaks to Us Through Submission to the Spirit

Not only does God communicate His specific will to us through His Word and through prayer and fasting, He also speaks to us through His Spirit. God's Word and His Spirit always work together in revealing what Jesus' will is. Together, God's Word and His Spirit are known as the "truth"--the Word that becomes the Deed. *God's Word contains His will, and His Spirit is the One who interprets it for us.* In other words, God's Spirit works alongside God's Word, not only showing us what His will is, but also giving us personal understanding of how it applies to our life.

Most of us have repeatedly heard the phrase "we must submit to the Lord." What exactly does this mean? The word *submit* means *"to surrender or yield to the authority or power of another."* When one army submits to another, they surrender their power and strength, and they willingly place themselves in the hands of the superior force.

When we *initially* submit to God and ask Him to come into our life, we become "born again" as John 3:3 explains, and we receive God's Spirit and His new Life.[123] This is the time that the Holy Spirit comes to dwell in our spirit within our hearts. As we begin to yield, submit and relinquish ourselves to Him, moment by moment, He will be able to control and direct our lives and we will begin to hear His voice.[124]

An Example: George Muller

Of all the wonderful books I have read in researching this material, the biography of George Muller was, by far, one of the most fascinating. I will probably use his example many times.

Back in the 1800s, Mr. Muller was a young German Christian who answered the call of God to help poor children in Bristol, England. He had already mastered six languages and was brilliant in his own right, but never received a salary for what he did. Nevertheless, he established three orphanages, housed almost 2,000 orphans, ran six day schools, helped 24 others, gave away over 6,600 Bibles and one million tracts.

The only way funds came in for his projects was by his constant submission to the Spirit of God, the reading of God's Word and prayer. In answer to George Muller's faithfulness, God provided all the funds he ever needed. His primary goal for submitting to God and living by faith was to show others that God is trustworthy and that He does answer prayer. Mr. Muller was a wonderful example to all around him, because he looked to God only to meet his needs, and God always did.

The times that he was sick, his prayer was not, "Lord, heal me," but, "Lord, bring me closer to You through this sickness." He constantly told those he worked with that praying and submitting to God's Spirit "brings God remarkably near." Before he ever would pray or read God's Word, he always would cleanse his heart and make sure that his conscience was clear by the blood of Christ. He used to declare, "You can't trust in God, if your conscience is weakened."

He would seek the Lord for days on end about a particular issue. In fact, he entreated the Lord for 607 days *before* he moved to build the last orphanage. But because of his dependence upon the Spirit of God for guidance, not only were all his finances taken care of, but also the Lord gave him the wisdom to manage the work. God's glory was always his aim, and it certainly was always the result.

"Whatever ye do, do all to the glory of God."
(1 Corinthians 10:31)

All communication with God occurs in our spirit, not in our soul. When our soul and spirit are sanctified, we will be able to hear God's voice. However, the minute we choose to ignore God's voice and follow the voice of our own human emotion or reason, God's Spirit within us becomes quenched, which then blocks His leading and guiding.[125] At this point, we often complain that God is no longer speaking to us. Yet, the truth is that we were the ones to first hang up the phone!

Restoring Spiritual Communication

How do we then open up the lines of communication again? How can we once again unleash the flow of God's Spirit within us?

It's very important to understand that *before* we can hear God's voice again and *before* He can direct and control our lives again, we must cleanse our hearts.[126] How do we do this? It's simple. By adopting a lifestyle of confession and repentance.[127] As we continually confess and surrender our wrong choices to God, He will faithfully restore our spiritual sensitivity to His voice and leading. Repentance can actually be described as a kind of "Divine Draino," because it unclogs our spiritual "pipes" and, once again, restores the clean free flow of God's Spirit in and through us. It allows us to once again communicate directly with God's Spirit--spirit to Spirit.

For details to the cleansing of our souls and spirits--"being renewed in the spirit of our mind" (Ephesian 4:23)--please see *The Inner Court Ritual* in the Appendix.[128] Renewing our minds means the same thing as purging our souls and purifying our spirits.[129]

"Peace" seems to be the barometer that God uses to confirm that we are doing is His will. When we are in line with His will, He gives us "a peace that passes all human understanding." When we are not, He removes that peace. Just as the Lord guided the Israelites with His pillar of cloud and fire, we will begin to sense not only His blessed presence, but also His specific will. As we learn to simply submit to His Spirit and listen for His voice, He will be able to live His Life out through us, and we will experience a new found freedom--a freedom from having *to work at* living the Christian life. We will simply rest in His arms while He lives the Christian life out through us.

God Speaks to Us Through Counsel and Our Circumstances
(Acts 9:23-25; Proverbs 24:6)

God not only shows us His individual will through His Word, through prayer and fasting and through submission to His Spirit, but He also communicates His will to us through godly counselors and sometimes through our circumstances.

It's important to understand that we can't trust our circumstances *alone* to show us God's will. Although circumstances can confirm God's will, they must not be judged apart from the other means of confirmation (His Word, prayer and fasting and submission to His Spirit). For example, setting out some kind of "fleece" for God to show us His will through our circumstances can be just another form of divination, if it's not accompanied by Scriptural confirmation and guidance through prayer.

When circumstances are wonderful, it's so easy for us to say, "Oh, I know this situation must be from God! Everything is perfect. It must be His will for me!" A man or woman of faith knows how to maintain trust in God *even when his circumstances are bleak.* Although a young Christian may be sideswiped by a harsh situation, a person of faith will remember that God loves him no matter what his life experiences at the moment are telling him. A mature Christian won't try and squeeze God's will out of the circumstances that surround him.

Real trust is like that eagle on the cover of this book, who soars high above the storms of earth and keeps his eyes only upon the sun!

Scriptural Examples:

Throughout the Bible, God has rewarded this "eagle" type of faith, by allowing some believers to actually *see Him* in the midst of harsh circumstances.

For example, there's the extraordinary story of Stephen, who preached a bold and fearless message of salvation to the Sanhedrin, and then was quickly executed for his beliefs. Scripture assures us that Stephen was so full of the Holy Spirit, that when he was being stoned to death, he *saw* the heavens opened, and the Son of man "standing on the right hand of God." (Acts 7:55) Stephen loved God more than he loved his own life. Thus, God allowed this faithful servant to see and experience the glory to come, even while he was dying.

Also, there is the incredible example of the three young men who refused to bow down and worship King Nebuchadnezzar. While remaining faithful to God, they were thrown alive into a fiery furnace. In those very flames, the king recorded that "they [had] no hurt" and that there was a fourth man standing *with them in the fire* whose appearance was *"like the Son of God."* (Daniel 3:25)

These young men would have lost their faith had they measured God's Love by their circumstances. Yet, because they trusted in the Name of the Lord, He sent His Son to stand with them in the fire. Not only were Meshach, Shadrach and Abed-nego saved that day, but also the king himself paid homage to their all-powerful God. (Daniel 3:28)

Finally, there was the example of Moses in Exodus, Chapter 3. After Moses had been ridiculed by his own people over his killing the Egyptian, he fled to the land of Midian. (Exodus 2:15) After 40 years of exile there, God appeared to him in the wilderness of mount Sinai and gave Him the ten commandments. In the middle of those 40 years, had Moses tried to understand God's specific will for his life, he probably would have been confused and frustrated. But he remained faithful to God during those long arduous years in the wilderness, and God rewarded his faithfulness by allowing him to see Him "face to face."

The key here is, that *before* God reveals Himself to us, we must *first* be willing to unconditionally obey Him. Stephen, the men in the fiery furnace and Moses had done exactly that. And this seems to be the Biblical order of things that God has instituted within His kingdom from the very beginning. The more we trust and obey Him, the more He leads and guides us; the more we allow Him to lead and guide us, the more we will get to know Him; and the more we get to know Him, the more we'll experience (and see) His presence in our lives.

Godly Counselors

God not only validates His will through our circumstances, He also often uses godly counselors.[130] Although these counselors can be professionals, pastors or laymen, they should *always* be Christian men and women who are walking by the Spirit of the Lord. These counselors certainly don't have to be "perfect," for no one is, but they should, at least, be living what they are counseling. That way, Jesus will always be in the *center* of their counseling situations. If He is not, we are simply wasting our time.

Our pastors, counselors and doctors, no matter how good they are, cannot tell us exactly what God's will is for us, nor can they heal us. Only Jesus can do these things for us. Our counselors can help to confirm from the Scriptures and by prayer and by the witness of the Spirit what they believe God is saying, but: 1) only Jesus can see our hearts;[131] 2) only

Jesus can show us the real root causes of our problems; 3) only He can remove those roots as far as the east is from the west; 4) only He can align our feelings with our choices and make us genuine; 5) only He can give us the Love we need to go on as if nothing has happened; and, 6) only He can show us His specific and individual will for our lives.

If more Christians would learn how to "renew their minds" on a daily basis, we would not have the massive counseling industry that we have now; and I also believe more people would be healed genuinely and permanently.

The world, and much of the church, is currently being led astray by much emotional counsel and soulish mercy. While secular counselors seek our comfort, we must keep in mind that worldly counsel (even though it might be good advice), is often just the opposite from what God would tell us.

Over and over again in the Bible, God warns us to beware of "other" voices that we hear. These may come in the form of other people's opinions, our own minds or the voice of the enemy. It's imperative that we always hold these thoughts up to the light of Scripture and check them out. We are not to trust these voices until we validate them with God's Word and through prayer.[132] If the Bible does not confirm what we heard, then we should immediately set it aside. If it's truly from God, He will bear witness to it in many other ways.

Discerning God's Will When We Have to Move Quickly

In our walk with the Lord, we will encounter many life situations where we don't have the liberty to wait for God's specific will or His answers on a particular issue. In other words, we don't have time to seek His will through His Word, through prayer and fasting, or through godly counsel. If this is the case, then, there are four important things we can do:

1) Pray and acknowledge that God is in control of your life.
2) Let Him know that you have to move quickly, but you're not sure yet what His will is.
3) Tell Him what you are about to do.
4) Humbly ask Him to "shut the door" if it's not His will. (He is great at slamming doors!)

This is an especially good time to hold onto the words of Proverbs 3:5 and 6: "Trust in the Lord with all thine heart; and lean not unto thine own understanding. In all thy ways acknowledge Him, and He shall direct [your] paths."

Waiting for God's Answers

As we submit to God's Spirit and wait for Him to speak, lead and guide us, it's important that, even in that waiting period, we align our wills with His. How do we do this? By going through *The Inner Court Ritual*[133] and making faith choices to do God's will, even though we don't feel like it yet. The answer is always to be cleansed and submitted to God's Spirit, then, we can kind of float weightlessly until we *see what He will do.*[134]

Some good questions to ask ourselves in the meantime are: *Have I prayed? Is my will surrendered? Have I waited for the Holy Spirit's answer? Are my motives pure?*

If you are still unsure of His will, here is a list of other good questions to ask yourself:

> Will this hinder my spiritual progress? (Hebrews 12:1)
> Can I see Jesus doing this? (1 John 2:6)
> Will this bring glory to God? (2 Corinthians 10:17)
> Will this offend another Christian or cause him to stumble? (Romans 14:21)
> Could I do this in Jesus' Name? (Colossian 3:17)
> Would I want to be found doing this when Jesus returns? (1 John 2:28)
> Will this be a help or a hindrance to Christians around me?
> Will this bring harm to my body? (1 Corinthians 6:19-20)[135]

Remember, our ability to discern God's individual will is affected greatly by our love for Him. To love God means to *totally give ourselves over to Him*. It's not an emotional feeling, but an entire surrender of our body, soul and spirit. The more we love Him, the more we totally give ourselves over to Him, the more sensitive we will become to the thoughts of our Beloved, and the more willing we will become to listen for the sound of His voice.

When we willingly put God first in our lives, He graciously imparts to us the wisdom of His ways. Therefore, let us order our lives so that God can say of us: "...he has loved Me, therefore I will deliver him; I will set him securely on high, because he has known My name. He will call upon Me, and *I will answer Him*...." (Psalm 91:14-15)

To Hear His Heart

"Lord, I would soar like an eagle
Where thirsty souls can sing.
There taught by Your Holy Spirit
And hidden beneath Your wing.
Higher than earthly pleasure
Deeper than sorrow and care
Sweeter than a hearts dear treasure
May I, Your secrets share?
Father, I long to know You
With intimate tender love
And soar like an eagle with You
To lofty places above.
Draw me nearer precious Spirit
Lest I wander from His side
Mold my heart into His likeness
That I would be my Savior's bride."[136]

Key Points of This Chapter:

- God shows us His specific will (to attain holiness) by four means.
- He speaks to us through His Word, the Bible.
- He communicates to us through times of prayer and fasting.
- He directs us through being submissive to His Spirit in our lives.
- He also directs us through our circumstances and the counsel of others.

Section Three:
What Is Faith?

"By faith he [Moses] forsook Egypt, not fearing the wrath of the king: for he endured, as seeing Him Who is invisible." (Hebrews 11:27)

Chapter Five
Why Is Faith So Important?

Being Fully Persuaded

Few subjects in the Bible are more important for us to understand than that of *faith*. The dictionary tells us that faith is "confidence or trust in a person or thing." Since human trust has been greatly abused in this world, many people have chosen to put their faith in "some*thing*" rather than "some*one*." This should <u>never</u> be true of the believer.

God has not called His people to rally around *a belief system*, but to place their trust in a Person. If Christians are to endure to the end, we must understand that the one and only key to our survival is faith--faith in the Person of Jesus Christ.

As George MacDonald once wrote: "It is Thyself, and neither this nor that, nor anything told, taught, or dreamed of that keeps us living."

Faith is developed over the years by the various trials and testings that God allows into our lives. Many Christians have wrongly chosen to associate faith with their feelings. This kind of *emotional faith* can survive <u>only</u> as long as life is understandable and within their "control," but what happens when the rug of human understanding is pulled out from under them and events in their lives turn chaotic or uncontrollable? These Christians then sink because their faith is built on emotionalism, not on the solid rock of faith in Christ. True faith is being able to keep afloat in the dark sea of circumstances.

True faith must be closely interwoven with our will or our choices. Faith is strengthened when we choose to believe in the unfailing character, faithfulness and perfect Love of God, no matter what events surround us. When we choose to wallow in fear and doubt, however, faith is weakened. All unbelief and all debate concerning the integrity of God must be repented of and all argument and controversy concerning God's promises must be abandoned. We must choose, by faith, to believe that God will *forever* be true to His Word.

God is not only the *author* of our faith, He is also the *finisher* of our faith.[137] Faith begins and ends with Him. Faith is not something we can manufacture within ourselves, something that resides in our personality or something that is determined by heredity, intelligence or even religious belief. *Faith is simply being fully persuaded that God is able to do all that He has promised.*[138] Although each believer receives a measure of faith upon conversion, our capacity for faith will be enlarged or diminished by our own individual choices. Thus, it's imperative we be completely *convinced* that God will keep His Word and do the impossible, regardless of how we feel or what we think. Any hesitancy or staggering on our part comes from unbelief and doubt.[139]

A Scriptural Example: Abraham

Abraham in the Old Testament is a perfect example of one who had unshakable belief in God. He got to the point where he offered no arguments, no debate and no questions when God told him to do certain things. This automatic obedience needs to be our response also.

Abraham wasn't always a man of unwavering faith. In fact, he once lied to protect himself from the Egyptians (Genesis 12:11-20), and fhe ought with unbelief concerning the personal promise God made to him (Genesis 16). But in his later years, this same man agreed to sacrifice his son in perfect obedience to the Lord (Genesis 22:11-18). As the story of Abraham's life unfolds, we see this flawed man moving steadily from cowardice to faith, from fear to love and from doubt to obedience.

This response is surely the one God wants from every one of His children. We can either choose to trust and mature into an Abraham, or doubt and diminish into a Judas.

The Bible tells us that faith works only by love.[140] This means, not only God's Love for us, but also our love for Him. We are to love Him and have faith in Him, no matter how crushing the weight of our circumstances and no matter how much our emotions tell us to run and hide. In other words, the only motive that should ever move us is our love for God, not our circumstances, others' responses or human expectations and presumptions.

As George MacDonald so beautifully reminds us: "Every common day, we have to fight the God-denying look of things, to believe that, in spite of their look, they are God's and God is in them, and working His saving will in them."

When the Lord told Abraham to sacrifice Isaac, I'm sure Abraham's every thought and emotion was screaming, "No!" Yet, he obeyed without question. How could a loving father willingly sacrifice his son? The only possible explanation is that *Abraham loved God more than he loved his own son, and he loved God more than he loved his own life.* A fierce love for God is the only true motivation for obedience.

Abraham was simply a human being who diligently practiced loving and receiving God's Love every day of his life, and from that practice emerged an overcoming faith and an unquestioning obedience. As Francis de Sales wrote: "You learn to speak by speaking, to study by studying, to run by running, to work by working, and just so *you learn to love God and man by loving.* Begin as a mere apprentice and the very power of love will lead you on to become a master of the art." (emphasis added)

Only by faith in God's divine promises can we be made "partakers of His nature." Only through faith can we be "kept by the power of God." And, only by faith can we obtain "the salvation of [our] souls." (1 Peter 1:5, 9)

Definition of Faith

My favorite definition of faith is summed up by the words of Paul in Romans 4:21, "being *fully persuaded* that, what [God has] promised, He [will be] able also to perform." Regardless of what we see, hear, feel or think, true faith is choosing to believe that God will do whatever He says He will do! Consequently, faith is a radical reliance upon God.

The farmer plants seed in complete faith that there *will* be a harvest, and believers bury their loved ones in faith that God *will* raise them up in eternity. Our choice to believe is based upon the character of God. Just as Abraham believed God would be faithful to His promise and make of his offspring a "great nation," so he chose to believe God would somehow save his son in order to accomplish that promise.

We are asked to believe in, act upon and walk out God's promises by faith. And, even if we might not see them being fulfilled in the way we thought, He still calls us to believe.[141]

Other Scriptural definitions of faith are:

"Faith is the substance of things hoped for, [and] the evidence of things not seen" (Hebrews 11:1), or, as another translation put it, "faith is being sure of what we hoped for and certain of what we do not see."

Faith is "judg[ing] Him faithful Who [has] promised." (Hebrews 11:11)

Faith is "endur[ing], as seeing Him Who is invisible." (Hebrews 11:27)

Can you see the giant *leap* that is required to move from our natural thought processes to a supernatural faith in God? Be assured, this kind of faith comes from experience. A high jumper doesn't start with the bar at maximum height, but little by little, He raises it until the day his body achieves excellence. If he is faithful in the small things, then his skill will be steadily increased. And it's the same with us. If we are faithful in the small things, then our faith will also be steadily increased.

St. John of the Cross expresses it this way:

> "Faith is a gift from God that enables us to go *beyond* our reason into the reality of the Divine...It's a personal loving relationship with God and becomes the *bond* that links us to others."[142]

The question we must ask ourselves is: Are we building our lives upon *faith in God*, or are we building our lives upon *faith in our own natural skills*, strengths, intelligence and abilities?

How do we build our lives upon faith in God? By daily choosing to walk in childlike dependence and trusting Him, even in the smallest of ways (Matthew 18:3); by being obedient to His Word (1 John 3:22); by appropriating His promises (Matthew 21:22; John 14:13-14; John 15:7); and by loving others in His Name (Matthew 22:37).

Real faith is not feeling, not seeing, not understanding and not knowing but still trusting God. Real faith is being convinced that no matter what we see happening, no matter what we understand to be true, and no matter how we feel, *God will be faithful to His Word and He will perform His promises to us, in His timing and in His way!*

Real faith is allowing God to be God. It's allowing God to do in our lives all that He needs to do, good or bad from our point of view, in order to conform us into His image. Real faith is allowing God to strip us, flay us and crucify us, if that's what is needed to purge and sanctify our soul from sin and self.

David Hazzard clarifies what real faith is:

> "There is a clear line of distinction between true faith, which is set on things above and cannot be shaken, and the meager thing we call faith, which rests on our human understanding--and so it is a thing that is rooted in our life here below. If you want to grow in spirit, you must cross this line. What we normally mean by faith is really only our soul's ability to form thoughts about God. *Real faith is the ability to see with the eyes of [our spirit].*"[143]

The classic verse that validates Hazzard's declaration is Romans 8:28: "And we know that all things work together for good to them that love God, to them who are the called according to His purpose."

True faith allows God to do *all* that He needs to do in order to make us holy so that we can dwell in and enjoy His presence. True faith accepts God's *night seasons* as part of His will towards us in order to accomplish His will in us. And, at the same time, faith clings to God's promises of a future "new" day.

Faith is the unequivocal strong conviction that, no matter what happens, God will never leave us or forsake us.[144] True faith ravishes the heart of the Lord, and the man or woman who exhibits such faith will surely *"walk through the wilderness leaning on the breast of their Beloved."* (Song of Solomon 8:5 NAS)

An Example of True Faith: Diana

Again, the example of Diana Bantlow comes to mind as someone who truly, "walk[ed] through the wilderness *leaning on the breast of* [*her*] *beloved.*" We spoke earlier about Diana, who was terminally ill with leukemia.

Throughout her ordeal, no matter what the circumstances were, no matter how much pain she suffered and no matter what her emotions were saying, Diana continually chose to trust her God and to lay her will and her life down to Him. Having such tremendous faith, she was confident that God would never leave her or forsake her. She also knew that He would never allow anything into her life that was not "Father-filtered" and that would not eventually bring Him glory. So she trusted Him in everything.

Because everyone saw in Diana an intimacy with Jesus that none of us ever had experienced, during the last six months of her life she was invited to teach a woman's Bible study. Now, others might have chosen to spend those last precious moments at home with their families. But not Diana. After she prayed about it, she felt strongly that God wanted her out there sharing her faith and describing to others exactly what He was doing in her life.

The Bible study instantly grew to about 50 people. At the time, I had been a Christian for over 15 years, yet I had never met or seen anyone like Diana. She loved God and it was apparent to all of us that God loved her specially. Her life and walk constantly reflected that knowledge.

She often came to teach the Bible study after her chemotherapy sessions to teach the Bible study. To ease her pain we would prop pillows up behind her so she could sit more comfortably. With a radiant face, she would then begin to tell us about God's Love and His faithfulness and trustworthiness. There was never a dry eye in the room.

Of course Diana experienced natural human emotions, like the rest of us. But her faith and love of God kept her making faith choices to give those things over to Him and, instead, trust Him implicitly. Truly, Diana *did* walk through the wilderness "leaning upon the breast of [her] beloved."

Diana's story proves that *pure faith is simply accepting a situation that we cannot understand and no longer being troubled by it.* Diana's kind of faith means accepting everything that happens to us as coming from the hand of God and being convinced that God will use it all for His glory.

Faith Is Not a Feeling

As we said before, faith is not a feeling: it's simply the power to believe. Faith is the ability to see everything through God's eyes, just as Diana did. The only way our eyes ever get dim is by sin and self. This is why Scripture always exhorts us to walk by faith and not sight. Through faith everything will eventually be turned to sight and understanding. Only faith allows us to become freed of things "seen."

Only through faith can a human being leave his familiar comfort zone and move out into the realm of the unknown. Hebrews 11 is a powerful chronicle of those who faithfully stepped out into the unknown by listening to and obeying the voice of the Lord: *By faith* Noah prepared an ark...*by faith* Abraham went out...*by faith* Sarah received the ability to conceive...*by faith* Moses kept the passover...*by faith* the people of God passed through the Red Sea...*by faith* the walls of Jericho fell down...*by faith* Rahab the harlot did not perish.

Only faith can give us the strength to lay aside our own agenda and stand on the solid foundation that is Christ. Noah laid aside his reputation to build the ark; Abraham laid aside his wealth and property to follow God into the desert; Moses laid aside the treasures of Egypt to pursue his destiny; and Rahab laid aside her cultural identity to seek refuge with the people of God. In every case, these men and women chose to follow God in a completely "unreasonable" route, allowing their faith to silence all protest coming from their own thoughts and emotions.

Faith is letting go of the familiar and consenting to the new and the unknown. Faith is what integrates the *knowing* and the *unknowing*. Faith is learning to leave ourselves in order to find ourselves. It's deliberately choosing to move off of ourselves and to stand on Jesus. Faith is synonymous with abandonment to God's will, and that means being "obedient unto death." (Philippians 2:7-8) It's looking away from ourselves and looking only to Him. Diana did this. Abraham did this. Can we do it?

An Example: Joe

"I have a love-hate relationship with God," wrote Joe Hallett, an incredible Christian man who recently died of AIDS. "He asks things of me that no sane, reasonable or rational person would ever ask. It really annoys me. This God of ours keeps asking me to hope in the impossible. He invites me, or rather commands me, to push through to a place that is completely beyond my understanding and my experience--a place of scalding and naked brilliance. Oh, He's gentle and polite about it, but He's still inviting me to lay down my life. He's still asking me to die."

How accurately Joe describes our human reaction to the words of Jesus in John 12:24 and 25, "Verily, verily, I say unto you, Except a grain of wheat fall into the ground and *die*; it abideth alone; but if it die, it bringeth forth much fruit. He that loveth his life shall lose it; and he that hateth his life in this world shall keep it unto life eternal."

Faith is trusting in God's Love even when we've been stripped of reputation, comfort, family, position, finances and even our last ounce of understanding.[145] Faith is getting to the place where we can vow and mean, "[*let*] *none of these things move me*," even when that means letting go of all that we hold dear. (Acts 20:24) The Lord brought this Scripture to my heart the beginning of last summer and I made it my life verse. He knew that I would really need it for what He was about to allow in our lives.

An Example: Our Beloved Chip

In August of 1998, God allowed one of the biggest tests of our faith ever--probably the hardest thing we will ever have to face. As we sat around the dining room table eating dinner one Saturday night, we got that dreaded phone call: "We are very sorry to inform you that your son, Chip, has just died."

Our beloved "Chip," our firstborn son--Charles Jr., while out jogging had suddenly died of a heart attack. He was only 39 and he leaves behind a beautiful wife, Elizabeth, and two precious little girls, Emily, four, and

Madeline, one. Chip had not seen a doctor for five years. He had been in excellent health and had no prior medical problems. He had run for fun and pleasure all his life, from high school races to recent city-wide events.

There is no reason on earth why this tragedy should ever have happened. There is simply no human understanding for it and we could spend years trying to figure out "why" God allowed it. The fact is that He did, and only He understands the full ramifications of "why." We have chosen to leave all our "whys" and all our "questions" at the cross, and by faith, we have chosen to trust Him in it.

We have cried, we have grieved and we have cried some more. Words are inadequate to describe the depth of how much we loved our son. He was the "hub" around which this family lived and laughed and moved. We miss him beyond words. But God has supernaturally carried us through, filling us with a peace that passes all understanding. Somehow, in God's overall scheme of things and from His eternal viewpoint, this was Chip's time to come "home."

What Chip's death has done for me personally is to bring heaven and earth closer together. I now have one child in heaven waiting for all of us to come home, and three children here on earth, waiting to go home. The reason death is so difficult for so many of us, I believe, is because we are so preoccupied with the here and now. We see only our 30, 40, 50, 60, 70 etc., years here on earth. God, however, sees the "whole picture," and *that includes our life in heaven.* Thus, when He says "all things work together for good," He is figuring in the heavenly perspective, something we are totally incapable of doing.

> "While we look not at the things which are seen, but at the things which are not seen: for the things which are seen are temporal; but the things which are not seen are eternal."
> (2 Corinthians 4:18)

As Erwin Lutzer states in his excellent book on death, "What is life, but [simply] preparation for eternity."[146]

Several people have asked me, "Are you mad at God?" I must answer them honestly and say, "No, I actually find myself closer now to God than ever before" (I don't know how else one would survive something like this without Him carrying you through). I am experiencing more of His Love and more of His peace than ever before, probably due to the fact that I've had to trust Him to a deeper level than ever before.

I constantly have a choice: either to believe that God somehow *is* in these circumstances and knows exactly *why* He has allowed them, or to crumble in doubt and anger and fear that this is all just a cruel joke and that life has no meaning at all.

If I choose to doubt God's Love for me in all of this, then I immediately crash and burn and experience overwhelming depression. I become emotionally wiped out, not only for the moment, but also for anything I do in the future. My faith affects every choice, every thought and every action I take, not only for today, but also for tomorrow. When I choose by faith (not feelings) to believe and trust that what God says in His Word is true, that He loves me and that He will work these circumstances out in my life for His glory, then I'm able to experience, once again, His presence and His peace.

It's a fact that our faith is never more alive then when what we are experiencing in our spirit contradicts what our senses are saying. Faith is trusting that God loves us and will work out every detail of our lives for His glory, even if our senses are screaming just the opposite.

Chip's death has also forced me to determine in my own mind what exactly I believe. Do I really believe what the Bible says about eternal life? Do I really believe that one day we will be with our loved ones who have gone on to heaven before us? Do I really believe that the "present" is only a pre-cursor to what "real life" in the future is going to be?

Of all the thousands of loving cards, letters and poems that we received at that time, one particular poem has really ministered to our hearts. I'd like to quote it for you here because to me this message sums up everything:

> "When I am gone, release me, let me go. I have so many things to see and do. You mustn't tie yourself to me with tears. I gave you my love, you can only guess how much you gave to me in happiness. I thank you for the love you each have shown. But now it's time I traveled on alone.
>
> So grieve a while for me if grieve you must, but then let your grief be comforted by trust. It's only for a while that we must part, so bless the memories within you heart.
>
> I won't be far away, for life goes on. Though you can't see or touch me, I'll be near. And if you listen with your heart, you'll hear all of my love around you loud and clear. *And then, when you come this way alone, I'll greet you with a smile and say 'welcome home."*

This I believe with all my heart. Soon we will be with our beloved Chip, and it won't be just for 39 years, but for an eternity.

When we study the lives of Abraham and Moses and Joshua, we quickly understand that faith is not something we hold onto, but rather *Someone* who holds onto us! True faith steps out of the crowd still clamoring for understanding, lays itself humbly at the foot of the cross and whispers, "Though You slay me, yet will I trust You."

> "There was a time in my life when I thought He was a hard Master," wrote George MacDonald. "But now that I have learned a little more of what He means with me...how He would make me pure of sin, clean from the very bottom of my heart to the crest of my soul...truly, I am no more content to merely submit to His will. Now, I cry out in the night, 'Thy will be done, Lord let it be done, I entreat Thee?' and in the daytime I cry, 'Thy Kingdom come, Lord, let it come, I pray Thee!'"[147]

Faith is giving God permission to penetrate our souls with His fire of Love and burn up all that is not of Him. Opening ourselves up to the true depths of reality--not only believing and trusting in what God does *through us,* but also believing and trusting in what God does *towards us* is faith in action.

Why is Faith So Important?

Because it affects everything we think, say and do, faith is important. Faith is the *victory that overcomes* the world, the flesh and the devil. (1 John 5:4) *Faith is the only way we are able to stand, the only way we are able to live and the only way we are able to love.*[148] Thus, the most important thing we can do as God's children is to learn how to understand, possess and walk in complete faith.

In his book *Combat Faith* Hal Lindsey sets forth a few of the Scriptural promises that come to us through faith:

> "We are born into eternal life through faith; we are declared righteous before God by faith; we are forgiven by faith; we are healed by faith; we understand the mysteries of creation by faith; we learn God's Word by faith; by faith we understand things to come; we walk by faith and not by sight; we overcome the world by faith; we enter God's rest by faith; and we are controlled and empowered by the Holy Spirit by faith.

The issue of faith pervades every aspect of our relationship with God and our service for Him. Faith is the source of our strength, our provision, our courage, our guidance, and our victory over the world system, the flesh and the devil. Faith is the only thing that can sustain us in the trials and persecutions predicted for the last days. It is therefore imperative that we understand exactly what faith is, how we get it and how it grows."[149]

Romans 10:17 tells us that faith comes by hearing, and hearing by the Word of God, which is another reason why being in God's Word on a daily basis is so important.

Faith Allows Us to "See" God

Faith is the telescope that scans the heavens for the majesty of God, as well as the microscope that magnifies His hidden wonders. Futhermore, faith is the code-breaker that allows us to interpret His Words and understand His meanings.

Faith is the only path that not only allows us to "see" God, but also to draw near to His presence and fellowship with Him. Only as we walk by faith can God make the darkness light before us[150] and enable us to see His handiwork.[151]

Therefore, faith is the only avenue that will bring us the intimacy with God that we yearn for and that He so desires.[152] Only as we see God as He truly is and see ourselves as we really are will we ever become truly pleasing in His sight. In other words, no prayer, no tears, no fasting *without faith*, will ever bless Him.

We Can Only Live by Faith

To separate faith from life is impossible because every choice we make comes either from faith in something or Someone, or from unbelief and distrust. The Apostle Paul declared: "I am crucified with Christ: nevertheless, I live: yet not I, but Christ liveth in me; and *the life I now live in the flesh I live by the faith of the Son of God*, who loved me and gave Himself for me." (Galatians 2:20)[153]

What Paul is stating is that "living by faith" is *our responsibility*.[154] Nonetheless, living by faith does not mean "blindly" believing in God, but "wisely" trusting Him to supply our every need. Believing that God has promised us a better world and by faith, we have chosen to hold Him to that promise is living by faith.

Job is an example of someone living by faith. Although Job groaned in his present circumstances, he didn't lose confidence in the future. He *never* stopped believing that God would act as his Vindicator, his

Advocate and his Avenger. In the midst of his greatest suffering, Job still avowed, "I know that my redeemer lives..." (Job 19:25) and this trust needs to be the "battle cry" of every believer in Christ.

God is constantly asking us to decide, "Will you live by faith, or will you crumble when you don't see or understand what I am doing?"

An Example: "Living by Faith"

We have spoken of George Muller before, but I can't leave the subject of "living by faith" without expounding further about the life of this incredible man.

Mr. Muller believed that faith rested upon the Word of God. He used to say, "When sight ceases, then faith has a chance to work." As long as there was any possibility of human success, he felt faith could accomplish nothing. Thus, his motto was, "God is able to do this; I cannot."

His greatest desire was to live a public life of faith so that others' trust in God would be strengthened. He felt it would be living proof that faith works, if he as a poor man, without asking the aid or finances of anyone, simply by prayer and faith, could have all his needs met.

When there was no money, as happened often, he would simply say, "The Lord in His wisdom and love has not sent help, but I believe, in due time He will." And, He always did!

As a result of George Muller's life of prayer and faith, he was given the necessary money to built three orphanages, house and feed almost 2,000 children, buy all the furniture and supplies needed to furnish and run the homes and schools, and hire all the needed personnel to manage the facilities. Muller expected God to answer and expected His blessings on his labor of love. And he always received it, because *he lived by faith*. Mr. Muller epitomized Galatians 3:11, "The just shall live by faith."

Even as Christians, much of our faith rests upon what we can *see* and *feel*. God knows that we can never truly live by faith as long as we are being manipulated by our senses. His Word reveals that the farther removed we get from our faith resting on the things that we see and feel, the more deeply we enter into a life of real faith in God.

Instilling naked faith is one of the reasons God allows "night seasons" in our lives. *When we are no longer able to "see," we will be forced to live by faith.* And, when our faith finally stops being dependent on the realm of our senses, we will be free to enter into the *rest of God*. God knows that the less we "see," the more faith we'll have to live by. As Jesus stated, "...blessed are they that have not seen, and yet have believed." (John 20:29)

Faith Reveals the Character of God to Others

When we reflect God's image--His joy, His wisdom, His Love and His peace--in every circumstance, good or bad,--the world will see Jesus through us. Remember the two nurses who came to Christ as a result of seeing Diana's faith in God, even as she was dying? Even in dying, Diana was living her faith. Like Diana, *the life of every believer should be a magnifying glass focused on Christ, because what we do tells the world what we believe.* Doing demonstrates our belief.

When our faith crumbles in the midst of hard circumstances, we are telling the world that God is not trustworthy, He is not faithful and He is not loving. If Christians display such a lack of trust, then how can unbelievers be expected to put their trust in Christ? Instead, we must show the world that faith in God is always *the answer*, and that He is *our only refuge* in times of trouble.[155]

Faith Enables Us to Be Overcomers

Faith not only enables us to overcome the flesh and the world, but also overcome the devil. Only faith can repel the enemy. Thus, when we lose faith, we leave ourselves wide open for his vicious attacks. Knowing that faith and doubt cannot co-exist, Satan does everything in his power to make us doubt God and His faithfulness. Doubt and unbelief affect every choice we make. Unbelief can destroy our sensitivity to God's voice, and if we choose to entertain this attitude, we'll end up spiritually shipwrecked.[156] Doubt can always be traced back to unbelief in God's Word and His promises. As Hebrews 4:2 puts it, "The word preached did *not* profit them [because it was not] mixed with faith."

Doubting the character of God will stop your spiritual growth and ultimately devour your faith. The only way you can ever counteract such doubt is by an act of will to believe that God will never let you down and never deceive you, no matter what He allows in your life.

An Example: Aggie

I'd like to share a story from one of David Wilkerson's newsletters,[157] that perfectly illustrates the danger of doubting God:

"In 1921, two young missionary couples in Stockholm, Sweden, received a burden to go to the Belgian congo (which is now Zaire). David and Svea Flood (along with their 2 year old son) joined Joel and Bertha Erickson to battle insects, fierce heat, malaria and malnutrition. But after six months in the jungle, they had made little or no contact with the native people. Although the Ericksons decided to return to the mission station, the Floods chose to stay in their lonely outpost. Svea was now pregnant and sick with malaria, yet she faithfully continued to minister to their one and only convert, a little boy from one of the nearby villages.

"Svea died after giving birth to a healthy baby girl, and as David Flood stood over his beloved wife's grave, he poured out his bitterness to God: 'Why did You allow this? We came here to give our lives, and now my wife is dead at 27! All we have to show for all this is one little village boy who probably doesn't even understand what we've told him. You've failed me, God. What a waste of life!'

"David Flood ended up leaving his new daughter with the Ericksons and taking his son back home with him to Sweden. He then went into the import business, and never allowed the name of "God" to be mentioned in his presence. His little girl was raised in the Congo by an American missionary couple, who named their adopted daughter "Aggie."

"Throughout her life, Aggie tried to locate her real father, but her letters were never answered. She never knew that David Flood had remarried and fathered four more children, and she never knew that he had plunged into despair and had become a total alcoholic. But when she was in her forties, Aggie and her husband were given round-trip tickets to Sweden, and while spending a day's layover in London, the couple went to hear a well-known black preacher from the Belgian Congo.

"After the meeting, Aggie asked the preacher, 'Did you ever know David and Svea Flood?' To her great surprise, he answered, 'Svea Flood led me to the Lord when I was a little boy.' Aggie was ecstatic to learn that her mother's only convert was being mightily used to evangelize Zaire, and he was overjoyed to meet the daughter of the woman who had introduced him to Christ.

"When Aggie arrived in Sweden, she located her father in an impoverished area of Stockholm, living in a rundown apartment filled with empty liquor bottles. David Flood was now a 73 year old diabetic who had had a stroke and whose eyes were covered with cataracts, yet when she identified herself, he began to weep and apologize for abandoning her. But when Aggie said, 'That's okay, Daddy. God took care of me,' he became totally enraged.

"'God didn't take care of you!' he cried. 'He ruined our whole family! He led us to Africa and then betrayed us! Nothing ever came of our time there, and it was a waste of our lives!'

"That's when Aggie told him about the black preacher she'd just met in London, and how the Congo had been evangelized through the efforts of his wife's one and only convert. As he listened to his daughter, the Holy Spirit suddenly fell on David Flood, and tears of sorrow and repentance began to flow down his face. Although God mercifully restored him before he died, David Flood left behind five unsaved and embittered children. *His anger towards God had totally wasted his life's potential, and created a tragic legacy for his family.*"

This story clearly illustrates the fact that we must *never* doubt God or base our faith upon our own human understanding of what God is doing. Had David Flood chosen by an act of his will to accept his situation as coming directly from the hand of God, who knows what awesome fruit God could have brought forth from his life? *God is involved in every aspect of our existence, and there is no sorrow so great that He cannot "recycle" it to bring forth blessing.*

The wise Christian believes that everything God allows in his life comes forth from God's Love, and has been designed to transform him into Christ's Image. Let's remember to keep in mind C. S. Lewis' words, "What seems to us good may therefore not be good in His eyes, and what seems to us evil may not be evil (in His eyes)."

[See further information on "doubt" in Chapters Seven and Eight.]

Faith Is the Victory That Overcomes

Faith is the key that opens the door to our spiritual victory and enables us to walk triumphantly with Jesus.[158] As mentioned before, only true faith can overcome the world, the flesh and the devil. To "overcome" simply means to be able to conquer our sin, our self, our circumstances and our trials through the power of faith. Overcoming faith means putting off anything "that is not of faith" and putting on Christ.[159]

The way God implements this kind of overcoming faith, is by removing everything in our lives that hinders and prevents our trusting Him completely. Even if the world collapses around us, God wants us to still stay faithful and able to cry, "Though You slay me, yet will I trust You."

Overcoming faith enables us to maintain an abandonment to God even in times of suffering. Even though "the earth should change, and the mountains slip into the heart of the sea,"[160] *overcomers know they are being held by God.* Overcoming faith places its hope and its expectation in God and God alone.[161]

The Shield of Faith
(Ephesians 6:16)

Every morning I prayerfully put on the "whole" armor of God. (Ephesians 6) But over the last couple of years, I have come to especially appreciate the *Shield of Faith* as one of the more important pieces of armor. I know that all the pieces are essential, but I have found a special benefit in taking up the Shield of Faith. This is the piece of armor that *prevents Satan's arrows from piercing my heart and life.* Whenever I neglect to pick up and "put on" my Shield, I immediately sense the mounting attack of the enemy.

If we love Jesus, if we want more of Him, we will be attacked. Satan's game plan is to do everything in his power to undermine our faith so that we drop our shields, leaving ourselves wide open for his arrows. Thus, when we lose faith in God and His promises, we will experience the sharp thrust of the enemy's killing sword.

When we learn to make faith choices, however, and trust in God *no matter what is happening all around us,* we hold up that Shield of Faith and it protects our hearts. Faith choices, remember, are non-feeling choices that give God the freedom to work in our lives. The wonderful thing about faith choices is that God, in His perfect timing and His perfect way, will eventually align our feelings with what we have chosen to believe and make us genuine.

Just as David believed, "The Lord is my strength and my shield," we, too, must believe. (Psalm 28:7)[162]

Note something very important: Faith seems to have *two parts*: First, that portion of faith that God places in our hearts when we are first saved. As Ephesian 2:8 asserts, "For by grace are ye saved through faith; *and that not of yourselves, it is the gift of God."* The Shield of Faith, the second aspect of faith, is only activated by our own personal choice, moment by moment, to trust and believe. (Ephesians 6:16) In other words, we literally raise our shield only by making faith choices or non-feeling choices to believe what God's Word says.[163]

Even though this Shield of Faith belongs to every single believer, many have gone off to battle having left their shields at home.

An Example: Onslaught of the Enemy

For a variety of reasons, this book has become more precious to me than all the others I have written. I have not only lived the material in this book for the past seven years, but my heart and soul are in it. Thus the enemy has constantly been roaring around (as you can imagine) looking for holes in which to attack me.

December 1998 came only a few months after Chip died. The hustle and bustle of Christmas shopping, getting ready for company, preparing the house and all the food, and my own fluctuating emotions, made for leanness in my own private time with the Lord. That, plus my being emotionally very fragile, all made it a very dangerous time for me. I should have had my armor on tighter, especially my Shield of Faith.

Right in the middle of this busy and vulnerable time, something extremely devastating happened that caused me to stop making faith choices and sent me straight into the pits. Obviously, I dropped my Shield of Faith.

What had happened caused me to have great insecurity about my own writing ability. And, of course, that was just the "hole" the enemy was waiting for. Because my shield was down, he found a perfect entrance and began to whisper things like, "Who do you think you are to write such a book as this?" "You're no theologian or scholar." "You have no professional training, who do you think you are?"

Then, of course, my mind raced to all the other contemporary writers who could do such a much better job of writing than I, etc., etc. At one point, I literally became "afraid" to write any more. It was obvious that I had dropped my Shield of Faith and Satan's arrows had gone right to my heart.

By the middle of Christmas I was truly "down in the dumps." One morning, as I was doing my daily devotionals and putting on the Armor of God, I began to recognize exactly what was happening. *I had dropped my Shield of Faith because I had stopped believing in God's promises to me.* Back in November of 1997, after seven years of waiting, God commissioned me to write this book. He not only told me to write it, He also told me that *He would be with me and that He would teach me exactly what to say and how to say it.*[164]

[Please see Chapter Fourteen for all the details of this encounter.]

I also remembered a Scripture that He had given me back then, "When the enemy shall come in like a flood, the Spirit of the Lord shall lift up a standard against him." (Isaiah 59:19)

Because I had been in such an emotional state, I hadn't recognized what was happening. The slide downward is always so very subtle. Once I began to make faith choices again, to give my insecurities and fears over to the Lord, even though I surely did not feel like it, I immediately raised my Shield of Faith and the enemy's arrows were stopped. Not only were they stopped, but God was faithful to keep the enemy at bay for the rest of the holidays and to restore the joy of my salvation. And, the best part of all, was that He blessed the fruit of my writing with His Wisdom, His Love and His comforting presence.

So I, too, can join George Muller in saying, "God is able to do this...I cannot."

Name of Jesus, Word of God and Blood of Christ

Although the Bible assures us that *the battle belongs to the Lord*,[165] the battle is *only* won if <u>we</u> make faith choices and hold our shields high in place. This way is the only way we can deflect the blows of the enemy. God will fight our battles for us, but <u>we</u> must constantly make those faith choices to shield ourselves from the onslaughts of the enemy.[166]

A few other things we can do to shield ourselves are:

1) *Humble ourselves and cast ourselves upon the Lord in complete trust.* (Isaiah 37:1)
2) *Pray constantly.* (2 Kings 19:14-16)
3) *Run to the Word of God because it's our only hope.*
4) *Use our weapons of warfare (the Name of Jesus, the Word of God and the Blood of Christ).*

An Example: Tasmania

Speaking of our weapons of warfare, I once traveled alone to Tasmania, Australia, for a speaking engagement. It turned out to be a wonderful and blessed time of ministry, and I think the enemy was infuriated.

On my way home to the United States, I had to spend one night in Sidney, Australia, for an early morning plane change the next day. I was so exhausted when I got to the hotel that I forgot to pray and anoint my room with oil. (I often do so when I am alone and in a new and strange environment.)

In the middle of the night, I was abruptly awakened out of a deep sleep and sensing or seeing in my mind a demon touching me on my shoulder. As I quickly turned over to see it face to face, I began to scream out the Name of Jesus over and over and over again, until it finally vanished. I leapt out of bed, anointed my room with oil, pleaded the blood of Christ over everything, read the Word and went back to sleep without further interruption.

I have used the Name of Jesus hundreds of times: when I am afraid; when I don't know what to say or how to pray; when I'm overwhelmed with sorrow or sadness, etc. So I know by experience that the Name of Jesus is a powerful weapon. When that Name is mentioned, all principalities and powers are scattered and vanquished. The apostle Paul emphatically states in Philippians 2:10 that "...at the Name of Jesus, every knee [shall] bow, of things in heaven, and things in earth, and things under the earth." Thus, we can use His Name to repel an onslaught of the enemy.

What Does Faith Do?

What exactly is the "work of faith" that is spoken about in 2 Thessalonians 1:11?[167] The work of faith that Paul is referring to here, I believe, is simply choosing, moment by moment, to believe upon, trust in and walk out the promises of God. *An active faith is made up of a series of moment-by-moment choices.* Only by the work of faith can we fully embrace God's promises, *even though we may never see them fulfilled in our lifetime.*

I know this statement declares a difficult truth, but look at the lives of Abel, Enoch, Noah, Abraham and Sarah. Hebrews 11:13 tells us that all of these saints *"died in faith, not having received [God's] promises but having seen them afar off."* In other words, they fully embraced God's promises even though they couldn't see them yet. Such belief is our work of faith.

One of the lessons that God is teaching me in my own life is that His promises are true, but they will be fulfilled in His timing and in His way. *My work of faith is simply to believe and trust in His faithfulness to do so.* God is in charge of the means, the manner and the way in which those promises will be answered, and I am learning to accept this fact by faith. I am learning how to "hide" the promises that God gave me on that mountaintop seven years ago in my heart just as Mary did in Luke 2:19. "Mary kept all these things, and pondered them in her heart." As I keep my eyes totally focused on the Lord, He will show me when I can bring those promises out and say, "This was foretold me by the Lord, and now it's come to pass." This focus is my "work of faith."

Faith lightens our path and leads us from the realm of the visible to the realm of the Spirit. *Hope* turns our attention forward to what we do not possess. And *Love* centers our affection on God, so that we <u>can</u> live the rest of our lives to His commands and to His will.

Key Points of This Chapter:

- Faith is the *key* to our walk with the Lord.
- True faith is interwoven with our will, our free choice.
- Faith is being fully persuaded that God will do as He promises.
- It's not a feeling we have, but the ability to discern things through God's eyes.
- Faith is important because it allows us to "see" Him.
- Total trust in God, no matter what our circumstances, is the only thing that enables us to be "overcomers."

"Workman of God! O lose not heart but learn what God is like,
And in the darkest battlefield thou shalt know where to strike.

Thrice blest is he to whom is given the instinct that can tell
That God is on the field when He is most invisible.

He hides Himself so wondrously, as though there were no God;
He is least seen when all the powers of ill are most abroad.

Ah! God is other than we think; His ways are far above,
Far beyond reason's height, and reached only by childlike love.

Then learn to scorn the praise of men, and learn to lose with God;
For Jesus won the world though shame, and beckons thee this road.

For right is right, since God is God, and right the day must win;
To doubt would be disloyalty, to falter would be sin."

Written by Frederick William Fabre,
(1815-1863)

Chapter Six
Faith in the Dark Night

What is "the Dark Night"?

To recap: God's will for all mankind is that we might come to have a personal and eternal relationship with Him through salvation; God's will for believers is that we might be conformed into His image by sanctification so that we can enjoy the fulness of Christ .

Because God loves us so much, He will do whatever is necessary in each of our lives to accomplish this transformation. When we willingly allow Him to purge our souls of sin and self, He can then easily accomplish His will. However, when we block and prevent God from doing these things in our lives, either out of ignorance or disobedience, sometimes He takes matters into His own hands, i.e., the night seasons.

The dark night or the night season is simply the *transition* we make from depending upon our sight and ourselves to a total dependence upon Christ and His faithfulness. This shift brings us into a new way of knowing God. During this time God moves us from simply "feeling good about Him" to a deeper awareness of Him. It's a period of testing in which our soul and our spirit are cleansed of every shred of self-interest.

Although we already belong to Christ and we already love Him, our union with Him will be incomplete as long as our mind, our judgment, our desires, our habits and our ideas are still our own. God wants to rid us of our preoccupation with sight and feelings, and all our other dependencies besides Himself, and bring us into a new freedom and liberty of faith. Unfortunately, this freeing process does not happen *automatically*.

Most of us will not jump for joy when faced with the prospect of brokenness. Naturally, most of us run the other direction. But God loves us so much that He doesn't let us get very far. The dark night is God's way of turning us around and forcing us to allow Him to do whatever is necessary in our lives to purge our souls and spirits so that we can have intimate fellowship with Him. God is not a "mean" guy up in heaven waiting to send us bad things. *He is a loving Father who knows exactly what we need in order to accomplish His will in our lives. He knows that we will never be content, never enjoy real freedom and never be truly fulfilled, until we are "experientially" one with Him.*

An Analogy

This analogy was E-mailed to me recently. It's called *The Moth and the Cocoon,* and I believe it's by George MacDonald:[168]

> "A man found a cocoon of an emperor moth. He took it home so that he could watch the moth come out of the cocoon. On the day a small opening appeared, he sat and watched the moth for several hours as the moth struggled to force its body through that little hole.
>
> Then, it seemed to stop making any progress. It appeared as if it had gotten as far as it could and it could go no farther. It just seemed to be stuck. The man, in his kindness, decided to help the moth. So he took a pair of scissors and snipped off the remaining bit of the cocoon. The moth then emerged easily. But, it had a swollen body and small, shriveled wings.
>
> The man continued to watch the moth because he expected that, at any moment, the wings would enlarge and expand to be able to support the body, which would then contract. Neither happened! In fact, the little moth spent the rest of its life crawling around with a swollen body and shriveled wings. It <u>never</u> was able to fly."

What the man in his kindness and haste did not understand was that the restricting cocoon, and the struggle required for the moth to get through the tiny opening, were God's way of forcing fluid from the body of the moth into its wings so that it would be ready for flight once it achieved its freedom from the cocoon. Freedom and flight would come only after the struggle. By depriving the moth of this struggle, he deprived the moth of health.

Sometimes struggles are exactly what we need in our life in order to make us all that God desires. If God allowed us to go through our life without obstacles, it would cripple us.

Different Labels for the Dark Night

This night season has been given several names:

    The Dark Night of the Soul
    The Dark Night of the Spirit
    Night of Confusion
    Jacob's Ladder
    A Secret Ladder
    The Night Season

The Divine Darkness
Journey into the Desert
Cloud of Unknowing
A Wall
God's Fire of Love

A Night of Love

I like to call the dark night a "night of love."

The dark night is a night of love because it's a time in which we come to know and perceive our Beloved *in a way we never have before.* Our intial surrender to God usually comes *before* we understand what abandoning ourselves to His will really means. Before we understand that He must not only purge the sin from our souls, but also crucify our own self-centered ways. When we first come to Christ and are saved, we are *positionally* united with Him, but we really don't know Him intimately.

There is a deeper and more abiding union--an experiential oneness with Him--that He desires for every one of us where we can *experience* His presence and His joy and rest in the midst of any circumstance. This experiential union, as we have said before, does *not* happen automatically, but only as we become more and more sanctified or holy in body, soul and spirit. In other words, in order to enter into the Holy Place of our hearts where God dwells and enjoy *intimacy with Him*, we, too, must first become holy as He is holy. *Holiness is the only "ticket" inward.* God cannot commune and fellowship with anyone who is not holy and sanctified.

As we saw earlier, God often dwells in darkness and covers Himself with darkness.[169] This means that we, too, in our journey inward towards intimacy and experiential oneness with Jesus, can encounter *darkness*. For us, this "darkness" can simply mean the absence of any understanding or knowledge as to what's happening to us or where we are going. It simply means being deprived of the *light* (the seeing, the feeling and the understanding) that we are so used to.[170] In other words, we're unable to see through this kind of darkness with our own natural mind which, of course, is exactly what God intends. He is teaching us to walk by faith and not by feelings or sight. As our faith begins to grow, the light of understanding will also begin to form.

I'm finding this lesson to be so true. The more "faith" I have in Jesus during the dark times, the more I'm able to "see" Him and the more "understanding" He gives me.

"Unto the upright there ariseth *light in the darkness*."
(Psalm 112:4)

This darkness, then, does <u>not</u> come from the enemy, but from God who loves us. God is the One who initiates the darkness. Remember Isaiah 50:10, "Who is among you that feareth the Lord, that obeyeth the voice of His servant, that walketh in darkness, and hath no light?"

Now, don't misunderstand me. Satan is often involved when difficult things occur in our lives. And he rejoices when we react poorly to God's chastening, cleansing and purifying process. What God allows in our lives for good, Satan obviously wants to use to destroy us.[171] So, yes, the enemy is definitely involved in the night seasons, *but he is not responsible for sending the darkness.* It's simply God's will *towards us.*

[See Chapters Seven and Ten for more information on demonic attacks during the "night seasons."]

Jesus Had His own Dark Night

All throughout the New Testament, we are told that we are to keep our eyes focused on Jesus, because He is our example. The apostle Peter makes this fact very plain:

> "Forasmuch then as Christ hath suffered for us in the flesh, arm yourselves likewise with the same mind [attitude]." (1 Peter 4:1) "For even hereunto were ye called; because Christ also suffered for us, *leaving us an example, that ye should follow His steps.*" (1 Peter 2:21)[172]

Jesus is not only our Savior, our Lord and our King, but also our "role model." He walked the Christian walk perfectly. He showed us how it should be done. Again, we will *never* be able to walk it "perfectly" as He did, but Scripture tells us we are to emulate or try to follow Him. Because of this truth, how can we overlook Jesus' own dark night in the Garden of Gethsemane? As one writer says, "Gethsemane was the dark night of the soul for Jesus Christ; it was the test of His ways."[173]

Jesus is not only our God, He is also our Mentor, our Leader and our Guide, and we must be willing to follow Him wherever He leads. Matthew 26:38 says, "Christ suffered for us, leaving us *an example, that we should follow in His steps.*"[174] *The way Jesus became perfect, complete or fulfilled (teleioo), is by suffering.* If He had to go through suffering and His own dark night, then it's reasonable that this will be our role also.

In Jesus' painful night, Scripture tells us that sorrow and deep distress so marked His inner spirit that He actually sweated drops of blood.[175] No one was ever called to greater suffering. Mark 14:34 tells us that He exclaimed, "My soul is exceedingly sorrowful unto death...." The magnitude of Jesus' agony is beyond our understanding. When the revelation of what He was about to endure became fully apparent, He fell on His face and prayed, "Father, if Thou be willing, remove this cup from Me; *nevertheless, not My will, but Thine be done.*" (Luke 22:42)

Jesus' life had been bartered for a murderer's; He had been outwardly despised, rejected, reviled, crushed, oppressed, afflicted, mocked, taunted and now He was to be crucified.[176] He had no heavenly visitation to support Him. No loving heart came forward to help Him. His disciples were asleep. Not one person was true to Him.

Finally, Jesus' night culminated at the cross of Calvary. When the Romans put Him on the cross, a pall of *thick darkness* cut Him off and He cried out, "My God, My God, why hast Thou forsaken me?" (Mark 15:34) It seemed that at the very moment Jesus needed His Father the most, God had left Him. Matthew 27:50 tells us it was then that Jesus yielded up *His Spirit* and the temple veil of the Holy of Holies was rent from the top down.[177]

Jesus endured what no other man has ever had to endure. But, as a result of the *gift of His Life,* His blood has atoned for the sins of all mankind. Only Jesus' faith allowed Him to survive the garden and the cross. His total commitment to His Father--who Jesus knew was there, even though He could not see or feel Him--is what saved Him. His mission was complete. *Because of His death, anyone who accepts His free gift of salvation now has full access to the Father at any time.* The result of Jesus' dark night is eternal Life for all of us.

Isaiah 53

Isaiah 53 is one of the most incredible chapters in the Bible. Although it was written six centuries before Christ lived and translated into Greek three centuries before He walked the shores of Galilee, it describes this night in perfect detail,. Isaiah 53 foretells us exactly what would happen when the Messiah came: He would be despised, rejected, a man of many sorrows, acquainted with grief, wounded, bruised, oppressed, afflicted, cut off--exactly what Jesus had to endure.

In verses 4 to 6 and verse 8 Isaiah continues his accurate description:

"Surely, He hath borne our griefs, and carried our sorrows; yet we did esteem Him stricken, smitten of God, and afflicted. But He was wounded for our transgressions, He was bruised for our iniquities; the chastisement of our peace was upon Him, and with His stripes we are healed. All we like sheep have gone astray; we have turned every one to his own way, and the Lord hath laid *on Him* [Jesus] the iniquity of us all...He was taken from prison and from judgment... For He was cut off out of the land of the living, for the transgression of My people was He stricken."

Then, in verse 10, Isaiah's words are absolutely astonishing. *"Yet it pleased the Lord to bruise Him; He hath put Him to grief. When Thou shalt make His soul an offering for sin...."* In other words, out of His infinite Love for us, God used the way of suffering to accomplish His will--salvation for all mankind. In like manner, God deals with us. He uses the way of suffering to accomplish His will--the sanctification of our body, soul and spirit.

Are you willing to endure a night season so God can accomplish His ultimate purpose through your life? Do you love God that much? Don't tell me your answer--tell God!

In his tape *Experiencing God*, Henry Blackaby suggested that when we read Isaiah 53, we should ask ourselves, "Am I willing to allow each one of the things that happened to Jesus to occur in my own life?" If we are, then, praise God, He will see to it that eventually we will experience a oneness and a unity with Him that we have never known before. However, if we are not willing to allow these things to happen in our lives because we want our lives to be under our own control, then we'll have to remain where we are and, like that moth, be deprived of health, fulfillment and intimacy with God the rest of our lives. It's our choice.

Isaiah 53:7 continues:

> "He [the Messiah] was oppressed, and He was afflicted, yet He opened not His mouth; He is brought as a lamb to the slaughter, and as a sheep before her shearers is dumb, so He openeth not His mouth."

This statement astonishes me, because this is God we are talking about here. He was in perfect control the whole time (just as He was in the garden and also at Calvary), and with one word He could have called down all the legions of heaven and struck His oppressors. *But, because He loved us so much, He was willing to pay the complete price for our salvation and for our freedom.* What an example for us, as 1 Peter 2:23 clearly shows:

"Who, when He was reviled, reviled not again; when He suffered, He threatened not, but *committed Himself to Him that judgeth righteously.*" (emphasis added)

An Example: Corrie ten Boom

An incredible example of someone who suffered greatly but who continually committed herself to God even in the harshest of circumstances is Corrie ten Boom. I'm sure most of you have read her book *The Hiding Place.* If you haven't, I highly recommend it; it will totally change your outlook. All the comforts we take so for granted will become very precious as a result of reading this beautiful book.

Corrie lived in Germany during the 1930s and 40s. She and her Christian family soon became sympathetic to the plight of the Jews and harbored some of them in their own home. Soon the ten Boom house became known as a "safe sanctuary." Eventually, finding out about the secret room in their home, the Gestapo began rounding up all who were involved in the scheme.

The police picked up Corrie, along with her sister, brother and father. They abused and slapped Corrie around as they tried to find out about the others involved. They finally ended up taking all the ten Booms to prison where they were put in "cages" 6 feet by 6 feet. Because the Germans believed that Corrie was the "ringleader," she was put in solitary confinement cell.

Corrie not only suffered the shock of being absolutely alone for months, she also was not allowed to talk to anyone. The only break in the monotony of her days without human contact, came when a little ant began visiting her. At first, he came alone. But, then, he came back with his family and friends. Corrie would actually get down on the floor and watch him for hours. The other thing that lifted her spirits was when she realized there was a window in the ceiling of her cell. Even though it had 28 squares of bars, nevertheless, she could occasionally see the sun.

What sustained her throughout her ordeal was the fact that she could read the Scriptures. When she had first come to prison, she had asked a nurse to get her a Bible. It, then, became her lifeline. Daily, she would read verse by verse until she had gone through the entire Word of God. Then she would begin all over again. Continually, she would ask herself, "What would Jesus do?" "How would He have handled this situation?"

Finally, one of the guards allowed her to speak to him. Then, after several weeks, he allowed her to talk to him about the Lord. This was the biggest and greatest blessing of all--not only to be allowed to talk to another human being, but to be able to talk about her precious Lord. The guard eventually opened up and shared how much he hated working in the prison. Because of this man's sensitivity, Corrie was finally reunited in the same cell with her sister Betsie, allowed to take a shower once a week and even given a new sheet.

Corrie suffered greatly the year she survived the horror of solitary confinement; nevertheless, she committed herself to God every moment of every day. And, just as He had promised, He was faithful to *never* leave her or forsake her. She used to point out, "there is no pit so deep, that Jesus is not deeper."

The lesson we can learn from Corrie is the same one Jesus taught us: "Who, when He was reviled, *reviled not again*; when He suffered, *He threatened not; but committed Himself to Him That judgeth righteously.*" (1 Peter 2:23 emphasis added)

Eventually released from prison, Corrie ministered God's Love to hurting people all over the world. In the same way, God desires to make our souls a reflection of His own. However, in order to reflect Him, we need to be willing to walk as He walked. He entered in by the "narrow gate" and He walked the straight and "hard road." *Are we willing to do the same?*

Someone said that there will be no revival, either personally or otherwise, until there is *first* a Gethsemene and a Calvary in each of our own lives.

This is "Brokenness"

A piece written by John Collinson about "the narrow road" quoted in Roy Hession's book When I Saw Him, I think sums everything up perfectly:

"Sometimes it is asked what we mean by brokenness. Brokenness is not easy to define but can be clearly seen in the reactions of Jesus, especially as He approached the cross and in His crucifixion. I think it can be applied personally in this way:

When to do the will of God means that even my Christian brethren will not understand, and I remember that "neither did His brethren believe in Him" and I bow my head to obey and accept the misunderstanding, *this is brokenness.*

When I am misrepresented or deliberately misinterpreted, and I remember that Jesus was falsely accused but He "held His peace," and I bow my head to accept the accusation without trying to justify myself, *this is brokenness.*

When another is preferred before me and I am deliberately passed over, and I remember that they cried, "Away with this man, and release unto us Barabbas," and I bow my head and accept rejection, *this is brokenness.*

When my plans are brushed aside and I see the work of years brought to ruin by the ambitions of others, and I remember that Jesus allowed them to "lead Him away to crucify Him" and He accepted that place of failure, and I bow my head and accept the injustice without bitterness, *this is brokenness.*

When in order to be right with my God it is necessary to take the humbling path of confession and restitution, and I remember that Jesus "made Himself of no reputation" and "humbled Himself...unto death, even the death of the cross," and I bow my head and am ready to accept the shame of exposure, *this is brokenness.*

When others take unfair advantage of my being a Christian and treat my belongings as public property, and I remember "they stripped him," and "parted His garments, casting lots," and I bow my head and accept "joyfully the spoiling of my goods" for His sake, *this is brokenness.*

When one acts towards me in an unforgivable way, and I remember that when He was crucified Jesus prayed "Father, forgive them; for they know not what they do," and I bow my head and accept any behavior towards me as permitted by my loving Father, *this is brokenness.*

When people expect the impossible of me and more than time or human strength can give, and I remember that Jesus said, "This is my body which is given for you..." and I repent of my self-indulgence and lack of self-giving for others, *this is brokenness.*"

The Fellowship of His Suffering

Just as Jesus "bore our griefs and carried our sorrows" (Isaiah 53:4), so we are to *participate in His suffering*--by barring ourselves from sin and self, and choosing instead, to follow what He would have us do.[178] "Suffering" simply means *barring ourselves* (or preventing ourselves) *from following sin and self.*[179]

The apostle Paul speaks to this topic in Philippians 3:10 where he declares, "That I may know Him, and the power of His resurrection, and the *fellowship of His sufferings*, being made conformable unto His death."

We are to identify with Christ, not only by verbally assenting to, ascribing to and holding on to what He did for us on the cross, but also by daily experiencing the crucifying of our own "self." In other words, we are to actually bear our own cross and follow Jesus, being faithful as He was faithful. (Matthew 16:24)

> "Though He were a Son, yet learned He obedience by the things which He suffered, And being made perfect [complete], He became the author of eternal salvation unto all them that obey Him" (Hebrews 5:9)[180]

Are you willing to learn obedience this way? It's costly! It might just cost you everything. But through it, you will not only gain *abundant life*, but also the ability to abide in the unutterable joy of His presence (*the fulness of Christ*). Paul could genuinely rejoice in his suffering, because he found the true meaning of it: *Suffering is simply filling up what is lacking in our faith.*[181]

Suffering is the way God has chosen to bring redemption to a fallen world. Jesus suffered for us, giving us His example to follow. We cannot "die to ourselves" without suffering. Suffering has as its goal the sanctification the purification of our souls and spirits. As a part of *God's will towards us*,[182] suffering comes about as God unrelentingly identifies the most potentially damaging hindrance to our relationship with Him, and then lovingly begins to strip that thing away from us. He crushes us, He breaks us, He shakes us and removes anything that is in the way of His accomplishing His will in and through our lives.

Most of the time, we neither realize *why* God has called us to suffer, nor *that* He has called us to suffer. C. S. Lewis puts it another way: "The question is not why the righteous suffer, but why some do not!"[183]

The Bible tells us that only through death, can there be life. Unless we are willing to participate in the fellowship of Christ's sufferings, we will <u>not</u> be able to participate in His exaltation. 2 Timothy 2:11-12 states, "It is a faithful saying: For if we be dead with Him, we shall also live with Him; *If we suffer, we shall also reign with Him....*"

Life Includes Suffering

For many years I purposely ignored the sufferings of Job because it scared me, for I didn't understand suffering's purpose. I can even remember one dear lady who came up to me years ago and shared that I was to look forward to "suffering with Christ." Well, back then I thought she was a crazy heretic, so I stayed clear of her.

Now, of course, I understand that she was speaking the truth; I just wasn't able to hear it at that time. Eventually, in God's timing, the story of Job became incredibly real to me as I began to experience deep suffering in my own life.

God put the book of Job, one of the longest books of the Bible, right in its center for a very good reason: it's an example of *faith in the night seasons.* God intends for us all to use it as a "road map" on our journey through the dark night, always keeping in mind that at the end of the road, *Job finally "saw" God as he never had seen Him before, changing his life forever.*

Life itself includes suffering.[184] Futhermore, as Ecclesiastes 9 tells us, all things come alike to all and time and chance happen to all. (verses 2, 11) *Suffering can come as a result of our own sin, the sins of others, the schemes of Satan or from the fallen state of the human race.* God is above all of these things, and He will use any or all of them as He sees fit to accomplish His perfect will in our lives.[185]

There are *two* ways we can respond to suffering: We can either 1) despise it; be defeated by it; give up in it and quit;[186] or we can 2) delight and rejoice in it;[187] be strengthened by it; and continue on in it by faith.[188]

The actor Michael J. Fox, who has recently gone public with the news that he has been battling Parkinson's disease for over five years, said: "There's no tragedy; it's just *reality.*"

Life includes suffering.

Some important points to remember when we are going through suffering, are:

> God allows our troubles to drive us to our knees and to bring us back to Himself.[189]
> Sometimes our troubles must get worse before freedom comes. Satan, obviously, does not want our freedom; therefore, he does everything he can to stop it.
> It's important to realize that we can't get ourselves out of trouble. If God has allowed this trial, then He is the only One who can get us out. Therefore, it's not our battle, but His.[190]

Our troubles should always push us towards God, not away from
Him.[191] If they push us away from Him, we should check to be
sure Satan isn't the instigator.[192]

Once we understand that God is involved, it should give us hope.[193]

God wants to use our trials as a way for us to learn His statues and
His laws.[194]

God always has a reason for the things He allows in our lives. He is
preparing us for a future which He alone knows. He is preparing us as
His "bride." He not only wants to make us perfect (holy), established,
strengthened and grounded in Him, but also joint heirs with Him.[195]

[See *Endnote* for the different purposes of suffering.[196]]

Conformed to His Death

By allowing suffering into our lives, God is conforming us unto His
death. Philippians 3:10 not only talks about the fellowship of His
suffering, but also goes on to say we are to be made *"conformable unto
His death."* Listen again, "That I may know Him, and the power of His
resurrection, and the fellowship of His sufferings, [*and by this*] *being
made conformable unto His death."*

The Living Bible translates it this way: "To find out what it means to
suffer and die with Him." Being *"conformed unto His death"* simply
means personally walking out Christ's death in our lives. It means
"dying daily" as Paul says in 1 Corinthians 15:31. It means constantly
setting aside our own thoughts, emotions and desires and all of our own
self-centered ways (belief systems, expectations, etc.) that are contrary to
Him. It's called "dying to self."

What Philippians 3:10 is saying is that in order to truly "know" Him
and the power of His resurrection, we must *first* experience the fellowship
of His sufferings *by being conformed unto His death*. The Bible always
teaches us that death must precede life. In order to have more of God in
our life, there needs to be less of self. If we don't *decrease*, then how can
God *increase?*[197] *In other words, for God to fill us with Himself, He must
first strip us of our old self.*[198]

God's will for believers throughout the Bible is that we might be
"conformed into the image of His Son." (Romans 8:29) This is God's
basic will and the goal of our instruction: that He might *reproduce* His
Life in us. Most of us talk very openly about this and pray for it in our
own lives. *However, what most of us don't realize is that in order to be
conformed into His image, we must first be conformed to His death.* This
is what Philippians is telling us.

In other words, in order to experience the fulness of Christ, we must each experience our own personal Garden of Gethesmane and Calvary.[199] Nothing is made alive or quickened unless it first dies. Listen to Christ's example in Philippians 2:5-9:

> "Let this mind be in you, which was also in Christ Jesus, Who, being in the form of God, thought it not robbery to be equal with God: But made Himself of no reputation, and took upon Him the form of a servant, and was made in the likeness of men: And being found in fashion as a man, He humbled Himself, and became *obedient unto death*, even the death of the cross. Wherefore God also hath highly exalted Him, and given Him a Name which is above every name."

Romans 6:5 validates this: "For if we have been planted together in the likeness of His death, we shall be also in the likeness of His resurrection."[200]

How comfortable it is for us to simply *preach* "Christ crucified."[201] The question we must always ask ourselves is, how can we preach Christ crucified if we don't really live it? There's no way we can communicate it, if we have not experienced it! Our daily prayer should be what Paul prayed in Corinthians, that we would know nothing but Christ crucified and that death would work in us, so that life could be formed in others. (2 Corinthians 4:12)

Again, life only comes from death. Just as Calvary preceded Pentecost, so death with Christ precedes the fulness of the Spirit. Jesus' cross must become our cross, so that what others see and hear in us will truly bear "the marks of Jesus." Otherwise, no "life" will ever be imparted!

As Paul declares in Galatians 6:17, "I bear in my body the marks of the Lord Jesus."

An Example: German Pastor

In the mid-1930s, a dear, sweet German pastor was abducted from his church. Suspected of harboring, abetting and aiding Jews, he was immediately taken to prison and put in a five foot cell. There was no hearing, no trial--not even time to let his family know what had happened to him.

For weeks, this gentle pastor asked the prison guard outside his cell door if he could use the pay phone at the end of the hall to call his wife and, at least, let her know he was alive. The guard, however, was a contemptible man who hated anyone and everyone that had to do with Jewry. He not only wouldn't let him use the phone, he also determined in his heart to make the pastor's life as miserable as possible.

The sadistic guard purposefully skipped the pastor's cell when meals were handed out; he made the pastor go weeks without a shower; he kept lights burning in the pastor's room so he couldn't sleep; he blasted his short wave radio hoping the intolerable noise would break the pastor; he used filty language; he pushed him; he shoved him; and, when he could, he arranged for the pastor to have the most difficult job in the labor gang.

The pastor, on the other hand, prayed over and over again to avoid letting hate consume him. He prayed instead to be able to love this guard with *real Love*. As the months went by, whenever he could, the pastor smiled at the guard; he thanked him when his meals *did* come; when the guard was near his cell, the pastor told him about his wife and his children; he even questioned the guard about his own family and about his own goals, ideas and visions; and, one time, for a quick moment, he had a chance to tell the guard about real Love.

The guard never answered a word, but, obviously, he heard it all.

After months of unconditionally loving this sadistic guard, real Love finally broke through. One night, as the pastor was again quietly talking to him, the guard cracked a smile; the next day, instead of his cell's being skipped for lunch, the pastor got two; the following evening, he was allowed not only to go to the showers, but also to stay as long as he wanted; the lights began going off at night in his cell and the radio noise ceased. Finally, one afternoon, the guard came into the pastor's cell, asked him for his home phone number, and he, personally, made the long awaited call to the pastor's family. A few months later the pastor was released.

Identifying with Christ in His sufferings and death is far different than I ever imagined it to be. It's not only talking about Christ's death as an objective fact; it's also *personally experiencing His suffering and His death in my own life*. It's picking up and carrying my own cross and following Him in whatever circumstances He allows in my life. We often make claims to understand Christ's substitutionary death without being prepared to personally identify with it. Our identification with Christ, and His sufferings and death, is our own personal willingness to fall to the ground and die, just as John 12:24 tells us. This is what "being conformed unto His death" is all about.[202]

Only by personally sharing in the likeness of Christ's death can we ever expect to intimately and experientially know Him and the power of

His resurrection. As Jesse Penn Lewis says in her book *Climax of the Risen Life*, "It's only in proportion as we get down into His death, that in spirit we ascend to that life within the veil."[203]

The Fire of His Love

The dark night can be likened to God "salting us with fire." In the Bible, God is often spoken of as an all-consuming fire. Listen to Deuteronomy 4:24, "for the Lord thy God is a consuming fire."[204]

For this reason our night seasons can sometimes be referred to as "a baptism of fire." It's *God's way of making us "experientially" one with Himself*. The fire is God's loving way of purifying, refining and cleansing away the dross in our souls. He is a *consuming fire*, a living Flame, that "in love" burns to ashes anything that is contrary to His will. At no other time does God express His Love more for us than when He allows these night seasons into our lives. He loves us so much He takes the risk that we might misunderstand Him and walk away.

We could call this fire the fire of His Love. His fire of Love does two things at the same time: *it not only consumes by burning, it also transforms into itself whatever it touches*. In other words, the Lord's fire of Love <u>consumes</u> (or burns up) all that is necessary in order to <u>consummate</u> (or perfect) that which is left. It's interesting that these words, *consume* and *consumate* come from the same root <u>consum</u>.[205]

When Jesus declares in Mark 9:49 that "everyone will be salted with fire," He means that at one time or another, all of us who want more of Him will have our souls purified by His fire of Love. Just as the priests of Solomon's temple offered their "salted" sacrifices on the Brazen Altar, so too we must offer our bodies as living "salted" sacrifices, an idea continued in the New Testament.[206]

> "I beseech you therefore, brethren, by the mercies of God, that ye *present your bodies a living sacrifice*, holy, acceptable unto God, which is your reasonable service." (Romans 12:1)

Salt (*halas*) was to be offered with every sacrifice as a symbol of *the holiness of Christ*, and also as a token of the reconciliation of God and man by Christ's death on the cross. It stood for a believer's character and condition and was an emblem of their fidelity and friendship.

The "baptism of fire" means staying on that Brazen Altar until everything that is unholy is burned up and consumed. Only then, we will be allowed to enter into the Holy Place where God dwells and experientially fellowship with Him.

What so often happens, however, is that we jump up on the Brazen Altar and offer ourselves as a "living sacrifice," but when God turns up the fire, we quickly jump off. *The dark night is a time when God puts us on that altar, and leaves us there. Only then will that fire have consumed all that is necessary in order to transform that which is left into itself!*

An Example: Sue

The Way of Agape book shares a wonderful story that exemplifies the complete oneness God desires through our sanctification and purification. Sue is a dear Christian friend of mine who, after a painful divorce, decided to move to the East Coast.   Jim, her Jewish ex-husband, continued to live in Southern California with his girlfriend, Joy.

A year or so after the divorce, Sue took a business trip back to California. She could hardly wait to see all of her old friends again. When she found out a party was being planned, she was doubly excited about seeing "the old gang," most of whom were Jewish. However, after she arrived in California, Sue learned that Jim and his girlfriend were also going to be at the party. Feeling extremely angry and upset at the people who invited them, she thought to herself, "How dare they ask Jim and his girlfriend to come! There's no way in the world I am going to go now!"

For one entire week Sue argued with God. She knew in her heart that He would have her deal with her sin and her self-centered ways, pick up her cross and follow Him. She also knew down deep that God wanted to pour out His Love on those precious Jewish people who didn't know Him and that He probably wanted to use her to do that. Sometimes, however, it's almost impossible to do what God asks us to do right away. Sometimes it feels good to just feel sorry for ourselves and to "wade for awhile in the muck and mire."

God is so wonderful, though, and He loves us through these difficult times--even when we are being "brats." He patiently waits by us with His hand outstretched, never leaving us or forsaking us, until we just can't stand the "pig sty" any longer and we finally give in, grab hold of His hand and choose to do it His way.

That's just what happened with Sue. After an entire week of wrestling with God, she was finally convinced that it *was* His will that she attend the party and be a witness of Him. After reconciling herself to the Lord's desires, Sue told God, "Okay, I'm willing to go to that party; I'm willing to give you my sin and self, but it's absolutely impossible for me to love them. *"You're going to have to do that for me."*   Well, that's all God needed.

When Sue arrived at the house where the party was to be held, the first person she met at the door was Joy, Jim's girlfriend. Sue said later, "It was absolutely wild. My body stayed outside the door when it opened, but something deep within me stepped inside, reached out to Joy and in total genuineness said, "I am so glad to meet you. I have heard so many nice things about you," which, evidently, was true.

Going inside, the two of them sat on the couch talking comfortably for about an hour and a half. Jim must have wondered what on earth was going on as later he, too, asked Sue if they could talk privately. Once alone, he began to share his real heart and feelings about their marriage.

Later, when Sue was relating this story to me over the phone, I stopped her and asked, "But Sue, how did you feel when Jim began to share all those painful things with you?" Sue's answer was one I will never forget, "Nancy," she said, "it was incredible, *there was not a 'me' (self) there.*"

Sue was so completely *at one with* God (conformed to His image) that for those few moments it was God's Life and His Love that came forth. *God's fire of Love had so consumed her sin and self that, that which was left had been conformed into His image.*

As 1 John 4:17 says, "... as He is, so are we [to be] in this world."

So, again, it's <u>not</u> the devil hassling us or trying to tear us down through these night seasons, even though he's always there roaring around to find some "hole." God Himself is burning up everything in us that is not of Him and replacing it with something far greater: His own Self.[207]

Thus, the fire of God's Love not only purifies, cleanses and refines our soul, at the same time, it also enlightens our spirit. In other words, fire produces <u>heat</u> and <u>light</u> at the same time! Just as Acts 2:3 talks about fire descending as "cloven tongues" and resting upon the people, God's fire does not afflict us, but rather enlightens and enlarges us.[208] *God's ultimate purpose for His fire of Love is not to destroy us, but to consummate* (or perfect and complete) *us in glory.*

Peter exhorts us in 1 Peter 1:7-9, "That the trial of your faith, being much more precious than of gold that perisheth, though it be tried with fire, might be found unto praise and honor and glory at the appearing of

Jesus Christ, Whom, having not seen, ye love; in whom, though now ye see Him not, yet believing, ye rejoice with joy unspeakable and full of glory, receiving [as] the end of your faith, even the salvation of your souls."

Through the baptism of fire, God desires to consume everything in *our soul* that is not of Him. By doing so, He will make us experientially "one" with Himself and we will finally intimately know His presence.[209] This sanctification and perfection of our souls only occurs when our *acts* and our *ways* have been laid at the foot of the cross and burned by His Love.

Results of The Dark Night

In Chapters Eleven, Twelve and Thirteen we will talk exclusively about the *blessings and the benefits* that God desires for us as a result of our night seasons. However, before we go on and talk further about the dark night of the soul and the dark night of the spirit, I believe it would be helpful to give a brief summary of some of God's incredible blessings right now. If we can keep these goals and purposes in mind, it will make it much easier to get through the darkness.

So, this summary if offered simply like a movie "preview," so that you'll want to stay tuned for the main feature. We will explain each of these results in greater detail in later chapters.

Through our night seasons, God desires for us to:

> Be conformed into His image and, thus, experience the abundant Life.
> Experience His presence and, thus, the fulness of Christ.
> Experience true faith and dependence upon Him.
> Experience His unconditional Love and resurrection Power.
> Experience intimate knowledge of Him, i.e., seeing Him in all things.
> Experience the joy of the Lord.[210]
> Experience the rest and contentment of God.
> Experience the beauty of His holiness.
> Become true worshipers of God (worshiping Him in the spirit).
> Become true lovers of God.
> Become fruitful and able to genuinely comfort others.[211]
> Be "overcomers."
> Experience the peace that passes all understanding. (Philippians 4:7)

G. D. Watson, a Wesleyan Methodist minister wrote a piece in the 1800s that has blessed many followers of Christ in their "dark nights":

Others May, *You Cannot*

"If God has called you to be really like Jesus, He will draw you to a life of crucifixion and humility, and put upon you such demands of obedience that you will not be able to follow other people, or measure yourself by other Christians, and in many ways, He will seem to let other good people do things which He will not let you do.

Other Christians and ministers who seem very religious and useful may push themselves, pull wires, and work schemes to carry out their plans, but you cannot do it; and if you attempt it, you will meet with such failure and rebuke from the Lord as to make you sorely penitent.

Others may boast of themselves, of their work, of their success, of their writings, but the Holy Spirit will not allow you to do any such thing, and if you begin it, He will lead you into some deep mortification that will make you despise yourself and all your good works.

Others may be allowed to succeed in making money, or may have a legacy left to them, but it is likely God will keep you poor, because He wants you to have something far better than gold, namely, a helpless dependence on Him, that He may have the privilege of supplying your needs day by day out of an unseen treasury.

The Lord may let others be honored and put forward, and keep you hidden in obscurity, because He wants you to produce some choice, fragrant fruit for His coming glory, which can only be produced in the shade. He may let others do a work for Him and get the credit for it, but He will make you work and toil on without knowing how much you are doing, and then to make your work still more precious, He may let others get the credit for the work which you have done, and thus make your reward ten times greater when Jesus comes.

The Holy Spirit will put a strict watch over you, with a jealous love, and will rebuke you for little words and feelings, or for wasting your time, which other Christians never seem distressed over. So make up your mind that God is an infinite sovereign and has a right to do as He pleases with His own.

He may not explain to you a thousand things which puzzle your reason in His dealings with you. But if you absolutely sell yourself to be His...slave, He will wrap you up in a jealous love, and bestow upon you many blessings which come only to those who are in the inner circle.

Settle it forever, then, that you are to deal directly with the Holy Spirit and that He is to have the privilege of tying your tongue, or chaining your hand, or closing your eyes, in ways that He does not seem to use with others. Now when you are so possessed with the living God that you are, in your secret heart, pleased and delighted over this peculiar, personal, private, jealous guardianship and management of the Holy Spirit over your life, you will have found the *vestibule* [entrance] to heaven."

Key Points of This Chapter:

- God desires that we experience *His abundant Life* and that we intimately come to know *His fulness*.
- Because He loves us, He will do whatever is necessary in our lives to accomplish these things.
- The dark night is the transition we make from depending upon "self" to total dependence upon "Him."
- The darkness that comes is not from the enemy, but from God who loves us and wants to make us complete.
- Jesus is our example and we are to follow in His footsteps.

Section Four:
The Dark Night of the Soul

"My soul is exceeding[ly] sorrowful unto death...."
But, "...nevertheless, not what I will, but what Thou
wilt." (Mark 14:34-36)

Chapter Seven
What is the Dark Night of the Soul?

Two Night Seasons

In the next couple of chapters we want to explore not only how we *feel* going through the dark night, but also what we are to *do* in the dark night. In addition, we want to highlight some of God's goals, purposes, benefits and blessings. If we understand a little of what He is doing and why, we might be able to get through this time more easily.

The dark night is <u>not</u> just a dry time in our walk, a period where we are having a few problems, or simply a trial from the enemy, it's a "season" sent from God to draw us closer to Him. As He says in 1 Kings 12:24, "This thing is [sent] from Me."[212]

In general, there seems to be two aspects to the dark night, two "winters" so to speak. In the first winter, the dark night of the soul, God focuses on our "outward man" and our *sinful acts*. In other words, He concentrates on *what we do*. During the second winter, the dark night of the spirit, He focuses on our "inward man" and our *self-centered ways*. This is where He highlights *who we really are*.

In the dark night of the soul, God asks us to surrender or to sacrifice to Him everything in our lives that is unholy, unrighteous and "not of faith."[213] *In this dark night, God seems to focus not only on our sin, but also on "outward" things.* Anything that we put first in our lives or that we rely upon other than Himself, such as our own natural strengths, physical attributes, possessions, friendships, gifts from Him, power for service, etc. These would be things He wants re-prioritized. *In the second night, God asks us to sacrifice or to hand over to Him every "inward" attitude that is self-centered or self-oriented.* In other words, He wants us to give Him *all our natural ways*--all our goals, expectations, aspirations, dreams, presumptions, reputation, etc. As Oswald Chambers reminds us, "Deliverance from sin is <u>not</u> [necessarily] deliverance from [our] human nature."

If you recall, Jesus suffered two dark nights: His first night was in the Garden of Gethesmane, where He sweated great drops of blood, crying out, "my soul is exceedingly sorrowful unto death." (Mark 14:34) His second night of agony was on the cross at Calvary where He cried out, "My God, my God, why hast Thou forsaken me?" (Mark 15:34)

A perfect analogy showing the difference between these two nights is seen in the pruning of a tree: the first night would be likened to a gardener's *pulling off the tree's branches*; whereas, the second night would be likened to the gardener's *pulling up the tree's roots*.

The response necessary to the first night season is, of course, *confession* and *repentance* to rid ourselves of any sinful acts. The response needed for the second dark night, however, is *crucifixion and death to self*. Again, Oswald Chambers describes it perfectly, "Our natural life is not sinful, but there must be an attitude of [complete] surrender and of giving it up."[214] God delivers us from sin, but *we* must deliver ourselves from self-centeredness by surrendering it to God. Only one choice is required for us to conquer sin: we must simply choose to give it to Jesus, but the crucifying of our "self-centered ways" or our human nature requires a lifetime.[215]

Even though we are "positionally" cleansed and sanctified by the blood of Jesus when we are born again, we will *not* experience this perfection, this completion, until the sin in our lives is removed, and also our self-centered ways are nailed to the cross.

Let's explore these two "nights" in more detail, beginning with the *dark night of the soul*.

What Is Our Soul?

Our souls are made up of all our thoughts, emotions and desires, making up the "self-life" that we have so often referred to. The Greek word for our soul is *psyche* which has a very interesting twofold meaning. *Psyche* means "it shall have life" or "it shall wax cold." This is a perfect definition because our soul will either be Spirit-filled and "have life" because of the free-flow of God's Life into our lives, or our soul will be empty and "waxing cold" because God's Life has been quenched and blocked from flowing into our lives. Therefore, you could say our soul is like a "neutral area" that can either be filled with God's Life if we have made *faith choices* to do His will, or filled with self-life if we have made *emotional choices* to follow our own desires.[216]

When we are born again, our spirit becomes "new" when it is united with God's Spirit. At this time, we also receive a new heart (filled with God's supernatural Life), and a new will power. *But our soul and body remain unchanged.*[217] They are redeemed by the blood of the Lamb, but they are <u>not</u> changed, renewed or renovated. This change is what the sanctification process (that we are all in now) is all about. As He sanctifies us, God is trying to teach us how to constantly surrender, relinquish and set aside our "self-life" so that His Life can come forth from our hearts.

Our soul and our body together make up what the Scripture calls the "flesh." It's important to understand that we can *never* be completely rid of our flesh; we can never eradicate it totally from our body. This is what makes us human. Romans 7:20-21 tells us that the power of sin dwells in our bodies and, thus, we never will be free of its influence until we receive our resurrection bodies. *The only way we can be free from the influence of the "flesh," is by recognizing it, crucifying it and then giving it over to God.* God's will is that our entire soul and body be sanctified, set apart and made holy, so that we <u>can</u> reflect Him in all we do.

What Is the Dark Night of the Soul?

In his book *Abandoned to God*, Oswald Chambers states,

"The mystics used to speak of 'the dark night of the soul,' as a time of spiritual darkness and dryness; not the direct result of sins committed, but rather a deep conviction of sin itself within the heart and mind. It's a time the person 'is being brought to an end of himself,' and made aware of the utter worthlessness of his own nature when stripped of all religious pretensions. Moreover, there was the willingness to abandon all for Christ's sake, to deny--not only his evil self but also his good self."[218]

During the season of the dark night of the soul, God initiates a purging, a cleansing and a purifying of our souls from everything that is not of faith. At this time, God crushes our self will, so that He can merge it with His own. In other words, it's our own private Gethsemane. As Jesus cried in the garden, "My soul is exceeding[ly] sorrowful unto death...Nevertheless, not what I will, but what Thou wilt." (Mark 14:34-36) During this dark season, God teaches us to say, just as Jesus did, *"Not my will, but Thine."*[219]

By depriving our soul of spiritual blessings, God can begin to transform our reliance on soulish and sensual things to things of the spirit.[220] He wants us to learn to walk by faith, not by our senses, our feelings or our understanding. God wants to teach us how to detach ourselves from all physical, emotional and spiritual supports, so that we will be able to respond with "Not my will, but Thine."

Because this season can often be a time of desolation, of dried bones and ruined hopes, many Christians--because they don't understand what God's will is or what He is doing--get so discouraged and defeated that they give up and turn back. Many will feel like Job who "looked for good," but only "evil came;" and for "light," but found only "darkness." (Job 30:26) Or like Isaiah, who uttered "We wait for light, but behold obscurity; for brightness, but we walk in darkness. We grope for the wall like the blind, and we grope as if we had no eyes; we stumble at noonday as in the night; we are in desolate places like dead men." (Isaiah 59:9-10)

If we can only remember that the Holy Spirit has led us into this darkness *on purpose*. He desires not only to "replace us with Himself," but also to make us holy so that we can fellowship and commune with Him. As Moses was led into the wilderness to experience God's presence (Exodus 20:21), so this dark season is the very path God has chosen to put us on. It's a path that will lead us to greater light than anything we have ever known before. "Unto the upright there ariseth light in the darkness." (Psalm 112:4)

The whole purpose of the sanctification process is not only to learn how to reflect Him, but also to learn how to have intimacy with Him--the fulness of Christ.

An Example: St. John of the Cross

When I think of someone who truly experienced the fulness of Christ and who allowed Him to be his "all and in all," I think of St. John of the Cross, a Carmelite priest who lived in the 1600s. He was beloved by his peers and his students, but despised by his superiors because of his efforts at reform and his obstinacy to obey their rules and regulations.

King Phillip of Spain had become involved in the reform of the religious order, which led to many misunderstandings. The king's ordinance read that those who had been made superiors, against the rules and regulations of the order, should be removed. Those resisting this order would be considered rebellious and disobedient. Because St. John fit this description perfectly, his superiors took advantage of this fact.

He was arrested, flogged, carried off blindfolded and put in a 6 x 10-foot cell with nothing but a Bible. He had to wear the same clothes for days on end, lice and endured months of freezing cold weather. In spite of these horrendous circumstances, St. John was touched by God as he devoted all of his time to discerning God's ways. "Faith and love will lead you along a path unknown to you, to where God is hidden," he declared.

Finally, he was able to escape and ultimately became a fugitive from his own religious order. Given a safe haven by some of his peers, he was able to continue his writings. He bore no animosity towards his captors and harbored no ill feelings, but simply saw God in all his circumstances.

Going on to establish seven more monasteries, he wrote incredible works of faith, among which are *The Living Flame of Love, The Ascent of Mount Carmel, The Spiritual Canticle, The Dark Night* and many poems and letters.

To illustrate the depth of his spiritual state, in one of his books he explains that he dared not speak further about the workings of the Holy Spirit in the soul because "I am aware of being incapable of doing so, and if I were to try, it might seem less than it is."

His main purpose in writing his materials was that he wanted everyone to find comfort in the thought that, however severe their circumstances might be, purification still is the work of God's gentle hand clearing away the debris of attachment, making room for His presence. Pain for St. John was not a misfortune but a value when suffered with and for Christ. The only appropriate response to suffering, he used to proclaim, was to have loving confidence in God.

St. John's writings have been a tremendous blessing to me throughout these past seven years. He is the one who first taught me to see God's hand in everything. St. John truly knew how to experience a oneness with God, no matter what was going on in his life. *He never seemed to allow exterior things to take away his interior peace.* As he explained it, "Trust in God should be so great, that even if the whole world were to collapse, one should not become disturbed." Oh, how I pray to have this kind of trust.

Who Experiences the Dark Night?

As we saw in Chapter Two, the Lord allows the dark night to happen to all of His beloved children, and especially those who are the most faithful, the most loving, the ones who want all of Him. As Revelation 3:19 states, God chastens those He loves.

This night season happens to people walking with the Lord for a long time; people who love Him with all their heart, mind and soul; people who have surrendered their lives to Him; people who are obedient to Him; and, people who fear Him. Again, remember Isaiah 50:10, "Who is among you that *feareth the Lord*, that *obeyeth the voice of his servant*, that walketh in darkness and hath no light?"

Joy Dawson, a wonderful author and Bible teacher, shares that if we live righteous lives, then there is an inevitability that *all* of us will, at one time or another, experience God's fire or a night of faith. Therefore, the longer we walk with the Lord, the more we can anticipate this experience, unless we choose to moment by moment surrender everything to Him.

Great Christians are made by great trials. Pain, sorrow and failure are what produce men and women of God. Those with the greatest dreams are often the ones who receive the greatest trials. Eternal lessons seem to require hard places. As Scripture declares, the way we are made "perfect," or whole or complete, is by suffering or by barring ourselves from sin and self.[221] Only by uncovering and exposing our defects, can God really heal us. First, He must take away all our external and internal supports other than Himself, then, He can then strengthen our inner man, enabling us to experience His fulness.

The dark night of the soul happens to people who have *already* accepted the Lord; those who have *already* given their lives to Him; those *already* filled with the Spirit; those who have *already* dedicated their lives to Him; those who have *already* asked for intimacy; and those who have *already* been set aside for God's purposes of ministry.[222]

Why Does God Send the Dark Night?

There seems to be three things that God is looking for in each of our lives: our conversion (or salvation), our conviction and our consecration (or sanctification).

God wants to know the full proof of us. He wants to know our *real* heart. Will we be obedient in all things?[223] Will we obey Him, even when we can't see Him or feel Him? Will we hold on to His truths even though we don't understand what He is doing?

The kind of Love that God wants from us is a love that reaches to the point of full and total surrender. Remember, to really love God means to totally give ourselves over to Him. If we are discontent with what God has allowed in our lives, it's a sure indication that we have not completely surrendered and abandoned ourselves to Him. Just as God had to keep testing and proving Israel, so He must continue to humble, abase and weaken us. That way, He will perceive if we love Him, and we will see our total inability to live without Him.

The Lord wants believers who have faith like Job, and who can utter like he did, "Though You slay me, yet will I trust You." When Job sought the Lord to know <u>why</u> the bad things were happening to him, he got no answer from God. And it's often the same with us. God only tells us that He *does* have a plan for our lives and even though we don't understand what that plan is or how it is going to work out, we must trust that He always has our best in view. We must learn to rely upon Him in spite of our circumstances, in spite of our logic and in spite of our human reason. Human circumstances, logic and reason are *not* sources for spiritual guidance. We must trust that only God knows what is best for our lives; therefore, whatever He allows into them He will use it for our good.

Lamentations 3:33 tells us that God does not afflict us to punish us or to be mean. He does so only to accomplish the sanctification that will ultimately bring us abundant Life.

An Example: Dutch

Let me tell you the story of "Dutch," a Viet Nam veteran who found the secret to the abundant life. Last year, Dutch came into our ministry bookstore looking for Chuck and me. This dear man had lost an arm, a hand, an ear and an eye, and had many other physical disabilities from the war.

Dutch has endured his own personal dark night over the last twenty years, as he has tried to understand God's will for his life. He has, understandably, suffered severe marital and relationship problems, financial problems, as well as serious physical problems.

When he saw Chuck and me, he grabbed the two of us and burst into tears. He shared that he had been a Christian for the past 18 years, but had struggled for most of those years trying to find the real meaning and purpose of his life. He became a part of many of the major tangents of the Christian church, trying to find fulfillment. But, he explained, "something was always missing."

Then, someone gave him *The Way of Agape* book, and he stated that *his life changed forever*. Through that book, Dutch learned that God's purpose in choosing him was to conform him into His image of Love, so that He could love others through him. Dutch testified that he received incredible fulfillment as God began to work this message of Love into his life. He said he finally found his real meaning and purpose as a Christian: to be an open and cleansed vessel so that God's Life can flow in and through him to others. Then, he went on to relate, *"The neat part is, that it doesn't matter what that vessel looks like. The important thing, is that God's Love flows through it."*

Dutch found the secret to the "abundant Life." And, as he exemplifies, it doesn't matter what the vessel looks like that carries that Love, nor what his circumstances are. *If we are clean vessels, the abundant Life will always flow, because it's Jesus' Love--His Life--and not our own.*

Without such a night season, however, very few of us would ever consent to the refining process God must do in each of our lives. Nevertheless, because He loves us so much, He allows the "little foxes" to come so that we will come out of ourselves and into His loving arms. *The bottom line is that we must lose possession of ourselves in order that we might be fully possessed by God.*

As John 12:25 discloses, "He that loveth [hangs on to] his life shall lose it; and he that hateth [is willing to surrender] his life in this world shall keep it unto life eternal."

It's so important to remember in the middle of our night season, *who* has sent this to us and *who* will get us out of it. God is the only One who knows how to "perfectly" annihilate us; He is the only One who can be our guide through this time; and He is the only One who can get us through. As Psalm 105:19-20 declares, "The word of the Lord tried him" and "the King sent and loosed him." In other words, *if God sends the trouble, then only God can get us out.*

God is the One who has called us; thus, He is the only One who can perfect us and bring us into the inner chamber where He dwells.[224] The initiative is always in God's hands. No self-effort on our own part will ever work. Our *oneness* with Him will never be experienced until our soul is freed of itself and enabled to flow into God.

Goal and Purpose of the Dark Night

God's purpose for all of His actions towards us is that Christ might be formed in us and that we might experience intimacy and fellowship with Him.

God wants to purge our souls from sin and self, so that we will be open and willing to follow Him at any cost. As we explored in Chapter Three, our will controls everything in our lives. Thus, God wants us to have a will that is completely yielded and at one with His own. *One of the major purposes, then, of the dark night of the soul is to formulate an unshakable resolve in us, so that even if everything goes wrong in our lives and even if we can't see or understand a thing of what God is doing, we will still choose to cling unmoveably to God.* He wants us to be governed only by our choice of faith--a faith that proclaims whether I live or die, I choose to trust in You, not in my own thoughts and emotions.

God wants to produce in us a trust that can never be shaken. He is drawing us away from a life of senses and feelings and forcing us to turn to Him in *naked faith*, faith without feelings. He wants us to be able to constantly say and mean, "Not my will, but Yours" and "Though You slay me, yet will I trust You."

God is teaching us, by darkening us, that all that matters in this life is knowing and loving Him. He wants us to love Him and rely upon Him regardless of what we desire, regardless of what our intellect is saying and regardless of what we are feeling.

He wants us to be able to echo what Paul declares in 2 Corinthians 4:8-11:

"We are troubled on every side, *yet not distressed*; we are perplexed, *but not in despair*; Persecuted, *but not forsaken*; cast down, *but not destroyed*; Always bearing about in the body the dying of the Lord Jesus, that the life also of Jesus might be made manifest in our body. For we who live are always delivered unto death for Jesus' sake, that the life also of Jesus might be made manifest in our mortal flesh."

Our going through the dark night season and coming out even stronger in spirit, shows God that He alone is important. It shows Him that we have left "all," even ourselves, to follow Him.

Joy Dawson made an awesome audio tape entitled "In the Fire." In this tape series she describes God's *seven purposes for allowing the night seasons* in our lives. Understanding these seven purposes of God, help us tremendously in weathering our own night seasons. They are:

1) To melt hard substances and produce brokenness.
2) To destroy anything in our lives that is useless.
3) To reshape us and make us pliable for more use.
4) To make us more like Jesus, who is our example.
5) To endow us with more power. "Fire, glory and power are always linked."
6) To experience for ourselves the "fellowship of His sufferings," and
7) To teach us how to mentor and help others, by learning more about ourselves and our own responses to the night seasons.

Benefits of Dark Night of the Soul

The delights, blessings and benefits that God bestows upon us as a result of this dark night are a hundred thousand times better than the terror we experience in the middle of it. Job learned this lesson well:

> "He discovereth deep things out of [the] darkness, and bringeth out to light the shadow of death." (Job 12:22)

Some of the blessings and benefits that we experience in *our relationship with God* are:

> We will experience a purging and a cleansing of our soul from sin and unrighteousness.
>
> Our will will become one with His as we learn to choose "not my will, but Thine."
>
> We will experience His Life--His Love, His Wisdom and His Power.
>
> Our faith will become transformed and we will begin to have a radical trust in God.
>
> We will see the purposes of His cross more clearly.
>
> We will no longer be concerned about our own wishes, needs, mindset.
>
> We will be delivered from self-pity and self-righteousness.
>
> We will begin to have an overwhelming desire for God.
>
> We will learn more about His grace and acquire more understanding of His ways.
>
> The Scriptures will become alive to us as they never have before.
>
> We will begin to have deep compassion for others who are suffering and we will be eager to comfort them.
>
> We will develop more of His character--His patience and His long-suffering as never before.
>
> We will begin to know the difference between head knowledge and heart knowledge, and
>
> We will begin to experience a serenity and a peace that passeth all understanding.

By going through the dark night of the soul, we should be able to come with both a clearer understanding of ourselves, and a complete dependence upon God.

"Trust in Me"

Dan Marks wrote a song called, "Trust in Me." Listen to the words:

> "Though it's hard for you to understand
> All the mysteries in My plan
> And why things work out the way they do
> Why there are rooms we must go through
>
> But you must always keep one thing in mind
> I am working all the time

To bring about My perfect will
So I am asking you to still...

Trust in Me whatever may come
It's My job to see you through
Trust in Me
Whatever may come your way

There are times to laugh and times to cry
But as hard as things seem to be
You must leave them here with Me
See, all things are at My command
So just reach out your hand

Trust in Me whatever may come
It's My job to see you through
Trust in Me
Whatever may come your way."

Our Reactions Determine Our Walk

How do you react when your dreams, your plans and your hopes blow up in your face? What is your response when you were so sure you had heard from God and you thought He had encouraged you to move ahead, and then, all of a sudden, everything crumbled? How will you act when everything you read in the Bible confirmed your vision and then, out of the blue, your aspirations were destroyed?

How we behave during this time of affliction and crisis has everything to do with the results. *In other words, our "reactions" determine our walk with God.* How fortunate we are if we can, at least, understand God's overall plan. Then, even though we might not fully comprehend all the specifics of what He is doing, at least we know enough to stand still and trust Him through it.

If you are in a night season right now, the most important thing you can do is surrender. Believe me, I know. I fought God for seven years! Fighting only delays the whole process and makes you miserable in the meantime. In Chapters Eight and Ten, we will explore in detail not only how we *feel* going through our night seasons, but also what we are *to do* in them. We will also study God's purposes and all the other benefits that come from them.

God is drawing us into the realm of pure faith where we will have no feelings, no sights, no sounds, no smells, no guidance and no helps. *He is drawing us into a darkness where we'll have no other place to go, except to depend upon Him.*

Francois de Fenelon, the famous mystic of the 17th century, once stated:

> "We are a lump of clay and each stroke (from the Potter) we feel. Blow after blow descends upon us; we, the clay, do not understand how the Potter is shaping us or why He is chisling and cutting away at us. Only the Master Potter knows that. It's imperative, however, that we stay *immovable* and *endure* all that He sends us, because only He knows the perfect shape He is forming. Only He knows how to do it, we don't. We feel that each blow is ruining us (killing and destroying us), but the Master Potter knows it's the best thing for us."[225]

Don't Doubt God

The dark night of the soul often comes upon us suddenly without advance warning. This night will end up in either one of two ways. If we know what God's will is and we relinquish ourselves to Him, then we can experience the glorious eternal and continual presence of God even in the midst of our trial. However, if we are confused about what the dark night is and why God allows it, then we often will experience doubt, unbelief and, eventually, hardness and a falling away from the faith.

Remember, Aggie's father in Chapter Five. Because he did not understand what God was doing in his life when he experienced tragedy, he began to doubt God and His faithfulness. That doubt turned into bitterness and resentment that then hardened him for the rest of his life. He ended up not only personally living a very lonely, empty and unfilled life, but he also alienated the only family he had left, simply because he didn't understand God's purposes in the dark night of his soul. Thus, he closed himself off from the only Source of Life and Love there is and he died a spiritual death.

We must be aware. Unless we can continually look at our night seasons through God's eyes and remember His goals and purposes, we can slide into the darkness and never come out.

I've been at this point many, many times over the last seven years, and I know how hard it is to pull yourself up and cry, "No matter what is going on in my life, I choose to trust and believe in You, God, one more time." But, the bottom line is, *there really is no other choice! God is the only answer* unless, of course, we want to end up like Aggie's father.

Doubt in God's faithfulness and His Love will affect everything we do. Doubt quenches God's Spirit and brings us down faster than anything else. Doubt can devastate and paralyze us simply because it affects every choice we make. Even though they are opposites, doubt and faith affect everything we think, say and do--one for the good, and the other for bad.

Satan, as you are aware, will do anything he can to get us to doubt God's faithfulness. He begins by inserting suggestions like, "you're not special to God anymore." "He doesn't care about you." Or, as I shared last chapter in my own example, "who do you think you are to...!" Of course, when you are going through a night season, everything you feel and see at this time "validates" Satan's poisonous words. The enemy loves to agitate us, unquiet us and make things miserable and tormenting for us. Then, he moves in for the kill and begins to twist Scripture to confirm the doubts he is inflicting us with.

An Example: Shar

A dear friend of mine lost her oldest son last year in a horrible automobile accident. He was only 20 and he loved the Lord with all his heart. My friend had been a Christian for years, had taught numerous Bible studies, and had exhorted many others to know Christ. But losing her son absolutely crushed her--her own dark night. She could not understand how a loving God would allow this horrible loss to happen to someone who loved Him so much.

The more she questioned God, the more doubt and unbelief grew in her soul. Finally, she found herself at the lowest point in her walk with God. When she prayed, she couldn't hear His voice. It seemed as if He had covered Himself with a cloud, abandonng her in her deepest need. When she read the Bible, the enemy twisted its meaning to convey something totally opposite from what was intended. *Faith reads the word accurately; whereas, doubt allows Satan to give it a whole other meaning.* An example: When my friend read in Hebrews about our need to be disciplined by suffering, because of her doubt she thought it said that God took away her son to discipline her, which, of course, devastated her. And since she had no idea *why* she was being disciplined, she simply let go of God's hand. Her painful experience demonstrates that when our hearts and our spirits are covered by doubt and unbelief, we give the enemy huge holes and entrances into our soul.

My friend became so depressed that she wanted to die. She no longer cared about anything or anyone. When we cut our "life line," our lives become absolutely meaningless. The Lord in His Love, however, arranged some precious circumstances to show Shar how much He did care for her and to what extremes He would go to to communicate that

Love to her. Shar is slowly, once again, beginning to make faith choices acknowledging her doubt and unbelief and giving it to Him. These faith choices bar Satan's attacks and allow God to, once again, manifest Himself to her, minister to her and comfort her with His Love.

Again, Jesus is our example and we must remember what He did on the cross. In spite of what was going on with Him physically, He kept turning his head towards God; kept crying out to Him; kept abandoning Himself to Him; and kept praying to Him. Jesus never once gave up faith in His Father. Even though He felt as if His Father had abandoned Him, He continued to allow the Holy Spirit to minister to Him and to comfort Him. Even though He "felt" very little help from His Father at that time, He still abandoned Himself to Him and cried, "Father, into Thy hands I commend my spirit." (Luke 23:46)

We must do the same thing. Even though we feel and experience very little help from our Father in these night seasons, we must entrust our souls into His hands. Whether we sink or swim in this life, we must *never* let anything, anyone or any situation drive us away from holding on to God.[226] Only He can show us the way. If we doubt Him, we will never make it through our night season.[227]

Remember, when doubt becomes a part of our lives, then our own ideas, our own intuitions, our own work and our own inferences can also become sources of delusion.

If you are in the middle of a very difficult situation now, and doubt has already crept into your thinking, don't wait another moment. Turn to the Lord right now. Go through the *Inner Court Ritual* in the Appendix and make the appropriate faith choices to give your unbelief and doubt over to Him. There truly is nowhere else you can go for help-- to be healed, to be freed--but to God Himself, as Jesus taught us. And until you do, that doubt and unbelief will affect everything you think, say and do.

Sources of Doubt

Let's take a moment to point out the three primary sources of *doubt*, so we don't fall into the trap that Shar or David Flood did and end up quenching God's Spirit.

First of all, *doubt comes to us through the strategies of Satan and his demonic horde.* The devil has been active from the beginning of the world. He won his first victory when he convinced Eve to doubt in the goodness of God. Even though insinuating doubt has been Satan's best strategy since the Garden of Eden, human beings are still falling for it today! "Yea, hath God said...?" (Genesis 3:1) By destroying our trust in God's faithfulness, he devours our commitment to God. And when we surrender to doubt, we quickly become a backslidden statistic, wide open to deception.[228]

We must be diligent to guard ourselves against such thoughts as: "God doesn't love me"... "He doesn't care"... "He's not faithful"... "His promises are not true"... "God is mad at me"... "Others have fallen before me, how am I supposed to make it through?"[229]

Satan not only deceives us through our own questioning minds and through careless remarks of others, but also through our misunderstood circumstances, as in Shar's case. He is our mortal enemy, and when we are emotionally weak, physically exhausted, mentally confused and spiritually unprepared, he closes in for the kill. Thus, he thrives in our "night seasons."

Second source of *doubt comes from dwelling in a world saturated with human wisdom.* Worldly values are often the direct opposite of godly values[230] and human wisdom is often the opposite of the wisdom of God.[231] For instance, many Americans believe in evolution simply because it's what they were taught in school and, yet this popular theory is in direct conflict with the truth of creation.[232] Worldly wisdom can easily infect every aspect of our lives, and the only way to survive this contamination is to constantly renew our minds with the truth of God's Word.

A third source of *doubt comes from our own spiritual immaturity,* our own *doublemindedness.*[233] The Greek root word for *doubleminded* is *psyche,* which literally means *double-souled.* It means two lives are being lived. *God's Life* is still resident in our hearts, but because we have emotionally chosen to follow our own doubt and unbelief instead of what God has told us, *self-life* has taken over our souls. Doublemindedness is lethally dangerous, because it leaves us wide open for greater deception, which can ultimately lead to more doubt.[234] When we blindly follow Satan around by being doubleminded, we will eventually lose our faith in God and our hope in His promises.

Is It Okay to Question God?

Being honest with God is always best. During this difficult time of being in the fire, there will be many genuine, helpful and **good** questions that we will want to ask Him:.

> Is this darkness normal for the Christian walk?[235]
> Is it Scriptural?
> Is God really the answer to all my needs?[236]

> Does He know my thoughts and my feelings?[237]
> Is He going to help me?
> Does He see all that is going on?[238]

These questions are healthy, and it is my prayer that this book can help in answering many of them. However, watch out for speculation questions that have no answers, questions that lead us, once again, to doubt:

> Why is all of this happening to me?[239]
> Is God angry with me?
> How could a loving Father ever do this to His child?
> What did I do to deserve it?
> Doesn't He even care?
> Why has He forsaken me?
> What am I doing wrong?
> Why did He give me so much light and then turn it off?
> Why has He broken His promises to me?
> How can I ever trust Him again?
> Why has He made Himself out to be my enemy?[240]

Entertaining this type of doubting questions will pull us down faster than anything else. We must know that God is *always* ready and willing to help us.[241] He is really the only One who can help us.[242] We must know that He delights in us.[243]   And no matter what failures or our shortcomings, He promises that He will never leave us or forsake us. Even if He must take us through the valley of the shadow of death in order to reproduce Himself in us, He will never let go of us. He loves us so much that He has even engraved us on the palms of His hands.[244] He promises to bring us through any trial if we will only let Him.

The closer we get to Jesus, the more it seems we must suffer. Remember, Jesus is our example and Hebrews 5 tells us that even though He was a Son, He learned obedience by the things which He suffered. (verses 8-9) Thus, the only way we can learn obedience is by learning to bar ourselves from all the things in our lives that are unholy and not of faith. "Forasmuch then as Christ hath suffered for us in the flesh, arm yourselves likewise with the same mind; *for he that hath suffered in the flesh hath ceased from sin.*" (1 Peter 4:1)

Unless we begin to look at our trials through God's eyes, we can easily slide into the dark abyss of doubt and unbelief, never to come out. The purpose of this book is to help us "see through the night" from God's perspective and to see the many blessings that come from the darkness. It's critical that we not let doubt take root in us during this time, but allow the Holy Spirit to continually comfort us and minister to us. We must follow Jesus' example of entrusting our souls into the Father's hands and constantly proclaiming, not my will, but Thine.

Psalm 42 seems so appropriate here:

> "As the hart panteth after the water brooks,
> So panteth my soul after Thee, O God.
> My soul thirsteth for God, for the living God:
> When shall I come and appear before God?
> My tears have been my meat day and night,
> While they continually say unto me, 'Where is thy God?'"
> "...Why art thou cast down, O my soul?
> And why art thou disquieted in me?
> Hope thou in God: for I shall yet praise Him
> For the help of His countenance.
> O my God, my soul is cast down within me:
> "...Yet the Lord will command His loving-kindness in the daytime,
> And in the *night* His song shall be with me,
> And my prayer unto the God of my life,
> I will say unto God my rock, 'Why hast Thou forgotten me?
> Why go I mourning because of the oppression of the enemy?'
> As with a sword in my bones, mine enemies reproach me;
> While they say daily unto me, 'Where is thy God?'
> Why art thou cast down, O my soul?
> And why art thou disquieted within me?
> *Hope thou in God: for I shall yet praise Him,*
> *Who is the health of my countenance, and my God."*

Key Points of This Chapter:

- Our soul is our *self-life*--our thoughts, emotions and desires.
- The *dark night of the soul* is when God exposes of all our sinful acts. (He seems to focus on our "outward" man.)
- It's our own Gethesmene where we must surrender everything in our soul that is unholy, unrighteous and not of faith.
- God wants to cleanse our soul, so that Christ may be formed in us and we may experience His abundant Life.

Chapter Eight
Passing Through the Night

How Do We *Feel* Going Through This Night?

Now that we understand God's purposes for the dark night of the soul, we can go on to explore this night season in greater detail from our *own* perspective. Because this dark night shakes our consecration, our conversion and our commitment to God, we will be experiencing a wide variety of emotions. It's vitally important to express what we are feeling, because acknowledging our honest thoughts and emotions will help us understand what exactly we are to, then, confess and give over to God.

When I was at the depths of my despair, as I mentioned before, the only thing I could read were the Psalms, Job and parts of St. John of the Cross. It encouraged and comforted me to read the writer's thoughts and feelings. It comforted me to know that they, too, had experienced some of the very *same* emotions that I was feeling, and it made me realize that I was not alone. Psalm 88 describes exactly what I was feeling.

So this chapter is written primarily to comfort you with the thoughts and feelings of hundreds of others who have walked this same path, and secondarily to share some of the things *you can do* to get through this time easier. If we know that others have experienced what we are feeling, yet have come through the night season *even closer to the Lord*, that gives us hope and encouragement.

> "Blessed be God, even the Father of our Lord Jesus Christ, the Father of mercies, and the God of all comfort; Who comforteth us in all our tribulation, that we may be able to comfort them which are in any trouble, by the comfort wherewith we ourselves are comforted of God."
> (2 Corinthians 1:3-4)

The following are, first, some personal thoughts and emotions experienced by others going through this God-sent season, then, some Scriptural analogies, and, finally, *what we are to do.*

Confused and Resistant

One of the first mental emotions we will experience in the dark night of the soul is *confusion*. Not understanding what is happening to us is one of the hardest things to endure. In the past, we have always felt that God has generally shown us what He is doing in our lives. In this dark night, however, *understanding what He is doing* is the first thing that seems to go. And the confusion that is left in its place is both overwhelming and frightening. The lack of communication with God is like a vacuum. We talk to Him. We pray to Him, but nothing happens-- nothing changes. The comforting presence of God is gone, so we find no answers. Thus, we constantly question ourselves, "If the Lord be with us, *why* then is all this befallen us?"[245] We ask, "Is this thing really from God or is it from the enemy?" We are totally at a loss and completely confounded as to why we are being tested so severely.

Everything we do seems to produce chaos as God delays all our hopes and plans and dreams. We continually go from the heights of expectation to the depths of despair. As Alan Redpath expresses, "The depths of despair to which I sank were beyond description. Sometimes I spent hours each day weeping..."[246]

The psalmist puts it this way, "Thou hast lifted me up, and [then] cast me down." (Psalm 102:10) We literally experience this roller coaster every day. The truth is, God will never actually allow us to fall, although He permits *the terror of falling* in order to shatter our "self"-confidence.

Many of our troubles appear to be exacerbated or made worse by our *own resistance* to what God is doing. We forget that in the past, we have given Him permission to do whatever is necessary to conform us into His image. Once He begins His work, however, instead of remembering our commitment and seeing events from His perspective, we become tormented and consumed in ourselves. And, of course, the more we *hold on to ourselves*, the sharper our suffering becomes.

If we can just learn to surrender ourselves to God and permit the crucifying process to proceed, the purging will become much softer. God wants *Christ to be formed in us* so that we can experience His abundant life and we can have that intimate fellowship with Him. He has a plan for our lives, and we can't stop it, even if we wanted to. We must allow Him to complete what He starts. He, alone, knows what is best for us. Unfortunately for many of us, we recognize this fact far too late.

Because we don't understand what is happening or what God is trying to do in our lives, we fight Him the whole way which, of course, makes everything much worse. Resistance also causes God to have to teach us these *same* lessons over and over again, before we progress and move on. I was one of those.

To compound the problem, those around us do not understand what we are going through. How can they, if we ourselves don't understand? They also become troublesome like Job's friends. They make remarks like, "Get on with your life." "Snap out of it." "You're always so sad. What's wrong with you?"

Many believers turn back at this point, abandoning the road, because it's too hard, too narrow and too painful. Scripture tells us that only a very *few* will endure and finish the dark night and go on to experience the "the fulness of Christ" that God desires.

Like a Piece of Broken Pottery

Another way of expressing how we feel is like a piece of pottery that has been flung to the ground and broken into a million pieces.[247] God is shaking everything in us that can be shaken. Only that which is real and firm and of Him will be left. Thus, every waking moment is dominated by an overwhelming sense of emptiness and inexplicable loss as all our efforts at every turn are frustrated and our fruits are ruined.

No one is able to comfort our intense suffering, because it's as if our soul has been literally cast off and flung out into space. We find ourselves in a whirlpool of despair and loneliness. There is a deep bitterness within us that cries out like David in Psalm 51:8, "Oh, God, You have broken all my bones." We feel dismembered, in anguish, in a state of numbness and lifelessness, as if we are in a dark dungeon. In fact, we sometimes feel death would be a relief because what is happening in our eyes is cruel.

Formerly we found God in solitude, prayer and meditation, but now *none* of these acts brings us peace. Thus, because God's voice is silent, our sense of meaning and purpose is lost.

Oswald Chambers expresses it well in his book *Abandoned to God*:

"I longed for peace in my soul, but found only turmoil inside and out. I was misunderstood, shunned, avoided and became the object of whispers..."[248] "I was at the edge of a complete breakdown."[249] "God brought me to the point of utter despair and to where I did not care whether everyone knew how bad I was. I cared for nothing on earth, save getting out of my present condition. I had nothing. I was dry and empty with no power of realizing God or any witness of His Spirit."[250]

We read, but we don't understand what we read. We pray, but all our spiritual feelings are gone. We go to Bible studies, but we get nothing out of them as we used to. Even when we run to hear our favorite speakers or listen to our special worship music, nothing seems to move our hearts. All our old ways of edifying ourselves do not seem to work any longer. Even reading the Bible does not bring us the satisfaction it used to. Thus, we feel we have "lost" God. We are no longer "special" to Him, and certainly, not "loved."[251] We want to run, but *there is no place to go.*

The truth is, of course, that God is *not* missing during this time, even though we feel that He is. He has just hidden Himself from our view--*He is in the darkness.*[252] God never takes His eyes off of us, even for a moment. It's just that we can't "see" Him in the darkness. We forget the Scripture that tells us that God not only dwells in the light, but also *in the darkness.* For this moment, *darkness and light are the same to Him.* God would never lead us into a situation only to abandon us there. That's not His character! That's not His way.

As Hebrews 13:5 promises, *"I [Jesus] will never leave thee, nor forsake thee."* But, for this period of time, He has simply hidden Himself to test, strengthen and confirm our faith.

Like a "Nobody"

Another strong emotion that we will have during this period of time is the feeling that we are a *nobody* because, if we were *somebody*, then at least others would care.

What seems to compound the problem is that when we don't hear and see God as we once did, we naturally turn our eyes and our attention "horizontally" to our spouses, our families and our friends. Thus, we begin to stranglehold them for the love and the security and the identity that we once got from God and are now so desperate for. However, because they are not experiencing what we are experiencing, they don't understand what we are enduring, and they don't respond as we wish. This, of course, makes us feel even more insignificant, lowly and dispensable, creating tremendous insecurity, hesitancy and lack of confidence on our part.

On top of all this, many of our old "friends" seem to forsake us, acquaintances remain far from us and we become the subject of ridicule and gossip. False accusations, hurtful remarks and negative reports are hurled at us. As a result, we feel absolutely desolate and alone. We feel broken and shattered, smashed and pruned, chiseled and stripped of everything we hold dear. Psalm 88:8 expresses it perfectly, "Thou hast put away mine acquaintance far from me; Thou hast made me an abomination unto them: I am shut up, and I cannot come forth." And verse 18, "Lover and friend hast Thou put far from me..."

The horrible part is that there is no one we can run to. No one understands. God seems to have slammed His door on us. And, we certainly don't have "refuge" among our friends or our family, some of whom are now openly ashamed of us and don't even want to be seen with us. Some have even renounced us.

As David cried, "...for Thy sake I have borne reproach; Shame hath covered my face. I am become a stranger unto my brethren, And an alien unto my mother's children." (Psalm 69:7-8)

Our soul has literally become a battlefield of confusion, hurt feelings and broken dreams.

Like a Log on Fire

There are several excellent *analogies in the Bible* that perfectly describe how we feel, going through the dark night of the soul. They also explain a little more clearly *why* God has allowed these events to take place.

The first Scriptural analogy that conveys how we might feel at this time is, like a *"log of wood on fire."* First, the fire dehumidifies the wood; then it turns it black and ugly; next, it transforms the wood by burning it up; and finally, *the log becomes one with the fire.*

We could say that the log of wood is analogous to *our soul* and the fire is analogous to *God's Love.* The Bible often speaks of God as a consuming fire.[253] Because He loves us so much, the Word tells us that, at one time or another in our life, we all will be "salted with fire."[254] God wants all of our sin and self-centeredness to be burned up and to peel away, so that He can bring us into complete *union with Himself.* In other words, *He burns us up in order to make us "one" with Himself,* just like the log of wood eventually becomes *one* with the fire.

Lamentations 1:13 declares, "...He hath sent fire into my bones."

Being salted with fire means that God wants to "burn up" our dazzling outward complexion, so that all our defects will be exposed. Once they are exposed and we see them for ourselves, then we have the choice to either give them to God and be rid of them forever, or hold on to them and let them consume us. Unless we freely give these things over to God, we force Him to turn up the heat on us.

The Psalmist, himself, cried out, "My days are consumed like smoke, my bones are burned." (Psalm 102:3)

The baptism of fire exposes our imperfections and our defects, because this is the fuel that catches on fire, and these are the impurities that block and prevent our experiential union with God. Once these imperfections are gone, the fire will cease and our joy will return. *The fire of God's Love will not only consume and enlighten us, it will also transform us more into God's image (i.e., make us "one"), just like the fire and the log.*

Like Gold in the Refiner's Fire

Another great Scriptural analogy as to how we might feel going through the dark night is like *gold in a refiner's fire.* A refiner's fire is the only thing that can purify gold, separating the impurities and the foreign matter from the gold.[255] In other words, fire is the only thing that melts and dissolves the dross by force.

The refining process begins at a low heat and is then gradually increased. Over and over again, the gold must be cast back into the fire of the furnace[256] until, at last, every trace of pollution is gone. The gold must stay in the fire until there is *proof* that it no longer needs purification. *Only the refiner Himself can see the gold's impurities. Once the gold is finally purified, the fire will not be able to touch it any more and all future imperfections will simply "brush off."*

As we have learned, *God is a consuming fire* and He alone can refine us. On our own, we would <u>never</u> consent to the fire and its purging. Only God can separate the dross, the dregs and the slag of sin and self-centeredness in each of us. Only He knows our secret sins and the masked selfishness of our souls.

As Psalm 105:19 puts it, "The Word of the Lord *tried* him." The meaning of the word, *tried* conveys exactly what God is doing in each of our lives: *purging us in order to fuse us with Himself.* The fire of God's Love purges us in order to make us one with Him. As Job said, "When He hath tried me, I shall come forth as gold."[257]

In order for us to experience oneness with God, He must burn up everything in us that is not of Him. He must excrete all the "dross" because that's what prevents our alliance and our union with Him. Christ cannot be formed in us when there is impurity. *The names of this impurity are sin and self, and these are fatal to our union with Christ.* Thus, the fire of God's Love *burns* away all the impurities in us, and at the same time, He *brightens* (or enlightens) us and brings forth the gold of holiness.

Malachi 3:3 says it all, "He shall sit like a refiner and purifier of silver: and He shall purify...and purge them like gold and silver that they may offer unto the Lord an offering in righteousness."[258]

God purges our soul, as only He knows how to do, by breaking it layer by layer. Only when all the flaws are completely exposed and removed, will we be able to dwell in, enjoy and experience His presence and His fulness.

The crucible of God's fire is where all our hopes and dreams are dashed to pieces and broken, and where we sacrifice all that we have and all that we are to Him. But, *the furnace of God's Love is also where we receive, in exchange, all that God is and all that He possesses.*

All precious metals need to be tested. We are no different.[259] Did you know that a diamond was once a piece of dirty carbon and that it can be found in plain old gravel pits?[260] I was fascinated when I first heard this fact, because we, too, start off as a grimy piece of stone plucked up from the "wayside," but after many times in the Refiner's fire, we, too, can come forth as a diamond glittering and shining in God's eyes. God is a jealous God and He wants us perfect and complete for Himself.[261]

1 Peter 1:7 emphasizes this comparison: "That the trial of your faith, being much more precious than of gold that perisheth, though it be tried with fire, might be found unto praise and honor and glory at the appearing of Jesus Christ." (1 Peter 1:7)

Like a Sacrifice on the Brazen Altar

A third Scriptural analogy of how we might feel going through the dark night, is like *a sacrifice on the Brazen Altar.* In the Inner Court of Solomon's Temple, any sacrifice that was totally consumed by fire on the Brazen Altar was called an *olah* and gave off a sweet savor to God.[262]

All sin was dealt with by sacrificing offerings on the Brazen Altar. The sacrifices were first bound to the altar, then killed with a knife, cut, divided and the meat separated from the bones and muscle.[263] Then the sacrifice was "salted with fire,"[264] wholly and completely burnt and the resulting odor of sweet savor ascended towards God. Finally, the glory of God came down from heaven and consumed the offering on the altar, which meant that it was acceptable and well pleasing in God's sight.[265]

Any offering that was reduced to ashes meant that its acceptance was complete.[266] *To accept actually meant to turn to ashes.* The ashes from the sacrifice were a witness as to how entirely the sacrificial work had been completed. The priests would then remove the ashes from the

Brazen Altar to a clean place outside the camp, and they became the record of death.[267]

Isaiah 61:3 makes an interesting parallel, "To appoint unto them who mourn...to give unto them *beauty for ashes*, the oil of joy for mourning, the garment of praise for the spirit of heaviness; that they might be called trees of righteousness...that He might be glorified."

Romans 12:1 tells us that we are to offer our own bodies as a "living sacrifice." We are to climb up on that Brazen Altar and freely present our bodies as offerings in righteousness.[268]   Just like those sacrifices in Solomon's Temple, we are to allow ourselves to be bound to that altar; *we are to let God cut, divide and separate the soulish things in our lives from the spiritual*; we are to be salted with fire and, then, be wholly and completely burnt. This offering is the way God has designed for our sin and self-centeredness to be purged, so that we will be acceptable and well pleasing in God's sight.[269]

The problem I encountered in my own dark night was that I didn't stay strapped on that Brazen Altar. I had willingly gotten up there and had verbally offered my body as a living sacrifice to God, but when He began to cut and separate out the soulish things in my life, I screamed and jumped off. *Presenting our bodies as a living sacrifice is just the beginning. In order to enter the Holy Place of God's presence, we must not only present our bodies as living sacrifices, but also remain on that altar while God separates the soulish things from the spiritual.*[270]

Ephesians 5:2 tells us to follow Jesus' example, "Walk in love, as Christ also hath loved us, and hath given Himself for us *an offering* and *a sacrifice* to God for a sweet-smelling savor."[271]

What Do We Do?

The way we respond to this dark night determines our whole spiritual walk. Whether we advance, withdraw or simply stay where we are (which is actually impossible) will determine our degree of experiential union with God. The more passive and peaceful we remain during our night season, the quicker we will advance toward God.[272]

This is why it's critical that we endure, as patiently as we can, all that God allows into our lives. Some of us will <u>never</u> advance beyond this stage, because we will grow impatient and seek a means by which we can escape. This is detrimental to our walk! Rather, we must cooperate fully with God by bearing all that He allows.

We must stand still, rest in His promises, stop asking "why," cease doubting, cease fighting, guard against discouragement, stop blaming others, and, finally, put on the whole armor of God and begin to praise Him. Let's explore each of these suggested steps in detail:

Stand Still

One of the *first* things we must do in our crisis is to stand still. We must not move. We must stop all activity and cease striving.[273]

Remember Isaiah 50:10:

"Who is among you that feareth the Lord, that obeyeth the voice of His servant, that walketh in darkness, and hath no light?" Let's look at the rest of that verse and also at verse 11, "*Let him trust in the Name of the Lord, and stay upon his God.* Behold, all ye that kindle [your own] fire, [and] that compass yourselves about with sparks: [and that] walk in the light of your fire, and in the sparks that ye have kindled. This shall ye have of Mine hand; *ye shall lie down in sorrow.*"

So often in our night seasons, because we get impatient for God to "*do*" something, we begin to "*light our own fires.*" We try to find our *own* way out of the trial. And that's when the trouble really begins. When we resist what God is doing and begin to work on our own way out, that's when we find ourselves in an even bigger mess. The more we resist what God is doing by searching out our own ways, the more agony we will cause ourselves, the sharper our suffering becomes, and the longer we will prolong our trial.

We must stand still and wait for God to part the waters. We must stay quiet before God and keep walking in the direction in which we were going when our troubles first began. Nothing has changed between God and us except, perhaps, our *perception* of that relationship.

This kind of *standing still* is not sheer passivity, which so many of the mystics tell us is essential. (We will cover this in greater detail in Chapter Thirteen.) *What we are doing here is really the most active thing we can possibly do. We are choosing, by faith, to constantly remain quiet and cooperate with God, and this takes an enormous effort on our part.* Our natural inclination is to shove, fight, push, scream and yell. Standing still and *yielding our members to God* is the opposite of what we want to do emotionally and, thus, requires a constant and *an active* faith on our part.[274]

One of the ways we can most effectively stand still and surrender ourselves to God is by daily going through *The Inner Court Ritual.* (See *The Prayer Journal* in the Appendix for more details.) It's imperative that we take every thought captive, confess and repent of it, give it to God and, then, replace it with the truth of the Word.

Going through these steps every time we are confronted with a hurtful remark, painful situation, pride, fear, doubt, insecurity or whatever is not of faith, is the *only* way we can stay open and cleansed vessels so God can continue to form Christ in us and implement intimacy with Him.

Going through *The Inner Court Ritual* daily, and keeping a journal of all that God does will help keep us accountable. By writing down all that we feel and dealing with it, *sin* and *self* will not be able to accumulate. In other words, we won't be able to go on to the issues of tomorrow if we haven't first dealt with all the issues of today. This routine will help us "keep very short lists."[275]

> "...Reckon ye also yourselves to be dead indeed unto sin, but *alive unto God* through Jesus Christ our Lord. Let not sin therefore reign in your mortal body, that ye should obey it in the lusts thereof. Neither yield ye your members as instruments of unrighteousness unto sin: but *yield yourselves unto God...and your members as instruments of righteousness unto God.*"
> (Romans 6:11-13)

Rest and Hope in His Promises

At this point, it's very important to get our eyes off the monster, and simply rest and hope in God's promises.

The way we lay hold of His promises is, again, by making faith choices and knowing that He will align our feelings with our choices in His timing and way.[276] Other practical things we can do are: Cry out to Him;[277] quote Scriptures out loud to Him ("You said here..."); and then, listen for His answers in His Word.[278] All we can ask is that He keep His promises.[279]

We must not move out of the Spirit to do our own works. Struggling or becoming agitated just makes everything worse. God has not changed, even though He seems to have covered Himself in darkness.[280]

We must remain pliable, be attentive to God, with no self-effort on our part at all. Wait in peace and patience and faithfulness until God shows us what to do. Endure without complaint. If we simply trust and believe in the Name of Jesus and His Word, He promises to "make darkness light before [us]" and "crooked things straight." (Isaiah 42:16)

God will not lift the trial until He has completed the work in us that He knows must be done. Since He is the One who put us in this fire to begin with, He must be the One to take us out.[281] There is nothing we can do to speed things up, except to stand still, rest and hope in His promises. He will get us out of the fire in His timing and in His way. We simply must trust Him and let Him act.

Stop Asking Why

It's also imperative during this time, to stop asking "*why?*" Stop constantly examining yourself and thinking, "If only I had done this or that." Submit yourself to the confusion. Accept what is happening. Stay still for His Spirit to resolve it for you. *Love God without the need to see or understand why.*

Remember who God is and what He has done for you in the past. Remember His character. Remember that your reason cannot help you comprehend God. It's only by Love that we can reach Him, not by our understanding. So, by faith, we must choose to love Him and to totally give ourselves over to Him, without sight or feelings.

What we must understand is not what God is doing, but what God expects from us. The only way we can overcome our natural senses is by allowing Him to do all He needs to do while we are in the dark. As we focus all our attention on Christ in the darkness, our soulish life supply will eventually be cut off, and our own natural thoughts and emotions will become powerless.

Whenever a self-reflective thought comes, instantly reject it. Don't give way to imagination or reflection. Try to keep clearness of mind and purity of heart at all times. Don't allow negative thoughts to go unchecked to the point where you again dwell on them. Recognize these kinds of negative thoughts, and immediately choose to give them to God. Then get up and, by faith, do as God asks. During this time everything we dwell upon other than God will become an obstacle to our experiential union with Him. If our mind is cluttered with other attitudes and ideas, there will be no room for God.

Expect to get tired of the unrelenting struggle and battle. However, as we persevere we'll begin to have the encouragement we need. As we silently abide in the darkness, we will begin to see and experience God changing our motivations and healing our lives. Thus, the confidence that He is still working and that He still loves us will return.

Peace comes only when we accept what we cannot understand and are no longer troubled by it. Remember Diana's story? Peace comes when we leave everything up to God.

Cease Doubting

We have spoken about *doubt* several times already, but because this dark night is such a vulnerable time for us, doubt can become a major factor. It certainly was with me. We must not only cease striving in our own strength during this time, but we must also cease doubting Him. Don't ask God *why* you have to go through this fire.[282] This is not a time to speak to Him, but simply a time to humble ourselves before Him and suffer politely. Just know that what God is doing in you and through you is both very important and essential for your growth.[283]

It's also important not to run to a friend or to the phone first, but choose, instead, to be alone with the Lord. Reaffirm to Him that all that matters to you is knowing and loving Him. Quote Psalm 73:25 to Him, "*Whom do I have but You?*" Say in faith, as Job did, "For I know that my redeemer liveth and...in my flesh, shall I see Him." (Job 19:26)

Fast from any emotional or intellectual security of knowing, understanding and being right. One single attachment is enough to prevent you from attaining the union that God so desires. Be patient, believe in Him and listen for His voice. He knows about your every thought, emotion and desire.

The best thing you can do is to *accept* the trial graciously and stand back and see what God does. Surrender yourself to the suffering. Don't look for a way out. Stay in the trial if thats God's will and be willing to die to your "self." Be willing to be stripped naked and obliterated if that is what He requires.

Cease Fighting

There is an instinctive rebellion in us against what is happening. It's called "survival." We must stop all efforts to deliver ourselves and learn to *lean on His breast*[284] and trust in His Name, as Diana Bantlow did. Because we feel what is happening is not deserved, not warranted and not fair, this is the time we often take matters into our own hands by "lighting our own fires." This resistance we put up without realizing it, is the source of much of our trouble and as Isaiah 50:10 tells us, if we do this, "we will lie down in sorrow and be destroyed."

The less we struggle, the less it will hurt. We need to cease trying to figure out what God is up to and simply wait for Him to act. Cry out to

Him, "Lord, I give up. I can't fight. I confess my self-pity, my rebellion. It's all yours. I'm simply going to trust You."

Remember, the battle is not ours, but the Lord's. He has not forgotten us. He will always be faithful.[285] Thus, we must stop acting as if He has forgotten all about us and abandoned us.

We mustn't pray for relief from the trial, but rather pray for strength to endure it with courage, humility and love, and to be changed by it. We won't be able to weather the storms unless we are willing to persevere and overcome. Romans 5:3 tells us that *tribulation* brings about *patience*, and patience, if we allow it to, will bring about *hope*.

Much of our trouble springs from our not wanting to give up our attachments, our support systems and everything else we rely upon. The more we fight to save these things, however, the sharper our trials will become. If we can willingly surrender ourselves to what God is doing in our lives and permit the crucifying process to go unheeded, then the blows will be much softer and the process will go a lot faster. *It is God who holds us fast to the cross and it is God who will loose us from that cross when He sees fit.* No one can change His plans. We must simply seek His strength to endure.

Let's keep our eyes upon Him and run towards Him like that eagle. Even if we don't see Him or feel Him or understand His ways, He promises us that the darkness will eventually shrivel away and the light will begin to shine. "Unto the upright there ariseth light in the darkness...." (Psalm 112:4)[286]

All the trials and tribulations God has allowed are simply a part of the preparation process that He is implementing in each of our lives. These night seasons are a necessary part of learning *to love* and learning *to know God intimately*.[287]

Guard Against Discouragement

As we read the words of David in Psalm 38, we find this godly, righteous man discouraged and at the end of himself. Listen:

> "I am troubled; I am bowed down greatly; I go mourning all the day long...I am feeble and sore broken: I have roared by reason of the disquietness of my heart...My heart panteth, my strength faileth me: as for the light of mine eyes, it also is gone from me...I, as a deaf man, heard not; and I was as a dumb man that openeth not his mouth. Thus I was as a man that heareth not, and in whose mouth are no reproofs." (Psalm 38:6, 8, 10, 13-14)

One of the emotions I struggled with the most in my own night season *was* discouragement. Nothing seemed to bring me down faster than allowing disappointment and discouragement into my soul.

When we become discouraged and cling to our anxieties, our fears and our self-pity, it not only strengthens them, it also impedes what God wants to do. We must be careful not to fall into the mode of self-pity or wanting sympathy from others. Be assured, you won't get it. Besides, it does no good anyway--we only end up deeper in the pit than when we started. Our eyes cannot be on anyone or anything but God Himself. His approval and His support is all we need.

Our greatest failure during this time is in allowing our interior agitation and depression to become exaggerated. If we allow our negative thoughts to go unchecked, our agitation and our depression will not only quench God's Spirit and deprive us of hearing God's voice, but it will also become an obstacle to our union with Him.

A Small Example

I had such high expectations as to how God was going to miraculously perform His "mountaintop" promises of 1990 in my life. When things didn't turn out as I expected, I eventually became discouraged and disappointed.

A small example: In the middle of my dark night (1995-1996), a major book publisher asked to see all my books--the whole *King's High Way Series*. I was absolutely ecstatic! They read the entire series; they said they were thrilled with them; they said they were "just what they were looking for"; they said they were the "most important item on their priority list"; and they said they were eager to publish them. They promised to "get right back to me" with a contract.

Well, I waited and waited and waited, and waited some more. I never heard one word back from those people. I was crushed. I had told many people about the possibility because I was so excited. Well, God was dealing with my pride and He also was dealing with my natural, human expectations. If He wanted that publisher to do the books, He would have seen to it. But He was teaching me to be abandoned to His will, no matter how disappointing the circumstances. He was teaching me to relinquish *everything*, even my books and my ministry to Him.

You know, we say that we have already done that, but oh, how difficult it is when He actually puts us to the test in our actions. As it has turned out, K-House has done a great job of publishing the books and God has been a phenomenal CEO. We are now in our sixth or seventh printing of the series.

It's imperative to learn how to *"see"* in the darkness. We need to see and to understand not so much what God is *doing*, but rather *what He desires of us*. We must continue to walk abandoned to His will and wait upon Him without anxiety and without hunger for any experience. Our dependence must rest completely in His Love and faithfulness so that, no matter what events are transpiring in our lives, our spirit and our inner man remain at rest. This is one of the main reasons God wants our spirit strengthened, so that what happens to us on the outside in our soul, does not determine our composure on the inside.

Stop Blaming Others

Another important exhortation is that, during this time, we must stop blaming others. *When God has appointed us to suffer, He permits even the most virtuous people to be blinded towards us.* Thus, it's important to harbor no resentment or bitterness against those involved in our trials. By blaming others, we really only condemn ourselves and that, of course, breeds more insensitivity in us. It's critical that we not justify our own feelings or be governed by our self-righteousness.

God will repay those truly responsible for our troubles in His timing and in His way.[288] He is our defense and our avenger.[289] Psalm 94:22 tells us, "The Lord is my defense; and my God is the rock of my refuge." Only God knows the real truth and only He knows how to weave our lives together perfectly. We must try neither to vindicate ourselves, nor to help Him along. He will fight our battles for us.[290] We must simply stand still and watch.

Pray for the others involved; don't blame them; leave them in God's care and in His hands.[291] Thank Him in advance for delivering you out of their hands. And, above all, don't give way to grief.

Furthermore, don't speak about your problems to anyone else. It only deepens your bitterness, programs those negative thoughts in more deeply, and gives the enemy another entrance. Therefore, try to speak well of the other people involved. Ephesians 4:29 tells us, "Let no corrupt communication proceed out of your mouth, but that which is good to the use of edifying, that it may minister grace unto the hearers."

I know how very difficult this kind of behavior is to change, especially when we are "justified" by the world's standards for being angry and bitter. But, giving way to our feelings and emotions about others at this time only makes *us* more miserable, the enemy happier and the whole process prolonged. I know! I've been there!

Submit to the confusion, the *not* knowing, the *not* understanding and the *not* being right. Put your reason aside and look only to God. Our reason cannot cope with the dark night that God allows. We must live by faith and wait for the Spirit to resolve the darkness for us. *We must remain receptive and positive, not expecting to understand God's ways, but simply trusting Him in them.*

Put On The Armor of God

One of the most critical things we can do to endure--in fact, to stand effectively in--our night of faith is to *daily* put on the Armor of God!

> Ephesians 6:10 tells us: "Finally, my brethren, *be strong* in the Lord, and in the power of **His** might." (Ephesians 6:10)

Being strong in the Lord is our most critical imperative. This word *strong* is in the present tense which means it is to be *continuous*. It is in the passive voice, meaning that we *receive* the action; it's something that happens to us. *Twice* Paul emphasizes that to put on the armor includes *all* of the parts (not just our favorite pieces)![292]

As we consider this warfare we are engaged in, remember our combat intelligence insight: "For we wrestle not against flesh and blood, but against principalities, against powers, against the rulers of the darkness of this world, against spiritual wickedness in high *places*." (Ephesians 6:12)

So Paul details for us the seven elements of the Armor of God (Ephesians 6:10-18):

1) "...having your loins girt about with truth,";

In contrast with the myths and disinformation which dominates our contemporary society, we are to be girded with the only real truth: His. "I am the Way, the Truth, and the Life." (John 14:6)

2) "...and having on the breastplate of righteousness...."

The breastplate protected the vital organs; the penetration of this piece usually proved fatal. We need to be protected by *His Righteousness*, and not rely upon our own!

3) "And your feet shod with the preparation of the gospel of peace...."

Every battle requires preparation, and ours is no exception. We must choose, moment by moment, to "put off" our sin and self and, to "put on" Christ.

4) "Above all, taking the shield of faith, wherewith ye shall be able to quench all the fiery darts of the wicked."

Our shield of faith needs to be in good shape *before* the battle. Are there "holes" in our shield that need to be repaired? Are we making "faith choices" to believe what God has promised us in His Word? If we're not, our shield has holes and we are giving the enemy a perfect inroad.

5) "And take the helmet of salvation...."

Helmets are a form of security. Failure to wear a proper helmet can prove fatal. Our helmet was purchased just for us. We are entitled to it because of Christ and what He has done. We must realize who we are in Him and that He has paid the full price for our redemption. We have been redeemed; we have been paid for; we are no longer our own. Nothing protects us more from a blow to our head than our "helmet of salvation"-- His Life in us. Each time we step out our door, we must realize that we *have been* redeemed and that we *already* have eternal life. No one can take that away from us. Satan can't touch us! Nothing, by any means, can hurt us. Re-read Romans 8:28-39.

6) "...and the sword of the Spirit, which is the Word of God":

This sword, of course, a well-known idiom (Hebrews 4:12). Our sword is the *offensive* part of our armor. Notice that this sword is *two-edged*: it's intended to be used defensively as well as offensively. In addition to the "pulling down of strongholds,"[293] it is also used in the *defense* of the faith.[294] However, like any sword, its use also requires training and practice!

The heavy artillery:

7) " Praying always with all prayer and supplication in the Spirit...."

It is absolutely incredible that we each have a priority connection directly into the Throne Room of the Universe! It is amazing to realize that this astonishing resource is so available and yet so sparingly used.

It is unquestionably the most powerful weapon we could possibly have. And, it is *the deciding factor* in our spiritual warfare

Praise Him

And last, but certainly not least, we need to begin to pray and praise God in everything that concerns us. Most of us have heard quoted 1 Thessalonians 5:18: "In everything give thanks; for this is the will of God in Christ Jesus concerning you."[295] By faith, we need to act out this Scripture.

> "Rejoice in the Lord alway[s]: and again I say, Rejoice....Be careful for nothing; but in everything by prayer and supplication with thanksgiving let your requests be made known unto God. And the peace of God, which passeth all understanding, shall keep your hearts and minds through Christ Jesus." (Philippians 4:4, 6-7)

We need to thank Him, by faith, for what He is doing in our lives, for all that He has done and for what He will do in the future.[296] By doing so, we will pierce the darkness and the evil spirits will flee away. Scripture says that the enemy hates the Name of Jesus, he despises praises of God and anything to do with His Word. Try praising God and watch him flee.

The most important thing we can do at this time is to have a loving, blind desire to praise God in everything. Prayers like, "Jesus, You are my King, my Lord, my... I seek only You, my Love, my Life, my..." Tell Him, over and over again, how much you love Him. Let the Holy Spirit remind you of all the Names of God and all the one-syllable words about His character. Praising Him for these things will turn your mind from the depths of despair to being fully focused upon Him. (See the Appendix and the *Prayer Journal* for more specific suggestions.)

A Scriptural Example: Jonah

Jonah did this very thing.

God had told Jonah to go and preach at Nineveh, but Jonah refused and, instead, fled the presence of the Lord in a ship. God then took matters into His own hands and allowed Jonah to encounter a storm at sea. The men aboard the ship knew that Jonah was at fault for "fleeing the presence of the Lord," so they threw him overboard. God, however, had prepared a great fish that came along and swallowed Jonah.

God's ways are certainly *not* our ways!

Jonah literally hit bottom (pun intended). Now, he certainly had sufficent reason to believe that God had totally abandoned him. But when Jonah began to praise and thank God from the bottom of the sea, God heard his prayers and had the fish vomit Jonah out onto dry land. Jonah passed God's test of "praising Him in *all* things" and, thus, God released him. (Jonah 1; 2:9)

I remember years ago reading the book *Prison to Praise* by Merlin Carothers and thinking, "How on earth can I praise God for all the bad things that are happening in my life?"

I have since learned that what God wants us to praise Him for is not all the bad things, *but for who He is in the middle of the bad things.* He wants us to thank Him and praise Him for His goodness, His faithfulness, His righteousness, His power, His sovereignty, His Love, His mercy, His grace, His peace, His truth, His wisdom, His redemption, His Spirit, His strength, His salvation, His sanctification and all the other thousands of things that we can think of. This praise is what will get us through this trial in His timing and His way.

An Example: Fleas

Corrie ten Boom and her sister Betsie relate a wonderful example of praising God in "all" things in their book *The Hiding Place.*

They had just been moved to a new prison and a new barracks. As they approached the new quarters, Corrie screamed, "Betsie, this place is crawling with fleas! How can we ever live in such a room?" Betsie responded, "God has already given us the answer." She pointed to the Scripture she had just gotten that morning, "'In everything give thanks, for this is the will of God....' (1 Thessalonians 5:18) That's God's answer, Corrie."

Corrie couldn't believe her ears. "There's no way God can ever make me thankful for these fleas!" she thought to herself. She was sure Betsie was wrong this time. But eventually she made the choice to be thankful *by faith.*

The new building was a large dormitory, with many rooms adjacent to it. Corrie and Betsie's room held nine women, but was accessible to the main hall. As the ten Booms read their Bible each night, others soon began to join in. Soon, women from other wings of the dormitory also came. Some women would translate the Word, as they heard it, into their own language, so even more women could participate. Night after night they held their Bible studies and no guard ever bothered them. No guard even came near. In fact, there was no supervision at all!

One night, months later, Betsie said to Corrie, "I finally know why we never had any interruptions to our Bible studies and why we had so much freedom in the big room. It was because of the fleas! The room is crawling with fleas, and the guards won't step through the door!"

This is what it means to offer a "sacrifice of praise," a "sacrifice of joy" or a "sacrifice of thanksgiving."[297] These are sacrifices we make when we are not really thankful or joyful in the natural--we have nothing to praise Him for in our human understanding, but, by faith, we choose to do so anyway. By faith, we can praise Him for these things, as Corrie and Betsie did, because we know, again by faith, that He <u>does</u> love us and that He <u>will</u> be faithful to eventually work out all of the problems in our life according to His will and for His glory. He has not forgotten us. In fact, He loves us so much that, even in the middle of our trials, He has engraved us on the palms of His hands.

Conclusion

Our progress in God is always measured by our separation from sin and self. Suffering, then, is simply a means of "un-selfing" us.

Therefore, we are not lost in our night seasons, but actually found. The darkness does not come from the enemy who hates us, although he definitely tries to use it to crush us and annihilate us, but from God who loves us. God will not lift the darkness until He has accomplished in it and through it and by it all that He needs to do.

God never mortifies us, without giving us life as a result. And He never humbles us without bringing glory to Himself through it.

The question boils down to: "Will you let Him do these things in and through you? Can you pass the night of faith without lighting your own fire?"

Psalm 18 seems so appropriate here:

> "I will love Thee, O Lord, my strength.
> The Lord is my rock, and my fortress, and my deliverer;
> My God, my strength, in Whom I will trust;
> My buckler, and *the horn of my salvation*, and my high tower,
> I will call upon the Lord, Who is worthy to be praised:
> *So shall I be saved from mine enemies.*
> The sorrows of death compassed me,
> And the floods of ungodlly men made me afraid.
> The sorrows of hell compassed me about:
> The snares of death prevented me.

In my distress I called upon the Lord,
And cried unto my God:
He heard my voice out of His temple,
And my cry came before Him, even into His ears.
Then the earth shook and trembled;
The foundations also of the hills moved...
He bowed the heavens also, and *came down*:
And darkness was under His feet...
He sent from above, He took me,
He drew me out of many waters.
He delivered me from my strong enemy,
And from them which hated me...
He brought me forth also into a large place;
He delivered me, because He delighted in me."[298]

Key Points of This Chapter:

- The dark night shakes our consecration, our conversion and our commitment to God.
- We will experience a wide variety of emotions.
- Our reactions will determine our walk. We must stand still, trust in the Name of the Lord and stay upon Him.
- We do this by resting in His promises, ceasing to doubt, guarding against discouragement and refusing to blame others.
- We must put on the armor of God and praise Him in all things.
- God is in the process of making us *one with Him*--the log and the Fire.

Section Five:
The Dark Night of the Spirit

"We are troubled on every side, yet not distressed; we are perplexed, but not in despair; Persecuted, but not forsaken; cast down, but not destroyed; Always bearing about in the body the dying of the Lord Jesus, that the Life also of Jesus might be made manifest in our body. For we which live are alway[s] delivered unto death for Jesus' sake, [so] that the Life also of Jesus might be made manifest in our mortal flesh...."
(2 Corinthians 4:8-11)

Chapter Nine
Our Human Spirit

Introduction

One of the most important things that the dark night does is to highlight the glibness of "religion." It shows its hollowness and its emptiness. The dark night causes the breakdown of order and schemes. In the darkness, there are no guidelines and no maps to follow. No religious experience will get us through this time. If we want all of Jesus, we must be prepared to let all of our "religious" thoughts and traditions go.

Most religions concentrate on our souls or our *outward* man. Very few religious systems deal with the inward man or our spirit. Christianity is the one exception. Jesus tells us that the kingdom of God is within us--in our *inward* man.[299] Therefore, the further inward we turn towards God in our spirit, not only are we moving towards intimacy with Him, we are also moving away from our outward or soulish man.

Man's spirit was once "head" over the whole man. But because of Adam's fall, our soul and spirit became intermingled, with our soul being the dominant force. Thus, when the soul becomes defiled, unholy or unclean because of our emotional choices, it also defiles our spirit[300] and causes all communication, leading and guiding from the Holy Spirit to be stopped.[301] This blocked communication is what we mean when we say that the Spirit has become quenched or blocked.[302]

All communication with God occurs in our spirit, because this is the place where "He meets with us," this is the place where He dwells.[303] Thus, when our spirit is cleansed and purified, we are able to communicate and fellowship directly with Him. But as long as our spirit and our soul are intermingled (and not cleansed), our spirit will be suppressed by our soul's influence, and our spiritual walk hindered. Therefore, God wants to teach us *how* to allow our spirit, not our soul, to direct and drive our lives.

God wants us to glorify and reflect Him, not only in our bodies, but also in our spirits.[304] In order for this to occur, however, we must first understand what our spirits are and how God wants to set them free from the influence of our souls. So, before we continue to explore what the *dark night of the spirit* is, let's first understand what our spirits are, how they can be freed from the domination of our souls and what we can do to help speed up the process.

What Is Our Spirit?

Romans 8:16 tells us very clearly that we do have a human spirit. [305] "The Spirit Itself beareth witness with *our spirit*, that we are the children of God:" Thus, if we are the "children of God," then God's Spirit will always bear witness to us, lead us and guide us through our human spirit. [306]

Our spirit is like the *power source*, the *energy source* or the *light source* of our lives. It's analogous to a generator or the electric power plant in a huge building. Without its energy and power, nothing in the building will work. There will be no light or life at all! It's the same with us. Without a spirit, our bodies will have no life. Our spirit is a *life-giving power* that makes us alive, that quickens and gives us life. [307] It's removal means death. [308]

Our spirit exists independently in our body. It's not material; however, it does possess its own spiritual substance. [309] It can be likened to an electric light. As Proverbs 20:27 states, "The spirit of man is the candle of the Lord." In order to have light, however, Scripture tells us that our spirit must come in contact with and be united with the Spirit of God. The Spirit of God is the "Master Transformer;"[310] our spirit is simply the transmitter. So, apart from God's Spirit turning our spirit on, it remains darkened and unlit.

God gave us a body to interact and be *conscious of the world and others* around us; He gave us a soul that we might be *conscious of ourselves*, our own thoughts, emotions and desires; and He gave us a spirit so we could communicate and fellowship with God and be conscious of His will. In other words, our spirit is our "link" to God.

Watchman Nee gives us a great analogy of our body, soul and spirit in his book *The Spiritual Man*. He says the body, soul and spirit together are like a light bulb. The *electricity* is like the spirit or the source of light; the soul is like *the light that shines* (or the effect) of the electricity; and the body is like *the wire* or the material part of the bulb. [311]

This analogy is very helpful to me in understanding the separate functions of our body, soul and spirit and how they can (if we allow them to) "work together" as God intended.

What Happened at Creation?

Genesis 2:7 tells us that at creation, God breathed *the breath of life* (the spirit) into man (into his body) and man then became *a living soul*. In other words, our human spirit came forth from God, but our soul was produced after the spirit entered our body. "And the Lord God formed man of the dust of the ground, and breathed into his nostrils the breath of life; and man became a living soul."

Thus, in Adam, his spirit, soul and body were *perfectly blended together*--his soul being the *unifying factor*. In other words, his soul was not only in communication with his body, it was also in perfect communication with his spirit.

Even though Adam's soul was the "meeting point" between his spirit and body, *his spirit always remained the ruling power*. It controlled his whole body through his soul. God designed it this way. Man's spirit was to be the master, the head or the dominant force over man's soul and his body.

What Happened at the Fall of Man?

However, because God gave man a free choice or will of his own, instead of choosing to follow God's will by not eating of the *tree of the knowledge of good and evil*, Adam chose to partake of the forbidden fruit. With this act, sin entered and Adam lost his original union and fellowship with God. Adam's soul became inflated and his spirit suppressed. Adam choose independence, rather than dependence upon God, and thus his spirit died, or you might say, lost its sensitivity and communication with God.[312] Adam's spirit became cut off from its *source of power*--the Master Transformer (God's Spirit). Because the transmission of power was cut off, according to Watchman Nee's analogy, there was no more electricity.

At this point, Adam's spirit and soul became co-mingled, fused or joined, with his soul becoming the ruling and governing force. As a result, the spirit of man no longer controlled his body.[313] Thus, God could no longer communicate with man or rule him internally, and He had to resort to the laws of nature.

Man's spirit became simply a resident or a prisoner of his soul. Consequently, when we are born into the human race, like Adam, our soul is naturally the dominant force, controlling all that we do.

What Happened at Our New Birth?

When we ask Jesus Christ to come into our lives and become our savior and Lord, however, God gives us the gift of the Holy Spirit.

> "Repent, and be baptized every one of you in the Name of Jesus Christ for the remission of sins, and ye shall receive *the gift of the Holy Spirit*." (Acts 2:38)[314]

At this time God's Spirit unites with our human spirit and it becomes alive, quickened and regenerated. The electricity is turned on by the Master Transformer. Listen to Ezekiel 36:26: "I will put My Spirit within you, and cause you to walk in My statutes, and ye shall keep My judgments, and do them." This means that when the Holy Spirit infuses our spirit with new Life, our dead spirit becomes alive.

The Holy Spirit works with us *differently* than He did with Adam. When Adam received a spirit, he simply became a "living soul." This same thing occurs with us when we are born naturally. However, when we are *born again* of the Spirit, unlike Adam, we receive God's Spirit (the Holy Spirit) into our human spirit, which gives us a brand new spirit. This is what being "born again" really means.

God's Spirit uses our human spirit like a carrier or a transport to help carry out the process of sanctification and to restore spiritual communication in our lives. *The process of sanctification is simply the process of restoring our spirit to its rightful place, as director of our souls. This restoration is crucially important because until our soul is completely submitted to our spirit our communication and our walk with the Lord will be hindered.*

Our biggest difficulty, then, is that our spirit needs to be untangled from our soul, to break free from its influence and rule. The true spiritual man is one in whom the spirit rules, not the soul. God's will is that our regenerate spirit becomes stronger and stronger, so that it can work alongside of God's Spirit to control and govern our soul.[315] Then, the tables will be turned and our spirit can, once again, become the *uniting factor* between our souls and our bodies. Our spirit will be able to operate *outwardly* through our soul and communicate with the world, and it will be able to operate *inwardly* towards God and commune with Him.

The Holy Spirit (through our spirit) wants to permeate our souls with His Life and, thereby, establish "love lines" with others, and communion and intimacy with us. This is the "fulness of Christ" that we have so often referred to. We are "...to know the Love of Christ, which passeth knowledge, that *ye might be filled with all the fulness of God.*" (Ephesians 3:19)

Our spirit can only fill us, lead us and guide us, however, when the sensory part of our soul is weakened, crucified and annihilated. In order for this to occur, our soul needs to be brought through the darkness and death of its own ability. Thus, a spiritual Christian is one in whom the Spirit is allowed to lead, guide and direct; whereas, a carnal Christian is one who chooses to follow his own will and desires (his flesh) and, thereby, quenches the Spirit's leading. A carnal Christian still has God's Spirit in his heart united with his human spirit, but it's blocked from coming forth by sin and self. Thus, in this person the sanctification process is halted and all communication with God is stopped.

So, Christians will always have a human soul and a human spirit. The question is: which one is in control?

What Is An Unregenerate Man?

An "unregenerate" man, or a non-believer in Christ, is one who does not have the Spirit of God in him.[316] He has a human spirit, but it has not been quickened or made alive. Thus, he is both devoid of God's Life and dead to all things of God.[317]

> "He that hath the Son [Jesus] hath life; and he that hath not the Son of God hath not life." (1 John 5:12)

Proverbs 20:27 tells us that our human spirit is like a candle, *but until the Spirit of God comes into our spirit* (and we receive the Son), *that candle will remain unlit.* Once the Spirit of God comes into our spirit, then the light (or the power of God) can begin to shine forth.

After the fall of Adam, there was a kind of spiritual death and man's spirit lost both its power and its sensitivity towards God. Consequently, every person born into the human race inherited this problem. Therefore, if a person is never born again by the Spirit of God, he will not only be unable to communicate with God, he will always be controlled by his own soulish abilities.[318]

As a result, the life that this person produces will always be "human, natural life" generated by his own thoughts, emotions and desires; whereas, if he is an open and cleansed vessel, the life that a believer produces will be God's supernatural Life--His Wisdom, His Love and His Power.

What Are the Functions of Our Spirit?

Our spirit--the place where we communicate with God--has three main functions or operations that are essential to this communication: our conscience, our intuition and our communion.[319]

Briefly, our <u>conscience</u> is the place where God teaches us and speaks to us. This is where He lets us know what is right and what is wrong and what His individual will is. You could say that our conscience is like our *organ of faith*. Our <u>intuition</u> is where God guides and leads us and where we can discern His movements. This is the area where we develop true intimate knowledge of God and experience His revelation and His anointing. The third function of our spirit is where we <u>fellowship and commune</u> with God. This is where we are to worship the Lord in the spirit.

Let's explore these functions of our spirit in detail.

Conscience

All three functions of our spirit are very closely related, so each one depends upon and builds from the other. A pure conscience leads to an undefiled intuition and ultimately to open communion and fellowship with God.

Our conscience is like the inner voice of God. This is where God corrects and protects us.[320] This is also where the Holy Spirit reveals God's will to us. Our conscience is like God's inward monitor. It renders us uneasy when we don't choose to follow His will and gives us peace when we do. Our conscience reprimands us, reproves us, corrects us and approves us. It is designed to govern our lives and, by doing so, constantly show us what God's will is.[321]

Our spiritual conscience is our teacher. As Job declares, God's Spirit taught him things that he did not understand.[322] And I can say the very same thing. Throughout the writing of this book, God has taught me things by His Spirit that I neither knew or understood before.

The first step of salvation, then, is to awaken our comatose conscience. We need a conscience in order to convict us of sin and to make us sensitive to our self-centered ways. Hebrews tells us that Christ's blood has been shed over our conscience, so that we *can* have a cleansed and purified spirit.[323] A cleansed conscience is one that carries *no guilt*. Hebrews 10:22 tells us. "Our hearts [are] sprinkled [clean] from an evil conscience, and our bodies [are] washed with pure water."[324] Thus, a sprinkled and cleansed conscience is the only basis for our spiritual communion with God. A conscience that is tinged with offences will not only affect our communication with God, but also prevent our transformation. We cannot have the slightest accusation in our conscience, so we must make sure that every sin is atoned for.[325]

Someone once said, *"It's more important to be afraid of one reproach from our conscience than it is from all the condemnation of men in the world."*

The first step toward sanctification, then, is to abide by our "renewed" conscience, which will constantly tell us if we are clean or not. As we grow more and more into a spiritual man, our conscience will grow more and more sensitive and attuned to God's voice. Scripture states that our conscience will not only "bear witness" to us, it will also "condemn us."[326]

As our spiritual life grows, our conscience will begin to show us not only what is right and what is wrong, but also what is of God and what is not. Although many things will *appear* right in our own eyes, they are, nonetheless, condemned by God because they do not originate with His Spirit. Remember my incident with the false prophet in Chapter Four? This is a perfect example of the importance of learning to be sensitive only to only His voice and be willing to eliminate anything that does not bear witness to our spirit.

Now, please don't misunderstand me. We are never going to be perfectly clean or perfectly holy in this lifetime. *There is only One who is, and that's Jesus!* What I am referring to here is dealing daily with the sin and self that God shows us. Since God loves us and wants us completely for Himself, He will, moment by moment, lovingly point out more and more *self* that must be given over to Him. So, from now on, when I speak of a "sanctified soul," I do not mean a totally pure and completely holy person. That only happens at the resurrection. *I simply mean a person who has dealt with all that God has shown them for that day!*

We also don't have to wait until "all" sin and self is dealt with *before* we can have communion with God and enjoy His presence. That also will take a lifetime! We need only to be faithful to crucify the things that He shows us today! *It's not unknown sin that is going to hinder our communication with God. It's the known sin!*

Our conscience is limited by its own present knowledge. Therefore, it can only guide us by the knowledge it possesses now. God will continue to examine our actions and our motives and will reveal what He finds. Then, it will be up to us to deal with the things that "are not of faith."Thus, our sanctification is totally dependent upon our own willingness to accept the reproach of our conscience and to do whatever is necessary to correct it.

I do not believe it's God's will that we make some sort of a "blanket" or "general" confession by acknowledging *all* of our sins and *all* of our self-centered ways in some vague manner. I don't believe this is what cleanses our conscience. We need to let the Holy Spirit, daily, moment by moment, reprove and convict us of things that are "not of faith" and be ready, in or out of season, to give these over to Him.

An Example: Toni

I co-hosted several seminars with a woman speaker who lived a very self-centered life. She treated others very badly; she never read her Bible or prayed, except when she was going to give a speech, be on the radio or do a TV show. Just before these events, she would publically pray and very generally confess all her sins. Right after she spoke, however, she immediately went back to her hedonistic and self-oriented lifestyle.[327]

This used to really bother me. I knew it wasn't right and it always struck me as being so phony. I'm not so uptight about it anymore, because I realized that "God is never mocked." He knows exactly what is going on. He not only knows our specific sins, He also knows our motives and our "hearts" behind our words. Consequently, I believe, in His timing and in His way, the truth will come out.

But how many of us do the very same thing? We go as long as we can without confronting our sin and our self, but when we really *need* God, we quickly confess and repent of all the things we can think of; get what we want to from God; and then, go right back to the same old lifestyle. God wants us to daily and specifically confess and repent of our sins and self-centeredness, so that we can receive even more illumination from Him and enjoy the intimacy He has prepared for us.

Our conscience is like the window to our soul. If we allow Him to, God's light will shine brightly through this window, exposing our faults. If we heed what He shows us, that light will shine His light even brighter next time. If we <u>don't</u> obey God, then our conscience will be corrupted and our window clouded. After continuously quenching His Spirit, we won't be able to see God's heavenly light at all.

Paul is a perfect example of someone who had a Spirit-filled conscience. In Acts 24:16 he asserts, "I exercise myself, to have always a conscience void of offense toward God, and toward men." (Acts 23:1) And I believe God desires the same for us. Like Paul, we, too, need a clean conscience before God and man. In fact, Scripture tells us we can only serve God when we have a cleansed and pure conscience.[328] This is why we need to become more sensitive to our conscience, constantly paying special attention as to how it bears witness to us.

Maturity in Christ can be measured by our responsiveness to our conscience. A good conscience enables us to receive God's promises, walk by His Spirit and enter His presence. An evil conscience leads us to a lack of faith, being guilt-ridden and walking by the flesh.

Intuition

The next function of our spirit is our intuition. Intuition is the attaining of direct knowledge, perception or conviction, beyond the means of reason alone.[329] Our intuition and our conscience work closely together. One leads to the next. A pure conscience leads to a keen intuition. In other words, *we can't have discernment if we have a defiled conscience.*

Intuition is simply "spiritual sensing" or spiritual discernment. This is very different from following our own natural instinct or our soulish emotional feelings. Spiritual intuition is adhering to what the voice of the Spirit is saying, as this is how we receive God's instructions.[330] Many Christians do not have this intuitive knowledge because they don't know how to discern God's voice. They don't know how to "walk by or after the spirit." If we don't heed our spiritual intuition, then we'll naturally go back to walking after the flesh and adhering to our own soulish thoughts and emotions. *To live and walk by the Spirit means to live and walk according to our intuition.*

A pure spirit will disclose an unmistakable discernment[331] and this discernment is critical when fighting the enemy. *The enemy can attack us only through our outward man (our soul and body), through the motions of our flesh.* Therefore, if we are not sensitive and discerning of this vulnerability, he will always find a "hole" to keep us his prisoners. Those who adhere to the Spirit's leading, via their intuition, will be preserved from being deceived in times of confusion.

An Example: "Things Are Not What They Seem"

In the early 1980s, I met a woman who wanted to become my prayer partner. We had only known each other for a few weeks, so I should have been more discerning. I was mature enough in the Lord to have known better. But, because this woman "prayed like a saint," I thought it would be wonderful to learn from her.

When I passed the idea by God, I really didn't get peace about it. However, I was in a hurry and besides, I thought to myself, "One couldn't pray like she does and not be right with the Lord." Well, I was wrong. I stupidly overlooked God's "red flags" (something in my spirit said it wasn't right) and still said "yes" to this woman.

Now, when you pray with someone, you naturally let your guard down and share your innermost heart. I did just that. Big mistake! This woman turned out to be a "wolf in sheep's clothing" and nearly cost me my marriage and my ministry. (In hindsight, being able to pray like "a saint" is not proof that someone is "right" with the Lord; checking the "fruit" from their life is! If I had been more of a discerning *fruit inspector*, I might not have gotten into the trouble I did.)

God's discernment is absolutely crucial in everything we do.

Our intuition also gives us the ability to know God, and to know Him more intimately. God's Spirit bears witness with our spirit, as to what is of the spirit and what is of the soul. By that "revelation," we can see and confess our own sin and self, thus gaining greater intimacy with God. In other words, this kind of revelation is essential to greater knowledge of God. As we said before, *the purer we become, the clearer we can see Jesus.*

Communion and Fellowship

In review then, our *conscience* is where God teaches us what His will is; our *intuition* is where God leads and guides us and gives us supernatural discernment and revelation. The third function of our spirit, however, our *communion and fellowship* with God, is unique.

This operation of our spirit requires *our* participation. Teaching and guiding are aspects of God's communication *to us*; whereas, communion and fellowship require our communication *with God*. In other words, there is a response needed from us. *Communion is a two-way relationship!* Communion is our fellowship and our communication with God. Again, a sprinkled and cleansed spirit is the basis for this communion.

In order to communicate and fellowship with God, we must possess a similar nature, a spiritual nature. Scripture tells us that God is a Spirit and the only way we can have intimacy and fellowship with Him is through our sanctified and purified spirit. Therefore, if our spirit has been quenched, because of sin or self, then we won't be able to commune with Him. In fact, we won't even be able to hear Him; and He won't hear us. Lamentations 3:44 validates this, "Thou hast covered Thyself with a cloud, that our prayer[s] should not pass through."

Most of us attempt to communicate with God in a wide variety of ways. Naturally, we give our soulish thoughts and emotions first place. Consequently, we often overlook the most important way to fellowship with God, which is though our spirit. If we can learn how to constantly surrender and relinquish ourselves to God, then God will hear us and answer us *in the most miraculous ways.*

An Example: Eddie Rickenbacker

Captain Eddie Rickenbacker, the winner of the Congressional Medal of Honor, is well known in military circles for his daring exploits as a World War I flying ace. What is not known about him is an incident in World War II that led to his public declaration of faith.

In October 1942, he was on a special mission for the Secretary of War. As he was leaving California in a B17 to deliver a secret message to General Douglas MacArthur, the plane's tire blew out. Repairs were made, but what no one knew is that the accident had disturbed the plane's sensitive navigational instruments.

Unbeknown to anyone, the "damaged" plane took off for the long trip to Canton Island where MacArthur was stationed. When they approached the place where the island was supposed to be, there was no island and no land, only miles and miles of blue ocean. The aircraft circled trying to find where they were to land, but finally ran out of fuel and the plane crashed.

All eight men aboard the plane climbed into three small life rafts. They roped themselves together, but had no food or water. They survived for eight full days with nothing but a few oranges and Rickenbacker's copy of the New Testament. Every morning and evening, he insisted upon reading a few chapters and praying. At first, many objected. But as the days went on and the hardships became intolerable, they asked him to pray and read more.

On the eighth day, Rickenbacker was dazed and near death, but he felt something land on his head. Instinctively, he knew it was a seagull. Very slowly he reached up and grabbed it. That "gift from God" began the chain of survival that would otherwise have been impossible. God had heard their heartfelt prayers and had answered them. They divided the bird among them, used its innards for bait to catch fish, and those men survived for 16 more days until they were rescued.

Eddie Rickenbacker was convinced God had heard his spirit-led prayers and had kept him alive, so that he could serve Him for the rest of his life.[332]

A truly spiritual man is one who has a cleansed and sprinkled conscience, a sensitive and responsive intuition and is continually praying and fellowshiping with God in the Spirit. Our conscience tells us what is right and wrong; our intuition leads and guides us; both of which lead us to communion and fellowship with God. *Knowledge of God's will, followed by spiritual understanding and discernment and a two way fellowship, is a life that is both pleasing to God and one that will bear much fruit.*

Sanctification of Our Spirit

Now that we understand a little more about what our spirit is and what its functions and operations are, we can see the critical importance of allowing God to set our spirit free so that it can, once again, lead and direct our soul. *If our spirit does not grow stronger and the soulish things in our lives less and less, then we have not really grown at all. Real advancement is only measured by the growth of our spirit.*

Eloquent preaching, Bible knowledge and spiritual gifts do not increase our spiritual life. Only the cleansing and purifying of our spirit does. In other words, mental knowledge does *nothing* towards increasing a person's intimacy with Christ or his being conformed into Christ's image. Only the Spirit of God can do these things in our lives. Thus, God wants us to be sanctified not only in our soul, but also in our spirit.[333] He wants us not only to know His Life in our soul (the "abundant Life"), but also to have that intimate, experiential knowledge of Him in our spirit (the "fulness of God").[334]

Without the cleansing and purification of our spirit, however, we will never experience a pure conscience, a keen intuition or sweet fellowship with God. As the Psalmist declares, "Blessed is the man unto whom the Lord imputeth not iniquity, and in whose spirit there is no guile." (Psalm 32:2)

Sanctification, as we said before, is simply *the process of becoming holy, purified or consecrated.* It's the process of seeing Christ's Life reproduced in us. The word *sanctify* comes from the Greek root word *hagion* which means "holy place." This is particularly fascinating to me because the verb *hagiazo* (to sanctify) is used to describe the gold that adorns the Holy Place of the temple.[335] (You'll see the importance of this adornment in Chapter Twelve.)

Sanctification is the removal of anything in our lives that is unrighteous or unholy.[336] God is not only working to conform us into His image and to instill intimacy, He is also preparing us for His return as the Bridegroom. (Read the Song of Solomon.)

We begin our course of sanctification when we first become believers, but we don't finish this cleansing process until we are sanctified *wholly--*body, soul and spirit.[337] *Sanctification is simply the process of separating the soulish things in our lives from the spiritual.* God is the only One who can do this in our lives, because He is the only One who knows *what is spiritual* and *what is soulish.*[338] We could never accomplish this separation in our own strength or by our own wisdom. Only God can! And the way He implements this division in our lives is by literally applying Hebrews 4:12: "For the Word of God is quick, and powerful, and sharper than any two-edged sword, piercing even to the *dividing asunder of soul and spirit, and of the joints and marrow,* and is a discerner of the thoughts and intents of the heart."

God is the One who separates, divides and cuts away anything in our souls that is not of the spirit. This is what sanctification is all about.[339]

The Big Question

The question becomes, are we really willing to be sanctified body, soul and spirit? Are we prepared for what that really means?

A dear friend of mine, a missionary in New Zealand, wrote me a very provocative letter about this very subject a few months ago that I would like to share with you:

"I read 1 Thessalonians 5:23 in my daily devotions this morning and it really spoke to my heart. 'And the very God of peace sanctify you wholly; and I pray your whole spirit and soul and body be preserved blameless unto the coming of our Lord Jesus Christ.'

When we pray to be sanctified, are we really prepared to face the standard of these verses? All of us take the term sanctification much too lightly. Are we really prepared for what sanctification will cost us? *It will cost an intense narrowing of all our interests on earth, and an immense broadening of all our interests in God.* Sanctification means an intense concentration on God's point of view. It means every power of our body, soul and spirit must be chained and kept for God's purposes only. Are we prepared for God to do that in each of our lives? Are we prepared to separate ourselves to God, even as Jesus did?

Sanctification means "being made one" with Jesus so that the disposition that ruled Him (God's Spirit), can also rule and reign in us. Are we prepared for what that will cost us? *It will cost us everything that is not of God!*"

Dividing our Soul From Our Spirit

In order for our spirit to be sanctified so that our soulish ways are no longer entangled in our inward spiritual activities, it must be set apart, made holy and separated from our soul. In other words, there can be no mingling of our soul and spirit. Our greatest problem is *impurity*. We have become a "dual" man. Our outward man or soul continually affects our inward man or spirit and this cannot be. Our inward man needs to be released in order to direct our outward man.[340] In other words, our spirit needs to be set free. The only way this freedom is possible is to divide and separate the two.

In order for this division and this separation to come about, we must be able to "see" what God sees in us. *Seeing is the first step towards dealing.* Hebrews 4:12 tells us that only the Word of God can give us the revelation we need to see what God sees. Thus, the method God uses to sanctify our spirits is by the revelation of His Word, with the Holy Spirit as His agent.[341]

> "...all things are naked and opened unto the eyes of Him with whom we have to do." (Hebrews 4:13)

In other words, *to the degree that we allow God's Word and His Spirit to show us our "selves," is the degree to which our spirit can be purified.*[342]

Only God's Word can enable us to see what is of the spirit and what is of the soul, what is carnal and what is spiritual, what is natural and what is of God. Through His Word, God can reveal the motives of our heart and enable us to *see ourselves as we truly are.* Only He can expose, cut away and cleanse that which is soulish from that which is spiritual. *We are unable to do this for ourselves.* Thus, deliverance comes only when the light of God's Word helps us to see as God sees. And, the more of our soul we allow to be stripped away from our spirit, the clearer we will be able to see.

Just Like Separating Joints and Marrow

Hebrews 4:12 points out, "...the Word of God is quick, and powerful, and sharper than any two-edged sword, piercing even to the *dividing asunder of soul and spirit, and of the joints and marrow,* and is a discerner of the thoughts and intents of the heart."

According to this Scripture, our soul and spirit together are analogous to our *bones*, which consist of joints and marrow. In order to divide our bones, they must be broken, *dis-united* or separated.[343] God's Word is like His sword and He uses the power of His sword to cut, pierce and divide our soul and spirit, just as you would divide the joints and marrow of our bones.

To carry this analogy a little farther, we could say that our soul is likened to our *joints*; whereas, our spirit is likened to the *marrow* of our bones. A *joint* is a place between two parts, just as our *soul* is the place between our body and our spirit. A joint is where the separation takes place, just as our soul is the place where the separation of our spirit takes place. *Marrow* means the best part, the innermost part or the essential part from which all of our strength, vitality and life is derived, the richest portion of our bones.[344] And it's the same with our spirit. Our spirit is the best part, the richest, the most supreme part of our makeup, because it's where God dwells. Only as our spirit (the *marrow*) is separated away from our soul (the *joint*) can it be sanctified, strengthened and the Life of God truly come forth.

To separate the joints means to "cut across the bones." To divide the marrow from the joint means to "crack the bones" or to "break the bones." There are only two things harder to divide than the joints and marrow, and *that's our soul and spirit.*

As Job cries, "My bones are pierced in the *night seasons.*"[345] And, Lamentations, "He hath broken my bones." (3:4)[346]

Remember the priests of Solomon's Temple and how they cut, divided and separated the parts of the sacrifice upon the wood.[347] The knives of the priests penetrated to the innermost parts of the sacrifice by dividing the parts as closely united as the joints and the marrow. This is exactly what God must do with us. God's Word must divide the closely joined parts of our immaterial being (our soul) and penetrate even to the innermost parts of our spirit. Only the Word of God can do this. Only God's Word can separate the self-centered things in our lives that are not even perceptible to our own senses. Only the Word can lay our soul open and bare before God.

The deeper God is allowed to go with His sword, the deeper the cross can do its work. He must be allowed to expose even our most private and secret thoughts and intentions.[348] Again, our basic problem is impurity. God wants us to have a pure spirit, with no mingling of our soulish ways.[349]

Once this occurs, our spirit will be free to direct our soul, so it will no longer act independently of our spirit's leading. Every thought, emotion and desire will be governed by the spirit's control. At that point, God's Spirit will be free to communicate directly with our spirit, show us His will and to lead us into intimacy.

"My soul shall be satisfied as with marrow and fatness...."
(Psalm 63:5)

This cutting, cracking and breaking of our soul, however, requires our own willingness. We must come to the altar and we must present our bodies as a *living* sacrifice.[350] He then does the cutting, the separating and the dividing. The deeper we allow the light of His Word--His Sword-- to go, the more thoughts and intents of our heart will be exposed and the quicker our spirit can be sanctified.

The Word of God will reveal even our *hidden* purposes and motives. God wants our will to be His will; our thoughts and motives, His thoughts and motives; and our love, His Love. God's Word will even penetrate to the atomsof our being, if need be, in order to accomplish this union.

God's whole purpose is to refine us so that our spirit will not be influenced and affected by anything in our outward man or in our circumstances. He doesn't want *anything* to be able to move us from the peace and joy of His presence--from oneness of spirit.[351] He sanctifies our spirit and soul so that He might reproduce Himself in us and we might begin to experience His presence and His fulness, *no matter where we are and no matter what is going on in our lives.*

An Example: Tortured for Christ

An incredible example of experiencing God's presence no matter where we are, is that of a Romanian pastor named Richard Wurmbrand who spent 14 years in a Communist prison.

Pastor Wurmbrand was involved in the Christian underground movement. He met with groups of Christians in homes, basements, army barracks and in woods, knowing full well what the cost of his actions would be. The Communists, however, were determined to stamp out these Christians so that they could control the churches for their own purposes. Eventually, the pastor and his Christian brothers and sisters were exposed and captured.

Taken from his wife and son in 1948, Pastor Wurmbrand spent three years in slave labor, three years in solitary confinement and five more years in a mass cell. He was released after eight years, only to be arrested two years later and sentenced to 25 more years. He was finally released for good in 1964. His wife was confined to another prison where the women were repeatedly raped and made to work at hard labor. She was forced to eat grass and rats and snakes and stand alone for hours at a time. At the time of their arrest, their son, only nine, was left to roam the streets of their city.

Many of the Christians who were arrested at the same time lost their faith as they were brainwashed by the Communists. Some even ended up joining the party and denouncing their brothers and sisters. It was a tragic and horrendous time. The human torture was beyond anything one could ever imagine or that I could ever describe. One prisoner said, "All the Biblical descriptions of hell and the pain of *Dante's Inferno* are nothing compared with the torture in the Communist prisons."

Loving God with his whole being, Pastor Wurmbrand would *not* let any circumstance or any emotion separate him from his Beloved. Someone once asked him, "How did you resist the brainwashing?" The pastor replied, "If your heart is truly cleansed by the Love of Christ and your heart loves Him back, you can resist any torture." He went on to declare, *"God will judge us, not on how much we had to endure, but on how much we loved."*

Wurmbrand related that he was not frustrated by all the years that he lost in prison, because he said he also saw beautiful things happen there. He saw great saints and heroes of all kinds, much like the first-century church. "Christians could be happy even there," he said. The reason they could be happy was that they "saw the Savior in the midst of everything."

> "Wherefore glorify ye the Lord in the fires...." (Isaiah 24:15)

The lesson here is, that if the spirit is truly the *master* of the body, then God's presence is always with us, no matter what is occurring in our lives. The enemy, of course, wants to kill us with all the things that happen in our lives, but as we see in the above example, God wants to use our circumstances, no matter how bad, for His glory.

After his release from prison, Wurmbrand went on to write numerous books and is now the head of the international ministry called The Voice of the Martyrs, serving the persecuted church.

Just like the pastor, once we allow the sanctifying process to go unheeded, we can draw near God and dwell in His presence regardless of where we are walking. As Numbers 16:9 tells us, "Seemeth it but a small thing unto you, that the God of Israel hath *separated you* [set you apart] from the congregation of Israel, *to bring you near to Himself* to do the service...."

We can compare ourselves to the priests of Solomon's temple. After they had sacrificed their offerings on the Brazen Altar (and had become cleansed), they were allowed to *enter the Holy Place and God's presence.*

Once God begins to cleanse us and make us holy, we, too, can boldly approach God's presence in the Holy Place of our hearts.

Thus, the dark night of the spirit is a time where God sets us apart (in His loving arms) to make us purified, holy and consecrated.[352] This night of faith darkens us on the soulish level, but it sheds light to our spirit on another level. This night season becomes our own Calvary. Something we must always keep in mind, however, is that after Calvary, there was the Resurrection!

Attributes of a Sanctified Christian

Before we close this chapter, I would like to share a list someone gave me of all the attributes of a sanctified Christian. Test yourself and see how many of these attributes are in your character:

Radiation of Christ
Humility and selflessness
A servant's heart
Innermost heart of joy
Certainty of God's presence
Peace and rest
Abandonment to God
Unshakable trust in God
Love for God and others
Holiness

Other results of a sanctified Christian are: one who is approachable; one who confesses easily; one who is easy to talk to; one who is sensitive; and one who is easily edified.

> "Purge me with hyssop, and I shall be clean: Wash me, and I shall be whiter than snow. Make me hear joy and gladness; *That the bones which Thou hast broken may rejoice.*" (Psalm 51:7-8)

Key Points of This Chapter:

- Our human spirit has three functions: conscience, intuition and fellowship with God.
- Our spirit was once "head" over our whole man.
- Because of Adam's fall, our soul and spirit have become intermingled, with our soul the dominant force.
- God desires to separate our soul and spirit so He can, once again, communicate, lead and guide us through our spirit.
- In order to do this, God's Word and His Spirit must expose our self-centered ways.

Chapter Ten
What is the Dark Night of the Spirit?

Our "Root System"

As we mentioned in Chapter Seven, there seems to be two aspects to the dark night. The dark night of the soul is the time when God focuses on our "outward man" and *what we do,* whereas, the dark night of the spirit is when God focuses on our "inward man" and *who we are.*

Understand that God cannot be "boxed in" and that He will act upon each of us in His *own* way.[353] In other words, He will perform His own individual will in each of our lives as He sees fit. 1 Corinthians 12:11 tells us that God gives gifts "severally as He will" and I believe, it's the same with His plans for our lives. He accomplishes them as He alone knows best.

The difference between the two nights can be seen in the analogy of the fire and the log. In the first night (soul), the fire simply *blackens the log,* whereas, in the second night (spirit) the fire actually *consumes the log.* In the dark night of the spirit, God goes after our our human nature itself. He exposes our "root systems"--all of our preconceived belief systems, our secret habits, our hidden motives and all of our self-centered ways. God wants these things exposed and eliminated also.

Very often we are hindered from a life of freedom in the Spirit, because of what we think and perceive down deep. Much of what we "do" is based upon what we "believe." Our belief system not only undergirds and supports every thought and feeling that we have, it also influences every action we take. Thus, if we want to change our behavior, we must discover what untruths we are believing. Once we can expose, acknowledge and replace these, then our behavior will change automatically. For example, if we believe that God manifests His Love towards us by allowing only "good and wonderful" things to happen in our lives, then when something "bad" occurs, our belief system will tell us that God does not love us anymore. Therefore, it's imperative that we exchange the lies of our natural, soulish ways for God's absolute truth.[354]

So, it's not necessarily *sin* that God is focusing on in this second dark night (most people at this stage already love God and already are walking in fear of Him), but on our *human nature* itself--our natural self-orientation, self-reliance and self-love and all our "natural habits" that do not reflect

Him. These are the kinds of things that God wants to expose and eliminate because these are the attitudes that become the "roots" of our sin. So, the dark night of the spirit is when God fractures our inner being and strips us of our *inward* and sometimes *hidden* soulish ways.[355]

Job is a perfect example of this stripping. He was already daily confessing his sin when God allowed horrendous things to happen in his life. God even comments in the beginning of the book that Job was a "righteous man." He was "perfect" and "upright" and "one who feared God." (Job 1:8)[356] But, in the suffering and dark night that God allowed into his life Job died to his religious ways, his domestic affections, his rigid theology and his misconstrued views of God, all of which hindered his spiritual union with God.

The dark night of the spirit is the actual working out of Hebrew 4:12. It's God's way of dividing our soul from our spirit. It's the gradual penetration of God's spirit through the levels of our soul down to its innermost hidden depths. In this night, God forces us to look at things that we really don't see as being in conflict with God: our reason, our hopes, our affections, our views, our zeal, our narrow culture, our creeds, our churchism, our senses, our religious experiences and our spiritual comforts. These are some of the belief systems that often feed our pride and our ego and our self-life.

Oswald Chambers relates one incident in his own life when God showed him the motives of his own heart. The incident had to do with a time in Mr. Chamber's life where he desperately needed the power of the Holy Spirit and claimed it, but nothing happened:

> "I had nothing. I was as dry and empty as ever--no power or realization of God, no witness of the Holy Spirit. Later I was asked to speak at a meeting, and forty souls came forward. Did I praise God? No, I was terrified and left them to the workers, and went to Mr. MacGregor [his mentor] and told him what had happened. He said, 'don't you remember claiming the Holy Spirit as a gift on the word of Jesus? This is the power from on high.'"

> "...*I saw that I had been wanting power in my own hand, so to speak, [so] that I might say, 'Look what I have got by putting my all on the altar.'*"[357]

These habits and self-centered ways of ours will <u>never</u> change, unless God exposes them and uproots them. Again, these attitudes are not necessarily sin, but simply the result of being who we are--human. These natural ways come from our upbringing, from the influence of others in our life, from our preconceived value systems, from our habits and from our self-oriented thought processes. This "humanness" will never go away; it will always be there. It's called *the flesh*. Nevertheless, God wants to expose it to us, so that we will recognize the flesh and choose to crucify it at the cross. *In order to enter the Holy Place of our hearts where God dwells not only must sin be dealt with, but also self must be crucified.* Then, and only then, can we be filled with the "fulness of God" and begin to bear much fruit for the kingdom.

Examples of Our Self-centered Ways

God wants us to intimately know Him, not only in our soul where we experience His Life flowing through us, but also in our spirit where we will experience His presence. In order to accomplish this, He must <u>not</u> only expose all the *things we do* that are "not of faith" (i.e., our sin), but He must also expose all of our *self-centered ways* (who we are). *Even though they are not considered sin, these natural ways must be rooted out because they are the belief systems upon which we build our lives.* If not crucified, they not only can quench God's Spirit in us, but they also can prevent our intimacy with Him.

God wants all our self-interest, pettiness, spite, revenge, cruelty, foolishness, egotism, possessiveness, addictions and selfishness removed. These self-centered ways not only affect our communication with God, they also obviously affect our communication with others. Until these things are purged from our soul, we cannot have the union with Him that we so long for. We must become detached from all our self-centered thoughts, hopes, plans, yearning, preferences, sorrows, disappointment, praise, blame, success, failure and comforts, and dead to *all* desires but those of God.

As Lamentations 3:40 encourages us, "Let us search and try our *ways*, and turn again to the Lord."

Some examples of natural, self-centered *ways* are:

Presumption. Presumption is a preconceived belief about certain things, events or people. Presumption is taking something for granted or assuming something is true in the absence of proof to the contrary. In itself, this is obviously not sin. It's a behavior common to all of us. However, presumption can often be based on falsehoods that, if not dealt with, can lead us to disillusionment and bitterness, which *is* sin and which *will* separate us from God.[358]

For example: A woman may presume that her husband will treat her in the affectionate and kind way that her father treated her mother. When this proves not to be the case, the wife can easily become embittered and resentful. She had presumed something based on her previous experience that turned out not to be true.

Expectation. Expectation is very closely related to presumption. Expectation is a future hope in either things, events or people. Again, we all have expectations; it's characteristic of our own self-centered human nature. In itself, expectation is not sin. However, if our expectations are not fulfilled in the way we think they should be, they can lead to disappointment and doubt, which *can* end up quenching God's Spirit.

Disappointment. Disappointment is the failure to satisfy our own self-centered presumptions and expectations. Again, disappointment in itself is not sin. But if disappointment is not caught and taken care of (given to God), it, too, can lead to bitterness, resentment and depression which, of course, *will* block God's Spirit in us.

Comparing. Another characteristic of our human self-centered nature is making comparisons. This, too, is one of man's inbred, natural ways and, in itself, not sin. However, if not caught and given over to God, it, too, can open our senses (our soul) up to hurt, envy and jealousy. And these *will* quench God's Spirit in us.

Loneliness. It's certainly not a sin to be lonely. God has created the need for companionship in our human nature. As the Bible says, we were created for companionship and for love. But if we allow loneliness to consume us and rule our thoughts and emotions, it can lead to soulish manipulation and control, which again will quench God's Spirit in us.

There are impurities inside of us that actually rule us without our knowledge. These ambitions, hopes, dreams, goals, desires, expectations and presumptions[359] are beliefs, values and habits that sometimes we are not even aware of. However, they are often the pre-programmed responses upon which we build our lives. Therefore, it's vital that God expose and reveal these things to us, so that we can recognize them and surrender them to Him. Then, our spirit <u>can</u> be sanctified, freed and enabled to lead, direct and guide us in *God's ways*.

> "Search me, O God, and know my heart; try me, and know
> my thoughts; And see if there be any wicked way in me, and
> [then] lead me in the way everlasting." (Psalm 139:23-24)[360]

We might be able to fool other people on the outside by doing "good works," but if our spirit is tainted by any self-centeredness or self-love, it's going to be "wood, hay [and] stubble"[361] in God's eyes. "Every way of a man is right in his own eyes, but [only] the Lord weigheth the hearts [or ponders the heart]." (Proverbs 21:2)[362] Only God can see and know our hearts and only He knows our true motives and intents.[363]

A Deeper Death to Self

In the dark night of the soul, there is a death to sin, but in this dark night, there is an even *deeper death to self. This is our own Calvary.*[364] It's an interior crucifixion of self-love, self-confidence, self-reliance, self-trust, self-will, self- pity, self-grasping and any other self-interest, self-seeking, self-preservation and self-esteem that God sees.[365] Many of these things, as we have previously mentioned, are not conscious to us, but God knows about them and He knows the quenching effect they have on His Spirit and His Life through us.

Through this dark night, God not only wants to show us things about Himself, He also wants to show us things about ourselves.[366] He wants us to see *for ourselves* our self-centeredness and our selfishness. *Until we see these things through God's eyes, we really don't know ourselves.* Many of the qualities that we possess in the "natural" are really contrary to what God would have for us and, therefore, must be eradicated. In order to accomplish this, God must uncover things that we desperately want hidden and covered.[367]

Under all other circumstances, our human nature can hide, but in this dark night it all comes out in blazing color. God wants us to see our true inner motives and see just how far we have fallen from all that He desires for us. He wants us to see how much we still are in love with ourselves.[368] He wants us to see through this night season that we don't have that persistent, on-going faith that we thought we did, and how we we automatically run to "other things" besides Himself to fill our needs. *The more He enables us to "see" ourselves (our own incapacity), the more we'll realize we cannot live without Him.*

We cannot intimately know the One we love, except as we come to know ourselves as we really are. We must see our own nothingness next to His everything. Our soul needs to be completely undone, in order for God to instill "naked faith" in us--*a faith that is built on nothing else but Christ Himself.* This undoing is what this night of the spirit is all about.

An Example: Sarah

One of my favorite stories in *The Way of Agape* is about Sarah, who had this kind of faith--a faith built on Christ alone. A dear friend of mine, Sarah is only five feet tall and weighs about 100 pounds soaking wet. Many years ago before she was a Christian, she found out that her husband was having an affair with a woman who worked in his office.

Becoming violently angry, the next day Sarah marched down to her husband's office and literally beat the woman up.

A year or so later, after the affair was over and she and her husband had separated, God got hold of Sarah and, through a series of circumstances, she became a believer. Sarah was one of those people who immediately laid everything at the cross. She was open to God for whatever He desired to do in her life. One of the things God began to speak to her about was her actions to the woman at the office the previous year. He convinced Sarah that it was His will for her to go back to the office and ask this woman's forgiveness.

I remember being shocked when Sarah called to tell me what God had said and what she planned to do. I don't think I could have done that. Could you?

My dear friend *not only* chose to set aside her own "justified" feelings and emotions (her self), but she was also willing to humble herself, get up and do what God had asked her to do.

Well, when the woman saw Sarah coming, understandably she ran in the other direction. But Sarah pursued her, cornered her and they finally began to talk. First of all, Sarah asked the woman's forgiveness for beating her up the year before, and then she told her that she forgave her for "taking her husband away." The woman was so overwhelmed at what she was hearing, she broke into tears. Sarah sensed an opportunity to talk more and asked the sobbing woman if she would like to go to lunch. Amazingly, the woman agreed.

At lunch, Sarah had a chance to share what God was doing in her own life--how He was giving her such joy and peace in spite of her circumstances. The woman was at a "crossroads" in her own life, so she was intrigued to know more. Those two eventually became friends. (Only in God's kingdom could something like this occur!) I don't know if the lady ever became a believer or not, but the seed was planted. I believe this incredible incident occurred because my dear friend had faith enough in her Jesus to be "obedient unto death."

As Philippians 2:5-8 states:

"Let this mind be in you, which was also in Christ Jesus: Who, being in the form of God, thought it not robbery to be equal with God: But made Himself of no reputation, and took upon Him the form of a servant, and was made in the likeness of men: And being found in fashion as a man, He humbled Himself, and *became obedient unto death, even the death of the cross.*"[369]

In the years since *The Way of Agape* was published, some other developments have occurred in Sarah's life. Her ex-husband now has Alzheimer's disease and lives alone in a 12-foot trailer with no one to fix his meals or care for him. Sometime ago, God impressed upon Sarah's heart to, once again, be "obedient unto death" and be an extension of His Love to the person who had so devastated her so many years ago. *Because Sarah's faith is built upon Jesus and nothing else, when He asks her to do something, she willingly does it.* Sarah goes over to her ex-husband's trailer once a day--every day--and in God's Love and His strength fixes his meals, cares for him, shops for him and cleans his home.

Could you do that?

The dark night of the spirit accomplishes a much larger degree of self-renunciation, crucifixion and abandonment to God. God wants to show us that we don't have all the answers. He wants us to come to the place where we can admit and acknowledge that only He does. He wants to bring us to a place where we can admit only He has the "keys" to the abundant life and the fulness of Christ. He wants to bring us to the place where we can say, "I don't know who I am or where I am going. All I know is that *God is in control of my life and I am going to abandon myself to Him.*"

God wants to take all of us from a position of self-reliance to a position of total reliance upon Him--from self-centeredness to God-centeredness. He wants each of us to learn to detach ourselves from all other supports and all other guidance, so that we can enjoy something that is immensely superior--complete faith and trust in Him. When all our trust and hope in earthly and created supports have been taken away, then we will have no other place to run, except to Him. This is what the dark night of the spirit is all about.

Because God wants to be our sole support, He is burning up all else. In other words, God not only desires purity of life in our soul, He also desires purity of spirit in our heart. Many of us "know" these truths in our heads, but, oh, how different it is when God begins to work these truths out in our lives and our walks.

Life Comes Only From the Cross

God is not only desirous of making us holy by *removing all the sin* in our lives, He also wants to conform us into His image by *removing any character flaws, any belief systems, any habits or thought patterns* that prevent His Life from flowing through us. God accomplished both of these purposes by the cross.

Life comes only from the cross.[370] The cross is the heart of all Love and Love is the heart of the cross. The *foundation* of everything spiritual and the *end* of all things is the cross. The cross is the only way to rise *above* all that imprisons our soul and spirit. The whole purpose of the cross is to purge the soulish things in our lives (empty us out), so that God can fill us up with His abundant Life.

The cross must cut deeply in order to rid us of the things that prevent our fellowship and our life with Him. And, of course, this surgury hurts. If we don't "feel" the cross, however, then we really haven't suffered. Feeling pain is part of suffering, and suffering (barring ourself from sin) is a major part of the sanctification process. Without pain, there is no cross; and without the cross, there really is no exchange of life.

In the middle of our night seasons, we must learn to love the cross, because this is the way God accomplishes our sanctification. *Abandonment to God's will and the cross go hand in hand.* Sometimes we can bear the cross in His strength and proceed the way God desires. But, at other times, when we're weak, we must bear the cross by *faith*. Either way, *we must bear the cross* and allow God to do whatever He must do.

Throughout the Bible, the principle that "life only comes through death" is very apparent. For example, John 12:24:

> "Verily, verily, I say unto you, Except a corn of wheat fall into the ground and die, it abideth alone: but if it die, it bringeth forth much fruit. He that loveth [hangs on to] his life shall lose it; and he that hateth [is willing to surrender it] his life in this world shall keep it unto life eternal."

Just as Christ was raised from the dead after the cross, we too, can "walk in newness of Life,"[371] after being conformed to His death. [372] As we allow God not only to deal with our *sinful acts*, but also our *self-centered ways,* we too, can experience His resurrection Life.   God's desired outcome is that after the death of our self-life, we might "serve Him in newness of spirit."[373]

As Jesse Penn Lewis puts it, "Just as Calvary preceded Pentecost, so *death with Christ* precedes the fulness of Christ."[374]

The cross that cleanses us from *sin* is very different from the cross that deals with our *self.* Jesus made atonement for our sins by shedding His blood for us on that cross 2000 years ago. He paid the complete price and there is nothing else needed for our salvation. But, in order to be sanctified body, soul and spirit, we must also allow God to daily, moment by moment, expose our self and <u>we</u> are the ones who must nail it to the cross (crucify it).[375]

Again, Jesse Penn Lewis expresses it so perfectly in her book *Autobiography,*[376] "A jar must not only be clean, but [it also must be] empty."

Purification of Our Spirit

Only as we, moment by moment, crucify the flesh, can we truly walk by the Spirit. As 2 Corinthians 7:1 exhorts us, "Having, therefore, these promises, dearly beloved, let us cleanse ourselves from all filthiness of the *flesh* and *spirit*, perfecting holiness in the fear of God."[377]

Purification of our spirit simply means a spirit that is freed from all soulish influence. Our spirit gets polluted through our "flesh." God wants to purify and strengthen our spirit so that it can be freed of soulish influences or entanglements, and can, once again, begin to direct our soul. The only way this is possible is by cutting, separating and dividing away anything that contaminates it.[378]   Then we'll be able to have that complete spiritual union with God that He desires and that we yearn for.

In order for our spirit to become experientially one with God, there can be no adulteration from anything that is soulish. He wants us to know His will through our conscience, discern His leading and guiding through our intuition, and begin to fellowship and commune with Him in the spirit. He wants us to have a renewed and purified spirit, like Psalm 51:10 talks about. This is a spirit that has been cleansed of impurities, so that God's Spirit can freely work.[379]

All of our own self-justification, self-defense and self-orientation only betrays an *unbroken and unpurified spirit.* Until our spirit is purified, we will be full of ourselves, full of our own plans, our own ambitions, our own values, our own judgments, our own rationalizations, our own ideals and so on. Again, many of these things are not sin, but nevertheless, because we build our lives upon them, they can prevent God's perfect will from being accomplished.[380]

In contrast to our soul or our flesh being cleansed from sin, which can be *instant* (through our choice to appropriate what Christ has already done for us on the cross), spirit purification can continue for many months or even years. It reminds me of the difference between the "sin offering" (which was given *once a year* on the day of atonement when the priests actually carried the blood of the sacrifice into the Holy of Holies), and the "wholly burnt offering" which had to be offered *daily.*

The wholly burnt offering was an offering that had *already been cleansed*, it just needed to be killed, the bones and muscle separated and divided away, the remainder salted and wholly consumed by the fire. The aroma that resulted from this offering ascended to God in the fire and was accepted by God and well pleasing in His sight. Wholly burnt offering actually means "that which ascends to God in flame and smoke."

To me the *sin offering* is like our once-and-for-all acceptance of Jesus as the atonement for all of our sins. No matter what sins we have committed, past, present or future, if we give them to Him, they are already atoned for by His blood. Whereas, the *wholly burnt offering* (the most common offering) reminds me of our own, moment-by-moment responsibility to present our bodies as a living sacrifice. We must daily offer God our lives and ask Him to expose and to cut away the things that contaminate our spirit. This is what determines our intimacy or our experiential union with Christ. God wants us holy, not only in body but also in spirit, so that we might continually "meet with Him" and enjoy His presence.[381]

The dark night of the spirit is when we get up on that Brazen Altar and, out of faith and obedience, *we don't get off* until God says, "Okay, your offering is acceptable and well pleasing in My sight." The dark night of the spirit is the melting (by fire) of a vessel that is already filled with the spirit. It's being wholly burnt, in order to become "one" with God's Spirit. It's called *the way of the cross.*

How Do We Feel during This Dark Night?

The distress we feel during this dark night is beyond anything that we have ever experienced before.[382] In the past, it always seemed as if God protected us, shielded us and guided us. Now we feel as if He must be angry with us, because He has completely disappeared. As Job lamented:

> "How long will Ye vex my soul, and break me in pieces...God hath overthrown me, and hath compassed me with His net...He hath fenced up my way that I cannot pass, and He hath set darkness in my paths...He hath stripped me of my glory...He hath destroyed me on every side, and I am gone: and mine hope hath He removed like a tree." (Job 19:2, 6-10)

The feeling that we have been abandoned by the Lord is one of the most difficult emotions that we will encounter in this dark night. We feel that we have lost His Love, and there is absolutely nothing we can do about it. The reason this sense of loss occurs is because the work that God is doing is in the *realm of our spirit and not in our soul or our senses, therefore, we do not feel or see Him.* The truth is that God will never leave us or forsake us, but by withdrawing His presence from our senses, it produces the feeling in us that He has done just that.

Job talks about the suffering he experienced when he thought God had withdrawn His presence. "I cry unto Thee, and Thou dost not hear me: I stand up, and Thou regardest me not. Thou art become cruel to me: with Thy strong hand Thou opposest Thyself against me." (Job 30:20-21)

And it's the same with us. Our greatest suffering occurs when we feel God has "wounded" us and then left us and we don't understand why. It's as if He has placed a "cloud" (or a veil) over Himself[883] and has withdrawn His presence from us.[384]

As Gideon questioned in Judges, "...if the Lord be with us, why then is all this befallen us? and where be all His miracles which our fathers told us of?...but now the Lord hath forsaken us...." (6:13)

Abandoned by God

The horror of this dark night is the fear that real fellowship and real love with God is not something that is ever going to be possible again. Our torment is the feeling that God has become our enemy and that He has wounded us on purpose. As Job questioned, "Why have You set me as Your enemy?"[385]

One of the worst mental miseries one can ever experience is the feeling that we have opened ourselves up to our Beloved, thinking He will come and heal our grief, but instead He hides Himself, flies away and disappears. It's the feeling that we have followed God to the edge of a cliff and, at His command, jumped off, only to find He wasn't there to catch us or to protect us from falling. Instead, He has disappeared; He has gone; He has withdrawn Himself from us.[386] Isaiah experienced this:

> "For a small moment have I forsaken thee; but with great mercies will I gather thee." (Isaiah 54:7)

Remember the Shulamite woman in the Song of Solomon, "My beloved put in His hand by the hole of the door, and my bowels were moved for Him. I rose up to open to my beloved...I opened to my beloved; *but my beloved had withdrawn Himself, and was gone.*" (5:4-6)

It seems so cruel to attract us towards a "treasure," which we value above everything else on earth, only to be turned away from it when we come close. The pain this causes is unbearable. We can handle rejection from man, but once we have known God's touch in our lives, to feel His rejection is painful beyond imagining.[387] We have loved Him and walked obediently, yet during the dark night we feel lost and alone.

Job 34:6 talks about an "incurable wound." This is a wound of love and also a sense of loss. The dark night of the spirit is like suffering the *incurable wound*. St. John of the Cross expresses it so beautifully in his poem entitled "***The Bride***:"

> "Where have You hidden
> Beloved, and left me moaning?
> You fled like the stag
> after wounding me:
> I went out calling You, but You were gone.
>
> Shepherds, you who go
> up through the sheepfolds to the hill,
> if by chance you see
> Him I love most,
> tell Him I am sick, I suffer, and *I die*."[388]

These words must express the feeling Jesus suffered on the cross. It seemed like at the most important moment of His life, when He needed His Father the most, God abandoned Him and forsook Him. This is when Jesus cried out, "My God, my God, why hast Thou forsaken me?" (Matthew 27:46) As He hung there on the cross, it must have been the darkest night of His Life. He had never really known darkness up until then--the darkness of desertion. This was the culminating point of His anguish and the lowest pit of His misery. Jesus had lived in constant touch with God. He had always known the Father's conscious presence and His Love. Can you imagine what His sorrow must have been like at God's absence?

But then, Jesus does something that's completely opposite to our human nature: *He gave Himself completely over to God.* "...Into Thy hands I commend My spirit." (Luke 23:46)[389] Jesus surrendered His entire "Self" into His Father's hands. And this surrender needs to be our response also.[390]

Pastor Wurmbrand, whom we talked about earlier, was once asked how the Christians could endure the torture of the Communist prison camp. I loved the pastor's answer: "Christians could be happy, sing and dance there, because they *saw* their Savior in all things."[391]

> "...[they] endured, as seeing Him Who is invisible." (Hebrews 11:27)

Philippians 3:10 tells us that many of us will experience the fellowship of His suffering, which means that we, too, at some time, might experience the feeling of being abandoned and forsaken by God, just as Jesus did on the cross. David in Psalm 88:14 questions, "Lord, why castest Thou off my soul? Why hidest Thou Thy face from me?" People often say that grief of mind is harder to bear than any bodily pain, and that spiritual sorrow is the worst of all.

Charles Spurgeon once declared:

"A man can bear great depression of spirit about worldly matters, if he feels he has God to go on...But, if the Lord be withdrawn...there is a torment within his breast, which I can only liken to the prelude of hell. We can bear a bleeding body or even a wounded spirit, but a soul conscious of desertion by God is beyond conception unendurable."[392]

Abandonment was exactly what Jesus felt on the cross. It was the necessary consequences of standing in our stead and taking the punishment of sin for all mankind. Even though we might "feel" God's desertion, the truth is that *He will never leave us or forsake us*, as He had to His Son *on our behalf*. Most of us have become so attached to the good feelings we experience when we are right with God that when we no longer have those good feelings, we fear God has left us. The truth is that nothing at all has really changed, God is simply teaching us how to have "naked faith" (faith that doesn't depend upon feelings), regardless of the absence of spiritual supports.

Madam Guyon wrote a poem that's very appropriate here:

> "Be not angry--I resign
> Henceforth all my will to Thine.
> I consent that Thou depart,
> Though Thine absence breaks my heart.
> Go then, and for ever, too;
> All is right that Thou wilt do.
>
> This was just what Love intended;
> He was now no more offended.
> Soon as I became a child,
> Love returned to me and smiled.
> Never strife shall more betide
> Twixt the Bridegroom and His bride."[393]

If we insist upon God's presence being "felt" on the soulish level, we will never make it through the dark night of the spirit. Feelings, experience, sight, soulishness, emotions, touch and senses are all areas that God "darkens" at this time. These areas are also the ones the enemy uses to trip us up. During this dark night, when we can't find the soulish "emotional" support that we are so used to, we get more and more frustrated, until we finally let go of God's hand altogether, which is exactly what the enemy hopes we will do! Then he comes in for the kill! Thus, it's imperative that, in spite of our feelings, we constantly choose to believe that our union with God is still in place. The truth is--it is![394]

As God asks in Isaiah 49:15, "Can a woman forget her sucking child, that she should not have compassion on the son of her womb? Yea, they may forget, *yet will I not forget thee*...."

Disappointed Hope

One of the emotions that I experienced frequently during my own night season, besides the feeling of abandonment, was the feeling of *disappointed hope*.[395] The dictionary defines hope as "the anticipation of something or someone." Hope is a desire that is accompanied by confident expectation. It means looking forward to something, some occurrence, some condition, some prospect, etc. It's an anticipation of future events that combines certainty and tension. This is shown in Romans 4:18 when Paul refers to Abraham as one "Who *against* hope *believed* in hope." Disappointed hope would be a desired expectation that never was fulfilled.

When everything around me crashed and totally contradicted all that I thought the Lord had promised, instead of my faith becoming "sight" and giving me hope, I became disappointed, resentful and then even bitter towards God.[396] It's a horrible place to be, because in this state, we're unable to move forward, and yet, we can't turn back either. Hope in God is critical. As Scripture declares, "Where there is no vision [or hope for the future] the people perish..." and "hope deferred makes the heart sick." (Proverbs 29:18; 13:12)

An example of disappointed hope can be seen in the two disciples on the Emmaus Road who thought Jesus was going to redeem Israel and bring in the new kingdom. Instead, Jesus had been crucified and they were crushed and disappointed. As they walked together, they said to Jesus (not recognizing Him), "We hoped that it would have been He who..." (would build the kingdom, etc.). (Luke 24:17-21)

Disappointed hope!

Other Scriptural examples of disappointed hope are: The Jews in Lamentations 4:17, who looked for help "that never came." And David, in Psalm 42:3, where his friends and acquaintances made fun of him and taunted him, by saying, "Where is [your] God?" He made the mistake of listening to them and ended up in despair. "My tears have been my meat day and night..." Finally, in verse 5, he remembers that God is where his hope and faith ought to be. And, he says to himself, "Hope thou in God; for I shall yet praise Him for the help of His countenance."

Why is hope so important? Romans 8:24 gives us the answer. It says, "We are saved [delivered, protected, healed, preserved, made whole] by hope." And, Hebrews 6:19 tells us that "hope is the anchor of [our] soul."

Our hope, as Christians, can only be in God and His Word.[397] We must constantly have hope in God, *even when it contradicts all that is happening in the present moment*. Since Scripture tells us that it's impossible for God to lie, either God *is* who He said He is and will perform what He has promised, or He's not. There is no in-between. We must choose to believe one way or the other. It's impossible to live in-between.[398] Disappointed hope means doing exactly that--living in the middle, halting between two opinions![399] Hope in God is simply the *freedom from wanting anything or anyone but God*. For this reason, Paul tells us that we are "saved" by hope.

To the one who loves God, *hope is promised* and *is demonstrated by a new strength*. "They that *wait* upon [hope in] the Lord shall renew their strength; they shall mount up with wings like eagles; they shall run, and not be weary; and they shall walk, and not faint." (Isaiah 40:31)[400]

The word *wait* here means "to literally bind together by twisting." Hope is the anticipation of all God's promises being fulfilled and, yet, while we are waiting for them to be fulfilled, binding ourselves together with Him so that we become "one."

Hope--confidence that God will do as He says--must be the anchor of our soul.[401] Abraham demonstrates this fact when he "staggered not at the promise of God though unbelief, but was strong in faith, giving glory to God; And being fully persuaded that what He had promised, He was able also to perform." (Romans 4:20-21)

Hope in God is the *opposite of disappointment*.[402] With God, there is always hope in the end![403]

An Example: Joe

Joe Halett, a dear saint who was dying of AIDS, commented about disappointed hope:

"I have laid on the couch struggling with nausea and pain wondering what good could come out of all of this. I wondered where God was in the midst of my sorrow, pain and grief. I know that He promised to be with me in the midst of everything. But I couldn't feel His presence, and prayer was a towering obstacle that I could not overcome.

"I am reminded of Job (though I am not on his level) and how he suffered. The only thing he had was his life and he was loathe to keep that. He lost his family, his wife, his wealth, and his community standing. He even lost his health. Think of scratching off boils with a potchard! His neighbors accused him of being a sinner. They reasoned that since he was suffering so much he must be a deeply sinful person. Throughout the whole book, Job longs to see God vindicate him.

"Then God comes; but He *never* answers Job's question. He simply says that He is God. Job, however, is completely changed by this encounter, 'Surely I spoke of things I did not understand, things too wonderful for me to know...My ears had heard of You, but now my eyes have seen you. Therefore I despise myself and repent in dust and ashes.' (Job 42:3b, 5-6)

"It is the same way with me. I don't know why God is allowing me to suffer as I am. But in the midst of it I trust Him, though like a child, I do kick and scream now and then. I know enough about who God is to realize that no matter how it looks, He is using my circumstances for my good and the building up of my spirit, all for His glory.

"So, come celebrate with me the faithfulness of our God! For ten years he has kept me not only alive, but He has given me hope in the middle of a very difficult situation."

The apostles Paul and James, evidently felt the same way. "Brethren, count it all joy when you fall into divers temptations [various trials]." (James 1:2) Paul's joy and confidence expressed throughout Corinthians, Philippians and Colossians came from the Holy Spirit. And, because God the Holy Spirit was always present, Paul could be joyful and of good cheer all the time he was imprisoned. This meant that to Paul disappointment, despair and discouragement were unnecessary.[404] He felt that to submit to these things would be to dishonor his Lord, who delighted in maintaining an unbroken fellowship with him.

We are to look at our trials in the same way. We are not to look at the things which are seen, but at the things which are not seen, the "eternal things."[405] If our gaze falls from heaven to things around us, however, then there is much to be discouraged about and defeated by. But, as Paul, James and Joe found, if we are engrossed with eternal things, then we can walk on firm and stable ground, always finding confidence and joy in God's abiding presence. When we take our eyes off the Lord and look at the waves beneath us, we will surely be engulfed and consumed.[406]

Our human existence is not determined by the acceptance of the present or by the recollections of the past, but solely by the expectation of the future. People without a purpose or a goal or a vision do "perish" as Proverbs 29:18 tells us. This is why our heart often becomes sad, when our hope is deferred. Hope not only extends in this life, it also implies a future.

Hope comes as a result of *patience.* As Romans 5:3 says: *tribulation* brings forth *patience,* and patience brings forth experience, and experience *hope.* When our hope is fixed on God, it will secure our future expectations.

Despairing of Self

The dark night of the spirit occurs when the worst possible thing that we could imagine happens. As Job said, "The thing which I greatly feared is come upon me." (Job 3:25)[407]

The dark night of the spirit comes when our life is already in ruins, our hopes already destroyed and our hearts already broken.[408] Only God, out of His Love and compassion, knows how much more we can take. Only He knows the perfect timing and the perfect way to show us ourselves and to orchestrate all the events in our lives according to His will.[409] We, of course, feel that we are being unfairly stripped, flayed and laid out bare for everyone to see and that what is happening is cruel and completely undeserved.

Since we are already troubled with inexplicable confusion and humiliation, God's ways become totally incomprehensible to us. The desperation we feel at this time defies explanation and surpasses all sensory pain.[410]

Often we feel like just giving up, shutting down and dying.[411] In fact, we feel death would be a relief. We become numb, conscious of very little, except our own suffering and pain.[412] We hate what we see ourselves thinking and doing, and we feel we are the most miserable of creatures. We begin to experience great insecurity in doing the things that we used to do with great ease. We have the feeling that we are being cursed and crossed out by God, certainly not blessed. Thus, we despair of life itself.[413]

Paul understood this suffering. In 2 Corinthians 1:8 he writes:

> "For we would not, brethren, have you ignorant of our
> trouble which came to us in Asia, that we were pressed out
> of measure, above strength, insomuch that *we despaired*
> *even of life*."

No Consolation from Anyone

Not only do we feel abandoned by God, we also feel that our family
and friends have deserted us. As David cried out in Psalm 69:20,
"Reproach hath broken my heart, and I am full of heaviness; and I
looked for some to take pity, but there was none."[414] And Job experienced
the same thing, "He hath put my brethren far from me, and mine
acquaintances are verily estranged from me. My kinsfolk have failed, and
my familiar friends have forgotten me." (Job 19:13-14)[415]

Not only has our hope been cut off from God, it has also been cut off
from others. No one reaches out to us; no one takes pity on us;[416] and no
one takes the time to listen or counsel us.

> "All my inward friends abhorred me: and they whom I loved are
> turned against me." (Job 19:19)   "For it was not an enemy that
> reproached me; Then I could have borne it: Neither was it he that
> hated me that did magnify himself against me; Then I would have
> hid myself from him: *But it was thou, a man mine equal, My guide,*
> *and mine acquaintance* [my friend]." (Psalm 55:12-14)[417]

Often in the middle of all this horror, our reputation vanishes and we
become unable, for various reasons, to justify ourselves and clear our
name. Thus, we become even more repugnant to our friends and family.
I believe losing our reputation is one of the hardest experiences to endure.
Our reputation is difficult to let go of, because *it's who we are.*

Recently, the newspapers have carried stories about several very
prominent men who have committed suicide. The articles have explained
that these individuals were highly motivated and ego-driven men *whose*
reputations had become clouded and in question. In several cases, the
men's wives had also chosen to leave. Losing not only their families, but
also their own identity, was more than these men could handle. They
chose to "out."

An Example: Ann

Several years ago, a dear sister in the Lord came up to me at a
seminar. She was devastated because her daughter had inexplicably

become estranged from her and her husband and had been spreading vicious lies about them everywhere--throughout the family, at church, at her job, in the neighborhood. As Ann tried to tell me her story, she continually broke down and sobbed. This precious lady said there was no basis or logical reason for the stories that her daughter was spreading. They were all totally untrue. She had tried the best she could to counteract the waves of gossip, but they had already begun to spread like wildfire. This poor woman was completely undone. Her reputation was crucial to her, because it was *who she was.*

I shared with her that Chuck and I, too, had experienced similar public humiliation and the loss of our reputation. I shared about our public bankruptcy, all the bad press that we had received because of it, and all the gossip among our "friends." But I also shared with her what God had shown me through it.

God reminded me that Jesus, too, was humiliated and betrayed by His own family and His friends. His reputation was unjustly tarnished. However, Jesus' way of dealing with these things was not to run around and try to save and repair that which was already lost, but to simply relinquish Himself to God and trust Him implicitly. Listen to Isaiah 53:7 and 1 Peter 2:23:

> "He was oppressed, and He was afflicted, *yet He opened not His mouth....*" "When He was reviled, [He] reviled not again; when He suffered, He threatened not, *but committed Himself to Him that judgeth righteously."*[418]

This needs to be our response also--to commit ourselves unreservedly to God (in naked faith) and trust Him to carry us through.

It's a very painful lesson to learn that we can't always depend upon our friends and our family. How desperately we want to look *horizontally* for the support and the love we need, but God is graphically showing us that we must only look *vertically* to Him for our strength, our esteem and our love. Sometimes our loved ones will be there for us and those times will be wonderful; but, at other times, they will have their own issues to deal with and they will be unable to support us. *God, however, is always there for us and we must learn to look only to Him.*

> "Trust ye not in a friend, put ye not confidence in a guide: keep the doors of thy mouth from her that lieth in they bosom." (Micah 7:5-7)

This is something we all must constantly keep in ming. Just the other day, I was just speaking on the phone to a dear friend who was complaining that the people she works with are sometimes wonderful to her, but, at other times, they are hateful and mean. I told this young girl that we mustn't define our own self-worth by looking horizontally. Again, God is the only One who can give us the *consistent* Love, esteem and comfort that we need. So we shouldn't be crushed when others do selfish and mean things to us. God already told us they would (see above Scripture). We can be assured, however, that in the end the truth will all come out.

The bottom line is, how much do we trust God? Do we trust Him enough to give Him *everything* in our lives? Or, do we only trust Him with the things that don't really matter to us? This is what He is asking in our night seasons. Whether it's our reputation, our job, our marriage, our health, our children or our friends. God's question to all of us is, "Will you trust Me to carry you through?"

A Feeling of Rebellion

Another emotion we'll experience at this time, is rebelliousness. I know this was certainly true with me. As God began to work in my life and everything began to fall apart, I struggled and strained to "control" what was happening. At the time, I didn't realize I was fighting against God. I thought it was the enemy who was doing all of these things. I thought if I could just fight him harder, I would break free. Of course, just the opposite happened; the more I fought, the worse things got.

Now the truth is that the enemy is *always* at work in our lives. But when we have a situation where we have done *all* that God has asked of us (renewed our minds and put on the Armor of God, etc.), and the circumstances still don't improve, chances are these are God's circumstances and He is orchestrating them for His purposes. At this point, we must cease striving and struggling, and simply surrender, relinquish and abandon ourselves to God's will.

There is a fine line between *apathy and passiveness* and *relinquishment and abandonment*. I am not suggesting that we just lie back and do nothing. That's foolishness and certainly, not God's will. I am suggesting, however, that once we have gone through all the doorways that are open and available to us, and if there are no more options left, then we must rest in peace, knowing that God has allowed this particular thing into our lives. And we must know that He will work it out in His timing and according to His perfect will, if we lie still.

Our continued resistance should only prove to us how far we are from truly possessing the courage and the faith we thought we had.

Other Emotional Descriptions of the Night of the Spirit

People have described this night of the spirit in various ways. Here are a few of their descriptions:

"Sorrows of hell"[419]
"Entombment"
"Utter torment"[420]
"Black hole"
"Pulverized"
"Cruel spiritual death"
"Shadow of death"[421]
"Annihilation"
"Emptiness"
"Shattered expectations"
"Engulfed in an abyss"
"Forsaken by God"
"Crucifixion"
"Pangs of death"
"Unutterable sadness"
"Searing loneliness"
"Cut off from God"
"Inner torment"
"Mystical death"
"Brought to nothing"
"Gold in the crucible"
"Sheer wretchedness"
"Unrelenting pressure"
"Solitary confinement"
"Profoundly frightful"

What Do We Do?

Now, the big question, *"What are we to do?"* Many of the things God tells us to do in order to get through our night seasons have already been discussed in Chapter Eight, but here are a few more options. The *essential* answer is always, "trust in the Name of the Lord."

As Isaiah 50:10 says, "...[he] that walketh in darkness, and hath no light. *Let him trust in the name of the Lord, and stay upon his God."* In other words, we are to be still, know that He is God and commit ourselves to Him.[422]

As we said many times before, we are to be content to stay in and endure the darkness. We are to cease our own understanding and our own striving, lie still and let God accomplish in us the purification of our spirits that He desires. Our response should always be, "let it come." Because if we can *face it, accept it and rejoice in it*, then we will eventually make it through to experiential oneness with God. It's only by living through this dark time and discovering what magnificent things this night season can do in our walk with the Lord that we can truly understand why God allows it.

Even though our feelings are raging, our will must remain submissive to God. We must learn to trust in His plan for our lives and remember that there is no other remedy for this season, except complete faith in Him.[423] Now it takes incredible effort on our part to be able to remain faithful and to remain abandoned to Him in faith and Love when the only responses we get seem to be chastisement and rejection. *Staying abandoned to His will*, however, is the *key* to getting through this night season faster and the key to our victory.

What are some other things we can do to help this process along? Here are a few thoughts:

1) See the necessity of letting God divide our soul and spirit and consent to His work being done.
2) Entrust ourselves to the Lord. Let Him use the sword of His Word to do the necessary work.
3) Surrender our whole man as a "living" burnt offering on the Brazen Altar.[424]
4) Reckon ourselves dead to sin and self, and don't let them rein in our bodies.[425]
5) Take up our cross daily in all the circumstances of our life.[426]
6) Seek to walk only after the Spirit by discerning the good and refusing the evil.
7) Be in constant prayer and the reading of God's Word.[427]
8) Carry out in practice what God shows us. Refuse the soulish things and open ourselves up to the things of His Spirit.

In addition, we can:

1) Refuse all things that draw our spirit out of fellowship with God.
2) Choose instead, to keep a renewed, steadfast and upright spirit.[428]
3) Reject any form of sadness, disappointment, expectation, presumption, comparing, touchiness, grumbling, fault-finding, loneliness etc., knowing that these are the things that quench God's Spirit and that the enemy uses to distract our soul.
4) Should these things occur, immediately confess them and give them over to God.

5) Recognize that the enemy can only harass our soul; he cannot get to our spirit. (See more information on "Deceptions of the Enemy" at the end of this chapter.)

6) Finally, reject anything that would hinder our complete union with God's Spirit.

1 Chronicles 28:20 encourages us to always "...Be stong and of good courage...fear not nor be dismayed: *for the Lord God, even [thy] God, will be with thee; He will not fail thee, nor forsake thee....*"

Goal and Purposes of Dark Night of the Spirit

God allows the dark night of the spirit in our lives because *He wants us to experience the fulness of His Life and enjoy His presence through the complete union of our spirits.* Thus, God will allow us to remain in this dark night until His will is accomplished--until our spirit is purified and able to communicate freely and directly with Him. He wants our spirit freed from any soulish entanglements so that it can rightfully rule over our soul.[429] Once this occurs, then He can begin to lead and guide us and teach us "the deep things of God."[430] A purified and strengthened spirit will constantly be sensitive to God's voice; whereas, a polluted, tainted or weakened spirit will miss His leading and His guiding altogether.

We have already mentioned several of the purposes of the dark night of the spirit: to expose our often hidden self-centered ways, beliefs, habits and value systems; to separate the soulish things in our lives from the spiritual; to purify our spirit; and to accomplish a deeper death to self.

A few more goals of this night might be:

Freedom from Self-ownership

Not only does this dark night free our spirit from our soul's domination, it also frees us from self-ownership. God delights to hear us declare, "Do whatever You like with me, Lord, I belong to You. I abandon myself into Your hands. May all that You want and all that pleases You happen.

The dark night of the spirit serves to rid us of our own self-will, self-love, self-interest and self-energy. All our own plans and purposes, our own intellectual and emotional ways, our own egotism and possessiveness and our own inner talking, delusions and fantasies must go, so that we can rest and rely only upon Him. "Any high thing that exalteth itself against the knowledge of God" must go. (2 Corinthians 10:5)

The goal and purpose of this night of the spirit is that we might look only to Christ for our fulfillment, our satisfaction, our security, our strength, our meaning and purpose, etc., and nothing else. God wants us to rest in Him, not only in our *enjoyments* but also in our *adversities*. He wants us to be able to say, may "none of these things (people, events, feelings) move me." (Acts 20:24)

God desires that this dark night free us from all emotional entanglements, so that we can love others unconditionally without the shackles of self. Once we are freed from self, we no longer will have the need to judge others, be over-sensitive to them or over-react to them. Since self has been blotted out, God will give us the ability to love, without fear of rejection or longing for approval in return.

Instill An Unshakable Trust and Faith

The whole exercise of the dark night of the spirit is to instill in us *a real spirit of faith.*[431] The goal of this night is for us to be able to walk trusting in God, without seeing or feeling Him, but nevertheless, knowing that He is there. *When all around us is falling apart, if we can sit before Him without questions and without doubts, then the test of our commitment will be established.*

Only after every support is taken away--house, job, friends, family, husband, ministry, pastor, church, reputation, etc.--does our journey to real faith begin. "[He] made Himself of no reputation, and took upon Him the form of a servant, and was made in the likeness of men: And being found in fashion as a man, *He humbled Himself, and became obedient unto death*, even the death of the cross." (Philippians 2:7-8)

Now, again don't let the thought that God might take everything away from you make you afraid. This is not what Paul means here. He is simply saying that God wants *nothing* before Him in our lives. *If we willingly release these things to Him, He will have no need to take them.* Right? However, if we remain afraid to release them to Him, it shows Him that we don't trust Him and that we do have other "gods" before Him.

So many women come up to me and say, "What about my baby? I'm afraid God will take my baby, if I surrender everything to Him." My answer is always the same. "Who gave you your baby in the first place? And whose baby is it anyway?" It's God's baby! He made him and He gave him to you. God made him alive and He is the only One who can keep him alive. No matter how much you love that baby, you cannot keep his heart pumping and his lungs breathing. Only God can do that!

Our babies and our children--no matter what their ages--still belong to God. They are lent to us by God to enjoy for a certain period of time, but eventually we must give them back (as I learned last year). The safest way to enjoy our babies and our children as long as possible is to immediately (when God blesses us with that gift) give them right back over to Him and trust Him with their lives.

In this dark night of the spirit, God is testing our faithfulness. Will we believe and trust in Him when everything around us is in disarray? Or will we collapse in utter agony and disbelief and turn the other direction? God wants to get us to a place where we will *never* challenge His character or His nature again. He wants to build in us an *unshakable trust and resolve* so that no matter what happens in our soul, we know that He will never leave us or forsake us in our spirit.[432] Remember Pastor Wurmbrand's story. God wants us to no longer put trust in ourselves,[433] in others or in our circumstances, but only in Him. The further removed we can get from sight and from our faith's relying on our sight, the more deeply we will enter into real faith and intimacy with God.[434]

God wants us to cut off any reliance we have on other things besides Himself, and He wants us to get to the point where we can truly say, and mean, "none of these things move me." (Acts 20:24)[435] In other words, we won't allow any of the hard things in our life "move us" from the intimacy that we are experiencing with Christ. This attitude will begin to occur when we come to realize how much God loves us and that everything He allows in our lives is "Father-filtered." The ultimate place He wants us to be is where we can experience an unconditional trust and faith in Him in all things.[436] Then we will be able to say, no matter what is occurring in our lives, "Though [You] slay me, yet will I trust [You]..." (Job 13:15) "...because [You are always] at my right hand." (Psalm 16:8)[437]

The bottom line is, the further removed our faith is from resting on our feelings and our sight, the closer we are to true faith in God.

Abandon Ourselves to God's Will

One of God's most important goals during the night of the spirit, I believe, is to show us the difference between *relying upon our own human expectations and presumptions* and *being completely abandoned to His will.*[438]

The turning point in my own life came when I finally realized that abandonment to God's will and human expectations could not co-exist in my soul. In other words, if I put my eyes upon any other thing (any promises, any circumstances, any visions, any people) other than God and His Word, that human expectation would again become disappointed hope.

Our expectation can only be in God and His faithfulness, not in some promise or vision or prophecy. When we receive God's promises through various means, we often make the mistake of putting our hope in those things, rather than in the Creator who gave them. Our eyes, our hope and our expectation should only be in the Person of Jesus, His character and His Word.[439]

An Example: Oswald Chambers

Oswald Chambers is a perfect example of one whose hope was focused on only the Person of Christ, one who was totally abandoned to His will.

Chambers, the son of a Scottish minister, grew up in Scotland and England, attending the University of Edinburgh. He enjoyed writing poems and is the author of the now famous *"My Utmost for His Highest."* His life can be summed up in seven words: *"Many* people were added to the Lord." This is especially amazing, because Oswald died at a very early age due to complications from appendicitis. However, he is more widely known now and his books are more popular now than they ever were 80 years ago when they were written. Next to the Bible, *"My Utmost for His Highest"* is one of the most highly sought after books of all time. His books probably reached more people because of his early death.

Oswald never taught or talked about temporal things; he always talked about our relationship to Christ. He used to say, "When our hearts are open, then God can truly begin to change them." Like the apostle Paul, Oswald resolved to know nothing "but Christ and Him crucified." His message, just like Paul's, was not in wise and impressive words, but in a demonstration of the Spirit's power.

Oswald felt that God engineers and orchestrates our circumstances. Thus, he refused to worry or judge anything before God's time. They called him the "flaming prophet" because he didn't make his *own* plans or follow his *own* impulses, but was moved only by the Holy Spirit's direction.

Oswald Chambers is a perfect example of one who was totally abandoned to God's will and thus, lived a "restlessly restful life." This example was made possible only because he continuously surrendered his own life to God, and let Christ live His Life out through him by the power of the Holy Spirit.

This submission to God in all things, this abandonment, moment by moment, to His will, is the secret to the victorious Christian walk.

Benefits of the Dark Night of the Spirit

Some further blessings and benefits of the dark night of the spirit are:

A soul that radiates happiness that no earthly force can annihilate.
The promised peace of God.
Experiencing His presence.
Restored discernment, guidance and fellowship.
Knowing God intimately.
More Love and compassion for others.
Personal holiness, giving glory to God.
Deeper identification with Christ.
True worshiper of God.

Another insight that can result from the dark night, has to do with the accurate understanding of our internal makeup. Listen to how Gene Edwards in his book *The Inward Journey,* explains it:

"For a Christian to be denied the spirit's functionings within him is to have an opportunity to learn well just what parts inside of him are <u>not</u> his spirit but are, rather, the feelings of the soul, the rationale of the soul's mind, and the volition of the soul's will. Then to have the intuitive sense of the spirit return is a strong foundation upon which to begin to truly discern spirit from soul."

"...Soul and spirit are so intertwined, so similar in many ways, *yet utterly different in many ways*. Surely one of the major reasons He sends suffering into our lives is to reach those inward parts and cause us to learn a healthy differentiation between the two."[440]

How critical it is for us to discern, for ourselves, what is soulish and what is spiritual. Unfortunately, the only way this is accomplished is through experience.

Warnings and Deceptions

As in the dark night of the soul, there are several important areas to watch out for during this critical night season. Deception often follows the feeling that we have been forsaken by God, so we must be particularly careful. Here are three major areas of concern:

The first area to be particularly concerned about in this second night is *demonic lies.*

When our spirit is cleansed and purified, we will be able to commune directly with God. As we have learned, our spirit is the place where He meets with us and the place He speaks to us. *All communication with God must occur in our spirit, not in our soul. The reason this fact is so important is because the enemy has no entrance to our spirit.*

When we are born again, God gives us a *new* spirit, a spirit that is "positionally" united with God's Spirit, and a *new* heart filled with His supernatural Life--His Love, Wisdom and Power. Be sure to review *The Way of Agape* and *Be Ye Transformed* in regards to this subject.[441] This new heart is "...the hidden man of the heart...*which is not corruptible.*" (1 Peter 3:4)

Thus, our spirit and our heart are incorruptible and inviolate because they now fully belong to God.[442] This means that the enemy has no access here. Our soul and our body, the flesh, however, since they are not yet renewed, remain wide open to the enemy.[443] They are redeemed by the blood of the Lamb, but they are not yet made new by the Spirit of God. This cleansing is what the sanctification process is all about and why it's so important.

Satan's scheme is to get us to react emotionally to all that is going on in our lives. He does this by stirring up the sensory part of our soul with suffering or hurt or doubt or fear or bitterness or guilt or expectation or disappointed hope, etc. If he can stir up some fondness for our self and we fall for it, then he's got us. This is his battle plan: to stir up our senses in any way he can, in order to gain a foothold in our souls, cause a distraction and stop communication with God's Spirit. Then we will be forced to operate, once again, on a soulish level where the enemy can agitate and torment us immensely.

The devil can always interfere with soulish or fleshly communication, but never with spiritual communication. That's why all spiritual communication *should be* Spirit to spirit.

The Lord seeks to work through our cleansed and purified spirit; whereas the enemy seeks to work through our natural and unsanctified body and soul (the flesh). God works on us from the *inside out;* whereas, the enemy works on us from the *outside inward.* When the enemy is able to stir up our souls in one of these ways, we become "sitting ducks" for his deceptions. At this point, he can easily deceive us by giving us soulish visions, counterfeit words, revelations and prophecies, and, even at times, physical manifestations.[444]

In our night seasons, we are very vulnerable because we are so anxious to hear or see something from God. If we are operating only on the soulish level, then we become wide-open targets for the enemy's deception.[445] Because, if what was promised does not occur, on top of everything else we are experiencing at this time, there will be indescribable spiritual anguish. The resulting terror is greater than any other torment in life.

These conflicting soulish communications can snap us back and forth like a rubber band. We feel an unbelievable horror *because we begin to think that God has deceived us*. We feel like God tricked us into believing something, and when we chose to follow it (thinking God was in it), it turned out to be a lie. This type of pain goes far beyond any type of sensory pain we will ever experience.

Horrible thoughts keep coming back to us such as, "If I didn't hear God correctly this time, then I must never hear Him!" This kind of thinking produces a torment that is literally "hell on earth." The enemy makes it look like we have not only been abandoned by God, but now we have also been deceived by Him.[446]

"See what your God did now...He abandoned you...He dropped you." "How can you trust Him now?" "How can you believe in His promises now?" When we are guided only by our soulish senses, this kind of deception is impossible to avoid.[447]

The Scripture very plainly tells us, however, that it's impossible for God to lie.[448] There is only one who "lies" and that's the devil! He is a "lying spirit" and the "father of lies." (John 8:44)

For this reason, it's so very important that genuine spiritual communication with God occur only Spirit to spirit. Then there will be no room for soulish deceptions. (Be sure to see *The Inner Court Ritual* as to how to "renew our spirit.") The more removed from our senses we can become, the less the devil will be able to disturb us.

I would encourage you to set aside any spiritual predictions or visions, prophecies, words of wisdom, and so on that you have been given if you are not sure that they were received by your spirit. Then, if what was "promised" does not occur, you will not have opened yourself up to further disappointment and doubt. (Something that is received in your spirit by the Spirit of God will also be confirmed by His Word.) No matter what physical events transpire in our lives, we must always seek to have a pure dependence upon God's Spirit--Spirit to spirit--and His Word.

The second area to be concerned about is *false visions and false prophecies* during this sensitive night.

God allows the enemy to send us counterfeit visions and prophecies to enkindle the fire in our soul. He is testing our faith to see if we are *able* to be deceived, and also if we will believe the lies of the enemy. Satan wants to use all the things in our night seasons to destroy us; God, however, wants to use these things to crucify our soul, so that our spirits can be strengthened, purified and able to genuinely receive communication from Him.

As we mentioned, the dark night of the spirit is such a vulnerable time for us because we are so hungry to hear "anything" from God. This, of course, becomes a perfect opportunity for the devil, especially if we have given him an opening or a soulish entrance. He wants us to think that God has spoken to us. Of course, we are so desperate that we fall right into his trap. Thus, if we keep our eyes upon what was said, promised or shown us, and not on our Creator and His Word, we will find ourselves deceived.

God is always faithful to His Word and, if He makes us a promise, gives us a vision or a word, and it truly *is* from Him, then we needn't worry; *it will occur in His timing and in His way.*

It seems the closer we get to freedom of spirit, the more active the demonic lies become. The enemy knows that we are getting closer to experiencing intimacy with God and to sharing this newfound freedom with others;[449] therefore, he becomes more aggressive with his lies. Since many of his old ways do not work with us any longer, he spares no tricks in order to excite our senses and destroy what God is doing. The devil wants to block our capacity to receive and enjoy God's presence, and, above all, he wants to prevent our sharing this truth with others.

In order to thwart his tactics and prevent our deception, I might suggest that when we are given a promise, a vision, a word or a prophecy, we do as Mary did in Luke 2:19. She "...kept all these things, and pondered them in her heart." If the things come to pass, then, praise God, they <u>were</u> from Him. But, if they don't, we won't lose our faith because we haven't "acted" upon those things.

A final dangerous area during this critical period of time is demonic depression or the *feeling of quitting and giving up.* This period of time when the Lord begins to take away all our internal supports can be one of the most dangerous times in a Christian's life. Many believers become overwhelmed with discouragement and give up the journey here, which is exactly what the enemy wants. He wants us to be so downcast and so depressed that we'll throw in the towel and totally give up. We have talked extensively about discouragement and doubt. Remember, if we give the enemy a foothold in our soul by entertaining these attitudes, then we've had it. We are "dead in the water" before we have even begun. All the enemy needs is one small hole.

Now, the sad part is that many people give up just before they break through the darkness into the light, just before the victory. People often say that the hardest part of faith is the last half hour, just before the dawn. And it's certainly true here.[450]

Charles Spurgeon once remarked, "The wilderness is a way to Canaan. Defeat prepares us for victory. The darkest hour of the night precedes the dawn." Therefore, unless we look at this period of time through God's eyes (through His Spirit), and try to understand what His overall plan is, we can slide into the darkness and never come out. If we keep our eyes upon Him, like that eagle, He promises that He will eventually *turn the darkness into light.* "Unto the upright there ariseth light in the darkness...." (Psalm 112:4)

The book of Job represents a last day's believer to whom a series of events happened that seem totally opposed to the loving designs of God. Many of us are in similar circumstances. We have been stripped of everything: our children, our homes, our finances, our dreams, our hopes, our ambitions, our views, our feelings, our memories, our self-interest, etc. Although Satan desires to pour out upon us a spirit of fear and despondency at this time, just as he did to Job, God wants to use this time not only to conform us more and more into His image, but also to separate the soulish things in our lives from the spiritual and to bring us into experiential oneness. Then we will be able to "meet with Him" and enjoy His presence and He can give us the Love and the intimacy that we have been searching for all our lives.

As we close this chapter, listen to **Psalm 77**: 1-12:

"I cried unto God with my voice,
Even unto God with my voice; and He gave ear unto me.
In the day of my trouble I sought the Lord:
My sore ran in the night and ceased not:
My soul refused to be comforted.
I remembered God, and was troubled:
I complained, and *my spirit* was overwhelmed,
Thou holdest mine eyes waking:
I am so troubled that I cannot speak.
I have considered the days of old,
The years of ancient times.
I call to remembrance my song in the night:
I commune with mine own heart:

And my spirit made diligent search.
Will the Lord cast off for ever?
And will He be favourable no more?
Is His mercy clean gone for ever?
Doth His promise fail for evermore?
Hath God forgotten to be gracious?
Hath He in anger shut up His tender mercies?
And I said, 'This is my infirmity:
<u>But</u> *I will remember the years of the right hand of the Most High,*
I will remember the works of the Lord...
I will meditate also of all Thy work,
And talk of Thy doings.'"

Key Points of This Chapter:

- The *dark night of the spirit* is where God exposes all our self-centered ways. (He seems to focus on our "inward man.")
- It's our own "Calvary"--where we must nail to the cross all of our expectations, belief systems, hidden motives, etc.
- God wants to purify and strengthen our spirit so that we can experience intimacy with Him--Christ being all and in all.
- This is the time we often feel abandoned by God and despair, even of ourselves.
- During this dark night, God is bringing about the complete union of our spirits and instilling in us an unshakable trust in Him.

Section Six:
Life Within the Veil

"Surely the righteous shall give thanks unto Thy Name: The upright shall dwell in Thy presence." (Psalm 140:13)

Chapter Eleven
Dwelling in His Presence

"Who shall ascend into the hill of the Lord? Or who shall
stand in His Holy Place? He that hath *clean hands*, and a
pure heart; Who hath not lifted up his soul unto vanity...."
(Psalm 24:3-4)

The Journey Inward

Those of you familiar with my books *The Way of Agape* and *Be ye
Transformed* will remember the floor plan of Solomon's Temple. God
dwelt in the Holy of Holies, behind the veil and the priests only had
access to Him once a year on Yom Kippur, the day of atonement.

See Chart A

Because of Jesus' death and resurrection on our behalf, however, the
veil has been rent and the way to God opened. Scripture tells us God, the
Holy Spirit, now dwells in the Holy Place of our hearts. This means that
believers now have free access to God at any time and may commune with
Him as long as they like.[451] Such communion is not only our desire, but
God's will also. The Old Testament tells us that He came precisely to
dwell in us, and to fellowship and commune with us. This intimacy takes
place at the deepest level of our being where God now dwells.

Some call this inward journey towards experiential oneness with God
"Christian mysticism." *Mysticism* simply means a soul *in contact with* or
in union with God. Mysticism has had a very controversial history,
although it did play a vital role in the early church. Listen to how the
Encyclopedia Britannica expresses it, "The mystical aspect of early
Christianity finds its fullest expression in the letters of Paul and the
Apostle John. For Paul and John, the mystical experience always meant
union with Christ. It was Paul's supreme desire to know Christ and to
be united with Him.   Thus, the recurring phrase, "in Christ,"
[throughout Scripture] implies personal union, and a participation in
Christ's death and resurrection."[452]

True Biblical mysticism is simply contacting God in the deepest part
of our being where He now dwells. Christian mysticism, however, does
not mean experientialism. It does not mean visions or voices or dreams,
but simply an *all-pervasive awareness of God's presence*. It means

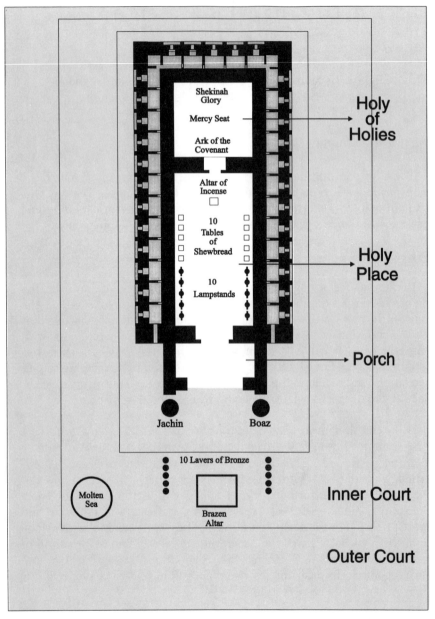

Holy
of
Holies

Holy
Place

Porch

Inner Court

Outer Court

Chart A

experiencing His nearness, His guidance, His revelations, His anointing, His Love, His Power, His peace and His joy. The only way to experience these blessings is not though techniques, introspection or experience, but humility, endurance and love for God.

The question that needs to be addressed then is: "Why are so many Christians running to and fro across the land trying to experience the presence of God if, all the time, *He dwells within?* Why don't we simply turn our attention inward, *not self-ward,* but inward to where God permanently resides?"

As Fenelon noted some 400 years ago:

> "All of us were made for God. But when people are told to seek God *within,* it's like telling them to go to another planet! *What is farther away and more unknown than the bottom of our own heart!"*[453]

I know how difficult it is in our busy, hustling and bustling lives, to abandon ourselves to God and seek to experience His presence. All the noise and clamor of our everyday lives try to constantly turn our attention elsewhere, and it becomes almost impossible to squeeze out time to spend with Him.

Intimacy with Jesus, however, does <u>not</u> mean that we are to turn our back on life and take flight from the world by secluding and sequestering ourselves and seeking only Him. Yes, there might be times that we want to do so but, in general, He wants us to "occupy" by living the reality of this life. *To occupy* means to dwell in or to reside in. Jesus wants us to dwell in and reside in this world, but at the same time, always have an *inner attitude* of communion and abandonment to His will. This "inward" love-relationship is what God desires and the only thing that will bring us the intimacy that we are searching for.

William Law expresses this relationship so beautifully in his book *The Spirit of Love:* "The one true way of dying to self wants no monasteries or pilgrimages. It is the way of patience, humility and (total) resignation to God."[454] God's primary purpose for each of us is to experience intimacy with Him, and then to share that Love with all those with whom we come in contact.

Is it possible in our modern times and our busy lives to live in constant communion and fellowship with God? Will He really teach, guide and commune with each of us personally? Can we actually meet with Him and dwell in His presence?[455]

The Bible says we can, and we must.

> "Surely...*the upright* [the just, the righteous and the straight] *shall dwell in Thy presence.*" (Psalm 140:13).

How Do we Get There?

The Psalms tell us that the only ones who are able to abide in His temple are those who have "clean hands, and a pure heart" and "that walketh uprightly, and...speaketh the truth." (Psalm 24:3-4; 15:1-2) In other words, the only ones who will abide in God's presence are the ones who are faithful, upright, just, holy and straight.   And only God knows just exactly who those ones are.

> "Blessed is the man *whom Thou choosest, and causest to approach unto Thee,* That he may dwell in the courts: we shall be satisfied with the goodness of Thy house, even of Thy holy temple." (Psalm 65:4)

As we have previously shared, once we accept Christ's death on the cross on our behalf, Scripture says we are made "positionally" righteous, holy, just and upright. "Experientially," however, it's another story! Since God is holy and cannot fellowship or commune with anything that is not holy, He must first make us holy through the sanctification process. He must be allowed to show us the areas that we need to surrender to Him so that we can be made holy. "Having, therefore, these promises, dearly beloved, let us cleanse ourselves from all filthiness of the flesh and spirit, perfecting *holiness* in the fear of God." (2 Corinthians 7:1)

Something important to keep in mind is that *the faithfulness, the uprightness and the holiness* that are spoken of in these Scriptures *are Christ's,* not our own. If our outer man (our soul) has been broken and our spirit purified and strengthened, then these attributes of God can also become ours. However, if the soulish things in our lives have not been cut away, separated and dis-united from the spiritual, then we won't experience Christ's character either.

Our journey inward towards "experiential" union with God is what the dark night is all about. This is the time that God burns up and melts away all our egotism and self-orientation and prepares us totally for Himself. All our own self-made strengths, self-oriented energies and self-centered activities must be consumed by His Love.

Again, the first thing we must remember is that *only* God can bring this union about. We are holy and pure only to the degree that we have allow God to cut away *self.* For the most part, after self has been severed, no separation will remain between God and ourselves, and for the moment, we can experience "oneness" with Him. Remember, our biggest hindrance to abiding in God's presence is our failure to recognize who He really is. He is Holy! Therefore, the only way we can approach Him is to become sanctified and holy. Anything short of His holiness cannot stand in His presence.

> "Who shall ascend into the hill of the Lord? Or who shall stand in His Holy Place. He that hath *clean hands* [soul] and a *pure heart* [spirit]." (Psalm 24:3-4)

Carried Like Hot Coals of Fire

Going back to the temple model for just a moment, Leviticus 16:12 tells us that after the sacrifice had been presented on the Brazen Altar, the priests took a censor (a fancy, silver shovel)[456] full of burning hot coals from that altar, and carried them into the Holy Place where they laid them on the Incense Altar.

The ritual of carrying the hot coals from the Brazen Altar to the Incense Altar connected the two altars.[457] The hot coals of fire that fed the Brazen Altar were the *same coals* of fire that burned the incense on the Golden Altar. As we mentioned earlier, the wholly burnt offering on the Brazen Altar testified of the acceptance of the offerer, just as the live coal on the Incense Altar demonstrated that all sin (and self) had been purged.[458] The resulting incense cloud and aroma that then arose was pleasing to God.[459]

The service of sanctification for the priests *began* by presenting a sacrifice on the Brazen Altar in the Inner Court and *ended* by the cloud of perfume rising towards God from the Incense Altar. And the same analogy can be applied to us. Our sanctification *begins* with the offering of ourselves as a wholly burnt sacrifice on the Brazen Altar[460] and *ends* with the cloud of incense and fragrance rising up before God's presence at the Incense Altar.

See Chart B

God wants us to *know* Him, not just in our souls (where we experience His abundant Life through us), but also in our spirits (where we experience His presence). *He wants us to be like those priests who did not stop at the Brazen Altar, but carried those hot embers of a wholly burnt sacrifice right into the Holy Place and presented them there before God's presence as a sweet smelling aroma.*[461] He wants us to willingly allow God to burn up all that He knows is necessary in our souls, so that we can *boldly* make our approach to Him in the Holy Place of our hearts.

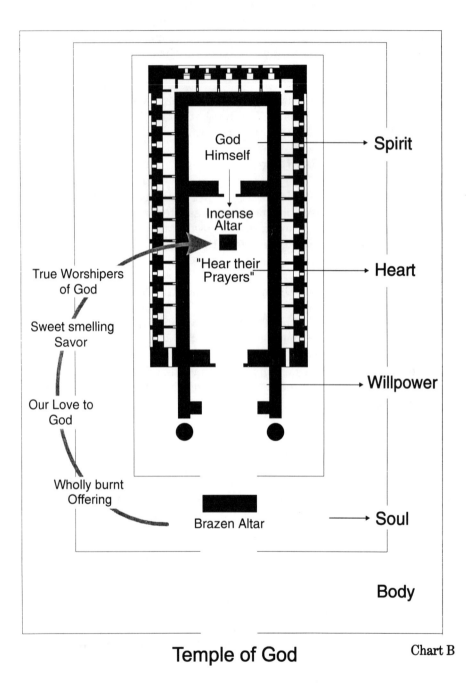

Temple of God   Chart B

The writer of Hebrews tells us:

> "Having, therefore, brethren, boldness to enter into
> the holiest by the blood of Jesus..Let us draw near [to God]
> with a true heart in full assurance of faith, having our
> *hearts sprinkled from an evil conscience,* and *our bodies
> washed with pure water."* (Hebrews 10:19, 22)

Because of Jesus and what He has done for us, the way to the Holy Place has already been permanently opened for us and we are already clothed in His righteousness.[462] But, in order for us to *enter the Holy Place,* we must be like that sacrifice, wholly and completely burnt. (Only the fire and hot coals were carried to the Incense Altar in the Holy Place.) There is <u>no</u> other access or pathway to God. *His death is the provision that opens the door for us, but only by personally passing the place of sacrifice are we allowed to enter the inner sanctuary where He is.*

No self-interests or self-centeredness are allowed within the veil. Only as we surrender our own goals, our own careers, our own future successes and our own desires, does the crucifixion of self become complete. Only as we bring the coals of our wholly burnt lives into the Holy Place and place them upon the Incense Altar, can a sweet fragrance arise towards God. Our soul has finally been melted by the fire of God's Love and we're able to experience His presence. We can then claim with the apostle Paul:

> "I am crucified with Christ: nevertheless I live; yet not I,
> but Christ liveth in me; and the life which I now live in the
> flesh I live by the faith of the Son of God, who loved me and
> gave Himself for me." (Galatians 2:20)

Our intercourse or experiential union with God can only come through the two altars! The holy fire on the Incense Altar, which causes the perfume to ascend, is the same fire which consumed the sacrifice at the Brazen Altar. There is no other pathway to intimacy with God. God makes us one with Himself only through the fire. In the words of Isaiah,

> "Behold, I have created the smith that bloweth the coals in
> the fire, and that bringeth forth an instrument for His
> work..." (Isaiah 54:16)

An Example: Betsie ten Boom

I have been so ministered to by Corrie ten Boon and all that she allowed God to do through her life. But, to me, the real heroine of her stories, and someone we don't hear too much about is her sister Betsie.

In spite of all the horrible conditions of their imprisonment, Betsie communed with the Lord constantly. She was like that hot piece of coal left over from the wholly burnt sacrifice and carried in to the Incense Altar and the presence of God.

Once when Betsie was whipped and beaten almost unconscious by a guard, as Corrie was running towards her to help, she screamed out, "Corrie, don't look at my wounds, look only at Jesus!" Betsie could "see Jesus," even in the middle of all the horrible events that took place in that German prison camp.

Sometime later, Betsie was taken very ill with a lung disease. It was absolutely critical that she remain on a particular medication which she was able to obtain secretly. The bottle of medicine was very small, holding about one month's supply. However, because of Betsie's total and complete abandonment to His will, God performed a miracle! He saw to it that that little bottle of medication lasted for four or five months until she was well.

Years later when Betsie finally died, Corrie described her beaten and swollen face as radiant, full and young. "The care lines, the grief lines, the deep hollows of hunger and disease were simply gone. She was finally happy and at peace--bursting with joy and health. Even her matted and tangled hair was meticulously in place." Betsie was a wholly burnt sacrifice, but she lived at the feet of her beloved in the Holy Place, like that hot piece of coal.

Just as the Incense Altar owed its standing to the blood of the atonement, we, too, owe our standing to the blood of the Lamb and His righteousness.[463] As Ephesians 5:2 exhorts us, "Walk in Love, as Christ also hath loved us, and hath given Himself for us an *offering* and a *sacrifice* to God for a sweet-smelling savor."

Entering His Presence at the Incense Altar

The Golden Altar of Incense, at the heart of the temple, was considered to be the most holy piece of furniture (except for the Ark of the Covenant with its Mercy Seat covering in the Holy of Holies). The inscription on the Incense Altar read, "He ever liveth to make intercession for us."[464] This Golden Altar sat in the Holy Place just before the veil and was called "the Altar before the Lord."[465] Consequently, it was considered to be *a part of, or belonging to,* the Holy of Holies.[466] Listen:

> "And he shall take a censer full of burning coals of fire from off the altar before the Lord, and his hands full of sweet

incense beaten small, and *bring it within the veil*. And he shall *put the incense upon the fire* before the Lord, that the cloud of the incense may cover the mercy seat that is upon the testimony...." (Leviticus 16:12-13)

The Golden Altar was a place of worship, communion and fellowship and it opened the way to the Holy of Holies where God's glory dwelt. There were no sacrifices on this altar, only the offering of incense. *Incense was the result of a sacrifice already given.* "For from the rising of the sun even unto the going down of the same, My Name shall be great among the Gentiles, and *in every place incense shall be offered unto My Name*, and a pure offering; for My Name shall be great among the heathen, saith the Lord of hosts." (Malachi 1:11)

Keeping the fire on this altar continually burning was necessary to symbolize uninterrupted communion and worship of God. Thus, because the priests needed ready and easy access to this altar, they placed it in the Holy Place as close as they could to the Holy of Holies. The priests had to offer incense three times a day as a fragrant memorial of the presence of God (in the morning, when they trimmed the lamps and at evening). Another reason this altar sat in the Holy Place and not in the Holy of Holies is because the High Priest was only allowed to go into the Holy of Holies once a year, on Yom Kippur.[467]

Incense is an aromatic compound that gives forth perfume or a sweet aroma by being burned. The essence of the offering, dissolving into vapor, ascended as a cloud unto God.[468] The perfume cloud symbolized the acceptance of the saint, his high standing and his potential communion with God.

Entering God's presence at the Incense Altar of our hearts is contingent upon the sanctification of our outward man and the purification of our spirit. Jesus' blood gives us the boldness to enter, but *our sanctification allows us to experience His presence.*[469] The veil has already been rent, so there is no barrier hindering our approach to Him.[470] Again the basis of our fellowship is dependent upon the cutting away of the soulish things in our lives. As Hebrews 10:19 and 22 urges, "Let us draw near with a true heart [a cleansed and purified heart] in full assurance of faith...[with] boldness to enter into the holiest...."

The willing surrender of our sin and self becomes our sacrifice and offering. "And He shall sit like a refiner and purifier of silver; and He shall purify the sons of Levi, and purge them like gold and silver, *that they may offer unto the Lord an offering in righteousness.*" (Malachi 3:3 emphasis added)

Jesus has always been before the Lord on our behalf.[471] Romans 8:34 validates this. But now that we have been allowed into the Holy Place, we will be able to experience His presence going before us and giving us peace and rest.[472]

The Place God Meets with Us

The Old Testament precept "Thou shall put it [the incense] *before* the vail that is by the ark of the testimony...*where I will meet with You,*" was fulfilled by putting the incense on the Golden Altar. (Exodus 30:6, 36) We are enabled to "meet with God" when we bring the hot coals of our wholly burnt lives to the incense altar of our hearts.

One of the reasons why God has us in the sanctification process in the first place is so that He might bring us near to Him. Listen to Numbers 16:9: "Seemeth it but a small thing unto you, that the God of Israel *hath separated you* [consecrated you] from the congregation of Israel, *to bring you near to Himself....*"[473]

Scripture tells us that "God will bring us near to Him" and "meet with us" at three different places: at the Ark of the Covenant (Exodus 25:22); at the Incense Altar (Exodus 30:6, 36); and at the Brazen Altar (Exodus 29:42). Therefore, even though we might "feel" abandoned and alone when we are going through our own night seasons, we must remember that *God is always in the midst of the fire with us,* just like He was with Moses, Jonah, Joseph, and Elijah. And just as He promised never to leave them, so He promises never to forsake us.

An Example: Amy Carmichael

Amy Carmichael learned early on in her life that closeness and nearness to the Holy Spirit was indispensable in an intimate walk with God. The phrase "grieve not the Holy Spirit" became very important to her, because she never wanted to lose His nearness and His presence.

Appointed as a missionary to Japan, Amy then spent the next 55 years as a missionary in India. In India, she became aware of an unfolding sense of a "Presence" or a "Listener," as she called Him. It seemed to her that God was looking for someone to listen to Him and commune with Him. She realized that God had created us for His pleasure, both to dwell in us and to fellowship with.

Any was called "the lover of children," because the Jesus in her reached out through her to the children. Children always seem to know the "genuine" article, they know when it's the real article and when it's not. Amy felt Jesus weep for the children she ministered to. She learned to sing to them and they loved her for it.

One of her favorite verses was, "In all things [God and His Spirit shall] have the preeminence." (Colossians 1:18) The source of her radiant, powerful and overflowing life came from her intimate walk with God and her being able to constantly sense His presence.

Amy loved to write poetry such as the following:

> "Give me the Love that leads the way,
> The faith that nothing can dismay,
> The hope no disappointments tire,
> The passion that will burn like fire,
> Let me not sink to be a clod:
> Make me Thy fuel, Flame of God."[474]

Sweet Aroma of Love

When sin and self no longer form a barrier preventing our approach to God, then a sweet aroma comes up before Him.[475] We will have been wholly burnt and, thus, His Life can come forth as a sweet savor.

Sacrificing ourselves as a wholly burnt offering on the Brazen Altar, carrying that hot piece of coal as a symbol of our burnt and crucified life, placing it on the Incense Altar, and watching as the perfume and the fire become one, is a graphic picture of how we become "experientially" one with God. This is what it means to truly love Him.

The verb *agapao* (to love) in Scripture means "what we totally give ourselves over to"; what we put first in our lives; or *what we become "one" with*.[476] As we offer God the incense of our wholly burnt lives, the cloud of our human fragrance mingles with the cloud of His divine glory and we do become "one" just like the fire and the log. The cloud enveloping the offering means that God has accepted the love gift of our lives. Remember the pillar of cloud and fire in the Old Testament?[477] The intertwined and intermingled cloud and fire always stood as a symbol of God's presence. That same pillar of cloud and fire, the Shekinah Glory, dwelt in the Holy of Holies over the Ark of the Covenant. When the incense was offered, the perfume cloud intermingled with the Shekinah Glory, becoming a pleasing aroma unto God.[478]

For this reason, I believe, the Incense Altar represents our "union with" or our "experiential oneness with" God.

Incense is also always associated with our prayers.   Throughout Scripture our prayers are said to ascend to God like a sweet incense.[479] Listen to Revelation 8:3, "And another angel came and stood at the altar, having a golden censer; and there was given unto him much incense, that he should offer it with the prayers of all saints upon the *Golden Altar which was before the throne.*"

An Example: Incense for Diana

Years ago, when Diana Bantlow's cancer was made public, many of us began praying around the clock for her. One of Diana's dear friends, Dottie, prayed faithfully every night for her just before she went to bed.

One particular night, Dottie's prayer time was especially anointed, so she stayed with the Lord longer than usual. After she was finished, she went around the house locking up and turning all the lights off. As she did, she noticed a very strong smell of incense throughout the house. Dottie never used incense, nor did she have any in the house, so she was very puzzled as to where the aroma might be coming from. She opened all her cupboards, looked in all her closets and even in her bathroom shelves, but found nothing.

Finally, the scent bothered her so much that she decided to wake her husband and see if he, too, smelled it. He definitely did. Together, they began to search the house, every room, every closet, every place they could think of where this aroma might be coming from. By this time, it was so strong that they couldn't stop until they found its source.

After almost an hour of searching, they finally gave up and went to bed. In the morning, the aroma was gone. But, during that day, God confirmed to Dottie through two different sources that the incense was a result of her prayers for Diana, they had been heard and that they were pleasing to God. Without her even being aware of it, dottie had been obedient to the Psalmist's command:

> "Let [our] prayer be set forth before Thee as incense; and
> the lifting up of [our] hands, as the evening sacrifice."
> (Psalm 141:2)[480]

I've never forgotten that story.

When we become experientially one with God's Spirit, He will hear our prayers, because they are now in accordance with His will. We can ask anything we want, because we will be asking *in His Name* and *in His Character.* Thus, we can be assured that He not only will hear us, but that He will also answer us in His timing and in His way.[481]

Fragrance of Christ

Incense in the Bible symbolizes the *fragrance of a life*. A bad savor means an unholy or impure life; a good savor means a holy and pure life.

In 2 Corinthians 2:14-16, Paul tells us that God manifests the savor of His knowledge by us in every place. In other words, when we are loving God and others as He desires, we will manifest His Life and His fragrance wherever we go. Now, to some people, this will be the "savor of Life" and they will be drawn towards Christ as they fellowship with us. To others, however, the fragrance of our life will be the "savor of death," because those people are offended at Christ in us, and often they will flee from our presence.

I knew a man who loved Jesus so much that he was a continual offense to his non-believing family. He never really did anything outwardly to insult them or offend them, yet the aroma of Christ's Life through him made him offensive to them. It's helpful if we can understand this, so if others possibly find us offensive, it's not necessarily us they are objecting to, but *Christ in us*.

Incense stood for a life that was pure and holy and good. As Exodus 30:36 tells us, "It [the incense] shall be unto you most holy." When we love God (and become "one" with Him), then we not only radiate the fragrance of His Life, but also the "beauty of His holiness." As 1 Chronicles 16:29 commands:

> "Give unto the Lord the glory due unto His Name; bring an [incense] offering, and come before Him [His presence]: worship the Lord in the beauty of holiness."

Something very important to note here is that holiness belongs only to Jesus. When we are cleansed, however, He can shine His Light through us and we become "partakers of His holiness."(Hebrews 12:10) Consequently, a true worshiper is one who draws near to God at the Incense Altar of his heart. True worship can occur *only* in our spirit and *only* if we are holy. This is what is meant by "worshiping God in spirit and truth."[482] (We will talk further about worshiping God in "the beauty of holiness" in the next chapter.)

I find it interesting that all of Israel had access to the Outer Courts of Solomon's Temple, but only the sanctified priests had access to the Incense Altar in the Holy Place. And it's the same with us. The whole redeemed Church of God has access to the Outer Courts and the Brazen Altar, but only the sanctified and consecrated believers have access to the Incense Altar of their hearts where God now dwells.

Strange Incense

Before we move on, it's also interesting to note that the Old Testament talks about offering "strange incense" to God. (Exodus 30:9) Strange incense, according to the Bible, is a perfume which people made for themselves, in order to satisfy their own desires and their own requirements.

Leviticus 10:1 tells us the story of Aaron's sons who offered "strange incense" before the Lord. Verse 2 says that God was so displeased over their deception that fire went out from Him and devoured them.

Numbers 16 also relates the story of Korah and 250 "renowned" men from Israel who manufactured their own incense to offer the Lord. These men had arrogantly confronted Moses for "taking too much upon himself." The truth was that the Lord *had* sent Moses to do all that He had done; he did not do them of his own mind. Nevertheless, these men did not believe Moses, nor did they trust God. Therefore, Moses directed these men to take their censors, put their own incense in them and bring them before the Lord and He would show who was "holy" and who was not! Korah and his men soon found out what happens to those who make their "own incense" for their own desires. The ground literally opened up and swallowed Korah, his cohorts and even their families and houses. Then fire came down from the Lord and consumed the other 250 men who had offered the "strange" incense.

God makes the rules. All of them are written in His *instruction manuel*--the Bible. Our only responsibility is to follow His rules--not make up our own!

Experiential Oneness with God

Our soul's natural strength is broken and dealt with on the Brazen Altar, but it's not until we reach the Incense Altar that God can truly rule and reign in our lives. *The Incense Altar symbolizes or represents our experiential union with God, the complete union of our spirit with His.* It represents our oneness, our communion and our intercourse with Him. Complete union of spirit means that our spirit has been sanctified and strengthened, so that it is now able to freely direct our soul in all things.

This deeper experiential merging of our spirit with God's is what God desires with each of us. This is why it's crucial to allow Him to burn up all that He needs to in our souls, so this complete union can take place.[483] Two containers, or two wills, in one body do not work! God wants us "one," not only in *fact*, but also in *experience*.

This union becomes the climax of our relationship with Him. We have finally not only positionally but *experientially* become one. (Even if it's just for a moment.) This is the completion, the perfection and the fulness of God that He has designed for every one of us. Everything on the *inside* and on the *outside* has finally become Christ's.[484]

Now, please don't misunderstand me. We never become God or even "little gods" because of this union. Just as the perfume retained its own unique properties, but was simply united with, mingled with, fused with or joined with the cloud of fire, so we retain our individuality and our humanness when we are united with God.

As John 17 expresses it, "...That they all may be one, as Thou, Father, art in Me, and I in Thee, that they also may be *one in us*...Father, I will that they also, whom Thou hast given Me, *be with Me where I am,* that they may behold My glory, which Thou hast given Me...." (verses 21, 24)

An Analogy: The Act of Love

In review, when we are initially born again, God's Spirit unites with our spirit and we become one spirit with Him.[485] "Experientially," however, in order to enjoy the completeness, the perfection and the oneness of spirit that God has designed for each of us, we must become holy as He is holy through the sanctification process.[486]

A perfect analogy of this oneness might be "the act of love" in a marriage. In a marriage, wives can make love, enjoy it and *even* bear children without ever having experienced the fulness, the intimacy and the ecstacy of complete union with their loved one. *Positionally,* yes, they are one with their husbands, but experientially they don't have the slightest clue as to what it means to truly be "one."

As I travel and teach across the country, I am constantly amazed at how many wives come up to me and share this very thing. They love their husbands, they are happy in their marriages and they have children, *but they never have really experienced intimacy with their husbands.* They have never really known the indescribable euphoria that occurs when two people truly become one, not only just physically, but also spiritually and emotionally. All other thoughts, worries, pressures, circumstances are, for a moment, set aside as two people are completed-- body, soul and spirit. God has designed the marriage act as a little bit of heaven here on earth.

In like manner, with our union with Christ, we can be born again and possess Christ's Life and His Spirit in our hearts, but not until we fully abandon ourselves to Him will we ever experience the ecstacy that goes along with full and complete union of our spirits. This kind of intimacy is what real love is all about!

God uses *marriage* throughout Scripture to convey His most intimate truths. Therefore, I don't believe it's an accident that the different aspects of the marriage "act" perfectly exemplify the differences between having *beginning knowledge of God* through salvation and *knowing Him intimately* through sanctification.

Throughout Scripture, marriage is used to symbolically represent our union with God. This is one of God's "word pictures." It's a piece of life that we can all understand and relate to. I believe God designed the euphoria of the climax of the marriage act to be exactly what He desires our intimacy with Him to be like. Only when we *experience* the union of our spirit with God's, will our spiritual marriage be completed or perfected so that we are able to know and understand the fulness of Christ that most of us have only read about. As Ephesians and Colossians exhorts us:

> "...know the Love of Christ, which passeth knowledge, that
> ye might be filled with all the fulness of God." (Ephesians
> 3:19) And that, "Christ [may be] all, and in all." (Colossians
> 3:11)[487]

At this point, we are united, fused and intermingled--the fire and the wood, and the fire and the incense cloud.[488] We are being loved and we are loving just as He desires. We have become enveloped and possessed by God.

Again, please don't misunderstand me. We <u>never</u> experience this complete union of our spirits permanently. There will always be more sin and self for us to deal with. Only Jesus could enjoy permanent union with the Father because He was God. *Full, eternal and incorruptible union happens only when we reach heaven.* But we <u>can</u> begin to experience here on earth the completeness and the fulness of Christ that Scripture talks about in an ever-increasing depth.[489] If we deal with the things that God daily shows us, then we will be able to experience His presence more and more. This "perfection" is the finished product that Jesus said was the goal of our instruction.[490]

An Example: Madame Guyon

Few people in history have attained the high degree of spirituality that Madame Guyon managed to reach and write about. This godly lady, who lived in the 1600s, was persecuted every step of her life and her career. She was forsaken by all her friends and acquaintances, betrayed by her family and even deserted by the church. She was born and reared in the Roman Catholic Church, yet she was tormented, afflicted, maltreated, abused and imprisoned for years by the same. Her sole crime was that of supreme devotion and unmeasured attachment to Christ. She loved Him with her whole being.

As a solitary woman, it's amazing to see how she subverted all the machinery of the kings, laughed to scorn the papal inquisition and silenced and confounded the more learned religious establishment of the day. While she was enjoying oneness with Christ, they were floundering in darkness. The only dignitary that opened his heart to her and extended a hand was Archbishop Fenelon. Over his objections, the church imprisoned her for ten years.

Her punishment was to write out her view of Christianity. They had intended to try her in court on these records. God, however, had another plan. He used her writings to preserve her thoughts and deeper experiences with Christ for posterity. Her writings were subsequently put into many books--*Experiencing the Depths of Jesus Christ, Union with God, Final Steps in Christian Maturity, Song of the Bride*, just to mention a few.

In Jeanne Guyon's books and St. John of the Cross's books I first heard the term "the dark night of the soul." Even though Madame Guyon loved God more than anything else in the world, God allowed her to experience a very great "night season." Thus, whenever I think of someone who truly knew what it meant to be "one" with God and experience His fulness, Jeanne Guyon is the one who comes to my mind. She shows us that no matter what our circumstances are, we can still experience a oneness with God in our spirit.

Perfection ("Completion")

Scripture tells us that suffering is what makes us "perfect"[491] and "complete," because, through it, we learn to bar ourselves from sin and self, and cling to God.[492] Just as Jesus became "perfect" by barring Himself from following His own ways and clinging to God, so can we.[493] As God begins to separate and cut away all of our self-centered ways, it will hurt and we will suffer. But until our souls are melted, annihilated and freed from every soulish thing, the consummation of our marriage with God will not occur.[494] The only way completion and oneness with God are accomplished is by abandoning ourselves to Him in all things. 1 Peter 5:10 declares that, "The God of all grace, who hath called us into His eternal glory by Christ Jesus, *that ye have suffered awhile*, [will] make you perfect, stablish, strengthen, settle you."

The word *perfection* is *theleioo* in the Greek and it means to achieve some goal or to attain some standard; to make a full end; to be brought into completion; to be full grown; and to be lacking nothing. When we are "perfected," our marriage with Jesus will be truly consumated.[495] Christ will have become our "all and in all."[496]

The definition of perfection that I really like is *to be exactly what God is looking for.* Perfection means *everything on the inside and everything on the outside has been changed into God's image.*[497] When our union with Him is complete, perfect, final and full grown,[498] we won't necessarily understand all of God's designs, but simply be willing to submit to them. This is the "fulness of God" that we have spoken so much about and that Ephesians 3:19 refers to.

Perfection describes not only a sanctified soul, but also a purified spirit. Again, only One has ever reached this spiritual level completely and that, of course, is Jesus. *Perfection can only be found in Him.*[499] The reason we will <u>never</u> reach this state of perfection or total completion here on earth is because we are not God, we are human, and we will always be human. In other words, we will always have the flesh to contend with. No matter how "holy" we become, our flesh will always remain intrinsically imperfect.

The Bible tells us, however, that *Jesus* is our example and that we are to emulate Him. We are to follow in His footprints. Jesus experienced this perfection and the "fulness of the Godhead." (Colossians 2:9) And John 1:16 tells us that *"of His fulness have we [also] received."* In other words, we are to strive in a positive sense for this *completion* and this *perfection* in our own lives--"to be exactly what Christ is looking for." Everything on the *inside* and everything on the *outside* should be changed into His image.

As we learn to "bar ourselves" from following sin and self, and learn, instead, to surrender our imperfections to the cross, we will "taste" more and more of this fulness, this completeness and this perfection of Christ. And, the more we taste, the more we will want.

Knowing God Intimately

Experiencing God's fulness is exactly what it means to have intimate knowledge of Him. In the Bible, there are two Greek words for the word know. They are *ginosko*, which means "beginning knowledge," and *oida*, which means "intimate, experiential knowledge."

For years, I've experienced intimate knowledge of God's supernatural Life flowing through my soul. *The Way of Agape* and *Be Ye Transformed* both cover this subject in detail. I've experienced His *Agape* Love enabling me to love people that I did not naturally care for; His Wisdom giving me understanding in areas that were completely "dark" for me; and His Power giving me His strength to do things I never could do in my own ability. But, I never imagined the intimacy, the fulness and the unsurpassed peace and joy and rest that would come as I have begun to intimately know Jesus' presence in my spirit. It's unparalleled to anything I have ever experienced before.

> "Thou wilt show me the path of life. *In Thy presence is fulness of joy*; at Thy right hand there are pleasures for evermore." (Psalm 16:11)

Intimacy means a constant, continuous communion and fellowship with the Holy Spirit. It's experiencing His leading, His guiding and His anointing continually. Intimate knowledge of God is dwelling in His presence, no matter what our circumstances are, and experiencing a peace and a joy that passes all human understanding.

Like Madame Guyon, Betsie ten Boom and Richard Wurmbrand, nothing else matters in life once we have come to experience the ecstasy and the euphoria that surrounds us when we abide in the presence of Jesus, the God of the Universe. The Psalmist says, "His loving-kindness [becomes] better than life."(63:3) Experiencing intimacy with God is truly the climax of our Christian walk.

Sanctification is simply the preparation of the saint for heaven. *Once we are sanctified--body, soul and spirit--heaven will simply be a continuation of the intimacy with Christ that we have already begun here on earth.* Thus, we are the ones who determine the degree of intimacy we will have with God. We can be as close to Him as we *choose* to be. If we want intimacy, the question becomes, are we willing to pay the price for it? It's costly.

As Jesus tells us in Luke 9:62, "No man, having put his hand to the plough, and looking back, is fit for the kingdom of God."

David Hazzard expresses it this way:

"Determine in your heart that you want to reach the highest place in God. By that, I mean, learning how to live each day in pure, *loving oneness* with Him. And once you have set your heart on this upward path, *you will have to choose it every day, and many times during each day.* For indeed your desire to rise to higher places in spirit will face many obstacles."[500]

Intimacy comes from two acts: an increased cleansing of our soul from sin, and a purification of our self-centered ways (in our spirit).[501] God's Love is the only constant that will draw us to this kind of intimacy. And God's Love is the only power that will keep us there. Nothing will ever fulfill us or give us the security and identity, meaning and purpose like intimacy with the Creator of the universe. Everyone else in our life will let us down because they are, like us, human. Only God can be that "perfect" Father, Friend, Companion, Lover, Spouse, who will never let us down, never leave us or forsake us.

Intimacy has four degrees: 1) Approaching the mountain, but unable to ascend (Exodus 19:11-12); 2) Having an intimate vision of God, but that's all (Exodus 24:9-11); 3) Proceeding halfway up the mountain (Exodus 24:13-14); and, 4) *Seeing God face to face* at the top of the mountain (Exodus 33:11).[502]

Is experiencing this fourth kind of intimacy a prize worth sacrificing everything? This is a question only *you* can answer before the Lord. *We'll be able to "see" God only in proportion to how much sin and self we have lost*!

As we mentioned before, God often uses the marriage and the sexual intimacy in marriage to convey His most intimate truths. The different aspects of the marriage act, I believe, describe the difference between simply having *beginning knowledge* of God and experiencing ultimate, *intimate knowledge* of Him.[503]

Do We Really "Know" God?

First, we must ask ourselves is it even possible to intimately know the God of the universe? Can we truly fellowship with Him moment by moment? Can we really experience His presence?

Again, the Bible says we can. And we must.

Isaiah 5:13 tells us that God's people will "go into *captivity*" if they don't know God intimately. And Hosea 4:6 warns us that if there is no intimacy with God among His people, *"they will be destroyed."* "Captivity" simply means bondage. It means that the soulish things in our lives are preventing us from experiencing the full union with Christ that God desires and, because of it, we'll be "destroyed."

If we are really honest with ourselves, many of us would admit that we have no idea what the fulness of Christ is or what it means to know God *intimately*.

Listen to what Alan Redpath says in his book *Victorious Christian Faith:*

> "I had known, believed and preached for many years...[504] but I had become more concerned about knowledge of faith than about knowledge of God.[505] To me God had become more of a theoretical and doctrinal figure, than a saving, experiential companion."

Many Christians feel the same way. They have become born again. They know they are "positionally" united with God. They even experience some enjoyment with Him and have borne some fruit. But very few have any clue as to what intimate knowledge of God really means. Very few really understand what it means to dwell in His presence, or to experience the ecstacy of seeing Him.

As Ezekiel 33:31 declares, "...they come unto Thee...they sit before Thee as My people, and they hear Thy words, but they will not do them: *for with their mouth they show much love, but their heart goeth after their covetousness.*"

We often do just the same. Oh, yes, we all *talk* about "intimacy" and many of us pray earnestly for it and exhort others to it, but how many of us *really* have that daily, personal, intimate union with God that the Bible talks about? How many of us are willing to be stretched? How many of us are willing to "off load" the *baggage* that prevents our personal growth?

Most of us do not know God on a personal, daily, intimate basis. We know what we have read and been told about Him, but it's an intellectual knowledge that lacks spiritual experience. Thus, we don't "act" like we believe in Him. He is not the most important one in our lives. Our spouses, our children, our families, our relationships, our homes, our jobs, our goals and our aspirations are! *This* is the reason we are faltering, failing and getting captured and destroyed when our faith is tested to the max. And this is why we are crumbling in the night seasons.

As I look at the church as a whole today, I grieve because believers are only experiencing a fraction of the *fulness of God* that the Bible speaks about.[506] As Oswald Chambers lamented (speaking about the Christians he knew at the time):

> "I knew *no one* who had what I wanted...but I [also] knew that if what I had was all the Christianity there was, [then] the thing was a fraud."[507]

And he is so right. So many churches strive not for intimacy with God, but rather for experience, power, prophecy and miracles; for rituals and methods; for debates over doctrine; for the business of church building and all the other soulish endeavors of intellectualism and impressive preaching. These are some of the substitutes that we have entangled ourselves in that have replaced our own personal, intimate relationship with God. Consequently, many of us know *about* Christ and we possess His Name, we have that "beginning knowledge", but very few really intimately *know Him*. We are not yet experientially "one" with Him.

Therefore, because God loves us so much, He often takes matters into His own hands and begins to allow heartache into our lives that will put us on the journey towards "intimacy" and towards experiencing His fulness. God desires to commune and fellowship with us in the innermost part of our being where He now dwells.[508] He doesn't save us only to show us how much He loves us; He saves us so that we can get to know Him intimately and begin to return that love.[509]

The process works like this: the more we intimately get to know God, *the more we will see Him*. The more we see Him, *the more we will love Him*. The more we love Him, *the more we will trust Him*. And the more we trust Him, *the more we will obey Him*.

Experiencing His Presence

Eido is the Greek word that means "to see" and comes from the root word *oida* which means to know intimately. Remember Job, who acknowledged after all his trials, "I [had] heard of Thee by the hearing of the ear [beginning knowledge of God], but now mine eye *seeth* Thee [now I have intimate, experiential knowledge of You]."[510]

Remember, the fire of God's Love not only consumes us, it also *enlightens* us! When we enter the presence of God, we will "see" (*eido*) all that we have only known so far by "faith." The fire of God's Love will allow us to see and know Him *as we never have before*. Matthew 5:8 states it perfectly: the "pure in heart [and spirit] shall *see* God." In other words, the more our soul is stripped away from our spirit, the clearer we will be able to see Him. Purity is a prerequisite for seeing Him. Only when our soul and spirit are cleansed can God's light shine forth and we'll be able to see Him. Indeed, Hebrews 12:14 declares:

> "Follow peace with all men, *and holiness, without which no man shall see the Lord*."

The presence of God is *only* seen through faith, not through our own abilities or our own understanding. By faith, we will *see* Him in every circumstance; by faith, we will be conscious of His closeness all the time; by faith, we will be trying to please Him in all we do; and by faith we will seek to be moved only by His Spirit.

A Scriptural Example: Moses

Our goal should not simply be the security of our salvation, but the ability to see God face to face, just like Moses. "He is always before my face, that I shall not be moved." (Acts 2:25)[511]

The Lord talked face to face with Moses out of the fire. (Deuteronomy 5:4) Moses was so touched and so changed by the encounter that his face shown. His face shone on the outside because of what was happening to him on the inside. And the same thing can occur with us. Maybe, not to the degree that it happened with Moses, but we all have met those special people whose countenance glows because they have been with Jesus. They have been in the presence of God and it shows.[512]

In this wonderful state of seeing and experiencing and knowing God's presence, we will begin to watch Him repay our painful times with His unfathomable Love and affection. We will also begin to realize that in our dark seasons, He <u>never</u> really left us at all. He had to do what He did, in order to get us to this point of intimacy.[513]

This truth alone should render us *incapable of doubting* and give us the assurance that He loves us unconditionally.[514]

> "...And ye shall know that I have not done *without cause* all that I have done...saith the Lord." (Ezekiel 14:23)

Further Benefits of Intimacy

We have already covered many of the benefits of experiential intimacy with God, but here are a few more:

"Sight" becomes swallowed up by faith
Holiness allows us to *see* God
Hope grows stronger
Faith grows more active
We'll enjoy freedom of spirit
We'll experience no more "soulish" captivity
We'll see answered prayer

We'll distrust of things "seen"
We'll enjoy unclouded vision

And this list goes on and on.

Abiding in His Presence

In Chapter Thirteen, we will spend a great amount of time exploring how we stay in this experiential union of spirit with Christ. But, again, I would like to give you a short introductory preview.[515]

The following are some simple guidelines to follow:

> Have faith to stay abandoned to His will.
> Don't let anything move you away from that.[516]
> Ask God to expose your *sin* and self-centered *ways*.
> Go through the *Inner Court Ritual* daily.
> Live a pure and holy life.
> Continue to mortify your souls and "put on" Christ.
> Continue to choose to yield your members to God.
> Don't allow yourself an entrance to anxious cares or concerns.
> Keep faithful to God in all things.
> Look to God before you begin any task, and then, thank Him upon finishing it.
> Offer words of praise and adoration to Him.
> Have no expectations, other than in God.
> Keep your eyes fixed on Him.

Psalm 140:13 declares that, "[Only] the upright [the holy and the pure] shall dwell in [His] presence."

In closing this chapter, listen to **Ephesians 3:14-19**:

"For this cause I bow my knees unto the Father of our Lord Jesus Christ, Of whom the whole family in heaven and earth is named, That He would grant you, according to the riches of His glory, to be strengthened with might by His Spirit in the inner man; That Christ may dwell in your hearts by faith; that ye, being rooted and grounded in Love, May be able to comprehend with all saints what is the breadth, and length, and depth, and height; *And, to know the Love of Christ, which passeth knowledge, that ye might be filled with all the fulness of God.*"

Key Points of This Chapter:

- We can enter God's presence only by the complete surrender of our souls at the Brazen Altar.
- Then, we can worship and love Him at the Incense Altar of our hearts and enjoy intimacy with Him.
- This "experiential" union of our spirits is what He desires.
- Having intimate knowledge of Him is the purpose of our existence. The log and the Fire have finally become one.

Chapter Twelve
Results of Intimacy

One of God's purposes for the sanctification process is that He desires our intimate fellowship. Thus, He works *through our spirit* not only to conform us into His image, but also to establish a love-relationship with us.

In order to accomplish this, He draws us to Himself in a variety of ways: After He *quickens* our spirit, He then *purifies, renews* and *strengthens* our spirit. Once this process is completed, His Holy Spirit is free to come forth and *fill us and empower us.* This filling is what leads us to intimacy, communion and a love-relationship with Him that we never thought possible (the fulness of Christ). Also part of this relationship is the privilege of *worshiping Him in the spirit.*

Let's explore each of these ways that God works through our spirit. Then, we'll come back and examine some of the results of spiritual imtimacy.

Our Renewed Spirit

In review, our spirit is *quickened* or made alive when God's Spirit unites with our human spirit and we are "born anew."[517] A *purified spirit* is one that has been cleansed and all soulish entanglements have been separated.[518] A purified spirit and a *renewed spirit* are very closely related. A renewed spirit is simply a purified spirit that has been taken one step farther, not only being cleansed, but also released and freed to serve God.[519]

To be renewed simply means to "stand back up again" or to "reset to zero." It means a spirit that has been restored to its original image. As Psalm 103:5 declares, "...thy *youth* is renewed like the eagle's." What makes this Scripture so interesting is that after an eagle molts and loses its feathers, as his new feathers come in, he literally regains new physical strength.

Paul notes in 2 Corinthians 4:16, "...though our outward man [soul] perish, yet the inward man [spirit] is renewed day by day."

As we unconditionally surrender ourselves to God, we can expect a similar experience. Once our soulish powers are deflated (or we lose our "feathers" so to speak), our spirit can once again be renewed, strengthened and endowed with power.

Remember, our spirit can only be released according to the degree of brokenness in our lives. Consequently, the more we are broken, the more God can release our spirit, and the more sensitive we can become, not only to Him, but also to others. Unless we have been truly broken and our spirit released, not only will our communication with God be hindered, but also our spiritual fellowship with others will be quenched. Other's will not be able to hear or see *Jesus* through us. Our conversations will simply be "soulish communication." Therefore, unless we share *spirit to spirit*, we will not be able to touch the heart of another person.

The Spirit alone is who makes people "live." The Spirit not only quickens life,[520] but also enables us to know God's Word better. It's what gives us discernment and helps us communicate with God.

To have a renewed spirit means: our *conscience* has become cleansed, our *intuition* heightened and our *communion* sweetened. Thus, we *can* truly "serve God <u>with</u> our spirit." (Romans 1:9)

Our Clear Conscience

A renewed spirit means that our conscience (the inner voice of God), is once again opened and cleansed. Remember we said that our conscience enables God to teach us, to guide us and to communicate with us. In other words, if our conscience is defiled, we won't be able to discern either His voice or His will.

Consequently, the purer our conscience becomes, the clearer we will hear God's voice and the more He can teach us.[521] Romans 8 tells us that the Spirit of God alone knows the Mind of Christ and He alone can make intercession for us according to the will of God. (verses 26-27) In other words, when we're not sure how to pray, what to pray or what His will is, the Spirit of God will intercede for us.[522] He is in the process of teaching us how to do His will from our heart (from our spirit), as Ephesians 6:6 exhorts us: "Doing the will of God from the heart...."

Do you remember the story of Stephen in the book of Acts? Stephen was so surrendered and yielded to God and so full of His Spirit that he knew exactly what God's will was and spoke accordingly. All the people who heard him were amazed at what he said and, thus, they couldn't resist the wisdom by which he spoke. They knew what he said was from God. (Acts 6:8-15)

Like Stephen, when our spirit is cleansed and renewed, the Spirit of God will intercede for us and tell us what to say and how to say it. But if we do not obey the Spirit of God when He reveals things to us, then we will grieve Him and quench any further spiritual communication.

This is why it's so very important to deal with even the slightest accusation in our conscience; otherwise, our spirit will be quenched. Our conscience needs to be totally pure, both in order to hear God correctly and in order to know right from wrong. We should actually be more afraid of a reproach from our conscience than what all the men in the world might say about us.[523]

An Example: Chris

I recently read an incredible example in the newspaper of a man who desperately needed a clear conscience. Chris was a young man who, accidently, killed a girl 25 years ago. Only 17 at the time and "high" on drugs, he miraculously escaped the authorities. The incident so scared him, however, that he turned his life around and never spoke of the incident to anyone.

He eventually became a Christian, married and had a family. He became very active in his church and a model family man. When he first married, he told his wife that there was "something bad" in his past that he was ashamed of, but he never told her specifically what it was.

As they began to grow in the Lord, one day his wife mentioned to him, "How can you serve God with a clear conscience if you never have taken care of that 'bad thing' in your past?" As time went on, he found he couldn't do the things that he used to without feeling guilty. He knew God had forgiven him for the murder, because when he had become a Christian that's the first thing he confessed and repented of. But, taking his confession one step farther and turning himself into the authorities was something he never considered--until his wife's comments.

After months of wrestling with himself over this issue, he finally shared with her what the "bad thing" was. For a long time, they both prayed about what God would have them do. Incredibly, they both came to the same conclusion, that Chris would never have total peace within himself until he turned himself in. So, 25 years after the murder, Chris went to the authorities and confessed his crime.

The whole town--the police, the sheriff and all the authorities--already knew Chris as a model citizen and family man. They were completely shocked and didn't want to imprison him. Ultimately, the courts gave him a very lenient sentence, only ten years in prison.

Now Chris' conscience is clear and he is at peace with God.[524] He hopes to be paroled early for good behavior. Perhaps, God had some work that He wanted Chris to do for Him inside those prison walls. I'm sure Chris's life will touch and affect many lives.

A reproach in our conscience that we don't follow can cause us to miss God's will, misunderstand His ways and ultimately lose our fellowship with Him. Only under the Holy Spirit's control can our conscience grow more and more in tune to God's voice and His commands. This is why a Spirit-filled conscience is the organ of our faith.[525]

Our Supernatural Intuition

When our spirit is renewed, our spiritual intuition becomes heightened. Remember that our conscience and our intuition work hand in hand: our conscience advises us what is right and wrong and our intuition leads and guides us in God's way. Proverbs 3 exhorts us to, "Trust in the Lord with all thine heart, and lean not unto thine own understanding. In all thy ways acknowledge Him, and *He shall direct thy paths*." (verses 5-6) A sensitive intuition will give us discernment of those "paths."

Can God really direct our paths? Not unless we have a receptive and heightened intuition. And, this does not happen naturally. Scripture tells us that, "There is a way which seemeth right unto a man, but the end thereof are *the ways of death*." (Proverbs 14:12) This means that to the "natural man," his own self-centered ways are fine. He has no understanding that down the road, his pleasure-seeking life will eventually take its toll and, consequently, he will find himself separated from God. This is why it's critical for believers to continually renew their spirit and listen for our spiritual intuition to lead and guide us.

Only God knows the "right way" for us to walk and only He can guide us along that path that He knows is best for us.[526] The moment God's Spirit says "stop," we must be sensitive enough to stop. When He says "be careful," "watch out," or "something is amiss here," we must heed His nudging. In my own life, every time I have overlooked God's "red flag" and His gentle squeeze on my shoulder, I have gotten on the wrong path.

Secret Revelations

God reveals His will to us both through His Word and through His Spirit, not through our own reason or our own thoughts.[527] This is a hard concept for many very intelligent people, but the Bible tells us that it's "not by might [or our own strength], but by God's Spirit" (a heightened intuition) that things are made known to us. (Zechariah 4:6) According to 1 Corinthians 2:10-12:

> "God hath revealed them [identified them] unto us by His Spirit: for the Spirit searcheth all things, yea, the deep things of God...Now we have received, not the spirit of the world, but the Spirit who is of God; that we might know the things that are freely given to us of God."

Therefore, the more abandoned and the more surrendered we can become to God's Spirit of discernment, the more insight and revelation we will have.

Everyone who walks intimately with God will enjoy His secret communication and the bestowing of His revelations. This is often called God's anointing or, simply, "His presence to give light." The Old Testament word for anoint" means *oil producing light*. And this is exactly what God means here. God anoints us with His presence and, thereby, gives us His supernatural revelation--supernatural wisdom and understanding. Happening in our spirits, this annointing enables us to know God's thoughts which gives us supernatural understanding. Our natural mind cannot even conceive of all "the deep things of God" that He wants to bestow upon us. These things can only be given to us by supernatural *revelation*.[528]

This book has been an exercise in "revelation" for me. God has consistently revealed new and wonderful spiritual insights as I have endeavored to stay in His presence. Scriptures that I have read for years are popping off the pages with new meaning. Sometimes He wakes me up in the middle of the night to pour out pages upon pages of specifically worded sentences, thoughts and ideas. Other nights I'm unable to sleep because I'm so excited to see what He is going to reveal the next day.[529] That sounds so silly, but it's the truth. Constantly, if I am faithful to wait upon Him with a pure and renewed spirit and ask for revelation, God fills in the "gaps" for me; He teaches me deep things I don't understand with my natural mind.

I think of revelation as God simply "turning the lights on" for us. In other words, only God's Spirit knows God's thoughts. Man in his natural state can never comprehend the "deep things of God," they require special spiritual enlightenment.[530]   Only through our spirit, our heightened intuition, can we perceive the wondrous things of God. And, only through our spirit, can He lead and guide us as He intends.

An Example: Trish

A precious friend of mine is a missionary in New Zealand (8000 miles away). One morning last summer while she was in church, God impressed upon her that I was in "great need." She immediately wrote me a letter expressing her concern:

> "So, sister, what is going on in your life? Seems like the Lord has given me a heavy burden on my heart for you. *I know these are not my own thoughts.* When the Lord spoke to me this morning, I heard three words: lonely, hurting and uplifted. I wrote them on my pad during the sermon. I truly was trying to listen, but it seems the Holy Spirit was having His own agenda with me. Even though we are 8000 miles apart, I feel very close to you right now and I am writing this letter from my heart, not my head. I know how we can be in the midst of millions of people and yet, still hurt. I know you know all this, but I just want you to picture Jesus always being there with you and holding your hand. *I don't know what is wrong, but I know you are hurting*, and I just want to uplift you...."

Our son Chip had died that very day.

Trish had no way of knowing this by natural means! Yet, she wrote to me "as an extension of God's Love" almost to the *very hour* of his death.

Remember this story the next time God lays someone on your heart to pray for or to write a love note to. Supernatural revelation is simply a knowing in our spirit that, otherwise, would be impossible to know.

God's Word and His Spirit Work Together

God's Spirit works alongside God's Word to give us supernatural revelation about others, as well as about our own selves.[531] In other words, God's Spirit enables us to see our own selves as we truly are.[532] Only by His Word and His Spirit working together can our lives begin to change *from the inside out.*

Repentance and the cross is the way God has laid out in Scripture for us to deal with our sin. We are to recognize it, confess it, repent of it and take it to the cross. *Revelation and the cross* is the way God has chosen for us to deal with our <u>self</u>. Through our renewed spirit, God will reveal what part of our self needs to be dealt with. Then it's our responsibility to bring that self to the altar or to the cross and surrender it to God.

An Example: Karen

A dear friend of mine went on a vacation with three of her best friends. She had a wonderful time, but there was one woman, she told me later, that "absolutely bugged her." After seven days of being with this woman, Karen finally said she could not tolerate being around her any longer. Some of the self-centered things she did, infuriated Karen.

Finally, angry and frustrated, Karen went to the Lord in prayer about her own reactions. "Why is it that what my friend does bothers me so much?"

God will always be faithful to give us personal revelation about ourselves in His timing and in His way. One night as Karen was reading the Word of God, God gave her insight as to "why" the woman's behavior angered her so much. It was the exact same behavior that Karen's husband complained about in her.

God was simply magnifying this behavior through her friend, so that she could see, for herself, what her husband saw in her. It was a painful lesson, but God's revelation was the first step she needed to take in order to deal with her own sin. *We can't deal with our sin, if we don't know what it is.* We need God's revelation, His spotlight, to highlight them for us. And He is often very creative in the ways He chooses to do so.

If we are quick to obey God's Spirit, God's Word promises us that in the end, great and wonderful blessings will come.[533] He promises us that He will never humble us, but that He will exalt us in the end, another example of life coming out of death.[534]

Our pure conscience is where God teaches us, speaks to us and tells us what His will is. Our heightened intuition is where God leads us and guides us and gives us His revelation. Again, notice that these two functions of our spirit are *one-sided*--it's <u>God</u> communicating to us. However, the third operation of our spirit, communion and fellowship, differs, involving a *two-way relationship*. Our spirit is the place where God not only communicates with us, but also where <u>we</u> return that fellowship. There can never be real communion and fellowship, without two people involved.

Our Restored Communion and Fellowship

One of the greatest blessings of a purified and renewed spirit is the resulting communion, fellowship and friendship with God. When we learn to intimately commune with God, a friendship is established. *Friendship simply means a union of two wills.* Friendship begets intimacy and intimacy comes from abiding and sharing common ideals, goals, objectives and secrets.

Friendship with God, like human friendship, means not allowing anything to hinder our face-to-face relationship. It's being governed and constrained purely by our love for each other. A friend of God is one in whom God confides and shares secret things. It's not only experiencing His company, but also conversing with Him and doing all that He asks.

Jesus declares in John 15:14-15, "Ye are my friends, if you do whatever I command you. Henceforth I call you not servants; for the servant knoweth not what his lord doeth; but I have called you friends; for all things that I have heard of my Father I have made known unto you."

Some great Biblical examples of friendship with God are: *Abraham* in Genesis 17:3 where he talks with God and in James 2:23 where he is called "a friend of God"; *Gideon* in Judges 6:22 where he sees the Lord "face to face"; and, of course, *Moses* in Deuteronomy 5:4 and Exodus 33:11 where he, too, sees God's face.[535] (As a result, Moses's own face began to shine with the glory of God.)[536] All these anointed men had the privilege of "seeing" God and "knowing" His presence.[537]

Our face, too, will shine as we dwell in God's presence. An unusual serenity and peacefulness will spread over our souls as it becomes apparent that the God of the universe is continually at our side.

Our Strengthened Spirit

God desires to break our outward man so that our spirit can be purified, renewed and then strengthened so that, once again, it can rule and reign over our soul. As we yield and forsake every doubting aspect of our soulish life and willingly obey God, our spirit will gain control of our every thought, emotion and desire.

As Ephesians urges, we are to "be strengthened with might by His Spirit in the inner man" (3:16) and we are to be "strong in the Lord and in the power of His might." (6:10)[538]

God's Spirit energizes our spirit, endowing it with power so that it is enabled to govern our whole man.[539] This strengthening of our spirit occurs through the Holy Spirit at the Incense Altar of our hearts. *Strengthened* is the word *kratos* in the Greek, meaning *power to rein in, mastery over self, self-control* or, better yet, *spirit-control.*[540] God's Spirit gives our spirit strength to *put off* the habits of our flesh and to *put on* Christ.

The Old Testament word for *strength* is *gibbor*, which means *to overcome*. Overcomers are simply those who choose, no matter what is going on in their lives, no matter how they feel and no matter how others are treating them, to "put off" sin and self and "put on" Christ. *An overcomer is simply one who is freed from self to serve God.*[541] Thus, we must close the windows of our spirit to all other resources, and be strengthened only by God's Spirit of strength.[542]

Some Christians have a *strong* spirit--a cleansed and quickened conscience; a heightened intuition and an on-going communion with God. These Christians have allowed God's Spirit--through their strengthened spirits--to keep their soul under control. Unfortunately, other Christians, even though they have God's Spirit in them, have *weak* spirits. They have not allowed God to purge their soul or purify their spirits; therefore, they don't know right from wrong; they can't discern God's ways and they have no fellowship with Jesus.

Consequently, despite superficial appearances, if our "soulish ways" are not broken and our spirit has not been set free and strengthened, then we really have <u>not</u> grown at all. *Real advancement with God is only measured by the growth of our spirit.*

The Outpouring (or release) of God's Spirit

Major trouble occurs in all of us because our outward man and our inward man have become so entangled. What influences us outwardly usually disturbs us inwardly. God wants these two areas to be separated--our soul from our spirit--so that *nothing* on the outside will be able to affect, move or disturb us on the inside. Therefore, God allows circumstances in our lives to lovingly bring about the breaking of our outward man and thus, the release of His Spirit.

> "Verily, verily, I say unto you, Except a corn of wheat fall into the ground and die, it abideth alone; but if it die, it bringeth forth much fruit. He that loveth his life shall lose it; and he that hateth his life in this world shall keep it unto life eternal."[543] (John 12:24-25)

Death of the outward man precedes life in the Spirit. In nature, if we take a corn of wheat, drop it into the earth and cover it with soil, it will eventually die. The elements in the soil, the heat of the sun and the moisture work on the outer shell of that seed. Soon, the outer shell breaks open and a little green sprout pushes its way out. The seed then disappears and a stalk of grain appears. Charles Stanley points out, in his wonderful book entitled *Brokenness*, if we replanted the fruit from that one grain of wheat, a million acres of wheat could be the result.

This is such a great analogy, because it's true: *We can do nothing as long as Jesus' Spirit is tucked nicely away behind the outer shell of our soul. In other words, without death, there will be no life! Our soul needs to be cracked wide open, in order for Jesus' Life to come forth and for us to sow much fruit.*

When we speak of *brokenness*, we simply mean the breaking of our "soulish" powers--all our self-strength, self-exaltation, self-love, self-acknowledgement, self-reliance, self-cleverness and pride. God's Spirit will be released according to the degree of brokenness in our lives.

We have been learning that God is doing a twofold work in all of us: He not only is breaking our outward man (our soul) by means of the *dark night of the soul*, which is a slow process and usually involves *discipline by the Holy Spirit* but , He is also separating and cutting away our inward man (our spirit) by means of the *dark night of the spirit*, which usually happens quite quickly and involves *revelation by His Word.*[544]

Once our spirit has been separated from our soul, renewed and strengthened, one of the most visible results will be a continual *outpouring* (or release) of God's Spirit. This is what Ephesians 6:19 means when it says "be filled with the fulness of God." In other words, *we will be filled inside and out with God and His Spirit of Love*[545].

Going back to the temple for a moment, one can easily visualize what it might have looked like when it was filled with the Shekinah Glory of the Lord. The Holy Spirit came forth from the Holy of Holies where He dwelt and filled the entire temple. This is exactly what happens with us, once our spirit has been released through brokenness. God's Spirit comes forth from the Holy of Holies of our hearts and fills our souls and bodies.

See **Chart C**

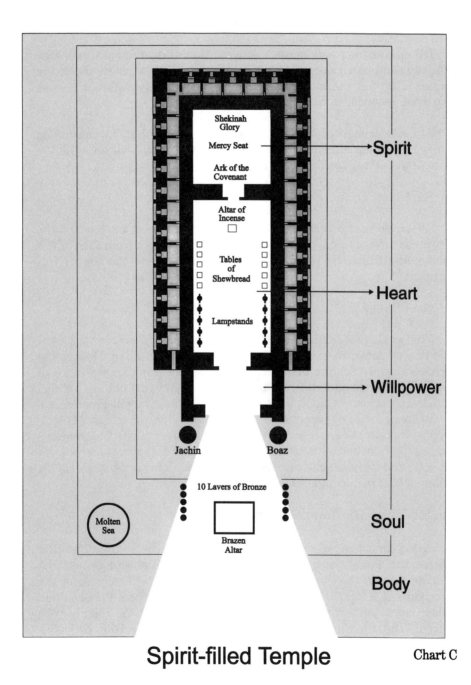

Spirit-filled Temple

Chart C

"Wherefore be ye not unwise, but understanding what the
will of the Lord is. And be not drunk with wine, wherein is
excess; but *be filled with the Spirit*." (Ephesians 5:18-19)

It's interesting to me to contrast what God's Spirit did at the *Brazen
Altar* in the Inner Court of Solomon's Temple with what He did at the
Incense Altar in the Holy Place, because two totally different actions
occurred, recorded in Scripture for our instruction.

At the Brazen Altar, God's Spirit came down from heaven, consuming
the wholly burnt offering in the Inner Court,[546] then went on to fill the
temple with His glory from the outside inward.[547]

See **Chart D**

At the Incense Altar, however, as the cloud of sweet incense and the
fire arose towards God, the Shekinah Glory came forth from the Holy of
Holies and filled the temple from the inside, where the source was
outward.[548]

See **Chart E**

This analogy is fascinating: The first *infilling of the Spirit* occurs at
the Brazen Altar when God first unites us with Himself and begins the
process of sanctification in our lives. As we allow him to purge our soul
and divide it from our spirit, we are enabled to carry that hot piece of coal
into the presence of God at the Incense Altar where we will experience a
complete union of our spirits. Thus, the *outpouring or release of God's
Spirit* occurs at the Incense Altar where our spirits are purified, renewed
and strengthened with might. *This outpouring of the spirit is the "fulness
of God" that we have so often referred to. It's result is our being full of the
Glory of God inside and out, just as the temple was.*

An Example: The Temple Institute

Last year when we visited Israel, we went to the Temple Institute
where the Israelis are actually rebuilding the furnishings and the
implements for the third temple. We asked them specifically about the
incident in 1 Kings 8:10-11 and 2 Chronicles 5:13-14 where the Shekinah
Glory came forth from the Holy of Holies and filled the temple. We
asked, "Did the Shekinah Glory come forth from the Holy of Holies
outward, or did He come from the outside *inward*?"

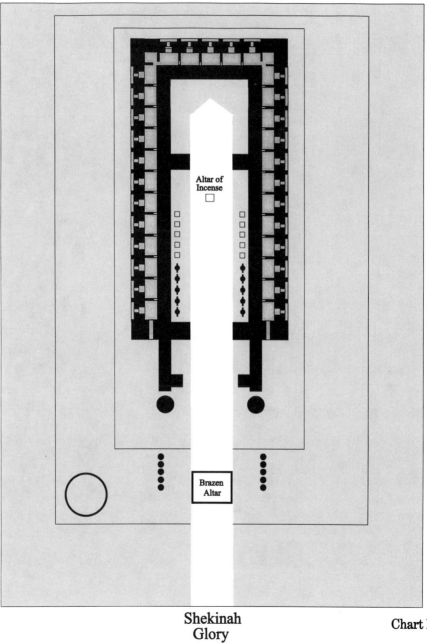

Altar of
Incense

Brazen
Altar

**Shekinah
Glory**

Chart D

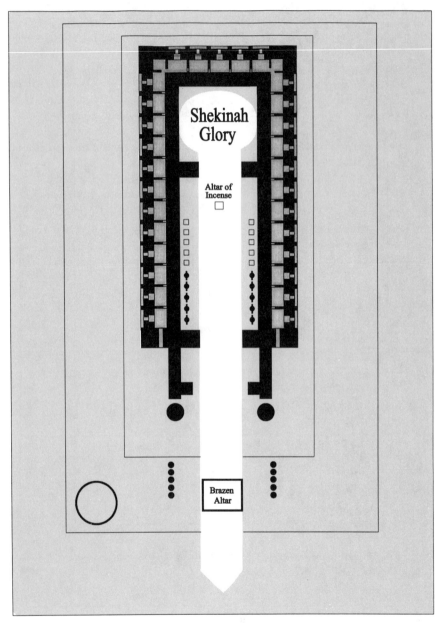

Chart E

They replied that the Shekinah Glory most definitely came forth *from inside outward*--from the Holy of Holies where He dwelt outward through the sanctuary till He filled the temple with His glory. They said the proof of this theory was that the temple windows (high around the inside of the sanctuary) were built in such a way (larger on the inside and smaller on the outside) so that they could capture the light and the glory of God's Spirit as He passed by and funnel it outward.

This answer thrilled me, because this process is exactly what God desires for each of us. To be filled with His Spirit from the *inside*--where the Source is--*outward* so that everyone can see Him.

Our outward man is broken and dealt with repeatedly on the Brazen Altar, but *it's not until our spirit is purified, renewed and set free at the Incense Altar that God's Spirit can be released through us to fill our souls and bodies.* Then, as Isaiah asserts, "Righteousness [can] go forth as brightness, and...salvation as a lamp that burns." (62:4)

The Empowering of Our Spirit by God's *Dunamis* Power

Once God's Spirit has been released, the miraculous *dunamis* power of God can come forth. This *dunamis* is the very same *resurrection power* of God that raised Christ from the dead.[549]

The *dunamis* power of God refers to His divine power or supernatural ability. We are endowed with God's supernatural power when we first receive His Spirit at our new birth, but this power is not released through us until our spirit is purified and renewed. *God doesn't give supernatural power to the old creation, but only to the crucified soul.* His supernatural power is just like His supernatural Love and Wisdom; we won't experience it until our spirits are renewed.

Therefore, one of the main reasons we lack power, even after we have been born again, is that our spirit (the residing place of God's *dunamis* power), has been quenched and blocked; we have chosen to follow our own self-centered ways over what God wants. Thus, not only God's Love and Wisdom are blocked from coming forth, but God's Power has also been stopped as well.

God had to bring Abraham to the end of his own power and ability for him to see that in himself he could do nothing. When Abraham was forced to look away from himself and trust God alone for His supernatural power, his life changed drastically. And it will be the same with us.

An Example: Charles Finney

When I think of the supernatural power of God, I can't help but think of Charles Finney and how he was filled with power from on high, but only after he became fully surrendered to God.

Charles Finney was a school teacher who came to a crossroads in his life at the age of 29. He believed in the Word of God but had much concern about his own salvation. He thus determined to settle this issue, by reading and by praying. His heart, however, continued to be cold. Finally, by faith alone, he told God that he accepted His free gift of salvation. Still he felt nothing. Again, he tried to pray and to give himself to God, but he couldn't. His cold heart was dead. Thus, a great discouragement came over him, and he sunk so low that he broke into convulsive sobbing. This allowed the Holy Spirit to completely break him by showing him his own sin.

Charles had always intellectually believed in the Word, but he had *never* understood what faith was a *voluntary trust, not an intellectual step*. He knew, this time, that God was speaking directly to him and so he cried out for more and more. This time, he felt assured that God had heard him. After he went home that night, he fell down on the floor and completely surrendered himself to God.

While lying on his face before God, he met Jesus face to face. The room in which he was praying had no natural light. The fire had gone out in the fireplace and the lights had not been lit, yet the room was ablaze with the radiance of the sun. Finney acknowledged that the whole experience was a mental state, yet to him, it was complete reality. He said the way Jesus kept looking at him broke him apart. The Spirit began to wash over him like "liquid love." Fire seemed to go right through him like waves of electricity. He began to weep like a baby full of joy and love. The waves kept coming and coming, till he thought he could bear no more. They continued all night long.

In the morning, the love bath began all over again. He got on his knees and wept some more. The Spirit kept saying to him, "Will you ever doubt Me again?"

From this encounter and this foundation, Charles Finney went on to become one of the world's greatest evangelists and preachers. He wrote that he felt that his "spirit was wedded to Christ." *The log had become one with the Fire!* When he preached, the Holy Spirit would not only empower him, but would fall upon the congregation. Thousands were converted to Christ. Revival began and spread abroad.

Power seems to be the mark of a disciple of Christ.[550] God's power, however, can often be concealed in weakness.[551] *Weakness* here simply means yieldedness, relinquishment and abandonment to God's will, so that His supernatural Power can be released through us.

> "My grace is sufficient for thee: for My strength is made perfect in weakness. Most gladly therefore will I rather glory in my infirmities, that the power of Christ may rest upon me." (2 Corinthians 12:9)

When we are weak or yielded, then we can be strong because it will be *Jesus' resurrection Power flowing through us,* just as it was with Finney. Therefore, *weakness is a prerequisite for divine power*.

Our Example: Jesus

Jesus, Himself, was crucified through weakness. *Weakness* means yieldedness and relinquishment of all soulish strength, so that the Holy Spirit can direct our lives. As Zechariah 4:6 so beautifully expresses, "Not by [my own] might, nor by power, but by My Spirit...."[552]

Jesus lived His whole life in obedience to this premise.[553] He was endowed with supernatural Power to heal and preach,[554] and He did everything in His ministry only by the Power of the Holy Spirit working through Him.[555] At any time, He could have called down all the legions of heavenly angels to do His own will. But He loved us so much that He chose, instead, to lay aside His strength, so that through the cross, He could give us His Life.

Interestingly, *the power of the spirit* is usually the first power we experience after we are born again, but actually it is the last power we come to understand. This has certainly been true in my own experience.

This kind of supernatural Power is only available when we surrender ourselves to God in faith.[556] Through weakness, the unspeakable *dunamis* power of God is enabled to come forth. God's power will allow us to handle and endure situations that we never could on our own, do things that we never could in the natural and fight the enemy in ways we never could imagine doing by ourselves.

God's Power must be the controlling force of our lives, not only in the visible world but also in the invisible world. Colossians 1:13 tells us that Christ has already delivered us from the power of darkness and translated us into the kingdom of His Son. And, this "kingdom" is not in words, but in *power*.[557]

God's Power will lead us to repentance and surrender and, thus, to real revival. Revival is simply the return of God's people to an obedient love of God and to being a vessel of His Power and Love. Those who evidence God's *dunamis* power in their lives are those who have allowed God to separate their soul and spirit. They have a purified, renewed and strengthened spirit. Thus, God's Spirit has been freed to come forth to direct their lives. *The goal of preaching is not eloquence or human wisdom, but that of personally exhibiting Christ's saving power in our own lives.*[558]

An Example: George Muller

George Muller's goal of preaching is evident from his writing:

"The anointing of the Holy Spirit helps me greatly when I preach. I would never attempt to teach the truth of God by my own power. One day before preaching at Teignmouth, I had more time than usual, so I prayed and meditated for six hours in preparation for the evening meeting. After I had spoken a little while, I felt that I was speaking in my own strength rather than God's power. I told the brethren that I felt as though I was not preaching under the anointing and asked them to pray. After I continued a little longer, I felt the same and therefore ended my sermon and proposed that we have a meeting for prayer. We did so, and I was particularly assisted by the Holy Spirit the next time I preached."

I am glad that I learned the importance of ministering in God's power alone. I can do all things through Christ, but without Him, I can accomplish nothing."

These are the kinds of sermons I love to hear--the ones that are directly from the Spirit of God.

Worshiping and Loving God in the Spirit

The whole purpose of being sanctified body, soul and spirit is twofold: *Outwardly* to reflect Him in all we do, and *inwardly* to commune, fellowship and experience intimacy with Him. Part of this intimacy is the privilege of worshiping Him in the spirit.

Only when our spirit has been renewed and strengthened and God's Spirit set free, can we truly worship God "in the spirit." Again, it's a two-way relationship. <u>God</u> quickens, purifies, renews, strengthens and empowers our spirit, so that <u>we</u> can then fellowship, commune and worship Him in the spirit. Jesus declared, "But the hour cometh, and now is, when the true worshipers shall *worship the Father in spirit and in truth*; for the Father seeketh such to worship Him."[559]

Worshiping in the spirit simply means adoring, praising and loving God in the same nature that He is. God is a spirit and only that which is spirit can abide and worship in His presence.[560]

So, are we really worshiping God when we close our eyes and lift our hands in church? Are we really worshiping Him when we run to renewal services where there is an outpouring of His Spirit? Are we worshiping Him when we pray in tongues and sing in the spirit? I believe worshiping God *in the spirit* means far more than any of us comprehends.

The Greek word for worship is *proskuneo* which means to bow, to stoop down or to prostrate oneself. Worship is not necessarily something we do on the outside, but something that we do on the <u>inside</u>--in our spirits. It's prostrating and bowing down our inner man before God. Worship is asking nothing of God, but losing ourselves in adoration, reverence and homage.

In contrast, serving God, *latreia,* is something we usually do on the <u>outside</u>--through our bodies and our souls. It's presenting our bodies and souls as a living sacrifice, so that God can be glorified through us in all that we do.

Worshiping and serving God are very closely related to *loving God.* Loving God is following, cleaving and so binding ourselves together with Him that we actually become "one." Again, we are reminded of the incense cloud and the fire and the log and the Fire as they intermingled with one another to become one. *Loving God is being so emptied out of ourselves and so intertwined with His Spirit that we actually become one.*[561] When we love as He desires, we get lost in Him.

> "Be ye, therefore, *followers of God*, as dear children; And *walk in Love*, as Christ also hath loved us, and hath given Himself for us an offering and a sacrifice to God for a sweet smelling savor." (Ephesians 5:1-2)[562]

Worship flows from that kind of love. Where this kind of love is deep, worship will overflow.

Worshiping God in the Spirit means carrying that hot piece of coal from the Brazen Altar of our soul into the Holy Place and worshiping Him at the Incense Altar of our hearts. Then we can cry, like Isaiah, "Woe is me! For I am undone, because I am a man of unclean lips, and *mine eyes have seen the King*, the Lord of hosts. Then flew one of the seraphim unto me, having a *live coal* in his hand, which he had taken with the tongs from off the altar [Brazen]. And he laid it upon my mouth, and said, Lo...thy sin [is] purged." (6:5-6)

Worshiping God means prostrating ourselves before Him in spirit. This is exactly what the priests of Solomon's Temple did before they even approached the Holy of Holies to minister. They lay flat on the ground. After the service was over, they left the room from that prostrate position.[563]

What Worshiping in the Spirit Is Not

Worshiping God in the spirit is an attitude we should have on all week long. It's not something we can instantly "put on" like clothing. How sad it is to say that we "worship God" Sunday mornings at 9:30 A.M. If we truly love God, *what happens the other six days of the week?* How can we expect to instantly worship God on Sunday mornings when we usually are not "in the Spirit" when we come? Most of us have just spent the last hour and a half yelling at our kids to get dressed on time, arguing with our husbands about what we are going to do that afternoon and feeling frustrated that we can't find the shoes that go with our outfit. Then, when we finally arrive at church, we are not given enough time to go before the Lord to get cleaned up--to get from the Brazen Altar to the Incense Altar![564]

Being in church, singing and raising our hands to God does not make us true worshipers. True worshipers are those who worship Him in the "beauty of holiness" all the time. (Psalm 29:2) The beauty of holiness occurs after God has purged our souls, and we have carried that hot coal into the Holy Place. Worshiping God in the beauty of holiness simply means *self* has been wholly burnt at the Brazen Altar and we can now truly prostrate ourselves before God at the Incense Altar.[565]

This is the adoration and the communion of Love that God deserves and that He desires. Then we are genuinely worshiping Him from the depths of our being--in our spirit.

Worshiping God doesn't have to be some long drawn-out affair that takes hours. This process can only take five minutes, if we truly allow God to purge our souls and purify our spirits. We can worship God in the spirit after spending only a few minutes genuinely going through *The Inner Court Ritual* and giving God all the sin and self that He reveals. But we do need at least five minutes and we should be perfectly quiet. 2 Corinthians 7:1 exhorts:

"Having, therefore, these promises, dearly beloved, let us cleanse ourselves from all filthiness of the *flesh* and *spirit*, perfecting holiness in the fear of God."[566]

Beauty of Holiness

Worshiping in the beauty of holiness means that sin and self have, for the moment, been set aside, so that Jesus' image--His rock-likeness--is coming forth.

It's important to understand that it's *Jesus' holiness*, not our own. Just as God's supernatural Love is not our love and His supernatural Power is not our power, this holiness is not our holiness. Jesus is the only One who is holy and He makes holiness beautiful. When we are clean and purified, He is able to shine forth His holiness through us.

In other words, we are *"partakers of His holiness."* (Hebrew 12:10) Therefore, *we* don't have to work at being holy, but simply relinquish ourselves to Him and allow Him to be holy through us. Holiness is the result of our constant repentance and sanctification,[567] meaning that the soulish things in our lives have been divided, separated and cut away, and only the spiritual things remain.[568]

This does not mean we will always stay cleansed and pure, which is God's will. But the reality is that none of us will be able to do that! Only Jesus could. However, we can go before the Lord at least every morning, go through *The Inner Court Ritual* and, then, set about our day not only conformed to His image, but also worshiping Him in the beauty of His holiness. Problems arise during the day that will send us fleeing back to the altar again, but at least we've started off the day renewed.

A holy person is one who is not afraid of the light. In fact, he invites the light. He avows, "I want all the hidden things in my life to be revealed, because I want all of me to be like Jesus." A holy person is one who continually prays, "Let death work in me, so that Life may be received by others." (Paraphrase of 2 Corinthians 4:12) As God's people, we are to forsake all darkness and all secrecy and are to become open books that can be read by all men.[569]

As Leviticus 20:26 adjures, "Ye shall be holy unto Me; for I, the Lord, am holy, and have severed you [sanctified] from other people, that ye should be mine."

An Example: My Diana

People often say that this kind of holiness takes a lifetime to achieve, coming only from a lifetime of brokenness.[570] This might be true for some people, but I don't believe it needs to take that long. Remember, my beautiful friend Diana Bantlow who died of leukemia whom I spoke about in Chapter Three? Diana had only been a Christian for two years, yet *she lived this kind of holy and set apart life.*

When we first met Diana, she and her husband were business acquaintances. Neither of them knew the Lord. In fact, at that time, Diana was very involved with the Women's Lib Movement. I remember having some pretty strong conversations with her about it!

After getting better acquainted and having several opportunities to share Christ, Diana and her husband joined a local "right on" church. There they heard more about Christ and His good news and both became believers. Diana, however, wasn't satisfied with just knowing *about* God; she wanted to "know Him intimately." Thus, she devoured everything she could get her hands about the spiritual walk, and, almost immediately, surrendered and relinquished everything in her life that "was not of faith."

After only one year of knowing Christ, she found out that she had leukemia and was given only one year to live. As I previously mentioned, everyone who saw Diana in those last few months of her life knew God was with her. She reminded me of Joseph in Genesis 39. All who saw Joseph knew "God was with him." Well, it was the same with Diana. People could see Jesus' beauty in Diana's face, His holiness in her actions and His Love and Power in all her ways.

Every week, after her chemotherapy sessions, she came straight to teach her Bible study. We would prop pillows around her so she could sit more comfortably, and then she would tell us about Jesus' Love and His faithfulness. Could you have done that? Could you have taught a Bible class after you had just undergone cancer chemotherapy treatments? In all honesty, I don't think I could. From all that I know about this terrible procedure, it robs you of "life" and leaves you unbearably weak. Not Diana! Because she was a "partaker" in God's holiness and His Life, His Power and Strength, she functioned beautifully. She was already yielded and relinquished, so He was able to flow through her magnificently.

In those last remaining few weeks in the hospital, the nurses saw in Diana Jesus' Life and His holiness. Though Diana was physically dying, the light and Love and Power that were being manifested through her showed forth the beauty of God's holiness.

Nothing is more beautiful than Jesus' Life coming through a cleansed and purified vessel. This kind of Life and holiness cannot be manufactured or conjured up. This is "the real thing"! This Life is what everyone everywhere is crying out for. This is "life," the way life is supposed to be.

This kind of life and this kind of holiness can be ours today. We don't have to wait to get it. *The number of years we've been a Christian has nothing to do with this kind of holiness. The main factor is how yielded and how abandoned we are to God.* The more we allow God to possess us, the more we will be made like Him and the more of His holiness will shine forth.

Holiness: Heaven's Term for Happiness

Holiness is simply heaven's term for *happiness*. The world is slowly finding out that happiness does not come from another person, from our circumstances or from our accomplishments. Happiness comes only from abiding in Christ and being all that He wants us to be. He is our Creator and only He knows what it will take to make us fulfilled and happy. In other words, He knows that only His continuous presence in our lives will bring us that *permanent and lasting* happiness.

As C. S. Lewis puts it:

"God knows that our happiness lies in Him. Yet, we will not seek it as long as there is any other resort where it can be looked for. When our life remains agreeable, we will not surrender it to God. [So] What can God do but make our life less agreeable...When He can love [through us] without impediment, we shall, in fact, be happy."[571]

Holiness comes through brokenness.[572] Unfortunately, there is no other way to attain holiness than to constantly set aside our own passions, our own possessions and our own power, and depend upon God for everything. The more complete our submission and our abandonment is to Him, the greater our holiness or happiness. As David cries out in Psalm 73:25, "There is none upon earth that I desire beside Thee." This is the holiness that brings true happiness.

Only God knows just how to perfectly bring about this holiness and happiness in each of our lives. In other words, only God can make us holy. It's a gift from Him; it's His work. We cannot attain it on our own.

As Jean Pierre Caussade exhorts:

> "If we only have sense enough to leave everything to the guidance of God's hands, we will reach the highest peak of holiness."

If you recall in Solomon's Temple, only the priests were allowed to enter the Holy Place where God's Spirit dwelt. These were priests who wore headpieces called *mitres*. Written on top of each of these headpieces was "Holiness To The Lord." (Exodus 28:36)

Praising and Thanking God in the Spirit

In Solomon's Temple, it's interesting to note that *after* the incense was offered and *after* the singers had praised and thanked God, the priests then offered their own prayers at the Incense Altar. The priests were then assured that their prayers would not only be heard, but also be answered because they were given in accordance with God's will.[573]

Jesus tells us the very same thing. "...If any man be a worshiper of God, and doeth His will, him He heareth." (John 9:31) In other words, when our prayers are according to God's will (which they will be, if we are at the Incense Altar), then He will not only hear them, He will also answer them.[574]

Besides worshiping God in the spirit, another blessing of intimacy is the praise and thanksgiving that is stirred up within us. As we worship, commune and fellowship with the Lord God of the universe, praise automatically arises from our hearts. Just as in the temple, after the priests had concluded their offering of incense on the Golden Altar, they burst into singing and praising the Lord.

> "It came even to pass, as the trumpeters and singers were as one, to make one sound to be heard in *praising and thanking the Lord*; and when they lifted up their voice with the trumpets and cymbals and instruments of music, and praised the Lord, saying For He is good; for His mercy endureth forever; that then *the house was filled with a cloud*, even the house of the Lord. So that the priests could not stand to minister by reason of the cloud; for the glory of the Lord had filled the house of God." (2 Chronicles 5:13-14)

And it will be the same with us. As we begin to experience God's presence and His Love and joy and peace on a continual basis, "rivers of living water" will rise up from our innermost being until we will be compelled to praise and thank God for all that He is doing.[575]

An Example: Me

It seems like such an paradox, but the more abandoned to God's will that I become, the more joyful and thankful I am. Now, the opposite is also true. The more I hold on to myself and don't let go, the more miserable and unhappy I become. This exemplifies John 12:25 all over again: "He that loveth [hold on to] his life shall lose it; and he that hateth his life [is willing to lay it down] in this world shall keep it unto life eternal."

As I am beginning to know God in this incredible new dimension of intimacy, I can hardly stop thanking and praising Him. Even in my sleep, I find myself constantly worshiping, adoring and praising Him in the spirit. It rises from my innermost being, like waves of living water and just naturally consumes and overflows me. What I am experiencing was promised in John 7:38:

> "He that believeth on Me, as the Scripture hath said, out of his [heart] shall flow *rivers of living water*."

For me, this joyful and thankful spirit is relatively new. It hasn't always been this way. Many times in the past, especially in the last seven years, I've had to make faith choices in order to praise and thank God for "all" things, because I certainly didn't feel like it. I knew God would accept my praises by faith,[576] and that they still would be incense unto Him, but I certainly didn't experience them. This new, joyful and overflowing praise is wonderful.

As I look back over the last seven years of my life, I can honestly testify that what God has done during my dark night has been the best thing possible for me. I can't believe I am saying this, because it's been such a difficult road, but to know Jesus and His sweetness and His fellowship and His friendship the way that I am beginning to know and experience Him *is worth everything I had to suffer.*

Truly, "the sufferings of this present time are <u>not</u> worthy to be compared with the glory which shall be revealed in us." (Romans 8:18) I am beginning to get a taste of knowing Jesus--spirit to Spirit--and I never want to leave.

I finally understand what the writer of Hebrews meant when he said that Moses "endured, as seeing him who is invisible." (Hebrews 11:27) As I am seeking to live what Brother Lawrence calls "practicing the presence of Jesus," *God* has become my everything--my Friend, my Father, my Husband, my Lover, my Companion, my God, my King and my Lord--my everything.

The Psalmist aptly expresses my thoughts:

"O bless our God, ye people,
And make the voice of His praise to be heard:
Which holdeth our soul in life,
And suffereth not our feet to be moved.
For Thou, O God, hast proved us:
Thou hast tried us, as silver is tried.
Thou broughtest us into the net;
Thou laidst affliction upon our loins.
Thou hast caused men to ride over our heads;
We went through fire and through water:
But Thou broughtest us out into a wealthy place [freedom]."
(Psalm 66:8-12)

Key Points of This Chapter:

- God desires our spirit be purified and renewed so that we can experience fellowship with Him--Spirit to spirit.
- A renewed spirit means that our conscience has become cleansed, our intuition heightened and our communion sweetened.
- Once our spirit has been renewed and strengthened, God's Spirit can be released through us to fill and empower us.
- Our response is to worship Him in spirit and truth and manifest the beauty of *His* holiness.

Section Seven:
The Love Affair

"I am my Beloved's, and my Beloved is mine."
(Song of Solomon 6:3)

Chapter Thirteen
Further Blessings from Intimacy

In 1 Peter 5:8-10, God promises us that after we have suffered and barred ourselves from sin and self, He will make us perfect (complete) and established (strengthened).[577] And it's true. After our God-sent period of brokenness, the inner darkness that has plagued us for so long will finally begin to fade away and the light will appear. The images of anguish and loneliness will be replaced by certainty, joy and the penetrating peace of God's presence. Thus, we will begin to see and understand that all things do work together and that God has been "in control" all along.

Because of the faith and trust we are now experiencing, we are able to forget about ourselves and focus our minds on Christ. We no longer think so much about what we want or what we feel, but are able to give ourselves over to God and His will. We find ourselves not reacting as we used to or, I should say "overreacting" as we used to. The little irritating things that others do that used to bother us so very much are quickly forgiven, dealt with and forgotten. We are beginning to experience the grace of God in a way we never have before. We don't exactly understand how it is all being accomplished, but we do see a drastic change in ourselves. We are being healed from the *inside out* and becoming a totally different person. God's Love has become tangible and real and we encounter it at ever turn.

A few months ago, I was speaking in Georgia. Both men and women were in the audience (my Chuck was there also) and, so, I particularly wanted my talk to be Spirit-led. As I was approaching the podium, praying in the spirit that my words and actions would be all His, I heard God say in my spirit, *"Don't worry so much. I love you and I'm right here."* What a wonderful thought to have just before I was about ready to speak to others concerning His Love!

It doesn't matter where we are, what we are doing or how we are doing it, God will be right there. Our being able to "hear" His voice and experience His presence, however, still depends upon "our own location" to God at the moment. Are we worshiping Him at the Incense Altar of our hearts or are we back at the Brazen Altar ready to be cut, stripped and divided? Having spent "much time" at the last altar, I'd much rather stay at the first--in the presence of Jesus.

Intimacy offers more benefits than we could ever possibly mention, but several important ones need to be highlighted here.

The Joy of the Lord

Scripture tells us that "joy" comes as a result of suffering. "I say unto you, Ye shall weep and lament, but the world shall rejoice; and ye shall be sorrowful, *but your sorrow shall be turned into joy.*" (John 16:20)

As we allow God to purge our soul and purify our spirit, we will suffer. Certainly during those difficult times of stripping and crucifying, we won't "feel" God's joy. But as God begins to restore our soul and renew our youth and we begin to see His presence in all things, we will experience an unutterable and unspeakable joy.

As the Psalmist says, "...weeping may endure for a night (*a "night season"*), but joy cometh in the morning." (Psalm 30:5) And that joy and strength is something that no man, no situation and no illness can ever take from us.[578]

A Small Example

A couple of weeks ago, I was in the fitting room of a major department store, trying on a pair of jeans for an upcoming trip to Israel. Over the intercom, the store began to play some old "disco" music. Well, I love music and I love to dance. So I just couldn't help moving and hopping with the beat.

Pretty soon, I was dancing all over that tiny dressing room. No particular reason just filled with joy, the joy of God's presence. I could hardly put each piece of clothing on, because I was dancing so hard. It was a riot. I'm 61 years old! Boy, if that department store had hidden cameras anywhere in that dressing room, they certainly got an eyeful!

Certainly Psalm 30:11 is very appropriate here, "Thou hast turned for me my mourning into *dancing;* Thou hast *put off my sackcloth,* and *girded me with gladness.*"

You cannot imagine the harvest of lasting joy and peace that will come when we learn to become free of our soul's "whining," when Jesus finally becomes real and tangible in our hearts and lives. *It's Jesus' presence that brings us this joy.* As Psalm 16:11 declares, only in His presence is *fulness of joy* or complete joy. *Joy is our response to experiencing His presence.*

As God's overflowing, abundant, buoyant, joyful happenings begin to flood our soul, the long, dark, dreary, hopeless and bleak years of frustration and disappointment simply fade away.

An Example: Tammy

I did a seminar a few weeks ago in Northern California. A precious young woman named Tammy came up to me to share one of the most joyful stories I've heard in a long time. I was so touched by her story that I asked her to get up in front of the audience and share.

Tammy and her husband had had severe marital problems for many years. Tammy was a Christian, but her husband was not. (In fact, he was Jewish.) They had been married for about ten years and had two young children, but their marriage had been on the rocks for some time. They fought continuously and each had threatened to leave many times. Tammy had cried out to the Lord, she had prayed, she had fasted, she had read the Scriptures and she had listened for His answers. But nothing seemed to change the situation. The problems persisted. Finally, everything just seemed to unravel and Tammy came to the end of her rope. She felt she had tried everything she could to save her marriage, but to no avail. Consequently, she decided to throw in the towel.

Out of desperation, Tammy called her pastor and told him that she just couldn't take it any longer and was going to leave. Her pastor was very wise and said, "Tammy, give it three days. See what happens in three days. If things don't turn around by then, do what you have to do."

Wanting to be an obedient Christian, Tammy decided to follow his counsel. The three days passed, but they were even more miserable. Both she and her husband kept saying, "We need to talk," which meant, "We need to decide who is leaving and who is staying."

The third afternoon, Tammy was again crying on her bed (they had planned to have their "big talk" that evening). She really didn't want him to leave, nor did she want to leave. She still loved her husband; she just couldn't stand living with him. As she lay there praying, her eyes glanced down on a book she had had for over a year called *Why Should I be the First to Change?* She never had gotten around to reading it. The title intrigued her. How did it get on her bed now? She was sure she had packed it away with her other books.

She picked it up, read a few pages and was hooked. Through that little book, God began to expose all the things in her own soul that she had kept hidden and secret. His Spirit began to peel back all the veneer that concealed her real self--her real feelings. For the first time, she began to see herself through God's eyes. As a result, she began to feel such remorse over the way she had treated her husband. She began to cry and couldn't stop. She said she cried more in the next three hours than she ever had before. She felt horrible over some of the things she had done to her husband. She repented before God and cried even more out of sorrow.

Later, Tammy went downstairs for the "big talk," but instead of deciding which one was to leave and which one was to stay, Tammy was so full of the Love of God that she led her Jewish husband to the Lord. He was so overcome by the supernatural Love he felt from his wife that he wanted that same Gift of Love. Instead of leaving, he found His own personal Messiah. Since then, Tammy shared, her marriage has not only been reconciled, but it's been radically changed and healed from the inside out. Both of them are now following God's *Way of Love*.

As Tammy shared this story, the joy of the Lord not only filled her own countenance, but overflowed on to all of us in the audience. She was crying and laughing at the same time as she shared all that God had done. She was so full of the Spirit, we thought that at any moment her legs would just give way and she would collapse. Two of us ended up going up onto the stage to hold her up, reminding me of the incident in Exodus 17 where Aaron and Hur held up Moses' arms so that Israel might win the battle.

Tammy's story was one of the most joyous I've ever heard. I believe it turned out as it did, because of her obedience through a long, hard and dark night. Only through the shedding of our self life, can we truly enter God's presence and His joy.

> *"Thou wilt show me the path of life. In Thy presence is fulness of joy; at Thy right hand there are pleasures for evermore."* (Psalm 16:11)

Next time God allows a trial in your life, remember Tammy's story. Offer God the "sacrifices of joy" (Psalm 27:6) and know that, by faith, you will make it through, if you stay abandoned to His will. Remember the times He brought you through before. He will be faithful to also do it this time. Remember *joy, peace and love do not come from the absence of trials, but only from the presence of Jesus.* Jesus' presence during our hard times will enable us to say, "I am exceedingly joyful in all [my] tribulation." (2 Corinthians 7:4)[579]

This joyful, deep and lasting union should continue in the midst of any circumstance, even if our emotions fluctuate for the moment. No pain or outward circumstances should ever be able to prevent the peace and tranquility and unmoveableness of His presence. His presence is simply a habitual, uninterrupted, silent and secret conversation with Him that becomes a normal part of our daily experience.

When we begin to experience this kind of intimacy and begin to see that He truly is at our right hand, even in the midst of our troubles, this confidence will flood our soul with such joy that even death, itself, cannot hold us. Thus, the sting is taken out of our greatest enemy.

Joy, peace and faith are all linked together. Joy comes from the presence of the Lord; Peace comes from being fully persuaded that God will do what He has promised. And, faith comes from seeing God in all things.[580]

Fruitfulness

Another wonderful blessing that comes from knowing God intimately is the ability to genuinely share Jesus' Life and Love with others. Scripture tells this is one of our primary goals and purposes as Christians.

> "Now the end [goal, purpose] of the commandment is Love out of a pure heart..." (1 Timothy 1:5)

Jesus' presence brings us a commitment and a desire to share the Lord's burden--to share the gospel with others. Just as Paul's encounter with Jesus on the Damascus Road changed his life forever, we, too, will have an intense desire to share the gospel with others, not only in words, but also through our actions.[581] Christ has become our life, thus, it will be as natural for us to share what He is doing in our lives as it is to share family news or other happenings of the day.

When we are experiencing intimacy with Jesus by dwelling in His presence, we'll have a far greater capacity to genuinely feed and teach others[582] and our teaching and sharing will be done by *example*, not just by our *words*. As we said earlier, many instruct others on the "crucified life," but if they never have personally experienced it, how can they ever expect to give to others? Only the Spirit of God can touch and affect another's life, not our own soulish endeavors. The communication must be Spirit to spirit. This is the only way real *Life* is imparted.

Many mothers have written me in the past and asked how they can teach their children *The Way of Agape*. "Which book can I get?" "What class would be best?" "Which teacher would you suggest?" My response to them has always been the same: "*Live it yourselves*. Show your children that *agape* works for you, and that it is the *only* answer!" Our life actions are a hundred times better than our words.

An Example: Our Kids

Years ago, when Chuck and I were going through all our own marital problems (see *Why Should I Be the First to Change?*), our boys were teenagers. Teenagers and non-believers, I believe, are people the most "sensitive" to hypocrisy. They can spot phoniness a mile away.

Even with all our personal problems, Chuck and I were still teaching Bible studies in our home. With our words we were telling others, "Jesus is our life," "He's the *answer* to all our problems." In our hearts, we believed this to be true with all of our being, *but behind closed doors, it wasn't true at all.* Our lives were totally falling apart and our teenage boys saw the whole thing.

You can't tell your teenagers, *"Do as I say,"* and not expect them to look at your life and see if it works for you. *If it doesn't work for you in your own life, how can you expect them to want it for their own lives? Our lives need to be examples of what we say.* Otherwise, it's not the truth! (The definition of truth is "when our words and deeds match and become one.")[583]

Now this doesn't mean that we have to be "perfect" (in the sense of "having it all together"). None of us are or ever will be! But, it does mean we need to be *running to Jesus* as the Answer to all our problems. Then we will be showing our kids that, in spite of all that is going on in our lives, *He still is the only Answer!*

There's an old saying, "If we have *head knowledge*, then all we can give is head knowledge. If we have *heart knowledge*, then we can give heart knowledge. But, if we have *feet knowledge* (if we are really experiencing what we are sharing), then we can truly pass along life knowledge.

In other words, *only those who have lived the cross can give the cross.* Only those who are intimately experiencing Jesus can teach about intimacy. This is why Scripture exhorts us to let our lives become "open books"--read by all men.

> "Ye [your lives] are our epistle, written in our hearts, known and read of all men." (2 Corinthians 3:2)

Our Present Relationship with God Affects Everything

Our present relationship with God affects everything we think, say and do. The impact we have on the world around us depends upon the impact Jesus is having in our own lives *at that moment.* We can't function now on something Jesus did for us twenty years ago. Our relationship and our intimacy with Christ needs to exist in the "now." It must be on-going and growing like any love-relationship. When our fellowship with Him is intimate and we are experiencing being loved and cared for, then we will be able to extend that same Love and forgiveness to others. When our relationship with God is strained or even non-existent because we are holding on to some hurt, disappointment or fear,[584] then our relationship with others will also be greatly affected. We won't be able to extend unconditional Love and forgiveness because we are not experiencing it for ourselves.

"Rejection of God seems to go hand in hand with the rejection of others."[585] In order to love and forgive others genuinely, we need to first be sitting at the Lord's feet and filled with His Love.

Now if we are going through *a night season*, and we are not "feeling" or "seeing" anything from God at the moment, by faith we need to make those choices to allow God to purge what He needs to in us and expose the self-centered things in our lives. Then, also by faith, we must walk in His Love and forgiveness. Eventually, He will align our feelings with our faith choices and make us genuine.

During the times spiritually weak and someone asks how I am, I will often say, "Well, I have made the appropriate faith choices, *but my feelings haven't aligned yet.*" I'm being honest with them, and yet I haven't disappointed God by my remarks.

Remember, the timing for our "feelings" to eventually match up with our choices is up to God. We *can't* change our own feelings or emotions, we can only put in charge the person who can change our feelings, and that's God.

A Reproduction of Christ

God doesn't just want a *revelation of Christ,* He wants us to be *a reproduction of Christ.* God wants to form Christ in us so that outwardly we can reflect Him in all that we do, and inwardly we can commune and fellowship with Him.[586]

The proof of our being like Christ is shown by *what we do.* All that we do--whether at home, at the office, shopping, on trips, every place we go and everything we do--will bear fruit and show that we belong to God. It's not that our life will be a "piece of cake" and that we will breeze through (we definitely will not!), but that in all things, in all our experiences, our actions will prove that we belong to Christ and that we have an intimate Love-relationship with Him.

Paul expresses it so well in 2 Corinthians 6:4-10:

"...Approving ourselves as the ministers of God, in much patience, in afflictions, in necessities, in distresses, In stripes, in imprisonments, in tumults, in labors, in watching, in fastings;

by pureness, by knowledge, by long-suffering, by kindness, by the Holy Ghost, by love unfeigned, By the word of truth, by the power of God, by the armor of righteousness on the right hand and on the left, By honor and dishonor, by evil report and good report;

as deceivers, and yet true; As unknown, and yet well known; as dying, and, behold, we live; as chastened, and not killed; As sorrowful, yet always rejoicing; as poor, yet making many rich; as having nothing, and yet possessing all things."

This describes a Christian who truly is a "reproduction" of Christ. And, the same thing can happen in our relationship with others. We can be a reproduction of Christ to them in everything we say and do.

An Example: Fruit of a Pure Heart

A few months ago, I was on a radio talk show and a young Christian man called in and asked a very provocative question. "How can I show my wife that I really love her?" He said his non-believing wife had never experienced real Love. He had bought her many expensive personal gifts and trinkets for their home, but she still was very insecure in his love for her. He just wanted to know what he could do to really communicate how much he loved her.

I thought about it for awhile and said, "You know what. All the fancy gifts, treats and frills that you might buy your wife to show her your love, will never compare with the natural fruit of a pure and loving heart. In other words, nothing is more precious for a wife than seeing an *adoring look* from her husband's eyes, than feeling *a soft and gentle touch* on her neck from his hands or experiencing other *silent, loving actions* that convey so much louder than words, 'I love you.' These are the things that mean so much more to a wife than all the gifts, the presents and the goodies you could ever possibly buy her." (I also told him, however, that once he had convinced her of his love, then *gifts are wonderful too!*)

By doing these kinds of actions, this husband will not only convince his wife that he loves her, but he will also be a "reproduction of Christ" to her.

Chuck has become just that to me. His embrace in the mornings, his adoring look over the dinner table and his affectionately taking my hand when we're walking, all communicate his love for me much louder than any gift he could ever buy. He not only has become a vessel of human love towards me, but he has also become an extension of God's Love towards me. As 1 John 4:12 reminds us: "No man hath seen God at any time. If we love one another, God dwelleth in us, and His Love is perfected [allowed to flow through] us."[587]

Contentment

Now that our inner man (our spirit) has been strengthened by God's might and our outer man (our soul) has been endowed with God's *dunamis* Power, we can begin to experience a contentment and a rest from our own labors.[588]

Contentment and rest occur when we finally realize that every circumstance that happens to us is "Father-filtered." When we come to understand this, we can be comforted by the fact that since God is in everything, *nothing can really hurt us,* and, in the end, we will have a much closer walk with Jesus. This again validates the importance of knowing what God's will is in the night seasons. Sometimes God <u>does</u> allow hard things into our lives, but it's only to push us into full and experiential union with Himself.[589]

Contentment is not determined by our circumstances, by the actions of others or by how we feel. Contentment only comes from knowing that God loves us and that no matter what our circumstances are or how we feel, He will be faithful to His promises and bring us through.[590]

A Scriptural Example: Paul

Paul understood both sorrow and joy, distress and comfort and anxiety and rest. He had more difficulty in his life than you or I will ever know in a lifetime.[591] But the way he bore up under all the pressure of these trials was in personally knowing God's faithfulness and Love. Through all his wild adventures, Paul learned that *an intimate walk with Jesus is independent of external circumstances.* His spirit had become independent of his soul and was leading and directing his steps.

As he declares in Philippians 4:11, "I have learned, in whatsoever state I am, in this to be content." And, in verse 6 he says, we must be "anxious for nothing." In other words, there was *nothing* in his environment that could ever change his inward contentment.

This is our goal as Christians.

The verse that has meant so much to my life lately, as I have mentioned before, is Acts 20:24. "Let none of these things (other people, circumstances or my own feelings) move me." (Nancy's translation) Paul learned how to do this--to be content in every single circumstance of his life.

> "We are troubled on every side, *yet not distressed*; we are perplexed, *but not in despair*; Persecuted, *but not forsaken*; cast down, *but not destroyed*." (2 Corinthians 4:8-9)[592]

This kind of contentment is something that no earthly force can ever emulate and it's available to every one of us.   Now, I'm certainly not where Paul was, but his prayer has become my prayer. "May none of these things (my circumstances, my feelings, or others actions, etc.,) move me" from the presence of Jesus. As a result, I am beginning to see God free me from things that I never thought possible. And this has given me the confidence that as long as I allow Him to, He will *continue* to free me from all the things that have, for so long, kept me in bondage.

Consequently, we have the continual choice to either dwell with God at the Incense Altar of our hearts, or dwell in our current circumstances and situations. Sometimes it seems as if we focus so much on trying to get God to *change* our circumstances, that we don't stop to listen to see what He is doing in us *through* our circumstances. And, unfortunately, if we don't learn these lessons the first time around, God will often make us go through another set of similar circumstances so that we learn the very same lessons all over again.

Contentment is a state of mind and it only comes from living a totally crucified life.[593]

An Example: Corrie's Sister, Betsie

After all the horrifying things that Corrie and Betsie ten Boom experienced in prison, and all the hideous things that the German guards had done to them, Corrie turned to her sister one day and said, "Don't you hate them for what they have done to us?" Betsie sweetly looked up at her sister and replied, "Corrie, what better way to spend our life than to share the gospel with men who need it the most?"

Contentment comes from daily, moment by moment, abandonment to God's will, no matter what is going on in our lives. It means the appeasing of all our desires, because we know that only God can fulfill them. This kind of contentment is not found in others and what they will do for us, in our circumstances or in our accomplishments. Contentment is *only* found in Christ and what *He* will do for us. *A contented person is one who has no other need and no other desire than to be possessed by God.* He has absolute confidence that everything God allows in his life is His will.[594]

The secret of contentment is knowing where our satisfaction comes from.[595] If Jesus is our only satisfaction--and we know that He will never leave us or forsake us[596]--then when we find ourselves in difficult times, we'll be able to say, "none of these [other] things move me." (Acts 20:24) If, however, we look to any other person, thing or situation for our satisfaction, then we'll open ourselves up for disappointment, frustration and sorrow. Contentment is doing only that which God desires and knowing that only He will supply all our needs. (Philippians 4:19)

Knowing Christ intimately--experiencing His presence and fulness--is the only way we can be satisfied in all things. Knowing Him in this way fills all our emptiness with contentment, joy and peace.

The Rest of God

Contentment in our lives leads us to the "rest" of God, or the *promised land* that we hear so much about in the Old Testament.[597] Remember, Israel wandered in the wilderness for 40 years and never could seem to find rest. Over and over again, God told His people about the "promised land," and urged them to go in and *possess* it. As I recall biblical history, that promised land was only a few hundred miles away from them the whole time they wandered in the desert. Yet the Israelites couldn't seem to find it. The reason? *Because, in their dark night, they didn't believe God.*

There is a very valuable lesson here for us. No matter what God allows in our lives, no matter how bleak, how black, how painful, how confusing or how hurtful, we must choose to believe that God still is in control of our lives and that He will still lead us through to His "promised land."[598]

"And it shall be, when the Lord thy God shall have brought thee into the land which He swore unto thy fathers...to give thee great and goodly cities, *which thou buildedst not*, And houses full of all good things, *which thou filledst not*, and wells digged, *which thou diggedst not*, vineyards and olive trees, *which thou plantedst not*; when thou shalt have eaten and be full." (Deuteronomy 6:10-11)[599]

At the end of our dark night, if we have allowed God to do the necessary work, we will find a state of rest. He will have brought us to the end of ourselves, to the end of our works. And, the greater our rest, the more we will progress in our walk of faith.[600] God's rest means coming to a place where we are striving for nothing, but are simply abandoned to His will. It's where we have no expectations, no presumptions and no ambitions, except in God and what He wants for us. Whatever we do, we want it to be only His will.

As Hebrews 3:19 tells us, *faith* is the key to this kind of rest. If there is any unbelief or doubt, then we will <u>not</u> be able to enter. God's rest comes by simply living our lives according to His will and constantly avowing, "*No matter what You allow in my life, Lord, I trust You.*"[601]

> "In returning and rest shall ye be saved; in quietness and in confidence shall be you strength..." (Isaiah 30:15)

The bottom line is: Do we believe God or not? God wants us to experience the kind of rest that is undepressed by sorrow, unaltered by temptation and unterrified by adversity. *He wants us to rest from all our fears and sorrows and accept everything that He sends into our lives. He wants us to be "fully persuaded" that He will work all things together for good.*[602]

When we first begin our walk with Jesus, we will only experience this kind of rest occasionally. But after we have tasted the beauty, the savor and the incredible peace that intimacy with Christ brings, the difference between this "restful" walk and our previous walk of anxiousness and striving is so acute that we will yearn to have this rest permanently.

> "Be careful for nothing; but in everything, by prayer and supplication with thanksgiving, let your requests be made known unto God. And the peace of God, which passeth all understanding, shall keep your hearts and minds though Christ Jesus." (Philippians 4:6-7)

Private Quiet Times

I believe there definitely is a correlation between having our own personal quiet times with the Lord and enjoying His rest. It's very difficult to enjoy the rest of God and the kind of contentment we have been talking about if we haven't *first* had our own prayer time with the Lord. Jesus told His disciples, "come apart to a desert place, and rest a while." (Mark 6:31)

This quiet place is our own prayer time with the Lord, where we put off our *sin* and *self* and "put on" Christ. It's the time we empty ourselves out and deal with the things that God has shown us are not of faith. It's also the time where the Lord is faithful to take the things we surrender to Him "as far as the east is from the west" and, then, fill us back up with Himself. Spiritual quietness and the rest of God go hand in hand.

Noises and distractions of all kinds *do* draw our attention and focus away from the important. A truth that is often cited is that, "the urgent preempts the important." Noises can cause tremendous frustration, anxiety and exhaustion in our soul, so the enemy loves to use these distractions to wipe us out. He knows that without quietness and solitude, we will *not* have the chance to be cleansed or renewed. Thus, he knows we will end up quenching God's Spirit, with a resulting shallowness and hypocrisy in our lives. This, of course, is exactly his goal.

An Example: A Wild Airplane Ride

In 1997, Chuck and I hosted 250 people on one of our yearly trips to the Holy Land. Our return flight scheduled a stopover in Amsterdam. Despite the fact that I was exhausted, I had to hand-carry my bags up five flights of stairs because an inadequate number of bell hops were available and Chuck had remained in Israel for a business meeting.

After my bath, bone-weary, I climbed into an European bed made up with a plush comforter and plumb pillows. The experience was blissful-- for about five minutes. Just as I began to pray, thanking God for the day, a group of drunk or high men noisily entered the room above me. Yelling and laughing, screaming at full throttle, they jumped up and down. Knowing I could not enjoy the sleep I so desperately needed, I prayed, "Please, Lord, do something."

They all went into the bathroom directly over mine. The sound of their raucous laughter as they turned the water off and on, echoed loudly in my room below. Suddenly, all was quiet. I heard not another sound from them the entire night, and I slept like a baby.

Seattle-bound the next day aboard a 747, I settled comfortable into a window seat preparing to write a speech for an up-coming seminar. The weather was gorgeous; I was rested and refreshed, so I anticipated an enjoyable flight.

Wrong!

Of all of the planes going to the United States, out of all of the planes going to Seattle, and out of all of the 400 seats abroad that airliner, guess who was sitting directly behind me?

Already half out of their minds from alcohol and/or drugs, my tormentors from the night before began to curse and joke crudely both among themselves and with other passangers. My seatmate remarked, "This is going to be a long trip."

The men continued to drink utter profanities and became physically annoying by bumping and pulling back my seat. Despite my polite request for quiet, so I could work, despite a glaring look from my seatmate, their boorish behavior escalated. When I requested assistance from a flight attendant, they made a pass at her.

I finally went before the Lord: "Lord, I desperately need this time to write. I can't think, let alone write, with this profane noise behind me. I've done all I know to do. Please do something."

I had no sooner uttered that prayer than the flight attendant came back with one of the captains who requested the ringleader to follow him. After some resistance, he finally abdicated. His removal acted to quiet down the other three and they quickly drank themselves into another stupor.

My seatmate, a business executive who traveled extensively, looked at me and remarked, "In all my flying, I have never seen that happen before." With their ringleader gone and his accomplices silent, I was able to write my speech in peace and calmness. The noises and distractions that had drawn my focus away from the Lord were silenced.

In order to experience peace and rest in our *lives*, we must first go to God in prayer and experience that same peace and rest in our *hearts*. It's in our times of quietness and rest before the Lord that we develop our intimacy with God. These are the times that He puts all of our circumstances into perspective for us; gives us clear direction as to what His will is;[603] and then fills us with His Love and Power.[604]

Again, be sure to check out the Prayer Journal and, in particular, *The Inner Court Ritual,* in the Appendix of this book as to *how* to have a quiet time before the Lord and *how* to deal with the things that are not of faith. Hebrews declares:

> "Let us, therefore, fear lest, a promise being left us of entering into His rest, any of you should seem to come short of it." (4:1)

The only path that leads to the rest of God is *the path of faith.* The reason many of us are unable to enter God's rest is because of a lack of faith. Faith always accompanies contentment and rest.

Freedom of Spirit

Another wonderful blessing of intimacy with Jesus is the freedom that it affords us, not only from sin and unrighteousness, but also freedom from self-seeking, self-importance and of self-love. The Spirit literally gives us freedom from slavery or bondage to the "flesh."[605]

> "The Lord is that Spirit: and where the Spirit of the Lord is, *there is liberty* [freedom]." (2 Corinthians 3:17)

Intimacy with Jesus gives us freedom from human expectations, presumptions and comparisons, and freedom from guilt as well.[606] It's imperative that we not take this blessing for granted. All of our sins--past, present and future--and our guilt over them can be taken care of by daily confessing, repenting and giving them over to God. Guilt is a crippling disease and can <u>never</u> be eradicated from our lives, except by the blood of Christ. What freedom *Christ in us*, brings us!

Intimacy with Jesus not only brings us freedom from guilt (a cleansed conscience), but also gives us the freedom *to admit our failures* and the freedom to forgive others of theirs. Oh, how the Christian body needs to experience this kind of freeing Love. It grieves my heart that so many of us are <u>not</u> walking out these truths. The body of Christ has become "lame" because we do not live out this kind of freedom in our relationships. There are more Christian divorces, more broken Christian relationships and more splintered Christian churches now than at any time in history.

How desperately we Christians need to experience the freedom from being ruled by our emotions--emotions of either rejection or approval. This kind of freedom is the only thing that will break the chains that bind us and allow us to be totally "other-centered," to hear and receive direction only from God and to care only about what He wants. This kind of liberty not only leads us to freedom from all things seen, but also gives us the ability to walk in the fear of God and not the fear of man.

A Scriptural Example: Joseph

Of all the examples of freedom of spirit that I can think of in the Bible, the one that stands far and above the rest is Joseph.

Joseph is the perfect example of someone who was supernaturally endowed with the freedom to unconditionally forgive. We talked about Joseph in Chapter Two. What we didn't mention was the fact that he unconditionally forgave his brothers for their evil deed against him, long *before* they ever asked for forgiveness. In Chapter 45 of Genesis, Joseph explains to his brothers, "it was not you that sent me here [Egypt], but God." (verses 5 and 8)

Joseph goes on to state, "you thought evil against me; but God meant it unto good, to bring to pass, as it is this day, to save much people alive." (Genesis 50: 20) Joseph then treats them kindly and gives them houses and provides for their families' needs. This is an incredible example of the freedom of forgiveness that God gives us when we experience intimacy with Him.

Another Example: Dead Men Walking

The Academy Award-winning movie *Dead Man Walking* is a true story about a beautiful young woman named Debbie Morris. Debbie is a great example of someone who, even though she had a real and despicable enemy, overcame her "justified" unforgiveness and was able to go on to experience real freedom of spirit.

Debbie was only 16 when she was kidnapped, terrorized and raped by a crazed madman, and her boyfriend mutilated, shot and left for dead.

Debbie has endured years and years of trauma and torment as she has tried to heal herself from this horrific incident. She has had to deal with memories that most of us will never even read about. In trying to find healing, Debbie attended her attacker's trial and witnessed his being sentenced to execution (he had killed a girl he raped two days before Debbie). She has suffered through years of medication, counseling and therapy, all trying to renew her mind.

Through a series of circumstances, God eventually brought her to Himself and began to minister His Love and forgiveness to her. As she began to trust Him with her fears, memories and unforgiveness, she began to get well. One of the hardest choices she ever had to make (and yet one of the most important) was to genuinely forgive "the man who ruined her life."

In an article she wrote about her life, she said someone asked her the question "What has helped you the most?" I thought her reply to be very provocative, "Justice (seeing her attacker get sentenced to death) didn't do anything for me. *Only forgiving him did.*"[607] Debbie realized the truth of John 8:36:

"If the Son, therefore, shall make you free, ye shall be free indeed." (John 8:36)

This kind of freedom comes only by faith--the faith to dwell in God's presence, no matter what the world tells us, what our emotions are saying or what is going on in our lives.[608]   Only faith is the victory that "overcomes." *Overcomers* are those who trust God and choose to do His will no matter what.

> "For whatsoever is born of God overcometh the world; and this is the victory that overcometh the world, even our faith." (1 John 5:4)[609]

Freedom from our Enemies

The reason faith is so critical is because it is the only thing that allows us to remain in God's presence, no matter what is going on around us. No one can touch us there--not our enemies, our foes, our feelings, our thoughts or our circumstances.[610]

The Bible tells us that Jesus came to set the prisoners "free."[611] In other words, He is the only One who <u>can</u> loose our bonds."

If you recall the floor plan of Solomon's Temple, the Holy of Holies, the Holy Place and the Golden Vestibule (or the porch) were inviolate (i.e., holy), which meant that no one but the priests were allowed to enter. In like manner, God has made our hearts and spirits impregnable.

In other words, the enemy has <u>no</u> access to these areas. Thus, if we remain in God's presence at the foot of the Incense Altar, the enemy cannot touch us. However, if the devil can, once again, stir up our soul or our senses in any way and we fall for it, then he will be able to capture us and make us his prisoners. Therefore, remaining in the Holy Place of our hearts is essential. As Jesus promises,

> "To him that *overcometh* will I grant to sit with Me in My throne, even as I also overcame, and am set down with My Father in His throne." (Revelation 3:21)

To be an overcomer simply means to experience freedom from self, freedom from others' reactions, freedom from our circumstances and freedom from the enemy's attacks.

As overcomers, our spirits can soar like the eagle above the clouds, because our eyes are only upon the Son. The eagle was intended for the heights, just as we are. When the eagle remains in the heavenlies, he is *safe* from harm. No enemy can touch him there. The same is true with us. Yet, rather than fly like an eagle above the clouds, many of us would rather huddle with the chickens in the barnyard.

God wants us free and soaring in the heavens. Are you?

> "Let all thine enemies perish, O Lord; but let them that love Him be as the [Son] when He goeth forth in His might." (Judges 5:31)

True Humility

The greatest freedom of all is humility.

Humility is the ability to accept the truth about ourselves. It's being able to see ourselves as we truly are. A truly humble person is one who is not afraid of failure, because he has perfect confidence in God's power and ability.

Humility is not shyness, hesitancy or timidness but an attitude of refusing to make ourselves the center of attention. A genuinely humble person is one who no longer is concerned about their own self-interests, their own reputation or being acknowledged themselves. They don't waste their time or efforts on defending these areas any more. They are fully content with personally taking a back seat and simply being filled with the fulness of Christ and sharing His Life.

Humility is putting God and what He wants above our own needs. The essence of pride is "I will." The essence of humility is "Thy will." The Greek word for *humility* comes from the root *phren*, which means "to rein in or to overcome." May God give us the strength and the humility to bring into captivity our sin and our self, so that Christ can be formed in us and we can enjoy His presence. However, if we are not willing and not humble enough to rein in our self, then we can't expect to experience either intimacy with Christ or His Life flowing through us.

Fenelon asserted:

> "Separation from the world means turning away from external things. When humility is formed in you, then you will turn away from your own *self*."[612]

The only route to humility, is the cross. *We are humble only to the extent that we lose ourselves in Him.* "For I [am] determined not to know any thing among you, save Jesus Christ, and Him crucified." (1 Corinthians 2:2)

When we look upon the world as something that is supposed to be focused on *us*, we will be imprisoned by self, unable to give or secure love. When God breaks through our darkness and destroys that self by the dark night, He sets us free to love and be loved the way He intended all along. We'll be free from needing love from anyone or anything, save God Himself, and we'll be free to initiate Love to others.

Only Jesus has ever loved perfectly. Humans will always fall short. But the more we learn to give ourselves over to God, the more capacity we'll have to be the initiator of that kind of unconditional Love.

In *The Way of Agape,* we speak of human love as being a "need love." In other words, we "need" that other person to return our love, whereas, we speak of God's *Agape* Love as a "gift of Love," free for the asking.

When we freely give away God's gift of real Love, we are, in a sense, being humble. At that moment, we are more concerned about other's interests and about what Christ wants, than we are about what we want. Humility is simply acting out "not I but Christ." (Galatians 2:20) When we display this kind of humility to the world, others *will* notice and others *will* want what we have.

This is the kind of love and this is the kind of freedom the world and everyone in it is desperately looking for, but very few are willing to pay the price of humility.

How Do We Stay in the Presence of God?

At some point, the question we want to ask ourselves is not "How do we experience oneness with God?" but "How do we stay there?" All of us have come in and out of intimacy with God at one time or another. To experience this state of intimacy is one thing, but to stay there for any length of time is quite another.

As one girl pleaded with me in her letter last week, "The Lord did a miracle in my life a little while ago (and I 'saw' Him), but I've lost it and *I don't know how to get back there and find Him!* Nancy, how do I find Him again?"

How do we stay steadfast and immovable in the presence of God?[613] Scripture tells us the only way we can remain steadfast in God's presence is by shedding all our attachments: self, others, friends, reputation, importance, wealth, delights, positions, control, comforts. Detaching ourselves from these is the secret to finding God's presence every moment.

I am not stating that God will always remove these things from our lives. He is not a vindictive God, but a loving God. *He simply must remove our "eyes" from being focused on these things for our security, our identity, our love and our fulfillment.* He wants us to remain unattached to these things, so that we can remain abandoned to His will.

Remain Abandoned to His Will

Just as Jesus, our example, always chose to do the will of the Father,[614] *the whole secret of the Christian walk is simply detachment from sin and self and abandonment to God's will.*[615] Only in this way, can we stay steadfast and immovable in the presence of God. *Relinquishment of sin is the "key" to the Inner Court, but relinquishment of self is the key to the Holy Place.*

We must leave the success or failure of all issues with God. Oh, how to do hard this for many of us, because we are such "doers." All the *doing*, however, must only be God's doing. The only "doing" that we are responsible for is the yielding of self. Then God can do *through us* all that needs to be done.

Abandonment to God's will means kind of floating weightlessly, having released all personal clutching for emotional and intellectual security, all personal needs to know and understand, all personal disturbances about being right, all personal humilations at being wrong, making mistakes and looking stupid, and all personal frustrations over being denied what we thought God promised. It's being completely dead to all our own interests, passions, prejudices, pleasures and reputation, and leaving everything in God's hands.

Abraham is an incredible example of this total submission to God. To me, the ultimate test of abandonment to God's will was when God asked Abraham to offer Isaac his only son. Genesis 22 tells us that Abraham amazingly did not fight God. He simply obeyed and trusted that God would "provide Himself a lamb." (vs. 8)

In verse 10, Abraham actually stretches out his hand to slay Isaac as God had told him to do, when an angel calls out to him (verse 12): "*Now I know that thou fearest God seeing thou hast not withheld thine only son from Me.*"

Ask yourself, could you have done that? I'm not so sure I could have gone that far. But this is what abandonment to the will of God means. It means walking in complete obedience and leaving everything else to Him. Abraham was completely abandoned to God's will, yet, he actively moved and did all that was required of him.

Again Fenelon expresses such abandonment perfectly:

"Inward peace comes [only] with absolute surrender to the will of God. *...The reason you feel so agitated is that you do not accept everything that happens to you with complete trust in God.* Put everything in His hand, and offer yourself to Him as a sacrifice. ...Until you reach this point of surrender, your life will be full of trouble and aggravation. ...So give your heart wholly to God and you will find peace and joy in the Holy Spirit."[616]

Be Surrendered, Not Passive

The abandonment to God's will that I am speaking about is <u>not</u> passivity or ceasing to resist altogether. It's not lying back and doing nothing. The abandonment to God that I am talking about *is actively seeking to carry out God's will, and yet willingly accepting all that He sends our way.* This kind of submission is <u>not</u> *apathy, indifference* or *immobility*, but simply a yieldedness and a relinquishment to God and all that He allows in our lives as if we were resting like a baby in His arms.

While we are resting, however, it's imperative that we continue to take up the offensive in our battle against the world, the flesh and the devil by *actively* making faith choices. We do so by making choices to love God, to love others, to put on the armor of God, and to fight the enemy by faith.

Abandonment to God's will occurs when our soul is surrendered and our spirit is in its rightful place, teaching, leading and guiding us. *The greater the abandonment, the more we will progress in our spiritual walk.* I mean that the more we learn <u>not</u> to fight what God is doing in our lives, but simply to resign ourselves to His workings, the faster we will progress towards experiential intimacy with Him. Had I understood this principle at the beginning, my dark night might not have taken me years to get through!

The Apostle Paul experienced such complete surrender. In Philippians 4:12 he avows, "I know both how to be abased, and I know how to abound: every where and in all things I am instructed both to be full and to be hungry..."

Abandonment to God's will ultimately means that we are so completely yielded to God, and to what He wants, that there is no room for anything else. There has been a complete exchange of energy! We have given God our all and He has given us His. A person who is intimate with Jesus, then, will <u>not</u> be destroyed when "bad" things occur in his life. He might be troubled, perplexed, persecuted and cast down, *but he will not be distressed, in despair, forsaken or destroyed.* (2 Corinthians 4:8)

Abandonment to God's will, again, is actively seeking to carry out His will, and yet willingly accepting all that He sends.

Abandonment to His will is the only way to live the Christian life, because it's the only way that works and the only thing that brings us peace! Confidence in God's Love, protection and friendship produces a certain strength in us which enables us to handle every situation that comes along. Being abandoned to God's will incorporates a mixture of faith, hope and love--all in one single act.

Let Go of Our Own Needs

Abandonment to God's will means that we have cast all of our cares, all of our needs, upon Him. We have aligned ourselves to what the Lord wants in all things, not what we want. It's letting go of our own needs, cleansing our hearts and giving ourselves unreservedly over to Him. It's letting go of our own desires, our own abilities, our own understanding, our own reason, our own rights, our own feelings and our own liking. Such abandonment requires simply forgetting about our past and leaving our future in God's hands.

Detachment and abandonment to God can occur only when we can honestly confront whatever comes our way without fear. We know that abandonment is present when we have peace, love and freedom in spite of what is happening in our lives. It's letting nothing interrupt our tranquility. *The obstacle to detachment is "self."* We must learn to constantly live like Paul, who said, "I am determined not to know any thing...but Christ crucified." (1 Corinthians 2:2)

Only a few short years ago, the words *detachment* and, *abandonment* would simply have been cliche's to me. But, after experientially getting a glimpse of what abandonment to God can really mean, I am beginning to see the glory one might experience if he remains yielded and surrendered consistently.

Again, we must remember that there is only One who was able to stay permanently abandoned to God's will and experience consistent oneness with Him, and that, of course, is Jesus. As long as we are in our human bodies, we will move in and out of that intimacy.

Letting go of our own needs frees us from any longer having to think about ourselves, *because our face is now turned in a completely different direction. Letting go of our "needs" means being lost in God and what He requires.*

An Example: Livingstone

One of the most poignant examples of one who set aside his own needs to be entirely surrendered to God's will was David Livingstone--an English physician in the late 1800s who felt a call from God to evangelize inland Africa. As you can imagine, he encountered many dangerous threats, including a lion who mauled his arm so badly, he was maimed for life.

Dr. Livingstone was a confirmed bachelor until he met and fell in love with Mary Moffat, the daughter of some missionaries stationed near by. They married and had four children. That David loved his wife passionately was apparent to all around him.

However, he felt strongly that God wanted him to open up the interior of dark Africa. His own desire was to settle down with his beloved wife and children, but he knew that God had a "call" on his life. Mary stayed with him for awhile on the mission field, but because she was fragile and in poor health, she eventually took the children back to England, where she stayed with her parents.

It was a very difficult time for them because they had to be separated from each other for *years* at a time. Gossip began, "Why is he always leaving her? Can't they get along? Something must be wrong with their marriage." Mary hated being in England, apart from her beloved. She desperately wanted to be with David, but her health would not permit it. She wrote to him often, begging him to return home to his family.

David, however, was at the crux of his career. And it forced upon him the realization that his call from God as an active missionary and his duties as a husband and father were two things that were incompatible. One or the other must be sacrificed.

David struggled for a long time over this horrible decision, but finally came to the conclusion his calling before God was more important. He felt that if he didn't follow through with what God had already begun in Africa through him, the interior would never again be open to the gospel message.

After five years, Mary finally joined David, only to die a short while later, nearly crushing Livingstone's spirit. Making one last visit to England, he disappeared in the deepest part of Africa for another five years.

He was not seen or heard from by anyone. Finally, an American editor who took an interest in the story traced Livingston for nearly a year. When he finally caught up with him, all Livingstone could say was, "I am a missionary, heart and soul and in God's service. There I wish to live and there I wish to die. Viewed in relation to my calling, the end of my geographical feat is only the beginning of the enterprise."

Livingston died shortly thereafter, but he remains a hero to all the English people for his incredible courage and determination in the face of extreme difficulties. His body lies in Westminster Abbey.

Livingston chose God and abandonment to His will over his own desires and needs. He forgot about himself, because his face was turned in a different direction.

Live for the Moment

As I mentioned before, the turning point in my own dark night experience occurred when I realized that *abandonment to God's will and human expectation cannot co-exist.* Abandonment to God's will is getting to the point where we assert like Paul, "None of these things move me, neither count I my life dear unto myself..." (Acts 20:24); whereas, human expectation is picking back up all the pieces of our lives and, once again, running around trying to fit them back together.

God brought me to the place where I finally saw that I couldn't do *both!* I couldn't have human expectations and be abandoned to God's will at the same time. Once I began to recognize this truth and began giving God all my expectations and chose to remain abandoned to His will, my life began to change. *I began to live for the moment--not for my own expectations, dreams, hopes and plans!*

Living for the moment is being content with the "here and now," no matter what it contains. We are satisfied with the present because we know it contains God's plan for us. It's His will for our lives at the moment.

I remember years ago, I remember picking up and reading *Practicing the Presence of Jesus* by Brother Lawrence.

Example: Brother Lawrence

Brother Lawrence was a lay brother at one of the Carmelite monastaries in France in the mid-1600s. While doing only the most menial jobs--washing, cleaning and cooking, he constantly enjoyed the "presence of Jesus." His only desire in life was to commune with God.

He could worship anywhere: in a cathedral or while washing dishes in the kitchen. He used to tell his brothers, "I live my life as if there is only He and I in the world." He felt that our only satisfaction in life should come from fulfilling God's will. Thus, he needed that unbroken fellowship with Him, in order to hear what that will was. He always left the "choice" to God, waiting in peace to see what that choice was.

The key to Brother Lawrence's intimacy with Jesus was that he believed no matter what happened, God would <u>never</u> deceive him and would only allow such things into his life that were good for him. *"Living for the moment"* was both his daily motto and the reason he was able to really "know" the fulness of God.

At the time I read Brother Lawrence's book, I didn't understand this principle of "living in the present," so I missed his whole point. I could see that what Brother Lawrence experienced was wonderful, but I didn't understand how to get there or how to remain there.

Now I see.

Living for the moment is coming to a place in your walk with God where you are not striving or reaching or pushing for anything. You're completely abandoned to God and His will, therefore, there's no room for expectations other than from Him.

Living for the moment is relinquishing ourselves to God's hidden guidance and accepting everything that comes our way as being from Him. We don't need to understand all that He is doing in our life, but only to accept it. *Living for the moment is accepting what we cannot avoid (or change), and enduring (with love and resignation) the things that would normally cause us weariness and disgust.*

Seeing God's hand in the apparent trivialities of the moment will bring us closer to God. What He does with us is entirely up to Him. The final stage of this interior life is where we finally enter the "promised land" of fruits and nuts and honey. There, we can enjoy the vineyards that <u>we</u> did not plant, the wells that <u>we</u> did not dig. (See Deuteronomy 6:10-11.)

Do Those Things That Please God

In 1 John 3 we are told that we are always to "do those things that are pleasing in His sight." (verse 22)

Since the King of Glory has become our sole focus of attention[617] we are not so much concerned about others' approval or their disapproval anymore, but only about pleasing and loving Him. Consequently, *we won't be loving others out of our desperate need to be loved by them in return*. We will be free from self-centered motives, thus, everything we do will be out of our love for God and our desire to please Him.[618] He has become the center of life for us. We have given Him our wills and our lives and there is no way we are ever going to take them back. Fleshly glory has lost its appeal because all our hopes and expectations are now focused on Him.[619]

Again, there is a paradox here that I find interesting. The natural outcome of loving and pleasing God first is that we will be putting others' interests and concerns before our own, i.e, loving them. The difference is that our motivation has changed. *We are not "loving others" in order to manipulate and get their approval or their love, but we are loving them simply as the natural outflow of loving and pleasing God.* It only works in this order, however. We love and please God first; He, then, enables us to genuinely love and please others.

Trust and Obey Him

Finally, in order to stay in this spiritual union, we must develop an unfaltering trust in and obedience to God.[620] We must not listen to the voice of our natural reasoning, but simply put all our reliance upon Him,[621] "hoping against hope," as Romans 4:18 says. Like a baby in his father's arms sleeping without fear, we unreservedly trust our Father. *"Perfect trust means you must turn your back on yourself."*[622] We are asleep in our Father's arms, with no thought of fear, but simply a willingness to follow Him anywhere. The more resigned we can become to His care, the more indifferent we will become to the conditions around us.[623] And, we won't be moved by the frightening occurences that we see, because we are abandoned to His will.

Jesus, again, is our example. He not only *chose* to be abandoned to His Father's will, He also lay down *His life* to the Father's will. And, thus, He enjoyed the Father's uninterrupted communion and intimacy.

As we, too, surrender our wills and our lives at the cross, along with all our fears, our doubts, our unbelief, our presumptions and our expectations, the result will be an unshakable trust in God's provision for us.[624] We will have come to the place where we are allowing God to possess us without holding anything back. We will have stopped "preserving ourselves," which was the cause of our suffering in the first place, and will be seeking to speak, act and live under the complete guidance of the Holy Spirit

Merely, *saying* with our words, "I trust you," is <u>not</u> enough. We must daily *prove* this trust in our lives. Matthew 16:24 talks about "following" in Jesus' footsteps. Listen:

> "If any man will come after Me, let him deny himself, and *take up his cross, and follow Me."*

To "pick up our cross and follow Him" means to relinquish everything to Him, even the things that we don't understand, and to develop *an unshakable trust in Him*. It means to enter into a commitment with Him that, regardless of our circumstances, we will face them without fear because we know *He will be there with us*.

An Example: Anita and Paul

My dear friend Anita is a beautiful example of this. She is a modern day "Diana."

Like Diana, Anita contracted cancer about three years ago, and was told there was not much hope left. Like Diana, Anita has sacrificed everything she is and everything she has for the Love of Jesus. Her only desire, like Diana, is to "please God in all things."

Anita and her husband Paul, in their late thirties, have four beautiful children. Even though the doctors gave them such a discouraging prognosis for her illness three years ago, Anita and Paul decided they would not give up by listening only to man's opinion, but would unconditionally trust and believe in God's provisions for a healing. Convinced that Anita's life belongs to the Lord, they believe that *He* will take her home *only* when He was ready, not just because the doctors have predicted it.

They began a path of healing, using many of the procedures that the doctors recommended, but also using their own homeopathic cures along with prayer, trust, obedience, surrender and relinquishment.

We have all watched in amazement as this beautiful sister in the Lord has made a miraculous recovery. From being hospitalized and completely bedridden three years ago unable to even sit up or eat, she went with 250 of us to Israel last year. She had no wheelchair, no walker and no cane.

She was the first one up every morning, the first one on the bus and the first one in line for whatever sightseeing climb or adventure was planned for that day.

Truly, Anita has picked up her cross, and she *is* following Jesus with an unshakable trust wherever He leads her.

God promises that He will return to us "a hundredfold" all that we have chosen to surrender to Him. "Verily I say unto you, There is no man that hath left house, or brethren, or sisters, or father, or mother, or wife, or children, or lands, for My sake, and the gospel's, But *he shall receive an hundredfold now in this time*, houses, and brethren, and sisters, and mothers, and children, and lands, with persecutions; and in the world to come eternal life."(Mark 10:29-30)

Practical Guidelines to Remaining Abandoned

Before we close this chapter, here are a few *practical guidelines* to help us daily remain abandoned to God's will. (Further details are covered in *The Inner Court Ritual* found in the Prayer Journal in the Appendix.):

Commit each day to be abandoned to God's will.
Daily, confess and repent of your sin and self and ask forgiveness.
Ask Him to deliver you from further self-centered feelings, thoughts and desires.
Have no expectations or presumptions other than in Him.
Reject all imagination, high things and useless thoughts that drag you down.
Hold your mind steadfast on Him.
Don't let distractions cause your thoughts and emotions to wander off.
Distrust your own strength and abilities; depend completely upon God's strength.
Humble yourself before Him and live so as not to offend Him.
Perform everything from a motivation of love for Him.
Worship and praise Him as much as you can.

――――――――

Psalm 145 seems so appropriate here. Note what *we* are to do; and then, see what *the Lord* will do:

"I will *extol* Thee, my God, O king; And I will *bless* Thy Name for ever and ever. Every day will I *bless* Thee; And I will *praise* Thy Name for ever and ever. Great is the Lord, and greatly to be praised; And His greatness is unsearchable. One generation shall *praise* Thy works to another, And shall *declare* Thy mighty acts. I will *speak* of the glorious honor of Thy majesty, And of Thy wondrous works. And men shall *speak* of the might of Thy terrible [awesome] acts: And I will *declare* Thy greatness. They shall abundantly *utter* the memory of Thy great goodness, And shall *sing* of Thy righteousness... All Thy works shall praise Thee, O Lord; And Thy saints shall *bless* Thee. They shall *speak* of the glory of Thy kindgom, And *talk* of Thy power; To *make known* to the sons of men His mighty acts, And the glorious majesty of His kingdom... *The Lord upholdeth all that fall, And raiseth up all those that be bowed down.* The eyes of all wait upon Thee; And *Thou givest them their meat in due season. Thou openest Thine hand, And satisfiest the desire of every living thing.* The Lord is righteous in all His ways, And holy in all His works. *The Lord is nigh unto all them that call upon Him, To all that call upon Him in truth. He will fulfill the desire of them that fear* [reverance] *Him: He also will hear their cry, and will save them. The Lord preserveth all them that love Him.*"

Key Points of This Chapter:

- Intimacy with God allows us to enjoy the *fulness of Christ*--He is all and in all.
- This intimacy brings us the joy of the Lord, the ability to share Jesus' Life with others and a contentment and rest from our own labors.
- Spiritual oneness with God brings freedom--freedom from self and freedom from our enemies.
- The only way we can remain in God's presence is by abandoning ourselves to His will and living for the moment.

Chapter Fourteen
My Own Love Affair with Jesus

"I am my beloved's and His desire is toward me."
(Song of Solomon 7:10)

The Great Hoshana

It was October 22, 1997, the day on the Jewish calendar that is called *The Great Hoshana*.[625]

The Great Hoshana is a Jewish festival on the *seventh* day of the Feast of Sukkot in the *seventh* month of the year.[626] It was a great and joyful feast to the Lord and commemorated the end of Israel's 40 years in the wilderness and their entrance into the "promised land" of *rest*.[627] After they had eaten unleavened bread for the six days of the festival, the seventh day, the Great Hoshana, was a day of joyous celebration--filled with praise, singing, and great rejoicing.[628] The feast symbolized Israel's prayers and hopes for a *good and bountiful harvest in the coming year*. Hoshana was also a special day of judgement during which God's decrees for the coming year would be finalized. The entire next year would be spent rejoicing, praying and studying God's Word.

As I began my own devotional reading this particular morning, I recognized that this was not only a very significant month and day for the Jews, it was also a very special month and year for me. I, too, had been a Christian exactly 40 years (1957)! And, I too, had wandered in the wilderness for most of those 40 years, never truly entering God's rest. I don't want to disparage *all the wonderful things* that God has done in my life over the last 40 years--learning to love Him; learning to love others; learning to renew my mind--but, in all candor, up to that point, I had never really known the complete abandonment to God's will that makes rest with Jesus possible. I had come in and out of wonderful times with the Lord, but never had really stayed there and rested at His feet for any length of time.

Next, I noticed on our Jewish calendar, that 1997 was considered by some to be a very special year for the Jews. Throughout Jewish history, every seventh year was called "a sabbath to the Lord" (Leviticus 25:4) and was very special because it was known as the "year of release."

(Deuteronomy 15:9)[629] It was the year the Lord designed to allow the land to lie fallow (to rest) and the year that every creditor could be released from debt.

Again, I noticed the personal parallel. Not only had I been a believer 40 years, but also I was in the seventh year of my own dark night, which began back in 1990. I prayed, too, that it might be my own "year of release." The Scriptures God gave me that morning in my devotion time seemed to confirm that He might be doing just that. Psalm 102 not only talks about the "set time to favor her has come," but also it says, "to *release* those appointed to death."[630]

I received several other Scriptures that morning that implied the very same promise. Oh, how I prayed that this would be my year to be "released." I prayed that I would have learned the lessons God was trying so hard to teach me and that I might be freed to share them with others.

Back in November of 1991, God had impressed upon my heart to write a book on the dark night. I was so excited to do it, but knew in my spirit that *it wasn't time yet*--I still had much to learn. I was fascinated, however, by the many saints whom I was learning about who had experienced such a "night season," and yet I found relatively few good books written on this important subject. I knew it wasn't yet God's timing for me to write, but I prayed that when I was ready, He would let me know. Somehow I knew that the ending of my own dark night was tied to the commission to write this new book.

I concluded my wonderful prayer time that morning with 1 Timothy 1:16 which declares, "...that in me first Jesus Christ might show forth all long-suffering, for a pattern [a model, an example] to them which should hereafter believe on Him."

That day I also received a letter from a friend back East whom I had not seen for over eight years who had no idea what was going on in my life. In her letter she had some wonderful, and also very interesting, words of encouragement for me about the coming year. Having just read about the Great Hoshana and what it symbolized--Israel's prayers and hopes for *a good and bountiful harvest in the coming year*--her words riveted my attention: "*...you are due for a good and bountiful harvest, beyond any you have ever seen or dared to ask for, hope for or imagine.*"

Could her "wording" simply be a coincidence? Maybe. Maybe not!

As I look back on that particular day, October 22, 1997, it amazes me all the things that God communicated to me and, yet, because I didn't understand all He was going to do, I missed completely. For example, just as the Jews spent the entire next year after the Great Hoshana feasting, rejoicing, praying and studying the Word, that's exactly what happened to me the following year. Once I received the commission to write this book (see next page), I had the privilege of being able to pray and study God's Word for hours daily and, consequently, was filled with unspeakable joy that continually overflowed my soul.

My Beloved

Two weeks after my own "special" Hoshanna, I had a seminar scheduled in the state of Washington. I had privately complained about doing this retreat, because I was going to have to rent a car and drive myself from the airport to the retreat grounds, two and a half hours away. Normally, the women in charge of a seminar meet me at the airport and then drive me to the retreat center or the convention center. This arrangement is always more convenient because I'm usually not familiar with the area. This retreat, however, had some special circumstances which made this impossible; thus, I needed to drive myself.

Well, it was a God *set-up!* The Lord had arranged these circumstances, so that "we" could have a weekend together that I will never forget as long as I live. I like to call my next three days with God *my love affair with Jesus.*

I had been reading a wonderful book on the Song of Solomon and learning some new things about intimacy with Jesus. Somehow, in my 40 years as a Christian, I never really thought much about the Lord being my own Lover. I had known Jesus as my Lord and Savior, my Friend, my Confidant, my Master, my Creator, my King, my Comforter, my Life and my Love, but the concept of *me* being His beloved and His spouse was really foreign to me. The next three days, however, would change all that.

The drive to the retreat was one I will never forget. It was one of those magnificent fall afternoons, clear and crisp with a bright blue sky and white bellowing clouds (very similar to the day I climbed the mountain in Big Bear). The scenery along the way was breathtaking and with the worship music that I had brought along, the ride was truly a little bit of heaven. Jesus, music and scenery, what else is there?

Jesus began to love me that afternoon as I have not ever experienced. There are no adequate words in my vocabulary to describe the joy and exilaration I felt in His presence. As Charles Finney expressed it, "It was like liquid love."

All I can say is that God's presence was more real to me that afternoon than my actual physical existence in that car. Many of you will know exactly what I am talking about. You can't help but feel that you are more a part of Him than you are yourself. That's exactly how it was. I can only liken it to Job's experience and the way he expressed it in Job 42:5. I had heard of Jesus before, *but now my eyes see Him*.

God witnessed to my heart that afternoon, "You will never find yourself again--because you are now completely mine." I felt like the Shulamite woman must have felt in Song of Solomon, "I am my beloved's, and my Beloved is mine ..." "... and His desire is towards me." (Song of Solomon 6:3; 7:10)

I would like to have stayed in that car forever!

The Commission to Write

The next morning at the retreat, in my prayer time, God gave me some wonderful personal promises.[631] Each of the Scriptures had something to do with "raising up God's standard of faith and Love"; with "casting up the highway;" with "removing the stones from the path"[632] and with being a "repairer of the breach." I began to get very excited because these were some of the very Scriptures He had originally given me back in 1991 concerning the writing of this book.

During the day, a Bible teacher, whom I had never met before, came up to me and told me she had "something from the Lord" for me. She told me that she had not planned to come to the seminar, but that God had prompted her to come and talk specifically with me. She then proceeded to give me the most wonderful and the most amazing prophecy I have ever heard. In it, she mentioned things that *only* God and I knew about. In the prophecy, God validated all the Scriptures that He had given me that very morning about raising God's standard, His light, His beacon; about casting up the "high" way; about removing the stones from the path and repairing of the breach. He encouraged me and re-assured me about "lifting up the standard of His cross," which seemed to be the major theme of the lady's message to me. She even called it "the statue of *liberty*."

"Coincidently" that same Saturday afternoon, several ladies came up to me and exhorted me to write a book on *faith in the night seasons*, especially concerning the dark night of the soul. Now, what made this so amazing was that up to this point, I had very rarely mentioned this subject in public. So this inquiry was terribly out of the ordinary. One of the women, who said she had been a Christian for over 20 years, mentioned that she had just been at a convention of about 300 women and many were crying out for a book like this.

I went back to my room and fell on my face, absolutely awed at what God was doing--all the Scriptures, all the messages, all the circumstances and the "timing" of all these things. He obviously was moving and speaking directly to me. My thoughts were, "Could He possibly be releasing me to write the book I so longed to write?" That night I wrote in my journal, *"November 8,1997, I have truly seen God today. I had heard of Him by the hearing of my ear; but now I see Him."*

That night, as I lay there in bed thinking about all that God had done during the day, my mind went back to that original call to write this book way back in 1991. I remembered so clearly the circumstances I was in and even the place where I was sitting.

I was on my way to Tasmania to speak, and had stopped over in Sydney, Australia, to visit a friend. In my friend's bedroom, I remember sitting up in her bed outlining this book and writing out the table of contents. I couldn't remember exactly what the date was. But I was almost positive that it was sometime in November of 1991.

Sunday evening when I arrived home, one of the very first things I did, was run to my old 1991 journal to see the date of that trip to Tasmania. Would you believe, there on the page of my journal was--you guessed it--**November 8, 1991!** Six years to the day, from *the call to write* to *the commission to write*!

Coincidence? Maybe. But, I don't think so! God is a God of precise detail, and in those details, He always communicates more of His unfathomable and infinite Love towards us. Truly, I had heard of God by the hearing of my ear, but *now I see Him*!

Psalm 30:5 tells us that, "Weeping may endure for a night, but *joy cometh in the morning.*" God truly has "turned for me my mourning into dancing...[and He has] girded me with gladness." (verse 11) "...there hath not failed one word of all His good promises which He promised..." (1 Kings 8:56)[633]

My prayer for this book began that weekend, and continues to be, that I might be used by Jesus to help cast up *His* way, remove the stones from *His* path, help repair the breaches of *His* walls and help lift up *His* standard of faith and Love.

Our Love Affair Continues

Now that I have begun to "see" Jesus more and more clearly every day, I've fallen more and more in love with Him. Since my own Hoshana (almost two years ago now), as I daily abandon myself to His will, I have felt a profound sense of intimacy, inner peace, joy, contentment, rest and Love more so than I have ever experienced before.

To me, intimacy with Jesus means sensing His presence continually-- being filled and absorbed with His Love.[634]   It means constantly fellowshiping, talking and communing with Him. It's hearing His still, small voice and even His correction, when a thought or motive is not of Him. It's seeing Him leading and guiding me and giving me supernatural discernment in things I never would see on my own. It's experiencing continual worship and praise flowing forth from my inner being as it never has before--rivers of living water. And, more than anything else, it's knowing, without a shadow of a doubt, that He will <u>never</u> leave me or forsake me, no matter what turns life may bring.

As I am beginning to understand *how* to know His will, *how* to sense His direction and *how* to hear His voice, I am learning what it means to experientially be "one" with Him in spirit.   I am experiencing a oneness with God, not only in my soul--in my thoughts, emotions and desires,--but also in my spirit. As God is exposing, revealing and changing my own self-centered ways, I am learning how to really love and worship Him at the Incense Altar of my heart.[635] 1 Chronicles 16:29 states just how to do this:

> "Give unto the Lord the glory due unto His Name; bring an offering, and come before Him; worship the Lord in the beauty of holiness."

Not that I stay in this perfect experiential union all the time, *I do not*. It's my desire to do so, but only Jesus Himself enjoyed the presence of God permanently. I still quench God's Spirit often when I choose to follow my hurts, fears or any of my own self-centered ways. But, because I know *how* to renew my mind, how to allow God to purge my soul and purify my spirit, I find getting back to the Holy Place much easier.

Since I have tasted what it's like to dwell in God's presence, it's easier for me to choose to get back there--*because I know what I am missing!* Before I experienced intimacy with Him, I wasn't sure what I was striving for or working towards, as I had never really been there. It's difficult to choose to do something when you have never experienced it before. But now that I know what intimacy with Jesus is like, I can hardly wait to "turnaround" and get back there. And praise God, it seems my "turnaround time" is getting shorter and shorter.

My life verse has become Acts 20:24. "But none of these things move me, neither count I my life dear unto myself, so that I might finish my course with joy, and the ministry, which I have received of the Lord Jesus, to testify the gospel of the grace of God...." If I can continue to do these *two things*--"let none of [my circumstances, my emotions or other people] move me," and "not count my life as dear unto myself"--then intimacy with Jesus will be assured.

Someone once said, "God's Love is a consuming fire and it will burn to ashes all that is contrary to His will. A soul kindled with fire cannot live, but in God's presence." *I have become that kindled soul,* because I don't want to live anymore without His presence. The more I allow Him to burn away all the soulish things in my life, the clearer I am able to see Him. It seems that the "log" and the "Fire" are finally beginning to become *one.*[636]

"...for He is [my] Life." (Deuteronomy 30:20)

I Am My Beloved's and He Is Mine

In spite of all that He has allowed in my life over the past seven years, I feel very loved, very special and very much His beloved. In fact, I know He has "engraved [me] on the palms of [His] hands." (Isaiah 49:16) I no longer fear losing Him as I once did. I *know* that He will never leave me or forsake me, no matter what happens in the future. All that has become important to me is knowing Him more and continually abiding in His presence. Truly, the Love of God has consumed me and,

> "I am my beloved's...and [He] is mine."
> (Song of Solomon 6:3)

This love relationship is available to every single one of us. We were designed for this kind of Love, for this kind of relationship and for this kind of intimacy. God desires that we not only receive *His Gift of Love* (Jesus) into our hearts and allow that "Love Life" to flow through us to others, but also that we return that love and worship to Him. This is what the kingdom of God is all about.

> "For the kingdom of God is not meat and drink, but righteousness, and peace, and joy in the Holy Spirit." (Romans 14:17)

Flying Above the Storms

We began this book with a story about an eagle. It seems only appropriate that we end this book with another story about an eagle:

The eagle was born with the instinct to know exactly how long before an approaching storm actually breaks. He will fly to the highest spot he can find and then wait for the winds to come. When that storm finally does come, the eagle sets his wings so that the wind will pick him up and lift him high above the storm.

While the storm rages beneath, the eagle is soaring in the sky above, with his eyes directly upon the sun. Therefore, the eagle does <u>not</u> escape the storm, but *simply uses the storm to lift him higher.* In other words, he rises on the winds that brings the storm.[637]

We, too, can soar like the eagle in the midst of our storms. *It's not the burdens of life that weighs us down, it's how we handle them. All of us experience the storms of life. However, if we can keep our eyes upon the Son and use the storms to lift us higher, then we can soar like the eagle in the sky <u>above</u> the storms. The storms will not have overcome us, but actually empowered us into the presence of Jesus.*

"For the Lord God is a sun and shield..." (Psalm 84:11)

God is the One who enables us to ride the winds of the storms that bring sickness, tragedy, failures and disappointments to our lives. The only way we can soar above our storms is by setting our eyes firmly upon God and having *FAITH IN THE NIGHT SEASONS.*

"They that wait upon the Lord shall renew their strength; they shall mount up with wings as eagles; they shall run, and not be weary; and they shall walk, and not faint." (Isaiah 40:31)

In closing, my prayer for you is **Ephesians 3**:

"...I bow my knees unto the Father of our Lord Jesus Christ. Of whom the whole family in heaven and earth is named. That He would grant you, according to the riches of His glory, to be strengthened with might by His Spirit in the inner man; that Christ may dwell in your hearts by faith; that ye, being rooted and grounded in Love, may be able to comprehend with all the saints what is the breadth, and length, and depth, and height; and to know the Love of Christ, which passeth knowledge, that ye might be *filled with all the fulness of Christ.*" (Ephesians 3:14-19)

Endnote Section:
Chapters 1 - 14

1. Story written by Claudia Lovejoy, 1998.

2. From a tape by James Payne, Oak Park Church, Hermitage, Tennessee, 1997.

3. Exodus 19:4; Deuteronomy 32:11

4. For the most part I will be using my own King James Reference Bible (see Bibliography for particulars). However, in a few places, I will use the *New American Standard* version because it expresses more clearly the meaning I am trying to convey.

5. Gene Edwards says in his epilogue to Madame Guyon's book, *Experiencing the Depths of Jesus Christ*, "...most of the truly helpful Christian literature penned on the deeper Christian experience, was written after 1500 and before 1800. Virtually nothing of lasting worth has been written in either this century or the last." (Page 147) He continues, "...this age has simply recorded no such people...Historically, this century must be catagorized as the most universally shallow age ever to parade across the pages of church history." (Page 151)

6. Psalm 30:5

7. Ephesians 3:19

8. John 10:10

9. Ezekiel 14:23

10. 2 Corinthians 1:4; 2 Corinthians 4:17

11. Hebrews 13:5

12. Colossians 1:19; 2:9; 3:11, 19

13. *Biblical Psychology*, Oswald Chambers, page 180.

14. Isaiah 40:3

15. John 16:13-14; Psalm 32:8

16. 2 Kings 22:5

17. Job 5:14; Isaiah 59:9

18. John 3:3 says that only believers will be able to "see" the Kingdom of God. Other Scriptures are Matthew 3:2 and1 Corinthians 4:20.

19. Romans 14:17

20. Psalms 32:7; 91:1-10; John 14:23; Romans 8:9; Deuteronomy 33:27

21. Psalm 140:13; Colossians 3:3

22. Acts 14:22

23. From *Final Steps in Christian Maturity*, by Madame Jeanne Guyon, found in the book, *Burnout* by R. Loren Sandford, page 115-117.

24. 1 John 1:5

25. Exodus 24:16; Job 38:1; Psalm 18:11; 97:2; 2 Chronicles 6:1

26. There are three kinds of "darkness:" unbelievers (John 3:19); demonic powers (Luke 22:53; Acts 26:18; Ephesians 6:12; Colossians 1:13); and the "darkness" allowed by God that we are talking about in this book.

27. Psalm 139:12

28. Psalm 131:2

29. John 8:36

30. *Victorious Christian Living*, Alan Redpath, page 15.

31. Job 42:5

32. *Burnout*, Loren Sandford, page 126.

33. Genesis 39

34. Isaiah 45:7

35. Psalm 42:9

36. 1 Kings 19:4

37. Luke 22:44

38. Exodus 24:15; Deuteronomy 5:22. Moses stayed seven days on the mountain. On the seventh day, God called him. (Exodus 24:16) The Spirit of the Lord was like a devouring fire.

39. Exodus 33:11

40. Genesis 50:20

41. *Abandoned to God*, Oswald Chambers, page 79.

42. *The Seeking Heart*, Francois Fenelon, page 11.

43. *John of the Cross*, Wilfrid McGreal, pages 28-30.

44. Acts 2:23

45. 1 John 1:7

46. Hebrews 10:10, 12, 14

47. Romans 8:21

48. *The Open Bible*, page 1762.

49. 1 John 4:8

50. *The Problem of Pain*, C. S. Lewis, page 43.

51. This discovery is also the emphasis of our daily teaching, "66-40" broadcast nationally and on Audio Central.com.

52. Matthew 23:37-39

53. Acts 13:47

54. Romans 3:10-18, 23

55. Ephesians 2:3

56. Romans 5:12, 21; 6:17, 20; 7:17, 20

57. Romans 3:13, 24-25; 5:1, 8; 6:23; Galatians 1:4; Ephesians 1:7

58. Ephesians 1:7; Hebrews 9:12

59. Romans 8:9; Titus 3:5

60. Romans 8:9; John 14:23; Acts 2:38; 15:8

61. 1 Corinthians 6:17

62. *The Open Bible*, page 21.

63. 1 Thessalonians 4:7; 1 Timothy 2:15; Hebrews 12:14; 1 Peter 1:2

64. Delivered from the "power of sin." (Romans 6:1-2, 11; 7:14, 17-18)

65. (Zechariah 2:10; Exodus 25:8; Isaiah 57:15; Joshua 3:10) This is why God went to all the trouble to build the temple in the Old Testament--so that He might "dwell among us." (Exodus 25:22)

66. John 10:10

67. Ephesians 5:15-18; 6:6; Colossians 1:19; 2:9; 3:11,19

68. Natural life is our own human emotions, human thoughts and human ability.

69. Matthew 5:8

70. 2 Chronicles 23:19

71. 1 Thessalonians 5:23; 4:3, 7; 2 Thessalonians 2:13; 2 Corinthians 7:1

72. *Abandoned to God*, Oswald Chambers, page 75.

73. Galatians 4:19

74. Matthew 12:25

75. Luke 14:33

76. Colossians 2:6

77. Galatians 5:19; 1 John 5:17

78. Romans 6:14

79. God's supernatural Life is His *Agape* Love, His Thoughts and His Power; our natural self-life is our love, our thoughts and our strength and power.

80. Hebrews 10:10

81. 1 Thessalonians. 5:23; Colossians 1:21-23

82. 1 Corinthians 13:1-8; Jeremiah 31:3; Romans 8:35, 38-39

83. *The Seeking Heart*, Francois Fenelon, page 73.

84. Psalm 94:12-13; Revelation 3:19; 2 Chronicles 32:31

85. *The Problem of Pain*, C. S. Lewis, page 82.

86. *The Problem of Pain*, C. S. Lewis, page 83.

87. *The Practice of the Presence of God*, Brother Lawrence.

88. Acts 20:24

89. Romans 8:28

90. Lamentations 3:37-38; Deuteronomy 32:39; 1 Chronicles 29:14; Romans 11:36

91. 1 Corinthians 8:6; John 15:16; 1 John 3:16

92. 2 Timothy 1:12; Jeremiah 17:7

93. *The Seeking Heart*, Francois Fenelon, page 176.

94. Psalm 119:107

95. *The Problem of Pain*, C. S. Lewis, page 81.

96. 1 Thessalonians 5:19; Ephesians 4:30

97. Romans 7:25; 8:1-2, 4-6, 12-14; 1 John 2:16

98. John 3:6; 6:63

99. Romans 8:8

100. Galatians 5:24; 6:8; Philippians 3:3-4

101. Ephesians 2:10

102. Psalm 119:33: Isaiah 30:21; Proverbs 15:19

103. Joshua 1:8; Psalm 1:1-3; 2 Timothy 3:16

104. 2 Timothy 4:2

105. Colossians 1:9-11

106. Proverbs 6:21-22

107. And, I say like David, "Speak [Lord], for your servant is listening." (1 Samuel 3:10)

108. 2 Corinthians 12:7-8

109. *You Set My Spirit Free*, David Hazzard, page 114.

110. Genesis 17:22 and 18:10 are another example of God's promise to Abraham and Sara to have a baby in their old age. Although God's promise was true, it was not fulfilled until ten years later. (Genesis 21:2)

111. Genesis 49:33

112. Genesis 50:13

113. See also Jeremiah 20:7-18; Judges 20:11-48

114. Hebrew 11:13, 39

115. Proverbs 13:12

116. *You Set My Spirit Free*, David Hazzard, page 116.

117. Hebrews 10:36

118. *Pursuing the Will of God*, Jack Hayford, page 86-87 (emphasis added).

119. 2 Peter 3:9

120. 1 Samuel 15:29

121. 1 Kings 8:56

122. James 4:2; Psalm 143:8,10

123. 2 Corinthians 5:17; John 3:5; Titus 3:5

124. 1 Corinthians 6:19; Romans 8:9; Colossians 1:21-22; Ephesians 5:18; Acts 2:4; 4:31

125. 1 Thessalonians 5:19; Ephesians 4:30

126. Romans 12:1-2

127. 1 John 1:9

128. Psalms 139:23-24; 19:12-13; Romans 8:4-5, 13; 1 John 1:9; Galatians 5:16-17

129. *Nous* is the Greek word for mind in this Scripture. *Nous* means our whole conceptual process, from our spirit to our life actions. Please see *Be Ye Transformed*, Chapters Five, Six and Seven.

130. Proverbs 1:5; 11:14; 12:15; 13:10; 15:22; 19:20; 20:18; 27:9

131. Jeremiah 17:10

132. Matthew 7:15; Hosea 9:8; 2 Corinthians 11:13

133. See Prayer Journal in the Appendix.

134. Hebrews 13:21; Psalm 62:1-2, 5-8

135. From Moody Press, "Finding God's Will," Viggo Olsen.

136. Juanita Graham, Coeur d' Alene, Idaho, 1997.

137. Hebrews 12:2

138. 1 Corinthians 2:5

139. James 1:6

140. Galatians 5:6

141. John 20:29

142. *John of the Cross*, Wilfred McGreal, pages 61.

143. *You Set My Spirit Free*, David Hazzard, page 45 (emphasis added).

144. Job 13:15

145. Luke 13:33

146. *One Minute After You Die*, Erwin Lutzer, page 12.

147. I have looked everywhere to find where I got this quote, but I can't seem to find the book.

148. 2 Corinthians 1:24; Galatians 5:6

149. *Combat Faith*, Hal Lindsey, pages 21-22.

150. Isaiah 42:16

151. Psalm 19:1-3

152. Hebrews 11:6

153. Hebrews 10:38

154. Hebrews 11:11

155. 2 Timothy 4:7; 1 Peter 5:7; Philippians 4:6-7

156. 1 Timothy 1:19

157. *Times Square Pulpit Series*, David Wilkerson, "Are you mad at God?" 2/16/98.

158. 1 John 5:4

159. Colossians 3:5; Galatians 5:24; Ephesians 4:22

160. Psalm 46:2

161. Ephesians 1:19-21

162. Psalms 5:12; 30:20; 59:11; 84:9, 11; Proverbs 30:5; Genesis 15:1

163. Proverbs 30:5

164. Exodus 4:12

165. 1 Samuel 17:47

166. 1 Peter 5:8; James 4:7

167. John 6:28-29; 1 Thessalonians 1:3

168. This was sent to me by someone on E-mail and they thought it was by George MacDonald.

169. 1 Kings 8:12; 2 Chronicles 6:1; Exodus 20:21; 24:16; Job 38:1; Psalm 18:11

170. Job 10:22

171. Genesis 50:20; James 1:13-14; 1 Peter 5:8

172. Matthew 16:24

173. "Dark Night of the Soul," author unknown.

174. Luke 5:11, 28; Hebrews 2:10; Luke 9:23-26

175. Luke 22:44

176. Psalm 22

177. Matthew 26:39

178. Romans 8:17, 29; 1 Corinthians 15:31; 2 Corinthians 4:10; Galatians 2:20

179. 1 Peter 4:19

180. Hebrews 2:10; 5:8

181. Colossians 1:24

182. 2 Corinthians 1:5-7; Colossians 1:24; 2 Timothy 3:11; Hebrews 2:9-10; 10:32; 1 Peter 1:11; 4:1-2, 13

183. *Problem of Pain*, page 93.

184. 2 Corinthians 1:3-6

185. Genesis 22:1-2, 15-18; Hebrews 11:17; Psalm 118:18

186. Hebrews 12:5, 16

187. Acts 5:41; 2 Corinthians 12:9; 1 Peter 4:12-13; James 1:2

188. Hebrews 12:11-13

189. Exodus 2:23; Isaiah 63:9; Judges 10:16; Exodus 2:24-25

190. Exodus 6:6-8

191. Psalm 77:2; 119:67

192. 2 Chronicles 33:12

193. Ephesians 1:17-20; 1 Corinthians 2:9

194. Psalm 119:71

195. 1 Peter 5:10

196. There are various purposes for suffering: 1) To produce fruit (Hebrews 10:36; James 1:3; Psalm 30:5; 94:12; 126:6; 1 Peter 5:10). 2) To silence the enemy (Job 1:9-12; 2:3-7). 3) To glorify God (John 9:1-3; 11:1-4). 4) To conform us into His image (Philippians 3:10). 5) To deal with our sin (1 Peter 2:20; 3:17; 4:15; Hebrews 12: 5-9). 6) To enlarge our ministry (2 Corinthians 1:3-7). From *The Open Bible*, page 682.

197. John 3:30

198. Galatians 2:20

199. Philippians 1:29

200. Romans 6:6

201. 1 Corinthians 1:23

202. Philippians 1:29

203. *Climax of the Risen Life*, Jesse Penn Lewis, page 33.

204. Exodus 24:17; Hebrew 12:29

205. "God's Love is offered freely, [but] to experience it, costs everything." (*You Set My Spirit Free,* David Hazzard, page 11.

206. Luke 3:16

207. Jeremiah 1:10

208. Job 3:20; 10:22; 2 Samuel 22:29; Psalm 18:28

209. 1 Peter 5:10; Isaiah 24:15

210. Psalm 30:5

211. 2 Corinthians 1:3-4

212. Job 19:8

213. Romans 14:23

214. *Abandoned to God*, Oswald Chambers, page 38.

215. Titus 3:5

216. Please see *The Way of Agape*, Chapter 12.

217. Please see *The Way of Agape*, Chapters 10, 11 and 13; and *Be ye Transformed*, Chapters 8 - 10.

218. *Abandoned to God*, Oswald Chambers, pages 37-38.

219. Matthew 26:39, 42

220. Colossians 3:1-4

221. Hebrews 2:10; 2 Timothy 3:12

222. Song of Solomon 4:12

223. 2 Corinthians 2:9

224. Song of Solomon 1:4

225. *The Seeking Heart,* Francois Fenelon.

226. Job 4:3-5

227. Psalm 73

228. 1 Peter 5:8; Exodus 17:7-8

229. Psalm 42:3; Isaiah 36:18 '

230. 1 Corinthians 2:6

231. 1 Corinthians 2:13

232. 1 Timothy 6:20

233. James 1:6-8

234. Ephesians 4:17-18

235. See "Dark Night of the Soul" Scriptures listed in the Appendix.

236. Philippians 4:19; Deuteronomy 2:7; 8:7-10; Nehemiah 9:21, 25

237. Psalm 139:1-5, 17-18

238. Psalm 34:15, 17; 2 Chronicles 16:9; 1 Peter 5:7

239. Judges 6:13

240. Job 33:10

241. Psalm 86:5,7; Exodus 2:23-25; Deuteronomy 26:6-8; Psalm 18:19; Judges 3:7,9; 1 Samuel 12; 10-11

242. Psalm 139:7

243. Isaiah 62:3-4

244. Isaiah 49:13-16

245. Judges 6:13

246. *Victorious Christian Faith*, Alan Redpath, page 14.

247. Psalm 102:10

248. *Abandoned to God*, Oswald Chambers, page 76.

249. Ibid, page 82.

250. Ibid, page 83.

251. Psalm 88, Job 16:12-16; Job 7:20; Psalm 18:5-6

252. Psalms 139:7-8, 12; 88:6-7; Deuteronomy 5:22

253. Hebrews 12:29; Deuteronomy 4:24

254. Mark 9:49

255. Proverbs 25:4

256. Proverbs 17:3

257. Job 23:10; Isaiah 48:10

258. Psalm 66:10; 1 Corinthians 3:13

259. Isaiah 48:10; 1 Peter 1:4-5

260. *Encyclopedia Britannica*, Vol. 4, page 64.

261. Exodus 34:14

262. Leviticus 1:3-9; Hebrews 10:6, 8; Mark 12:33; Exodus 29:41

263. Genesis 15:17; Psalm 102:3

264. Mark 9:29; Luke 14:34

265. Leviticus 9:24; 2 Chronicles 7:1

266. Psalm 20:3

267. Leviticus 6:10-11

268. Deuteronomy 33:19

269. Psalm 20:3

270. Psalm 50:5

271. Matthew 9:13. We can build our "own" altar rather than the one that God has provided for us. (Joshua 22:29)

272. 2 Timothy 2:21

273. Exodus 14:13-14; Deuteronomy.8:2, 16, 3

274. Romans 6:13

275. 1 Corinthians 13:4-8

276. Ephesians 3:20; Matthew 7:9-11; Deuteronomy 30:14

277. Psalms 18:1-6; 30:2-3; 55:16-18; 81:7

278. 2 Chronicles 20:3

279. 2 Peter 1:3-4; Isaiah 41:10

280. Psalm 9:10; Proverbs 18:10

281. Isaiah 50:10

282. Isaiah 1:25; Psalm 66:10-12; 1 Peter 4:12-13

283. Psalm 66:9

284. Song of Solomon 8:5

285. Hebrews 13:8; Psalms 46:10

286. Proverbs 18:10; Psalm 9:10; 2 Timothy 2:13

287. Genesis 50:20

288. Romans 12:19

289. Psalms 5:11; 18:47; 89:18; Isaiah 35:4

290. Deuteronomy 20:4

291. 1 Samuel 24:17

292. Ephesians 6:11, 13

293. 2 Corinthians 10:4

294. 1 Peter 3:15

295. Hebrews 13:15; Psalms 4:5; 27:6; 2 Corinthians 7:4; Psalm 100; James 1:2

296. Psalms 107:22; 116:17; 95:2; 69:30-31; 100:4

297. Hebrews 13:15; Psalm 4:5; Psalm 116:17

298. Psalm 18:1, 2-7, 9, 16-17, 19, 28, 30, 32, 34, 39, 47-48

299. Luke 17:21; Matthew 12:28

300. Luke 11:17

301. 1 Thessalonians 5:19

302. Proverbs 17:22; 25:26; Romans 7:15, 19, 23

303. Luke 17:21; John 14:23

304. 1 Corinthians 6:20; 2 Corinthians 7:1

305. Zechariah 12:1; Proverbs 25:28; Luke 8:55; 1 Corinthians 14:14

306. 1 Corinthians 2:11; 5:4

307. Ezekiel 37:5-6

308. Psalm 104:29

309. Scriptures from *The Spiritual Man*, Watchman Nee, page 70. (Mark 2:8; John 4:23; 11:33; Acts 19:21; 1 Corinthians 2:11; 2 Corinthians 2:13; 4:13; Ephesians 1:17; Colossians 1:8)

310. Psalm 18:28

311. *The Spiritual Man*, Watchman Nee, page 21. See also the Appendix of *The Way of Agape*, "Hardware and Software of a Computer," page 323.

312. Jude 19

313. 1 Corinthians 2:14

314. Acts 15:8; Romans 8:11, 15-16; 1 Corinthians 2:12; 6:17; 2 Corinthians 5:17

315. 2 Corinthians 7:1

316. Romans 8:9

317. 1 Corinthians 2:14

318. Isaiah 29:24; 65:14; Daniel 5:20; Genesis 41:8

319. I owe much of my understanding in this area to Watchman Nee's book *The Spiritual Man*. So, be as the Bereans, check out everything that is shared.

320. 2 Corinthians 2:13; John 8:9

321. Joshua 1:7

322. Job 34:32; 1 Corinthians 2:13-14

323. Hebrews 9:14

324.   1 Peter 3:21; Acts 24:16

325.   Romans 8:33-34

326.   1 John 3:20; Romans 2:15; 9:1

327.   1 Timothy 4:2; Titus 1:15

328.   2 Timothy 1:3

329.   Mark 2:8

330.   1 Corinthians 2:11

331.   Mark 2:8

332.   *One Who Believed*, Dr. Robert B. Pamplin, pages 5-6.

333.   2 Corinthians 7:1; 1 Thessalonians 5:23

334.   1 Corinthians 7:34

335.   Matthew 23:17,19

336.   1 Corinthians 1:30; 1 Thessalonians 4:3, 7; Hebrews 10:10; 12:14; Colossians 3:12

337.   2 Thessalonians 2:13; 1 Peter 1:2; 1 Corinthians 1:2; 6:11

338.   John 2:25

339.   John 17:17

340.   Ephesians 3:16

341.   John 17:17, 19; Psalm 105:19; 119:9; 2 Thessalonians 2:13; 1 Peter 1:2; Romans 1:9

342.   John 13:15; Ephesians 3:16; Romans 8:13; Matthew 11:29

343.   The Greek word for "dividing" here is *merismos*, which means to separate, *to disunite* or to reach beyond. (Isaiah 38:13; Lamentations 3:4)

344.   In light of this, Proverbs 17:22 makes so much more sense. "A broken spirit drieth the bones." It dries the bones, because without the spirit, *there is no marrow* (no life)!

345.   Job 30:17; 30:30; Psalm 31:10; 32:3; 34:20; 51:8; 162:3; Proverbs 3:8

346.   Psalm 51:8

347.   Leviticus 1:5-9

348.   For years, I did not understand the full ramification of Hebrews 4:12. I don't believe that God is talking about sin here in this Scripture, because He gives us a brand, new heart when we are "born again." (Ezekiel 36:26) What I believe He is talking about, are our *self-centered ways*--the deep-set and often hidden motives and intents of our heart. God is telling us in this Scripture that these things also need to be exposed, acknowledged and given over to Him.

349.   Hebrews 10:22

350.   Romans 12:1

351. Acts 20:24

352. 1 Corinthians 1:30; 1 Thessalonians 4:3

353. 1 Corinthians 12:11

354. Taken, in part, from a letter written by a woman teaching *The Way of Agape,* Linda Miller, Council, Idaho.

355. Jonah 2:1-2

356. Job 1:1; 2:3

357. *Abandoned to God*, Oswald Chambers.

358. Hosea 2:6; Psalm103:7

359. 2 K.19:34

360. 2 Corinthians 10:5

361. 1 Corinthians 3:12

362. Proverbs 16:2; Job 32:1

363. 1 Samuel 16:7; Psalm 33:10

364. 1 Corinthians 2:2; Galatians 6:14; Philippians 3:10; Psalm 116:15

365. 1 Corinthians 15:31

366. 2 Chronicles 32:31

367. Ezekiel 16:8-15

368. See *The Way of Agape*, Chapter Fifteen. (Ephesians 5:29)

369. Philippians 3:8-10; Revelation 12:11

370. 2 Timothy 2:11

371. Romans 6:4

372. Philippians 3:10; Romans 8:17

373. Romans 1:9; 7:6

374. *A Memoir*, Jesse Penn Lewis, page 26.

375. Galatians 5:24; Philippians 3:3; Romans 7:5-6

376. *An Autobiography*, Jesse Penn Lewis, page 52.

377. Psalm 139:23-24; 1 Corinthians 7:34

378. Psalm 32:2

379. 1 Peter 1:22

380. 1 Thessalonians 5:23; 1 Corinthians 6:9-10; 2 Corinthians 7:1

381. Hebrews 12:14; 1 Corinthians 7:34

382. Lamentations 3:1-18

383. Lamentations 3:8-9, 44

384. Matthew 27:46; Psalm 22:1

385. Job 33:10; 7:20; 30:21; Psalms 10:1; 88:4-8; Song of Solomon 5:7

386. Job 30:20

387. Psalm 22:8

388. *John of the Cross*, Wilfrid McGreal, page 35.

389. Psalm 31:5; Matthew 27:50

390. Song of Solomon 5:4-5

391. *Tortured for Christ*, Pastor Wurmbrand, page 59.

392. *Lectures to My Students*, Charles Spurgeon, page 39 emphasis added.

393. *Union with God*, Madam Guyon, "The Dealings of God," page 92.

394. Isaiah 41:9-10; 54:7-8

395. Job 6:20

396. Lamentations 3:18

397. Hebrews 6:17-19

398. 1 Kings 18:21

399. Proverbs 15:22; Psalm 42:5

400. Ephesians 1:17-20; 1 Corinthians 2:9

401. Hebrew 6:19

402. Romans 5:5

403. Jeremiah 31:17

404. 2 Corinthians 4:8

405. 2 Corinthians 4:18

406. Psalms 77; 102:3-11

407. Isaiah 59:10

408. Psalm 88; Job 30:16, 27

409. Isaiah 54:7-8

410. Job 23:16-17

411. 1 Kings 19:4

412. Psalm 88:4-7

413. Job 10:1

414. Song of Solomon 5:7

415. Luke 21:16; 2 Timothy 4:16; Micah 7:6

416. Job 19:21

417. Psalm 109:1-5

418. Ezekiel 22:4; 2 Samuel 22:48

419. Psalms 88; 55:15; 18:4-5; Job 16:12, 16; Lamentations 3:1-20

420. Ezekiel 24:10

421. Psalm 23

422. 1 Peter 2:23; Psalm 31:5

423. Psalm 34:4, 17-19

424. Philippians 3:10

425. Romans 6:1-14; Galatians 5:24

426. Matthew 10:38-39

427. 1 Peter 1:22

428. Psalm 51:10

429. 2 Corinthians 12:10; Psalm 32:2

430. 1 Corinthians 2:10, 12

431. 2 Corinthians 4:13

432. Hebrews 13:5

433. 2 Corinthians 1:9; Psalm 18:2; 26:1

434. Psalm 34:4, 17-19

435. 1 Thessalonians 3:3; Psalm 16:8

436. 2 Corinthians 1:8-9

437. Psalms 33:18: 34:15; 142:7

438. 2 Corinthians 2:9

439. Romans 8:24; 5:5; Colossians 1:27

440. *The Inward Journey*, Gene Edwards, page 192.

441. See *The Way of Agape*, Chapters 10-13; and *Be Ye Transformed*, Chapters 8-10.

442. Ezekiel 36:26-27

443. (1 Corinthians 15:42-44; Philippians 3:20-21) Also see *Be Ye Transformed*, Chapters 11-12.

444. Exodus 8:7, 18; 7:20-22; 1 Kings 22:22

445. Jeremiah 20:7

446. Jeremiah 4:19

447. Psalm 71:10-12

448. Hebrews 6:18

449. Daniel 3:12-15; Esther 3:5-6

450. Psalm 103:7

451. 1 Corinthians 3:16; 2 Corinthians 6:16

452. *Encyclopaedia Britannica*, Christianity: History of Christian Mysticism, Vol. 16, page 372.

453. *The Seeking Heart*, Fenelon, page 180.

454. John 12:24-25

455. 2 Chronicles 6:18

456. Leviticus 9:24

457. Deuteronomy 33:10

458. See Isaiah 6:5-7

459. Isaiah 56:7; Hebrews 10:19; 1 Peter 2:5, 9; Revelation 5:8; 8:3

460. The Brazen Altar could be analogus to the Cross in our lives. The Cross is where we deal with our sins. The Cross is also where we crucify our "self" after God has exposed it.

461. Song of Solomon 8:6

462. 2 Corinthians 5:21

463. Exodus 30:10

464. *The Holy Vessels and Furniture of the Tabernacle of Israel*, pages 39-42.

465. Hebrews 9:3-4; Leviticus 4:7, 18; 16:12-13, 18; Revelation 8:3; 1 Kings 9:25

466. 1 Kings 6:22; Exodus 40:5

467. Hebrews 9:7

468. Revelation 8:4

469. 1 Chronicles 6:49

470. Matthew 27:51; Hebrews 10:20

471. Hebrews 9:24

472. Exodus 33:14

473. Numbers 16:9; Exodus 40:13

474. *They Found the Secret*, Amy Carmichael, page 30.

475. Exodus 30:34-37; 2 Chronicles 2:4

476. See *Way of Agape*, Chapter Eight.

477. Exodus 13:21; 14:19; 16:10; 33:9; 40:36; Numbers 9:17; 10:11; 12:5; 16:42; Deuteronomy 1:33; 31:15; Nehemiah 9:12; Psalms 78:14; 105:39; Isaiah 4:5

478. Malachi 3:3-4

479. Acts 10:4

480. Revelation 5:8; 8:3-4

481. John 14:14

482. Hebrews 10:19-24; 1 Peter 2:5,9; Revelation 5:8

483. Psalms 55; 118:13-17; Proverbs 16

484. Romans 6:6, 11

485. 1 Corinthians 6:17; 2 Corinthians 5:17

486. Colossians 1:28; 1:19; 2:9

487. Colossians 1:19; 2:9; 3:19

488. John 17:24; 1 John 4:17

489. Exodus 33:14

490. John 17:21, 23; Hebrews 6:1

491. Hebrews 2:10

492. James 1:2-4

493. 1 Peter 5:10; Colossians 4:12; Hebrews 13:21

494. Song of Solomon 6-8

495. Ephesians 4:13; Colossians 1:28

496. 2 Corinthians 13:9

497. 1 John 4:12

498. John 17:24

499. Philippians 3:9

500. *You Set My Spirit Free*, David Hazzard, page 49 emphasis added.

501. 1 Corinthians 2:2

502. Exodus 24:15-17; Numbers 12:8

503. Ephesians 4:13; 2 Timothy 1:12

504. *Victorious Christian Faith*, Alan Redpath, page 15.

505. Ibid, page 16.

506. Luke 12:19

507. *Abandoned to God*, Oswald Chambers, page 82.

508. John 14:23; Ephesians 3:17-19

509. Philippians 3:10

510. Job 42:5; Genesis 32:30

511. Psalm 16:8; Exodus 33:14

512. 2 Corinthians 3:18

513. Romans 8:28

514. Colossians 1:17; Psalm 112:6; Acts 22:14

515. John 3:21; John 15:14-15

516. Acts 20:24

517. Ezekiel 36:26

518. Psalm 32:2

519. Romans 7:6; Psalm 51:10; Isaiah 40:31

520. 2 Corinthians 3:6

521. Nehemiah 9:20; Psalm 143:10; 1 Timothy 1:5

522. Psalm 48:14

523. 2 Timothy 1:3; 1 Peter 2:19

524. 1 Peter 3:16

525. Acts 23:1; 24:16

526. Proverbs 16:9; Hebrews 5:14

527. Ephesians 3:3

528. 1 Corinthians 2:9-16

529. Psalm 149:5

530. Colossians 1:9-10

531. John 17:17

532. Proverbs 20:27

533. Job 12:22

534. Hosea 6:1

535. There was no one like unto Moses who knew the Lord face to face (Deuteronomy 34:10).

536. Exodus 34:29, 35

537. 2 Chronicles 20:7; Isaiah 41:8

538. Philippians 4:13; 1 Timothy 1:12; 2 Timothy 4:17

539. Psalms 63:5; 32:2

540. Psalms 65:6; 18:32, 39; 1 Samuel 2:4

541. Revelation 12:11; Psalm 84:5, 7

542. Isaiah 11:2

543. Isaiah 53; 2 Corinthians 5:17; John 5:26

544. Romans 7:22; Ephesians 3:16

545. Acts 4:31

546. 2 Chronicles 7:1-3

547. Exodus 40:34-35

548. 1 Kings 8:10-11; 2 Chronicles 5:13-14

549. Philippians 3:10; Romans 13:1

550. Acts 1:8; 1 Corinthians 2:4; Romans 9:17

551. 2 Corinthians 13:4

552. 1 Corinthians 1:24; Psalm 89:17

553. 2 Corinthians 13:4

554. Acts 4:7, 33; 6:8, 10; 1 Corinthians 6:14; Psalm 110:2

555. Luke 4:14, 36

556. Luke 4:32; 9:1

557. 1 Corinthians 4:20

558. 2 Thessalonians 1:11

559. John 4:23; Philippians 3:3

560. Psalm 32:2

561. John 3:30

562. 1 John 3:16

563. *A House for All Nations*, Chaim Richmond.

564. Matthew 23:25-26

565. Psalm 96:9; 1 Chronicles 16:29

566. Psalm 139:23-24; John 3:20-21; 1 John 3:22

567. Ephesians 1:4

568. There is an interesting incident in Nehemiah 13:3-9 where the temple priest prepared a chamber in the temple for Tobiah, an evil man. When Nehemiah found out about it, he cast forth all Tobiah's household stuff and then cleansed the chamber. Then, he restored the vessels of the temple again to that room. The lesson here, is that the profane cannot be mixed with the holy. (Ezekiel 44:23)

569. 2 Corinthians 3:2

570. Isaiah 43:2; 1 Peter 4:12; Hebrews 11

571. *The Problem of Pain*, C. S. Lewis, pages 85 and 43.

572. Romans 8:8

573. John 14:14

574. Psalm 145:18-20; Hebrews 4:16

575. 1 Thessalonians 5:16-18

576. Hebrews 13:15

577. Hebrews 10:36

578. John 16:22; 17:13; Acts 2:28

579. Nehemiah 8:10

580. Hebrews 11:27

581. Acts 9:3-4

582. Philippians 3:8-14; John 15:5

583. See *Be Ye Transformed*, Chapter One.

584. See *The Way of Agape*, Chapter Fourteen.

585. *John of the Cross*, Wilfrid McGreal, page 56.

586. Romans 8:29

587. 2 Corinthians 4:11

588. Hebrews 4:10

589. Galatians 6:14, Philippians 3:9-10, 13

590. 1 Timothy 6:6-11

591. 2 Corinthians 11:23-33

592. Philippians 4:8-9

593. Philippians 3:9-10, 13

594. 1 Timothy 6:6; Philippians 3:13

595. John 4:34

596. Hebrews 13:15

597. Deuteronomy 1:8

598. Hebrews 4:9-10

599. Joshua 24:13; Nehemiah 9:25; 1 Kings 8:56

600. 2 Corinthians 6:4; 1 Corinthians 15:54

601. (Job 13:15). I find it interesting that God talks about entering His rest in Hebrews 4:9-10, and the following verses He tells us exactly *"how"* to do this--by allowing His Word to divide our soul and spirit.

602. Romans 8:28

603. James 4:8

604. Psalm 62:1-2, 5-8; John 15:5; Proverbs 19:20; Isaiah 55:8-9; Matthew 13:16; Deuteronomy 11:27

605. Romans 6:7, 11-14

606. Hebrews 9:14

607. Ladies Home Journal, "Forgiving the Dead Man Walking, Debbie Morris, October 1998, page 218.

608. Psalm 73:25

609. Daniel 2:24; Revelation 11:12

610. Revelation 12:11

611. Psalms 146:7; 116:16; Isaiah 42:7

612. *The Seeking Heart*, Fenelon, pages 46-47.

613. Psalm 15:1-5; Isaiah 57:15

614. John 4:34

615. Psalms 40:8; 143:10; Philippians 2:8

616. *The Seeking Heart*, Fenelon, page 175.

617. Song of Solomon 7:10

618. Hebrews 11:6

619. 2 Timothy 2:4

620. Philippians 2:8; 2 Corinthians 2:9

621. 2 Corinthians 1:9

622. *The Seeking Heart*, Fenelon, page 66.

623. Acts 20:24

624. 2 Corinthians 3:5

625. "Hoshana Rabba," Unger's Bible Dictionary, page 420; Encycopedia Judacia, Vol.8, Page 1026). *Hoshana* means "save, I pray." (Psalm 118:25)

626.   Leviticus 23:24, 34, 39; Numbers 29:12; Deuteronomy 16:13; Zechariah 14:16; Exodus 23:16; 34:22, John 7

627.   Leviticus 23:42-43

628.   Leviticus 23:40; 25:4-7; Deuteronomy 15:9; 16:14; 31:10; Exodus 23:10-11

629.   Deuteronomy 15:2; Exodus 23:10-11

630.   Psalm 102:13, 20; Isaiah 54:1-7; 62:10

631.   Isaiah 49:22; 58:12; 59:19; Luke 4:18; Psalm 112; Song of Solomon 7:10

632.   This comes from Isaiah 62:10. It's interesting to note that Jeremiah 18:15 talks about "paths that are not cast up."

633.   Hebrews 10:36

634.   Psalm 140:13

635.   Psalms 139:23-24;103:7

636.   John 17:11, 21-24; Hebrews 6:15

637.   Taken, in part, from *Parables*, "Bulletin and Newsletter Series," Winter 98.

Prayer Section

"Who shall ascend into the hill of the Lord? Or who shall stand in His Holy Place? He that hath clean hands, and a pure heart...He shall receive the blessing from the Lord, And righteousness from the God of his salvation. This is the generation of them that seek Him, that seek Thy face...." (Psalm 24:3-6)

"My voice shalt Thou hear in the morning, O Lord; In the morning will I direct my prayer unto Thee, and will look up." (Psalm 5:3)

"Whoso offereth praise glorifieth Me: And *to him that ordereth his conversation (his behavior) aright* will I show the salvation of God." (Psalm 50:23)

Steps to Peace with God

1) Recognize God's Plan -- Peace and Life

God wants us to know that He loves us. And He wants us to experience His peace and His Life. The Bible declares, "For God loved the world so much that He gave His only Son, so that everyone who believes in Him may not die but have eternal Life." (John 3:16)

2) Realize our problem -- Separation

People choose to disobey God and go their own way, resulting in separation from God. The Bible states, "Everyone has sinned and is far away from God's saving presence." (Romans 3:23)

3) Respond to God's Remedy -- Cross of Christ

God sent His Son to bridge the gap. Christ did this by paying the penalty of our sins when He died on the cross and rose from the grave. The Bible explains, "But God has shown us how much He loves us--it was while we were still sinners that Christ died for us!" (Romans 5:8)

4) Receive God's Son -- Lord and Savior

You cross the bridge into God's family when you ask Christ to come into your heart. The Bible promises, "Some, however, did receive Him and believed in Him; so He gave them the right to become God's children." (John 1:12)

The invitation is to:

Repent (turn from your sins) and by faith *receive* Jesus Christ into your heart and follow Him in obedience as your Lord and Savior.

Prayer of Commitment

"Lord Jesus, I know that I am a sinner. I believe You died for my sins. Right now, I turn from my sins and open the door of my heart and life. I receive You as my personal Lord and Savior. Thank You for saving me now. Amen."[1]

Prayer Journal

Prayer is essential!

Long ago, I learned that if I wanted anything at all to be accomplished, it must be brought before the Lord in prayer. But there is an appropriate *way to pray* and an appropriate *time to pray* that God has laid out for us in Scripture. When I follow His instructions, tremendous results occur. So, the following is not intended to be an in-depth thesis on prayer and worship, but simply some personal thoughts and ideas as to what has helped me in my own 40 year walk with the Lord.

Someone taught me years ago that when *I prayed the Scriptures,* God would do something very powerful, not only in me, but also in the ones I was praying for. Since it's always been difficult for me to memorize, I found writing the Scriptures out and then praying them, to be very helpful and beneficial. So, the following suggestions on praying and worshiping the Lord are just that--suggestions. If they minister to you, then praise God. If they don't, then you seek His face and see how He leads you. Above all, to allow the Holy Spirit to direct our times of worship and prayer is always imperative.

Remember, we are saved "by grace...through faith" (Ephesians 2:8) and "[we] are *not* under the law, but under grace." (Romans 6:14) Therefore, I do *not* mean to imply a "methodology" in order to work our way towards God. However, I do believe, God has given us a set of guidelines in Scripture, and by following His prescribed order, our worship and prayers will be acceptable to Him. Again, the Holy Spirit must always be free to lead us as He, alone, knows the *perfect* way.

My own personal prayer time is based upon the order of service and ministry that God instructed the priests of Solomon's Temple to do in order be cleansed of sin, reconciled to Him and enabled to approach His presence to worship Him. *The priests dealt with their sin and were reconciled to God in the <u>Inner Court</u>, but they worshiped and petitioned their prayers before His presence in the <u>Holy Place</u>.*

The order of service for the priests was as follows: Initially, they entered the Inner Court with praise and thanksgiving. Then, they went to the *Lavers of Bronze* where they washed their hands and feet (confessed and repented of their sins). After that, they went to the *Brazen Altar* where they sacrificed the animals in order to purge the sins of the people. Next, they went to the *Molten Sea* where they bathed completely by bodily immersion. Then, as we have explored in this book, they took the hot coals from the Brazen Altar, went back into the *Holy Place* where they changed their clothes and then sprinkled incense over the coals at the *Golden Incense Altar*. Finally, they worshiped the Lord in the "beauty of His holiness" in front of the Incense Altar and said their prayers.

Entering His Courts with Praise

So, the first place I begin my worship and prayer time is to, "*Enter into His gates with thanksgiving, and into His courts with praise: be thankful unto Him, and bless His Name.*" (Psalm 100:4)

Some wonderful Psalms for praising God are: Psalms 8, 9, 19, 32, 33, 34, 47, 48, 66, 89, 93, 96, 98, 100, 101, 104, 105, 111, 112, 113, 115, 118, 134, 135, 136, 138, 144, 145, 146, 147, 148, 149, 150.

The praise Psalms that the priests of Solomon's Temple actually prayed as they entered the Court were:[2]

On Sunday - Psalm 24
On Monday - Psalm 48
On Tuesday - Psalm 82
On Wednesday - Psalm 94
On Thursday - Psalm 81
On Friday - Psalm 93
On Saturday - Psalm 92

Praise God for Who He Is

Knowing some of the specific names and characteristics of Jesus is helpful. Then, as you praise Him for who He is and for what He has done in your life, you can meditate upon each of these names. Always let the Holy Spirit guide you as to which names to pray.

Alpha and Omega
Almighty
Anchor of my soul
Advocate
Avenger of Blood
Anointed One
All and in all
Author and finisher of my faith
Bread of Life
Beloved

Blessed above all
Bright and morning star
Creator
Counselor
Crown
Companion
Comforter
Consolation
Dwelling Place
Delight
Deliverer
Defender
Desire
Emmanuel (God with us)
Everlasting Father
Eternal One
Friend
Faithful One
Father
Fountain of Life
Firstborn
Foundation
Glory
Guide
Guilt-taker
Hiding Place
Holy One
Hoshana
Husband
Healer
Hope
Helper
Horn of my salvation
I am
Image of God
Immanuel
Joy
King
Lamb of God
Lord of lords
Light
Lion
Love
Life
Master
Messiah

Most High
Mouth
Mercy
Name above all names
Overcomer
Prophet
Priest
Prince of Peace
Great Physician
Preserver
Passover
Peace
Power
Prize
Pearl
Precious One
Perfect One
Pure One
Redeemer
Righteous
Refuge
Ruler
Resurrection
Ransom
Root of David
Redemption
River of Life
Rock
Rewarder
Restorer
Savior
Spirit
Sanctification
Strength
Sufficiency
Standard
Salvation
Son of David
Son of God
Son of man
Suffering Servant
Shepherd of my soul
Sacrifice
Shekinah Glory
Shiloh
Sceptor

Song
Triumph
Teacher
Treasure
Tabernacle
Truth
Unspeakable gift
Unchangeable
Unleavened bread
Vindication
Vine
Victory
Voice
Worth
Way
Wonderful
Wisdom

Blessings to Be Thankful for:

The following are some of the things that I thank God for every morning. Again, these are just suggestions. Be sure to allow the Holy Spirit to add to your list:

Jesus, I am thankful for:

Your soon coming--my hope
For my salvation--for Your Life in me
For being Your beloved whether I feel like it or not
For my relationship with You--the freedom You have given me
For Your Strength, Your Love, Your Wisdom, Your Power
For Your presence--our intimacy, fellowship and communion
For Your discernment and guidance
For Your rest, Your joy and Your peace
For continually cleansing me by Your blood--Your restoration
For Your protection
For my spouse
For my children
For my family
For my friends
For my health
For my home
For my situation--no matter what difficulties I face
For what You are doing through me
For the people I work with
For my job

The Inner Court Ritual

In the Inner Courtyard of Solomon's Temple, the priests went through a daily cleansing and purifying ritual that involved three pieces of furniture in the courtyard: *the ten Bronze Lavers, the Brazen (or Holocaust) Altar and the Molten Sea.* These three pieces of furniture represent the three cleansing agents that God has given us in order to deal with our sins and be reconciled to Him. 1 John 5:8 tells us that there are three forces at work in our own souls continually cleansing and washing away our sins: *the Spirit, the Blood and the Word of God.* The furniture in the Inner Court of Solomon's Temple represents these same three cleansing agents.

So, the following *steps* are not simply a procedure that I have made up or found in some psychology book, but they are the actual cleansing and purifying steps that I believe God has laid out for us in Scripture in order to deal with our sin and be reconciled to Him. This is why I call them *The Inner Court Ritual*.

[Please see *Be Ye Transformed* (Chapters 13-15) or *The Way of Agape* (Chapter 14) for an in-depth explanation of these essential steps and how they apply to us.]

Throughout Scripture, we are exhorted to "put off" the flesh and to "put on" Christ.[3] The practical application of just *how* we do this is *The Inner Court Ritual.* Moment by moment, dealing with our sin and our self is how we daily "renew our minds"[4] so that we <u>can</u> be transformed and so that Jesus' Life <u>will</u> be showing forth through us and not our own.

The Steps

1) **Recognize and acknowledge** the "sin" or "self" that has just occurred. Don't *vent* these thoughts or feelings and don't *push them down.* Get alone with God and give them to Him. Try to describe to God how you are feeling and what you are thinking. Ask Him to expose any "root causes" for your ungodly thoughts, emotions or actions. This is the step where it's imperative to experience your emotions (your humanness) so that you'll know exactly what to confess and what to give over to God.

2) **Confess and repent** of everything that God shows you is unholy, unrighteous and "not of faith" and choose to turn around from following these things. *Confessing* simply means "acknowledging" your sin and self. *Repenting* means choosing to "turn around" from following that sin and self and, choosing instead, to follow what God is

telling you to do. Just asking God to forgive you is <u>not</u> enough; you must *first* confess that you <u>have</u> sinned and, then, repent of it. *This is your own responsibility.*[5]

"I acknowledged my sin unto Thee, and mine iniquity have I not hid...I will confess my transgressions unto the Lord; and Thou forgavest the iniquity of my sin." (Psalm 32:5)

A part of this second step is that you must also **unconditionally forgive** any others involved. You have asked God's forgiveness for your sins; now you must forgive others of theirs.[6]

Both of these last two steps are patterned after what the priests did at the *Lavers of Bronze.*[7]

3) **Give over to God** all that He has shown you--not only your specific sin, but also any of your self-centered ways. Present your body to God as a "living sacrifice" (Romans 12:1), and ask Him to continue to expose, cut away and divide the soulish things in your life from the spiritual.[8]

At this point, I usually picture myself on that Brazen Altar, and I pray something like this: "My Jesus, I offer all that I am to You. I willingly surrender *my will* and *my life* to You. *May all that pleases You and all that You wish* and only that which You wish, *happen today.*"

You might also offer God the sacrifice of *praise* (Hebrews 13:15); the sacrifice of *righteousness* (Psalm 4:5); the sacrifice of *joy* (Psalm 27:6); and the sacrifice of *thanksgiving* (Psalm 116:17; 107:22). These are "sacrifices" because at this point we usually don't "feel" much like praising, being thankful or joyful.

This step is patterned after what the priests did at the *Brazen Altar.*

4) **Read God's Word** and replace the lies we have erroneously believed with the Truth.[9] As you read God's Word, He will cleanse and heal your soul with the "washing of water by the Word." (Ephesians 5:26) Only God's Word can totally restore you at this point. God is the only One who can wash you *in His Love*, minister to you and heal you with His Word. (*The Molten Sea*)

At this point, then, by faith, whether you feel like it or not, you have been "renewed in the *spirit* of your mind." (Ephesians 4:23)

This third step is patterned after what occured at the *Molton Sea* in Solomon's Temple. Because the priests had gotten all blood splattered from offering their sacrifices at the Brazen Altar, only bodily emersion in the Molton Sea could offer them the total cleansing needed.

Worshiping at the Incense Altar

Now you can proceed boldly into the Holy Place, where you can "change your clothes." You have put off your sin and self, and so now, you can *put on* Christ and boldly enter God's presence. And, you can carry those hot coals of your wholly burnt life right to the Incense Altar where "God will meet with you"--Spirit to spirit. Now, because you have "clean hands and a pure heart," you can truly worship Him in spirit and in the beauty of His holiness.[10]

Once you are at the Incense Altar, you can present your love to Him in worship, in song and in adoration. At this point, I often play my favorite hymns or worship songs or sing and dance before Him, just as David did.[11]

At this time you can offer your prayers and petitions and know, because they are "according to His will," He will hear you and He will answer. It's an acceptable time.[12]

The following, then, are some suggested Scriptures to pray for different types of needs:

Armor of God Prayers

Ephesians 6:10-19 exhorts us to daily put on the "armor of God" so that we might be strong in the power of *His* might and be able to withstand the wiles of the enemy.

"Having girt our waist with **God's Truth**. (His Word and His Spirit = Truth)

Putting on the **Breastplate of Righteousness** and Love. (1 Thessalonians 5:8) (God's Life in our hearts)

Having shod our feet (our soul) with the **Gospel of Peace**. (Putting off of the "flesh" and the putting on of Christ--*The Inner Court Ritual*--is how we wash our feet.)

Taking the **Shield of Faith** by which we can quench the fiery darts. (This is one of the most important parts of our armor because it's our choice to trust what God has promised us in His Word.)

The **Helmet of Salvation**. (This is the showing forth of God's Life instead of our own. It's His light that is shining forth. As Isaiah 62:1 says, "Salvation [is] a lamp that burneth.")

The **Sword of the Spirit** which is the Word of God. (The Word of God is our "battle ax" and the only way we are able to stand.)[13]

Praying always for all the saints. (We are to be constantly praying to God on behalf of all the saints.)

That utterance may be given to us to make known the **mystery of the Gospel** in everything we say and do."

Deliverance Prayers

The following are some Scriptures to pray for deliverance. Again, depend completely upon the Holy Spirit for guidance. (I have taken the liberty to paraphrase these Scriptures.)

Hebrews 4:16: I come boldly before Your throne in time of need.
Romans 8:26: The Spirit knows how to pray.
Isaiah 58:6: Loose the bands of wickedness.
Matthew 18:18: Whatever we bind (forbid) on earth will be bound in heaven.
2 Corinthians 4:4: The god of this world has blinded the eyes of those who don't believe.
2 Corinthians 2:10-11: We must forgive so that Satan doesn't get an advantage in us.
Luke 10:19: Jesus, You give us the authority over the power of the enemy so that nothing shall hurt us.
Galatians 1:4: You deliver us from this present evil world.
Colossians 1:13: You have delivered us from the authority of darkness.
2 Timothy 2:25-26: God give_____ repentance to the acknowledging of the truth, so that they may recover from the snare of the evil one.
1 John 3:8: You were manifested to destroy the works of the devil.
2 Chronicles 20:15: Be not afraid, the battle is not ours, but God's.
Colossians 2:15: God has defeated principalities and powers.
Matthew 12:29: How can we enter a strong man's house (the enemy's house), unless we first bind him and, then, we can spoil his goods.
Psalm 149:6-8: Let the high praises of God be in our mouths, and a two-edged sword in our hands, and may You (Jesus) bind the enemy's kings with chains.

Warfare Prayers

The following are some Scriptures we might pray for warfare:
Again, be Spirit-led.

Peter 5:8-9: Resist the devil (who is a roaring lion) knowing that all
Christians are in the same battle. You promise us, God, that
after we have "barred ourselves from sin," You will make us
perfect, established and strengthened.

James 4:7-10: Submit ourselves to God (go through *The Inner Court
Ritual*), resist the devil and he will flee from us. Draw close to
God and He will draw close to us. Cleanse our hands (body) and
purify our hearts (spirit). Humble ourselves in the sight of God
and He will lift us up.

Revelation 12:11: The way we overcome the enemy is by the blood
of Christ, the Word of our testimony and by "death to self."

1 John 4:4: Greater is He that is in us (Jesus) than he that is in the
world. Even the spirits are subject to us. (Also Luke 10:20.)

Psalm 144:1: Blessed be God, who teaches my hands to war. (Also
Psalm 18:34.)

Personal Prayers

Some personal Scriptures we might pray are: (Again, I've taken the
liberty to paraphrase these.)

Psalm 139:23-24: Search me and know my heart and my thoughts.
See if there be any wicked way in me and lead me in Your way.

Job 34:32: That which I cannot see, please teach me.

Psalm 45:17: I desire to make Your Name be remembered in all
generations.

Psalm 17:2: Let my sentence come forth only from Your presence.

Ephesians 4:29-31: Let no corrupt communication proceed out of
my mouth, but that which is good to the use of edifying, that it
may minister grace to the hearer. Let me not grieve the Holy
Spirit, whereby I am sealed. Let all bitterness and wrath and
anger and clamor and evil speaking be put away from me with
all malice.

Ephesians 4:32: Be kind to one another, tender hearted, forgiving one another, just as Christ has forgiven me.

Hebrews 4:16: Let me come boldly to Your throne in time of need and find mercy.

Psalm 119:133: Order my steps in Your Word. Don't let sin or self have dominion over me.

Romans 4:21: I choose to be *fully persuaded* that what You have promised me, You will perform.

1 Corinthians 2:2: I pray that I would know nothing but "Christ crucified."

Philippians 4:19: That You would supply all my needs according to Your riches in glory.

Matthew 22:37: I desire to love You with all my heart, with all my will and with all my soul, so that I can then love my neighbor as myself.

Romans 12:1-2: I offer my body as a living sacrifice, holy and acceptable which is my reasonable service, and I choose not to be conformed to this world, but to be transformed into Your Image (and show forth Your Life), by *the renewing of my mind*, so that I can (then) prove in my actions what is the good, the acceptable and the perfect will of God.

Psalm 138:3: Make me bold with Your strength in my soul.

Galatians 1:16: May You reveal Yourself in me, so that I might speak as You would have me.

Joshua 9:25: I am in Your hands, do what You will with me. Have Your way in me.

Philemon 14: Without Your opinion, I will do nothing.

Acts 2:28: That You would make me full of joy with Your countenance.

Colossians 3:4: Christ, You are my life.

Philippians 1:21: For me to live is Christ.

Family Prayers

In addition to your own daily personal prayers for each member of your family, here are some Scriptures you might want to pray for them. Again, let the Holy Spirit pick which ones.

> Ephesians 1:17-19: I pray for Your Spirit of wisdom and revelation for _____. I pray that the eyes of his understanding would be enlightened, so that he might know the hope of Your calling, the riches of Your inheritance, and the exceeding greatness of Your Power towards them who believe.

> Ephesians 3:16-19: I pray_____will be strengthened with might by Your Spirit in the inner man; that You might dwell in his heart and that he might be rooted and grounded in Your Love and able to comprehend the breadth, the depth and the height of Your Love, so that he might be filled up with the fulness of You.

> Philippians 3:10: I pray that_____may know You and the power of Your resurrection and the fellowship of Your sufferings, so that he might be made conformable to Your Image.

> 2 Timothy 2:25: I pray that You would give_____repentance to the acknowledging of the truth.

> Pray also: Acts 16:31; 1 Kings 8:23-53; Daniel 9:3-19; and, Colossians 1:9.

Other Suggested Prayers for Loved Ones

> Pray that God would "lift the veil" and give them a personal revelation of Jesus.
> Pray that the Holy Spirit would continue to hover over them and give them supernatural protection.
> Pray that God would put Godly people in their path.
> Pray that God would expose all pride and rebelliousness.
> Pray that God would expose all their hidden thought patterns-- religious prejudices, known strongholds and evil spirits, etc.
> Pray that God would bind Satan from taking them captive.
> Pray that He would place His armor around them, and that He would do all He could to bring them to Himself.[14]

Endnotes for Prayer Journal:

1. Taken from a Billy Graham tract, Billy Graham Evangelistic Association, P.O. Box 779, Minneapolis, MN. 55440-0779.

2. *A House of Prayer for All Nations*, Chaim Richman, the Temple Institute, Carta, Jerusalem, 1997, page 48.

3. Ephesians 4:22-24; Colossians 3:8-10

4. The Greek word here for mind is *nous*, which means our whole conceptual process.
    (Romans 12:1-2)

5. 1 John 1:9

6. Mark 11:25-26; Matthew 18:21-22; Ephesians 4:32

7. Note that the first and second steps of the Inner Court ritual are really only *one* step (all these things occur at the *Lavers of Bronze*). But, since there is so much that occurs in this first step, for convenience sake, I've made it into two separate steps.

8. Hebrews 4:12; Romans 8:4-8; 2 Timothy 2:21

9. Luke 11:24-26

10. John 4:23-24

11. Psalm 100:2; 2 Samuel 6:14

12. John 14:14; 15:7; Matthew 21:22; Acts 10:4, 31; 1 John 5:15

13. Jeremiah 51:20

14. Taken in part from the book *Intercessory Prayer* by Dutch Sheets.

"Confess your faults one to another, and pray one for another, that ye may be healed. The effectual fervent prayer of a righteous man availeth much." (James 5:16)

Dark Night Scriptures
"Night Season"
(Job 30:17; Psalm 22:2)

Purpose of Dark Night:

1 Peter 2:1-2: That we might cease from sin (and self) and live the rest of our lives to the will of God.

1 Thessalonians 5:23: That we might be wholly sanctified, body, soul and spirit.

2 Corinthians 1:9: That we might trust in God, not ourselves.

Psalm 140:13: That we might dwell in His presence.

Scriptures

Job 7:11; 10:21-22; 12:22; 17:1, 15; 19:2, 6, 8-14, 18-19, 25-26; 16:9-17; 17:12, 15; 19:8, 4-10; 23:4, 8-10, 12, 17: 30:15, 17, 20, 26-28, 30; 31:35; 42:3, 5-6, 11-12

Psalms 10:1; 13:1; 23:4, 6; 18:11, 17-18, 28; 22:1-2, 5-8, 11, 15; 33:19; 38:1-11; 39:12-13; 42:3-4, 6; 44:8-19, 17-22; 55:4-5; 63:1; 66:9; 77; 88:6-14; 89:46; 97:2; 102:3-11; 105:16, 25, 28; 107:13-14, 22-30; 110:3; 112:4; 139:11-12; 142:7; 143:1-4

Isaiah 7:9; 8:17-18; 24:11, 15; 26:9; 35:4; 42:15-16; 49:9, 14; 50:10-11; 54:7-8; 58:8, 10; 59:9-10; 60:1-2

Deuteronomy 4:11

2 Samuel 22:29

2 Chronicles 6:1; 32:31

Genesis 15:12

Lamentations 1:13-14, 20-21; 2:8; 3:1-18, 32-33

Exodus 20:21

Judges 6:13

1 Kings 8:12

<u>Song of Solomon</u> 5:4-6

<u>Micah</u> 7:7-8

<u>Hosea</u> 4:6, 14

<u>Numbers</u> 8:14-16

<u>Jonah</u> 2:3-8 (Jonah thought God had abandoned him)

<u>John</u> 6:17-20

<u>Hebrews</u> 3:17-18; 11:15

<u>Mark</u> 6:48; 14:34; 15:34

<u>1 Peter</u> 1:7

<u>Luke</u> 3:16

<u>2 Corinthians</u> 1:8-9

<u>Matthew</u> 27:43

Bibliography

Bibles:

The Amplified Bible, Zondervan, Grand Rapids, Michigan, 1965.

The Companion Bible, King James Version, Kregel Publications, Grand Rapids, Michigan, 1990.

The Interlinear Bible, Hebrew, Greek, English, Associated Publishers and Authors, Wilmington, Delaware, 1976.

The Open Bible, Thomas Nelson Publishers, Nashville, Tennessee, 1998.

The Septuagint Version: Greek and English, Sir Lancelot C.L. Brenton, Zondervan, Grand Rapids, Michigan, 1970.

The Thompson Chain Reference Bible, King James Version, B.B. Kirkbride Bible Co., Inc., Indianapolis, Indiana, 1988.

The Zondervan Parallel New Testament, Greek and English, Zondervan Publishing Co., Grand Rapids, Michigan.

Technical:

Berry, George Ricker, *The Interlinear Greek-English New Testament,* Zondervan, Grand Rapids, Michigan, 1971.

Botterweck, G. Joannes & Helmer Ringgren, *Theological Dictionary of the Old Testament,* Vol.1-3, Eerdmans, Grand Rapids, Michigan, 1974.

Bromiley, Geoffrey W., *Theological Dictionary of the New Testament,* Eerdmans, Grand Rapids, Michigan, 1985.

Douglas, J.D., *The New International Dictionary of the Christian Church*, Zondervan, Grand Rapids, Michigan 1974.

Edwards, Paul, *The Encyclopedia of Religion*, Macmillan Publishing Co., Inc., New York, New York, 1967.

Encyclopedia Judaica, (16 Vols.), Keter Publishing House, Jerusalem, Israel.

Henry, Matthew, *Commentary on the Holy Bible*, Thomas Nelson, Nashville, Tennesee, 1979.

Jamieson, Fausset & Brown, *Commentary on the Whole Bible*, Zondervan, Grand Rapids, Michigan, 1974.

Josephus, Flavius, *The Complete Works of Josephus*, Kregel Publications, Grand Rapids, Michigan, 1981.

Kellogg, S.H., *Studies in Leviticus*, Kregal Publishers, Grand Rapids, Michigan, 1988.

Richman, Chaim, *A House of Prayer for all Nations*, the Temple Institute, Carta, Jerusalem, 1997.

Richman, Chaim, *The Holy Temple*, the Temple Institute, Carta, Jerusalem, 1997.

Smith, Jonathan Z., *The Harper Collins Dictionary of Religion*, The American Academy of Religion, San Francisco, California.

Spence, H.D.M., *The Pulpit Commentary*, Eerdmans, Grand Rapids, Michigan, 1950.

Strong, James H., *Strong's Exhaustive Concordance*, Baker Book House, Grand Rapids, Michigan, 1985.

The Holy Vessels and Furniture of the Tabernacle of Israel, Samuel Bagster & Sons, Paternaster Row, London, 1880.

The New Encyclopaedia Britannica, Encyclopaedia Britannica, Inc., Chicago, Illinois, Vol.1-29, 1985.

Unger, Merrill G., *The New Unger's Bible Dictionary*, Moody Press, Chicago, Illinois, 1988.

Vine, W.E., *The Expanded Vine's*, Bethany House, Minneapolis, Minnesota, 1984.

Wigram, George, *The Englishman's Hebrew and Chaldee Concordance of the New Testament*, Zondervan, Grand Rapids, Michigan, 1970.

General:

Bilheimer, Paul, *Don't Waste Your Sorrows*, Bethany House, Minneapolis, Minnesota, 1977.

Blackaby, Henry T. & Claude V. King, *Experiencing God*, Broadman & Holman, Nashville, Tennesee, 1994.

Burrows, Ruth, *Ascent to Love*, Dimension Books, New Jersey, 1987.

Capps, Walter H. And Wendy M. Wright, Editors, *Silent Fire*, Harper Row, New York, New York, 1978.

Chambers, Oswald, *Biblical Psychology*, Discovery House, Grand Rapids, Michigan 1962/1995.

Chambers, Oswald, *Abandoned to God*, David McCasland, Discovery House, Grand Rapids, Michigan, 1993.

Christensen, Bernhard, *The Inward Pilgimage*, Augsburg Fortress, Minneapolis, Minnesota, 1996.

Cronk, Sandra, *The Dark Night Journey*, Pendle Hill Publications, Wallingford, Pennsylvania, 1991.

Dallimore, Arnold, *Spurgeon, A New Biography*, The Banner of Truth, Carlisle, Pennyslvania, 1984.

De Caussade, Jean Pierre, *The Fire of Divine Love*, Truimph Books, Liguori, Missouri, 1995.

De Caussade, Jean Pierre, *Abandonment to Divine Providence*, Doubleday, New York, New York, 1975.

De Caussade, Jean Pierre, *The Sacrament of the Present Moment*, Harper Collins, New York, New York, 1966.

Dent, Barbara, *My Only Friend is Darkness*, ICS Publications, Washington D.C., 1992.

Edman, V. Raymond, *They Found the Secret*, Zondervan, Grand Rapids, Michigan, 1960.

Edwards, Gene, *The Secret to the Christian Life*, Tyndale House, Wheaton, Illinois, 1992.

Edwards, Gene, *The Inward Journey*, Tyndale House, Wheaton, Illinois, 1993.

Edwards Gene, *The Highest Life*, Tyndale House, Wheaton, Illinois, 1991.

Fenelon, Francois, *The Seeking Heart*, The Seed Sowers, Sargent, Georgia.

Finney, Charles G., *Power From On High*, Christian Literature Crusade, Fort Washington, Pennsylvania.

Frangipane, Francis, *Holiness, Truth and the Presence of God*, Arrow Publications, Cedar Rapids, Iowa, 1986.

Grant, Patrick, *A Dazzling Darkness*, Eerdmans, Grand Rapids, Michigan, 1985.

Green, Deirdre, *Gold in the Crucible*, Element Books, Longmead, Shaftesbury, Dorset, England, 1989.

Guyon, Madame, *Autobiography of Madame Guyon*, Moody Press, Chicago, Illinois.

Guyon, Madame, *Experiencing the Depths of Jesus Christ*, Christian Books, Goleta, California, 1980.

Guyon, Madame, *Final Steps in Christian Maturity*, The Seed Sowers, Beaumont, Texas, 1995.

Guyon, Madame, *Song of Songs*, Whitaker House, New Kensington, Pennsylvania, 1997.

Guyon, Madame, *Song of the Bride*, The Seed Sowers, Sargent, Georgia.

Guyon, Madame, *Union with God*, The Seed Sowers, Beaumont, Texas, 1981.

Hayford, Jack, *Pursuing the Will of God*, Multnomah Books, Sisters, Oregon, 1997.

Hazzard, David, *You Set My Spirit Free*, Bethany House, Minneapolis, Minnesota, 1994.

Hession, Roy, *When I Saw Him*, Christian Literature Crusade, Fort Washington, Pennsylvania, 1975.

Ingram, Terrance N., *Eagle*, Metro Books, Michael Griedman Publishing Group, 1998.

Johnson, William, Editor, *Cloud of Unknowing*, Doubleday, New York, New York, 1973.

Kendall, R.T., *God Meant It for Good*, Morning Star Publications, North Carolina, 1986.

Lambert, David W., *Oswald Chambers*, Bethany House Publishers, Minneapolis, Minnesota, 1997.

Lawrence, Brother, *The Practise of the Presence of God*, Revell, Grand Rapids, Michigan, 1958.

Lindsey, Hal, *Combat Faith*, Bantam Books, New York, New York, 1986.

Louth, Andrew, *The Wilderness of God*, Abingdon Press, Nashville, Tennessee. 1991.

Lutzer, Erwin, *One Minute After You Die*, Moody Press, Chicago, Illinois, 1997.

Marshall, Catherine, *Light in My Darkest Hour*, Chosen Books, Old Tappan, New Jersey, 1989.

McGreal, Wilfrid, *John of the Cross*, Triumph, Liguori, Missouri, 1997.

Miller, Basil, *George Muller*, Bethany House Publishers, Minneapolis, Minnesota.

Muller, George, *Autobiography of George Muller*, Whitaker House, New Kensington, Pennsylvania.

Murillo, Mario, *Critical Mass*, Fresh Fire Communication, Danville, California, 1985.

Murray, Andrew, *Divine Healing*, Whitaker House, Pittsburg, Pennsylvania, 1982.

Muto, Susan, *The Dark Night*, Ava Maria Press, 1994.

Nee, Watchman, *Song of Songs*, Christian Literature Crusade, Fort Washington, Pennsylvania, 1965.

Nee, Watchman, *The Release of the Spirit,* Sure Foundation Publishers, Indianapolis, Indiana, 1965.

Nee, Watchman, *The Spiritual Man*, Christian Fellowship Publishers, New York, New York, 1968.

Pamplin, Dr. Robert B. Jr., *One Who Believed*, Christ Community Church, Newberg, Oregon, 1993.

Penn-Lewis, Jesse, *Soul and Spirit*, Christian Literature Crusade, Fort Washington, Pennsylvania, 1989.

Penn-Lewis, Jesse, *Life out of Death*, Christian Literature Crusade, Fort Washington, Pennsylvania, 1991.

Penn-Lewis, Jesse, *Climax of the Risen Life*, Christian Literature Crusade, Fort Washington, Pennsylvania.

Pratney, Winkie, *The Thomas Factor*, Chosen Books, Old Tappan, New Jersey, 1989.

Redpath, Alan, *Victorious Christian Faith*, Fleming Revell, Grand Rapids, Michigan, 1993.

Rolle, Richard, *The Fire of Love*, Penguin Books, London, England, 1972.

Sanders, J. Oswald, *Enjoying Intimacy with God*, Moody Press, Chicago, Illinois, 1980.

Sandford, Loren, *Burnout*, Examino Corporation, Concrete, Washington, 1998.

Schaeffer, Francis, *True Spirituality*, Tyndale House, Wheaton, Illinois, 1971.

Smith, Alice, *Beyond the Veil*, Regal Books, Ventura, California, 1996.

Sproul, R.C., *Surprised by Suffering,* Tyndale House, Wheaton, Illinois, 1988.

Spurgeon, Charles, *Twelve Sermons on the Cries from the Cross*, Baker Book House, Grand Rapids, Michigan, 1994.

St. John of the Cross, *Living Flame of Love*, Edited by E. Allison Peers, Truimph Books, Liguori, Missouri, 1991.

Stanley, Charles, *The Blessings of Brokenness*, Zondervan, Grand Rapids, Michigan, 1997.

Ten Boom, Corrie, *Defeated Enemies*, Christian Literature Crusade, Fort Washington, Pennyslvania.

Ten Boom, Corrie, *The Hiding Place*, Chosen Books, Minneapolis, Minnisota, 1971.

Thorald, Algar, *Self-abandonment to Divine Providence*, Templegate, Springfield, Illnois, 1959.

Tozer, A.W., *The Knowledge of the Holy*, Harper Collins Publishers, New York, New York, 1961.

Wardle, Terry, *Draw Close to the Fire*, Chosen Books, Grand Rapids, Michigan, 1998.

Wieland, Robert J., *Gold Tried in the Fire*, Glad Tidings Publishers, Paris, Ohio, 1983.

Williams, Rowan, *A Ray of Darkness*, Cowlely Publications, Cambridge, Massachusetts, 1995.

Wurmbrand, Richard, *Tortured for Christ*, Living Sacrifice Books, Bartlesville, Oklahoma, 1967.

Miscellaneous:

"Dark Night of the Soul," Author unknown, *Good News Magazine*.

Hallett, Joe, *Outpost Magazine*, Minneapolis, Minnesota.

Ospel, Margaret, "A Vessel for Honor," *Words of Good Cheer*, October 1997.

Payne, James, Pulpit Message called "God's Eagle," Oak Park Church, Tennesee, 1997.

Poems of St. John of the Cross, Christian Classics, Westminster, Maryland, 1993.

Porter, Dwight, Radio Message called "Learning to be Content," Sebastian, Florida.

Prayers of St. John of the Cross, New City Press, 1991.

St. John of the Cross Selected Writings, Paulist Press, New Jersey.

The Eagle Story, Institute in Basic Youth Conflicts, Oak Brook, Illinois, 1982.

The Collected Works of St. John of the Cross, Translated by Kieran Kavanaugh & Otilio Rodriquez, Discalced Carmelite Friars, Washington, D.C., 1991.

Lash, Jamie, Audio tape called *The Ancient Jewish Wedding*, Jewish Jewells, Ft. Lauderdale, Florida, 1997.

Wilkerson, David, *The Pulpit Series*, World Challenge, Lindale, Texas.
"The Nearness of God"
"The Making of a Man of God"
"Don't Waste Your Affections"
"Stand Still and See the Salvation of the Lord"
"The Salvation of Your Face"
"The Presence of God"
"The Sacrifices of Thanksgiving"
"Learning Through Affliction"
"How Not to Come to God"
"The Devil Can't Have You"
"Accusing God of Child Neglect"
"The Danger of Leaning on Your own Understanding'
"The Manifestation of the Presence of Jesus"

What is Koinonia House?

Koinonia House is a publishing ministry dedicated to creating, developing and distributing materials to stimulate, encourage and facilitate serious study of the Bible as the inerrant Word of God.

A certificate for an initial year's subscription to our monthly newsletter has been included at the end of this book.

For more information please write:

Koinonia House
P.O. Box D
Coeur d'Alene, Idaho
83816-0347

or call:
1-800-KHOUSE1

On the Internet:
http://www.khouse.org

The Way of Agape

Understanding God's Love

What is God's Love? What does it mean to "love" God?
Exploring these and other critical issues, Chuck and Nancy show
us how we can transform the failures of human love into the
victories of God's *Agape* Love.

In this audio or video version of *The Way of Agape*, Nancy
explains, in her warm and down-to-earth style, how understanding
God's *Agape* Love has changed her life and how it can change the
lives of others. The video series has a Leader's Guide and is also
available for a $25 rental fee.

Be Ye Transformed

Understanding God's Truth

What does it mean to truly renew our minds? What is the Mind of Christ? In this sequel to *The Way of Agape*, Nancy shares that the only way we can be set free from our hidden insecurities, fears and hurts that keep us in bondage and a continual prey for Satan, is by constantly *renewing our minds*.

In this audio or video version of *Be Ye Transformed*, Nancy shares, "Our efforts to change should not be focused on our wrong actions, but on our wrong thinking." The video series has a Leader's Guide and is also available for a $25 rental fee.

$20.00 Value FNS $20.00 Value

Certificate

This certificate entitles the person below to a full year's subscription to *Personal* **UPDATE**, a newsletter highlighting the Biblical relevance of current events.

(New subscribers only.)

Name: _____

Address: _____

City: _____ State: _____ Zip: _____

Koinonia House, P.O. Box D, Coeur d'Alene ID 83816-0347